Still Seeking the Magic Mushroom

Still Seeking the Magic Mushroom

FUNGI, PHARMACEUTICALS, AND MYSTICISM WITHOUT RELIGION

Hugh B. Urban

THE UNIVERSITY OF CHICAGO PRESS
CHICAGO AND LONDON

The University of Chicago Press, Chicago 60637
The University of Chicago Press, Ltd., London

Published 2026
Printed in the United States of America

35 34 33 32 31 30 29 28 27 26   1 2 3 4 5

ISBN-13: 978-0-226-85190-7 (cloth)
ISBN-13: 978-0-226-85192-1 (paper)
ISBN-13: 978-0-226-85191-4 (ebook)
DOI: https://doi.org/10.7208/chicago/9780226851914.001.0001

Library of Congress Cataloging-in-Publication Data

Names: Urban, Hugh B. author
Title: Still seeking the magic mushroom : fungi, pharmaceuticals, and mysticism without religion / Hugh B. Urban.
Description: Chicago : The University of Chicago Press, 2026. | Includes bibliographical references and index.
Identifiers: LCCN 2026008293 | ISBN 9780226851907 cloth | ISBN 9780226851921 paperback | ISBN 9780226851914 ebook
Subjects: LCSH: Mushrooms, Hallucinogenic—Religious aspects | Hallucinogenic drugs and religious experience | Psilocybe | Mysticism | Cults—United States—History
Classification: LCC BL65.D7 U73 2026
LC record available at https://lccn.loc.gov/2026008293

⊚ This paper meets the requirements of ANSI/NISO Z39.48-1992 (Permanence of Paper).

Authorized Representative for EU General Product Safety Regulation (GPSR) queries: **Easy Access System Europe**—Mustamäe tee 50, 10621 Tallinn, Estonia, gpsr.requests@easproject.com
Any other queries: https://press.uchicago.edu/press/contact.html

Contents

Figures

Preface

Any book is not so much a unique, single-authored entity as a complex amalgam or assemblage composed of many different voices, influences, and narratives. To use the central narrative of this particular book, it is more like a complex network of mycelia—a vast subterranean network of root-like fibers that stretch beneath the forest floor and periodically give rise to the fruiting body of mushrooms.[1] This book is very much the fruiting body that has emerged from such a vast network of complex relationships, which extend between many friends, colleagues, institutions, and archival resources. While I cannot promise that this book will inspire the sort of mystical, magical, and transformative experience described by many psychedelic mushroom users, I do hope that it might help us understand some of the complex cultural, historical, and religious networks within which these mushrooms have grown and evolved over the last century.

I approach this material both as a historian of religion, deeply interested in the complex development of various spiritual movements in their social, cultural, and political contexts,[2] and as an amateur mycologist, deeply interested in the complex role of fungi in their larger ecosystems. While I have been engaged in the academic study of religion for over thirty years, I have actually been engaged in the study of mushrooms for an even longer period of time. My interest in mycology was first sparked as a teenager during one particularly wet summer in my hometown in central Pennsylvania, and it gradually evolved into a lifelong fascination with all things fungal. I currently serve on the advisory board of the Ohio Mushroom Society and regularly assist with mushroom forays and identification. One of my motivations for writing this book is that it opens a space to explore both my lifelong interests in the study of religion, spirituality, and mysticism and my lifelong interests in fungi and their complex role in natural and human history. While psychedelic mushrooms such as *Psilocybe* are the primary focus of this book, I think fungi more broadly offer us some profound insights into the complex, interconnected, and symbiotic relations that comprise all of life. As such, they might provide us with some ways of reimagining our own place on the increasingly damaged and precarious planet that we now inhabit.

A few of the many people and organizations who have helped me with this project include Egil Asprem, G. William Barnard, Jeffrey Breau, Melissa Curley, Alan Davis, Erik Davis, Wendy Doniger, Patrick Dunn, Fritz Graf, David Hodges, Ben John, Paul Christopher Johnson, Sarah Iles Johnston, Jason Josephson-Storm, Travis Kitchens, Amy Koehlinger, Jeffrey J. Kripal, James McHugh, David Odorisio, Life Trek LLC, Bruce Lincoln, Sabina Magliocco, Paloma Martinez-Cruz, the Ohio Mushroom Society, Brian Pace, William Parsons, Christopher Partridge, Josefina Cuevas Pérez, Stuart Sarbacker, Patricia Sauthoff, Jason Slot, Walt Sturgeon, Kyle Wagner, and Isaac Weiner. I would also like to thank the curators of la Casa de María Sabina museum in Huautla de Jiménez and the librarians at Harvard University and Purdue University for their assistance in using their special collections.

[INTRODUCTION]

Mushrooms, Enchantment, and Mysticism Without Religion

In these decadent latter days, when fairies no longer haunt the groves as of yore, and when no more do witches career merrily on broomsticks overhead, it has been a pleasure to consider [mushrooms] for a moment, and with them the queer beliefs associating them with toadstools.

R. T. Rolfe and F. W. Rolfe, *The Romance of the Fungus World* (1925)[1]

Without the escape hatch into the transcendental and transpersonal realm that is provided by plant-based indole hallucinogens, the human future would be bleak indeed. We have lost the ability to be swayed by the power of myths, and our history should convince us of the fallacy of dogma. What we require is a new dimension of self-experience that individually and collectively authenticates . . . our stewardship of this small part of the larger universe.

Terence McKenna, *Food of the Gods* (1992)[2]

In case you missed it, we are in the middle of a psychedelic renaissance.

Rachael Petersen, "Taking Mushrooms for Depression Cured Me of My Atheism" (2019)[3]

In May 1957, *Life* magazine published a hugely popular and tremendously influential article entitled "Seeking the Magic Mushroom." Written by an affluent banker and amateur mycologist named R. Gordon Wasson (1898–1986), the article narrated the journey of an intrepid explorer who forayed deep into the mountains of southern Mexico, partook of secret rituals, and became "the first white man in recorded history" to consume the sacred mushrooms that lay at the heart of ancient mysteries.[4] Wasson's highly poetic account of the mushroom experience quickly inspired a generation of spiritual seekers and helped spark the massive interest in psychedelics that swept across North America and Europe during the 1960s. At the same time, Wasson and others inspired by his work began to speculate that psychedelic mushrooms lay at the foundation of other religious traditions—ranging from the Hindu Vedas to the Greek Mysteries—and perhaps even helped to catalyze human evolution and civilization itself. While most experts today are deeply skeptical of Wasson's work, his claims for a psychedelic origin of spiritual experience remain hugely influential and still circulate widely in popular discourse.[5]

Rather tragically, however, Wasson's publicization of the Mexican mushroom ritual also helped open the floodgates to massive numbers of journalists, tourists, and hippies who poured into the region and largely decimated its Indigenous culture and traditions. María Sabina, the local *sabia* (wise woman) who allowed him to participate in the rituals, was blamed by her community for the influx of foreigners. She was ostracized, and her home was burned down.[6] While Wasson himself later lamented the tragic effects of his publications on the community, he defended the need to bring the knowledge of these powerful fungi to light and to introduce them to a modern audience.[7] His work, moreover, clearly played a central role in the psychedelic revolution and counterculture that followed in the 1960s and 1970s. It also helped spark the first wave of psychedelic research, which began in universities such as Harvard in the early 1960s and flourished until the early 1970s, when psilocybin (the active compound in *Psilocybe* mushrooms) along with LSD (lysergic acid diethylamide) was labeled a Schedule I controlled substance, and most research into these drugs was shut down.[8]

In the early 2000s, some fifty years after Wasson's early publications, research on psilocybin was resurrected by scholars at Johns Hopkins and New York University. In 2006, Roland R. Griffiths and his colleagues published the seminal article "Psilocybin Can Occasion Mystical Experiences Having Substantial and Sustained Personal Meaning and Spiritual Significance," which helped spark a new wave of scientific research into psilocybin and other psychedelics.[9] Over the last two decades there has been a tremendous amount of research on the potential for psilocybin, LSD, and MDMA to treat a wide range of psychological disorders, including anxiety, depression, PTSD, and substance abuse. At the same time, not surprisingly, pharmaceutical companies have begun pouring millions of dollars into psychedelic research in the hopes of discovering a revolutionary new class of drugs.[10] Meanwhile, mushrooms both magical and nonmagical have also saturated popular culture, through films such as *Fantastic Fungi* and best-selling books such as *The Immortality Key*. Suddenly, it seems, the fascination with the magical possibilities of mushrooms is everywhere.

So, how did we get here? How did we get from some isolated Mexican healers using mushrooms in private rituals to the explosion of interest in psilocybin and other psychedelics that we see today in new spiritual movements, in scientific research, and in popular culture?

A Mycelial Genealogy

This book traces the history of the modern resurgence of interest in psychedelic mushrooms (primarily *Psilocybe* species) from the 1950s to the present, following its circuitous route from Wasson's article in *Life* magazine to the most recent research on psilocybin at universities such as Johns Hopkins today. While there is now a good deal of excellent scholarship on psychedelics and religion,[11] the story of this particular mushroom and its broader impact on spirituality, culture, and science remains to be written. In many ways, I argue, this genus of mushroom represents a kind of microcosm of many different cultural currents of the twentieth and twenty-first centuries. It lies at a critical nexus between the search for transcendence amid a seemingly rationalized, disenchanted world; the yearning for profound forms of mystical experience outside of traditional religious institutions; the ideal of some return to nature in an age of frightening ecological crisis; the deep faith in science, particularly new fields such as neuroscience, to explain all things; and the seemingly relentless power of capitalism and the pharmaceutical industry to transform everything into profitable commodities.[12] I want to follow the complex journey of these mushrooms from their traditional cultural contexts, to their reimagining as a form of "mysticism without religion," to the recent claims by scientists to produce mystical experiences in a laboratory setting, and finally to big pharma's marketing of psilocybin as a drug that could revolutionize the mental health industry.

Methodologically, I hope to engage in a kind of "genealogy," in Michel Foucault's sense of the term,[13] tracing the complex, often convoluted, and contradictory history of *Psilocybe* mushrooms as they made their way into the domains of spirituality, science, popular culture, and commerce. Throughout the book, I employ the metaphor of mycelia—the mycological term for the underground networks of fungal threads that extend throughout the soil and periodically give rise to the fruiting bodies of mushrooms.[14] In the chapters that follow, I trace the complex mycelial network of relations that extend between various human actors, spiritual communities, academic institutions, government agencies such as the CIA and FDA, and corporate pharmaceutical entities such as Compass Pathways and atai Life Sciences.

Along the way, the book will engage some of the most difficult questions that lie at the heart of religion, science, and culture more broadly. Among others, we will ask, To what degree are spiritual and psychedelic experiences really comparable? What does it mean to say that "mystical experiences" can be produced in a research setting? And is it ethical to take fungi and other substances that are used in ritual contexts by Indigenous cultures and market them as pharmaceutical drugs?

"We Have Never Been Disenchanted": Mushrooms, Magic, and the Myth of Disenchantment

Much of the recent fascination with the "magic" of mushrooms is tied to larger conversations about "disenchantment" and "re-enchantment" in modern societies.[15] The idea of the "disenchantment" or "de-magification" (*Entzauberung*) of the world was first expressed by the German sociologist Max Weber as part of his generally pessimistic view of modern life as a kind of rationalized "iron cage."[16] Throughout the twentieth century, this idea of disenchantment or "de-magification" became part of a much broader narrative that the modern Western world has become increasingly secularized, demystified and bereft of a deeper sense of the sacred.

In many ways, however, this narrative of disenchantment is itself a kind of myth that does not accurately reflect modern history. As Jason Josephson-Storm persuasively argues, modern Western societies have never really been disenchanted. Most of the great advocates of the narrative of disenchantment—including Weber and Sigmund Freud—were themselves fascinated with magical, mystical, and paranormal phenomena. And today we are arguably as fascinated with the realms of occultism, mysticism, and magic as we ever have been in the past. Polls consistently show that interest in phenomena such as psychic healing, ESP, haunted houses, ghosts, telepathy, clairvoyance, astrology, extraterrestrials, and witches remains surprisingly high even in the twenty-first-century United States.[17] We need only browse the myriad supernatural-themed shows on Netflix or look to best-selling series such as *Harry Potter* or *Twilight* to see that we remain intensely interested in narratives about magic, mystery, and the occult. "The single most familiar story in the history of science is the tale of disenchantment—of magic's exit from the law-governed world," Josephson-Storm observes. "As a broad cultural history, this narrative is wrong. Attempts to suppress magic have historically failed more often than they've succeeded. . . . In fact . . . we have never been disenchanted."[18]

In this complex narrative of the "de-magification," "disenchantment," and "re-enchantment" of the modern world, mushrooms play an important part. Throughout European folklore and mythology since at least the late Middle Ages, mushrooms have been closely associated with the powers of magic in both its most sinister and most benevolent forms. In English Romantic poetry, for example, mushrooms were frequently associated with feelings of decadence, corruption, and rot—"pale and fleshly, as if the decaying dead . . . had been animated," as Percy Byshe Shelley put it.[19] Yet mushrooms were also associated with the wonders of the spirit world, such as fairies, gnomes, and elves.

This ambivalent association of mushrooms with enchantment in both benevolent and malevolent forms appears throughout European folklore, popular narratives, and fiction. For example, the infamous witch of Russian folklore, Baba Yaga, is often portrayed surrounded by *Amanita muscaria* mushrooms, which are at once toxic and hallucinogenic, producing both

FIGURE I.1. Ivan Bilbin, illustration from *Vasilisa the Beautiful and the Baba Yaga* (1900).

FIGURE I.2. Arthur Rackham, illustration for *Alice's Adventures in Wonderland* (1865).

violent illness and visionary experiences.[20] In English literature, Lewis Carroll famously described Alice entering wonderland and encountering a hookah-smoking caterpillar seated on a giant mushroom, who invited her to consume the fungus in order to change shape and size. In short, mushrooms have long held a magical place in our imaginations and seemed to many to offer the sort of enchantment, mystery, and supernatural power that has been lost in the modern world.[21]

As we will see in what follows, this search for enchantment in the mysterious form of fungi is a recurring theme from the 1950s to the present. It runs not only through modern spiritual and countercultural movements, but also through current scientific research, which has in many ways led the charge in the latest attempt to re-enchant the world through the exploration of psychedelics and their potential to inspire mystical experiences.

The Appropriate Drugs: Mysticism, Nature, and Psychedelics

Contemporary debates over psychedelics and mystical experience comprise just one recent episode in the much longer and more complex history of "mysticism" as a category. The term "mysticism" itself derives from the Greek adjective *mustikos*, which originated in the various mystery religions of the ancient Greek and Roman world. *Mustikos* in turn comes from the root *muo*, meaning "to close," in the sense of closing one's eyes or closing one's lips (that is, remaining silent) in the context of the mystery rites.[22] The concept of *mustikos* was then elaborated in the Christian tradition, mainly to refer to mystical forms of biblical interpretation, to the mystical dimensions of the Eucharistic liturgy, and to a contemplative or experiential knowledge of God.[23]

Because of its roots in Greek, Roman, and Christian (or more broadly, Abrahamic) traditions, the term "mysticism" is in many ways problematic when applied to other traditions such as Hinduism, Buddhism, or Native American religions, where there is no precisely corresponding category.[24] As Richard King and others have argued, the category of mysticism was often deployed as a means defining and dominating other cultures, particularly in the context of European colonialism in the nineteenth and early twentieth centuries. For example, the stereotype of the "mystic Hindu" helped justify the need for strong, rational imperial rule in South Asia. Even as Hinduism was imagined as an irrational, exotic, effeminate realm of otherworldly mysticism, so too European Christianity (particularly Protestant Christianity) was reimagined as the realm of rational, orderly, civilized, masculine, and this-worldly religion: "The association of religions such as Hinduism and Buddhism with mysticism and the stereotype of the naval-gazing, anti-social, and otherworldly mystic has come to function as one of the most prevailing cultural representations of Indian religion and culture in the last few centuries."[25]

The category of mysticism and the ways in which mystical experience are defined are always tied to relations of power. The claim to have transcendent or otherworldly knowledge is a claim to a special kind of authority—one that may at times buttress and at times challenge more established forms of religious authority.[26] As we will see in the story that unfolds below, the claims to a kind of psychedelic mysticism and mushroom mysticism have also been bound up with complex questions of power and authority over the last several decades—questions such as, What counts as mystical experience? Who can claim such experiences? Who can define and interpret them? And how do psychedelic claims to mystical experience challenge or compete with more traditional religious claims to spiritual experience and divine authority?

Although *Psilocybe* mushrooms and other psychedelic drugs have long been portrayed as fringe, countercultural, and subversive substances, they have been a central part of the broader story of American spirituality and debates surrounding mysticism since at least the nineteenth century. One of the primary arguments of this book is that they are in fact a key part of "the American experience" and have deep roots in American attitudes toward religion, mysticism, nature, and drugs from late 1800s onward.[27] As Ryan Grim notes in his study of drugs in American culture, "If there's one certainty about American drug use, it's this: we're always looking for a better way to feed our voracious appetite for getting high—for something cheaper, faster, less addictive, or more powerful."[28]

One of the most important figures in the development of modern psychology—and a key figure in the study of both mysticism and drugs—is William James (1842–1910). In his attempt to map the complex terrain of religious experience in all its many forms, James identifies four primary qualities of mystical experiences: 1) ineffability, or the impossibility of communicating such experience in language; 2) a noetic quality, or a strong sense of direct insight into reality; 3) transiency, or the fleeting temporal nature of the experience; and 4) passivity, or the sense that the individual is in the grasp of some awesomely superior power.[29] According to James's eclectic and wide-ranging account, mystical experiences can be achieved in a variety of ways. For example, he notes that the beauty and wonder of the natural world is often a trigger for mystical states of mind, suggesting that "certain aspects of nature seem to have a peculiar power of awakening such mystical moods."[30] As James observes, this mystical power of nature is a common theme in American authors of the nineteenth century, such as Ralph Waldo Emerson and Walt Whitman. Emerson's highly poetic description of a nature-inspired experience, for example, would later reappear in twentieth-century psychedelic accounts:

> In the woods we return to nature and faith. . . . Standing on the bare ground—my head bathed by the blithe air and uplifted into infinite space—all mean egotism vanishes. I become a transparent eyeball. I am

nothing. I see all. The currents of the Universal Being circulate through me; I am part or parcel of God. . . . I am the lover of the uncontained and immortal beauty. In the wilderness, I find something more dear and connate than in streets or villages. In the tranquil landscape . . . man beholds somewhat as beautiful as his own nature.

The greatest delight which the fields and woods minister is the suggestion of an occult relation between man and vegetable. I am not alone and unacknowledged. They nod to me, and I to them. The waving bough in the storm is new to me and old.[31]

This image of the all-seeing "transparent eyeball" would later become a central trope in Wasson's famous 1957 article in *Life* magazine.

Beyond the splendors of nature, however, James devotes even more time to the mystical inspiration that can be derived from a wide range of drugs. He offers a lengthy discussion on the effects of alcohol, which he sees as a kind of natural stimulant to mystical states of consciousness (while acknowledging its proneness to abuse):

> The sway of alcohol over mankind is unquestionably due to its power to stimulate the mystical faculties of human nature, usually crushed to earth by the cold facts and dry criticisms of the sober hour. Sobriety diminishes, discriminates, and says no; drunkenness expands, unites, and says yes. It is in fact the great exciter of the yes function in man. It brings its votary from the chill periphery of things to the radiant core. It makes him for the moment one with truth. . . . The drunken consciousness is one bit of the mystical consciousness.[32]

James had even more optimism for the powers of nitrous oxide and ether. With the potential to "stimulate mystical consciousness in an extraordinary degree," nitrous oxide in particular seemed to have the power to reveal profound insights to its user, though these might be frustratingly difficult to retain after the drug's effects had subsided:

> Depth beyond depth of truth seems revealed to the inhaler; this truth fades out, however, or escapes at the moment of coming to. . . . Nevertheless, the sense of a profound meaning having been there persists; and I know more than one person who is persuaded that in the nitrous oxide trance we have a genuine metaphysical revelation.[33]

James provides several anecdotes from individuals who recalled having profound experiences while under anesthetic. In 1874, the philosopher and poet Benjamin Paul Blood described a mystical realization in which he saw that "each is all, in God," while the poet and literary critic J. A. Symonds achieved nothing less than "the vision of God, in all purity and tenderness and truth and absolute love."[34] As a curious aside, we might note that none other than L. Ron Hubbard—the controversial founder of Dianetics and the Church of Scientology—also claimed to have had a profound spiritual experience under the influence of the anesthetic. While undergoing a dental procedure in 1938, he allegedly had a near-death experience that revealed to him all the world's wisdom and resulted in his unpublished manuscript known as *Excalibur* or *The One Command.*[35]

In the first decades of the twentieth century, many authors also began to explore the mystical and psychoactive potential of the peyote cactus (*Lophophora williamsii*).[36] Used for millennia by Indigenous communities in central Mexico, peyote spread widely to many North American tribes in the late nineteenth century, primarily through the reservations in Texas and Oklahoma and via the new rail lines that linked these areas to the rest of the United States.[37] While peyote use faced increasing hostility and criminalization from the Bureau of Indian Affairs and various state governments in the US, many white authors also began to take a keen interest in the cactus. Among them was the infamous British occultist Aleister Crowley (1875–1947), who was arguably the most important figure in the modern revival of magic and also an early explorer of psychedelic drugs.[38] As Crowley recalled, "I made many experiments on peyote and with [peyote] in 1910 and subsequent years."[39] Indeed, he was inspired by his peyote experience to stage his own creative reimagining of the ancient Eleusinian Mysteries in a series of public performances held in London in 1910. His version of the mysteries included a special "Cup of Libation," which contained a potent mixture of peyote as one of several ingredients (along with alcohol and heroin). The point of using these substances was not mere intoxication but, in his words, to achieve the experience of "the soul itself . . . united to its God, and for this reason the rapture is more overpowering, the joy more lasting, and the resultant energy more pure and splendid than in aught earthly."[40] As such, Crowley was also one of the first authors to suggest a psychedelic origin for the Greek Mysteries, a thesis that was taken up again by Wasson, McKenna, and many other later psychedelic enthusiasts.

After James and Crowley, probably the most influential author to discuss the intersections between drugs and mysticism was the English novelist and philosopher Aldous Huxley (1894–1963). It would be difficult to overestimate the impact of Huxley's book *The Doors of Perception* on spirituality and popular culture over the next several decades, where it influenced everything from rock bands such as the Doors to early psychedelic explorers such as Wasson, Leary, and myriad others. Taking its title from a poem by William Blake, Huxley's book explored various means by which the "the doors of perception" might be opened to the infinite realm that lies beyond our narrow senses. Like James, he was interested in the various ways this expansion of consciousness might be achieved, including both conventional means such as prayer and potentially more expedient means such as "the appropriate drugs":

> It had always seemed to me possible that, through hypnosis . . . by means of systematic meditation, or else by taking the appropriate drug, I might so change my ordinary consciousness as to be able to know from the inside what the visionary, the medium, even the mystic were talking about.[41]

The drug described in *The Doors of Perception* was mescaline, which had recently been synthesized from the peyote cactus. Mescaline, we should note, is just one of many alkaloids found in peyote (and in other cacti), though it is the main cause of the psychedelic effects. First isolated in 1897, it was then synthesized by the Austrian chemist Ernst Späth in 1919. Huxley was introduced to mescaline in May 1953 while living in California, when a friend of his came to visit bearing the drug and looking for a "guinea pig" to test it. He eagerly took four-tenths of a gram with a glass of water and awaited the results. He recalls that he expected to experience something more aesthetic and picturesque such as "visions of many-colored geometries, of animated architectures, rich with gems, and fabulously lovely, of landscapes with heroic figures, of symbolic dramas trembling perpetually on the verge of ultimate revelation."[42] Yet what he actually experienced, as he sat gazing at a simple vase of flowers, was something more like a direct encounter with Being in its primordial state, which he compared to the mystical insight of Meister Eckhart and to the ideal Forms of Plato:

> I was not looking now at an unusual flower arrangement. . . . I was seeing what Adam had seen on the morning of his creation—the miracle, moment by moment of naked existence . . . *Istigkeit*—wasn't that the word Meister Eckhart liked to use? "Is-ness." The Being of Platonic philosophy . . . a bunch of flowers shining with their own inner light and all but quivering under the pressure of the significance with which they were charged . . . a transience that was yet eternal life, a perpetual perishing that was at the same time pure being, a bundle of minute, unique particulars in which, by some unspeakable and yet self-sufficient paradox, was to be seen the divine source of all existence.[43]

Huxley, we should note, was careful to state that the psychedelic experience should not be viewed as an end in itself, but merely as a kind of "gratuitous grace," which is not to be confused with the ultimate goals of enlightenment or the beatific vision. After his second mescaline experience in 1955, he also warned against the danger of becoming stuck in such contemplative states.[44] Nonetheless, as we will see in the chapters that follow, Huxley's account of the mescaline experience would be echoed in many descriptions of *Psilocybe*—including Wasson's *Life* magazine article published just a few years later.

Mysticism Without Religion

Much of the appeal of psychedelics in the twentieth and twenty-first centuries lies in the possibility of achieving a kind of profound spiritual experience, but one that can be achieved outside of traditional religious structures, without the need for priests, elaborate rituals, or dogmatic systems of belief.[45] This was a large part of the appeal of mysticism in the twentieth century, when it became the subject of intense interest and gave birth to a huge number of scholarly and popular works. To many living in a modern and increasingly secular world, mysticism seemed to offer the possibility of an intense spiritual experience without the trappings of religious institutions, a means of rediscovering all that is admirable in religion without the need for the more confining strictures of tradition and dogma. As the Buddhist historian Robert Gimello observes, "Mysticism has become fascinating to many of its students exactly because it has seemed to them to be an alternative to religion. It has come to be viewed as the repository of all that is best and still admirable in religion but one that is free from such no longer acceptable elements as dogma, authority, discipline, respect for tradition, etc."[46]

In this context, it is not difficult to see the appeal of psychedelics, which burst dramatically onto the scene in the 1950s and 1960s—right in the midst of the new interest in mysticism. Now available in the form of mescaline, LSD, and synthesized psilocybin, psychedelics seemed to offer an immediate route to mystical experience that might radically bypass traditional religious structures altogether. As psychologist William Richards recalls, for example, he first experienced psilocybin as a twenty-three-year-old when he volunteered for a clinical trial in Germany in 1963, during the very early days of psychedelic research. Though he had no particular spiritual expectations, he described an intense state of "mystical consciousness," complete with exotic visuals and feelings of infinite love:

> I felt immersed in incredibly detailed imagery, best described as Islamic architecture and Arabic script. . . . I seemed to fully become the multidimensional patterns or to lose my usual identity within them as the external brilliance of mystical consciousness manifested itself. Suddenly this consciousness was experienced as outside of time, a pinnacle from which history could be viewed. My awareness was flooded with love, beauty, and peace beyond anything I had ever known or wildly imagined to be possible. "Awe," "Glory," and "Gratitude" were the only words that remained relevant.[47]

Psychedelics thus gave birth to a new kind of spiritual revelation in their own way, a kind of counterreligion for a counterculture. In many ways, psilocybin and LSD helped create a new kind of religious rite of passage or initiatory ordeal—the "are you experienced?" trial by embarking on a psychedelic trip to depart from the known reality and entering into an alternative world of social, political, and spiritual possibilities. As popular historian Michael Pollan aptly puts it,

> The arrival of these [psilocybin and LSD] is also linked to the rise of the counterculture during the 1960s and . . . to its particular tone and style. For the first time in history, the young had a rite of passage all their own: the "acid trip." Instead of folding into the adult world, as rites of passage have always done, this one landed them in a country of the mind that few adults had any idea existed. The effect on society was, to put it mildly, disruptive.[48]

But the appeal of psychedelics as a kind of mysticism without religion is not simply a curious relic of the 1960s. It is perhaps even more relevant in the twenty-first century, as adherence to mainstream religious institutions continues to decline in North America, England, and Europe, even as interest in the supernatural and mysticism remains as strong if not stronger than ever. The recent interest in psychedelic exploration in the US has come amid a historic decline in church attendance, which has dropped from 70 percent in 1999 to just 47 percent in 2020, according to some polls.[49] Yet just as we have "never been disenchanted," we have apparently also not lost our curiosity about the realms of the mystical and the magical.[50]

In this sense, it would seem that the interest in psychedelics as a kind of mysticism without religion is closely tied to the broader phenomenon of the "spiritual but not religious" (SBNR), which is now one of the fastest growing trends in the United States. As Robert C. Fuller and William B. Parsons suggest in their study of the SBNR phenomenon in the US, the roots of this attitude lie deep in much older American spiritual and philosophical currents. Its antecedents include various liberal religious traditions, such as Transcendentalism, Unitarianism, Spiritualism, Vedanta, and Theosophy. It also reflects many of their broader spiritual values, such as individuality, solitude, meditation, ethical reform, creative self-expression, and the appreciation of religious variety. In the late twentieth and twenty-first centuries, these older spiritual currents merged with a variety of other forces, such as globalization, pluralism, secularization, the impact of visual and social media, and the pervasive networks of neoliberal capitalism. All of this, Fuller and Parsons suggest, produced a uniquely "American" version of spirituality, and one that is perhaps especially well-suited to the twenty-first century.[51]

At the same time, many young people in the US, have been increasingly turned off by the intense politicization of mainstream religion, which often seems to be less about love or connection to the divine than about political battles over abortion, sexual orientation, and children's books.[52] Many of those who identify as SBNR or Nones appear to be much less interested in dogmas or politics than in *experiences*; that is, they tend not to care so much about matters of correct belief as about a direct encounter with something transcendent. As amateur historian Brian Muraresku argues in his best-selling book *The Immortality Key*,

> A God that you can actually *experience* in a direct and personal way is a God that makes sense. A God that erases depression and anxiety like a cosmic surgeon, obliterates the fear of death, and sends a shock wave of love through your fragile heart is a God that lives in high definition. And a God that could hardly be expected to start a war against nonbelievers. More troubling is a God of organized religion and his army of spokesmen—those priests, rabbis and imams who stand between superficial definitions of heaven and a common-sense public who have every right to demand proof.[53]

It is not entirely surprising that many would seek these experiences in psilocybin and other psychedelics, which seem to offer the possibility of inspiring "profound mystical experiences, even among people who previously considered themselves atheists or long ago fell away from organized religion"—indeed, perhaps even "alternative communities of spiritual seekers moving beyond the tired dogma, divisive doctrine, and outdated denominations of old-time religion."[54] In the Bay Area, for example, there are now various groups such as the highly successful "Church of Ambrosia," which was founded in 2019 by pastor David Hodges, based on the sacramental use of both *Cannabis* and *Psilocybe* mushrooms.[55] Countless other new psychedelic communities have sprung up across the country and across the globe.

As the early psychedelic explorer Terence McKenna put it in his 1992 book *Food of the Gods*, traditional religious forms have increasingly lost their power to persuade modern secular human beings: "We have lost the ability to be swayed by the power of myths, and our history should convince us of the fallacy of dogma"; yet we now seem to have a kind of portal to other realms through psychedelics, which offer an "escape hatch into the transcendental and transpersonal realm . . . provided by plant-based indole hallucinogens."[56] Today, McKenna notes, there are spiritual entrepreneurs and neo-shamans all over the world who are opening these portals by growing their own mushrooms and distributing them widely. And he rightly wonders what this new explosion of DIY psychedelic mysticism might mean for the modern world:

> There are now many thousands of mushroom cultivators in the world. It is reasonable to suppose that more people are now actively involved in a religious quest using psilocybin than ever before in history. This is a complete rebirth of a religious mystery, and it has taken place in less than a decade! What are the implications of this emergence of a pagan mystery in the banal world of modernity?[57]

Much of this book will be devoted to exploring McKenna's question about the implications of this "old-but-new" mystery.

Fantastic Fungi: What Are *Psilocybe* Mushrooms? And What Is Psilocybin?

Psilocybe is a large genus of mushrooms containing over 150 species that are scattered on every continent of the globe.[58] The larger biological category of which *Psilocybe* species are a part is the kingdom of fungi—a vast realm that includes everything from yeasts and molds to fleshy, spore-bearing bodies such as mushrooms. In turn, mushrooms play several critical roles in various ecosystems. While some are *parasitic*, feeding upon and often killing other organisms, others are *mycorrhizal*, growing around the roots of trees and plants in mutually beneficial symbiotic relationships; and others, including *Psilocybe* species, are *saprobic*, meaning that they feed upon dead and dying organic material, helping to break down and recycle other organisms. *Psilocybe* species thus tend to favor and even thrive in areas that have suffered environmental damage, whether natural or human-caused, where there is a

FIGURE I.3. *Psilocybe cubensis*. Photo by Alan Rockefeller. CC BY-SA 4.0, https://creativecommons.org/licenses/by-sa/4.0/.

great deal of dead organic matter to break down. As such, they have tended to follow human civilization, feeding upon the wood chips and debris that surround our development, as well as our destruction of the natural environment.[59] "As humans destroy woodlands and engage in artificial construction," Paul Stamets explains, "Psilocybes and other litter saprophytes proliferate, feeding off the surplus of wood chips and refuse, especially in interface environments, wherever humans, forests and grasslands struggle to coexist. Since human development seems inextricably associated with ecological disturbance, Psilocybe mushrooms and civilization continue to coevolve."[60]

Psilocybe mushrooms are known, among other things, for their telltale blue-staining reaction when touched or bruised; this is believed to be the result of the oxidation of the compound psilocybin when the outer surface of the mushroom is breached.[61] In addition to *Psilocybe*, however, mushrooms in several other genera also contain some amounts of psilocybin. These include (among others) at least thirteen species of *Panaeolus*; six species of *Pluteus*; and sixteen or so species of *Gymnopilus*.[62]

The precise role of psilocybin in the mushroom's evolution and its place in the larger ecosystem remains a bit unclear. Some researchers have suggested that psilocybin may have served as a defense mechanism against mushroom-eating organisms, deterring them by its toxic and/or

FIGURE I.4. *Psilocybe ovoideocystidiata*. Photo by the author.

disorienting effects. Others have speculated that psilocybin may have actually helped the mushroom spread its spores more widely, by altering the behavior of animals who came into contact with it and so expanding its potential range of distribution.[63] In this sense, we might legitimately wonder if we human seekers of the magic mushroom are not simply helping the fungus—consciously or unconsciously—with its own reproductive work. By growing these mushrooms all over the world and consuming them widely in altered states, are we perhaps helping the mushroom to do precisely what it has evolved to do—that is, to spread its spores as widely as possible, if necessary through disoriented animals?

In comparison to other "classical psychedelics," psilocybin is sort of midrange in its potency among human consumers: while roughly ten times more powerful than mescaline, it is also about one hundred times less potent than LSD.[64] At low to moderate doses, individuals often report more intense perceptions of color, shifting visual patterns, and deeper emotional connections. At higher doses, individuals may report a more radical shift in their perception of conventional reality, seeing the world in a new way, and experiencing a sense of expanded or even boundless consciousness.[65] More daring psychonauts such as Terence McKenna recommend "heroic doses" of five grams or more for those who want to achieve what he calls "shamanic" experiences, including encounters with supernatural beings and profound insights into the nature of reality.[66]

However, exactly how psilocybin and other psychedelics produce their specific effects in humans remains somewhat unclear. As Michael Pollan frankly admits, we know that psychedelics like psilocybin and LSD seem to latch very powerfully onto a particular receptor in the brain called the 5-HT2A receptor; but beyond that, we don't yet have a very good explanation for the specific kinds of subjective effects and alterations of consciousness that they commonly produce:

> How do these psychedelics work? Well, the honest answer is we don't entirely know. But we know a few things. One is, they fit a certain receptor site, the serotonin 5-2A receptor, and they look a lot like serotonin if you look at the molecular models of them. And in fact, LSD fits that receptor site even better than serotonin does, and it stays there longer. . . . What happens after that, we don't really know. It's an agonist to that receptor, so it increases its activity, and this. . . . leads to a cascade of effects, which is a shorthand for don't really know what happens next.[67]

A somewhat clearer explanation is provided by researchers such as Matthew Johnson of Johns Hopkins University. Johnson explains that the psilocybin in the mushroom is converted by the body into another compound called psilocin, which in turn activates the 2A receptor. This appears to trigger a broader increase in communication across different parts of the brain, which may explain the experience of a kind of shift in perspective or new insights described by users:

> *Psilocybin* . . . converts to a related compound called *psilocin,* which is the thing that's actually hitting the brain receptors, and it activates a subtype of serotonin receptor . . . called the serotonin 2A receptor. And *psilocin* and the other psychedelics can latch onto that in the same way that our serotonin latches onto these brain receptors. So *psilocybin* affects *serotonin,* but then *serotonin* affects the glutamate system. And then at another level you have this massive increase in communication across these different silos in the brain. . . . There also may be increased

neuroplasticity in the system so that in the days following the psychedelic experience, people are more primed to learn new things.[68]

While the exact cause of psychedelic sorts of experiences—the sense of interconnectivity, loss of ego, transcendence of time and space, and so on—is not well understood, some researchers have offered possible explanations. The British psychopharmacologist Robin Carhart-Harris suggests there is evidence that psilocybin actually reduces brain activity, particularly in one brain system known as the "default mode network" (DMN).[69] A centrally located hub of brain activity, the DMN links parts of the cerebral cortex to deeper structures involved in memory and emotion. As such, it functions as sort of the brain's "orchestra conductor," capital city, or corporate executive in charge of managing the entire system. Many speculate that it is closely tied to our self-construct or what we commonly call the "self" or "ego": "The default mode is most active when we are engaged in higher-level 'metacognitive' processes such as self-reflection, mental time travel, mental constructions (such as the self or ego), moral reasoning, and 'theory of mind'—the ability to attribute mental states to others."[70] When psilocybin and other drugs reduce activity in this particular part of the brain, this can result in the sense of ego dissolution or transcendence of self commonly reported in psychedelic experiences—the melting away of the usual boundaries between self and world and the feeling of "Oceanic Boundlessness" or merging into some larger whole.[71] At the same time, the reduction of the DMN may also allow other parts of the brain to become to become more active. No longer held in check by the DMN, other material not usually available to consciousness may float to the surface, including emotions, memories, and buried traumas.[72]

It should be emphasized, however, that the precise understanding of how psilocybin and other psychedelics work remains murky at best, and there are many lingering questions about the complex physical, psychological, cultural, and religious factors that help produce these experiences. More critical scholars such as Brian Pace and Neşe Devenot argue that the social and political setting in which the mushrooms is consumed is as important if not *more* important than the brain chemistry itself. While many psychedelic enthusiasts see mushrooms as naturally aligned with a kind of progressive, leftist, inclusivist worldview, Pace and Devenot offer numerous examples of psychedelics being used by extremely conservative and even fascist individuals, often reinforcing a far-right-wing and staunchly hierarchical ideology. Psychedelics have also been used heavily by extremist religious groups that engaged in abuse, manipulation, and violence, such as Aum Shinrikyo and the Manson Family, to name but a few of the most infamous examples.[73]

As such, Pace and Devenot argue, psychedelics do not necessarily lead to any particular worldview but are instead more like "non-specific amplifiers of political set and setting." That is to say, they tend to enhance one's suggestibility and so can intensify whatever social, political, or religious ideology one happens to have or be surrounded by in the particular circumstance in which they are taken.[74]

Similarly, many anthropologists have argued that the communal, ritual, and aesthetic contexts in which psychedelic plants and fungi are consumed are as important, if not more important, than the specific chemicals they contain.[75] Thus, the religious and cultural set and setting of a Mazatec healing ritual would likely produce a rather different sort of experience than that of a university laboratory or an upscale psilocybin service center.

A Mycelial Narrative

This book follows a kind of mycelial narrative, tracing the complex journey of this particular mushroom through a series of interconnected social, cultural, historical, and religious encounters. The story that emerges is not so much a clear linear trajectory but a far messier, more tangled, and conflicted sort of genealogy, which also explores the tensions, fissures, and reversals in this narrative.

The narrative begins with an examination of the existing historical evidence for the use of *Psilocybe* and other mushrooms for religious purposes prior to the twentieth century. While *Psilocybe* species are found on every continent, they are not known to have been widely used for religious reasons in premodern times outside of Mesoamerica. The most detailed evidence comes from Spanish colonial contact with Mexico in the sixteenth century, where mushrooms of an unknown species (possibly *Psilocybe*) were reportedly used for both recreational and religious purposes. The Spanish Catholic clergy fiercely condemned the Indigenous use of the "flesh of the gods" (*teonanácatl*), which they saw as a demonic perversion of the Christian Eucharist. Yet some ritual use of mushrooms apparently continued in Mexico up to the time of Wasson's encounter with Mazatec healers in the 1950s. Particularly in the mountainous regions of southern Mexico, several Indigenous communities have been known to use various species of *Psilocybe*, as well as several non-hallucinogenic species, mainly for curing illness. Among the present-day Nahuatl, *Psilocybe caerulescens* is known by the poetic name *teotlaquilnanácatl* or "divine mushroom that paints or describes," leading some to speculate that it may be the same as the *teonanácatl* mushroom mentioned in sixteenth-century sources.[76]

Although a few other mushrooms such as *A. muscaria* were also used for shamanic purposes by some Siberian communities, there is actually fairly scant historical evidence for the widespread use of mushrooms for religious reasons prior to the modern era. The claims that fungi were the source of various other religious phenomena—ranging from the Eleusinian Mysteries to the soma beverage of the Vedas—remain at best ambiguous and elusive today.

Each of the subsequent chapters of the book covers roughly one decade and one or two key figures from the 1950s to the present. Thus chapter 2, "Seeking the Magic Mushroom," focuses on R. Gordon Wasson and his participation in mushroom rituals with the Mazatec wise woman María Sabina in the 1950s. As María Sabina later explained in interviews, she did not consume the mushrooms primarily for "mystical" purposes, and she flatly denied that they were used to "see God"; as a devout Catholic she went to Mass for her religion and instead used the mushrooms for more practical purposes such as healing and divination. Yet in his highly romantic descriptions in *Life* magazine, Wasson described the mushroom experience as comparable to the visionary experience of the biblical prophets and to the ideal Forms of Platonic philosophy. In so doing, I argue, Wasson helped to both *religionize* and *de-religionize* the mushroom experience. By "religionize" I mean that he redescribed it as a religious rite, comparable to the Christian Eucharist. But by "de-religionize" I mean that he also presented it as a mystical experience that anyone could achieve by simply consuming the mushroom, without participating in any ritual or institutional form of religion. Finally, Wasson also helped to imagine a kind of global mushroom mysticism, which he saw everywhere from ancient Greece to India and which he believed could explain the origin of human civilization and even consciousness itself.

In chapter 3, "High Priests," I then explore the ways in which psychedelic mushrooms were quickly taken up by researchers at Harvard University. While the controversial work of psychologist Timothy Leary is well known, this chapter focuses primarily on the less-well-known Walter Pahnke, who was a minister and PhD candidate at Harvard Divinity School in the early 1960s. Inspired by Wasson's work on *Psilocybe*, Pahnke based his dissertation research on psychedelics and mysticism. As part of that research, he organized the "Marsh Chapel Experiment," in which a group of Harvard Divinity School students were given psilocybin and asked to recount their various spiritual experiences. Building upon W. T. Stace's definition of mysticism, Pahnke created a quantitative metric for analyzing mystical experience, a version of which is still widely used in psychedelic research to this day. As such, Pahnke helped shape the discourse on psychedelics for the counterculture of the 1960s, claiming to provide quantitative evidence for a psilocybin-based spiritual experience. But perhaps more importantly, his metric continues to inform much of our current scientific discourse on psychedelics and mysticism—though often in ways that are extremely outdated and problematic.

Meanwhile, Pahnke's mentor Timothy Leary would go on to conduct even more wide-ranging and controversial experiments with psilocybin, which led to his dismissal from Harvard. Yet he would also create a new movement called the League for Spiritual Discovery, dubbing himself the "High Priest" and calling upon everyone to "create their own religion." As such, Leary was not only one of the most important figures in the American counterculture, but he was also a key figure in the broader push for a kind of mysticism outside of traditional religious institutions.

Chapter 4, "Neo-Shamans," turns to the decade of the 1970s and to the hugely influential work of the amateur ethnobotanist Terence McKenna. With his ingestion of "heroic doses" of *Psilocybe*, McKenna claimed to achieve a modern form of shamanic experience in which the mushroom could open "transdimensional portals" to other realities. Perhaps more than any other single text, his practical guide to growing *Psilocybe* mushrooms helped promote the widespread home cultivation and use of psychedelic mushrooms throughout North America and Europe. He offered, in short, the possibility for anyone to achieve a kind of DIY shamanic experience of other spiritual realms without any connection to conventional forms of religion. At the same time, McKenna also wove his neo-shamanism together with UFO narratives and the divinatory techniques of the *I Ching*, creating an eclectic worldview that clearly reflected (and helped shape) the hybrid landscape of New Age spirituality in the 1970s.

In chapter 5, "How Mushrooms Can Save the World," I turn to the decades of the 1980s and 1990s and to the work of the American mycologist and entrepreneur Paul Stamets. Arguably the world's leading "myco-evangelist," Stamets created his own company, Fungi Perfecti, and has done numerous TED Talks and other media appearances. In Stamets's bold, almost utopian vision, mushrooms can not only lead to higher states of consciousness, they can also literally "save the world," by curing cancer, boosting immune systems, remediating toxic soil, and even providing eco-friendly pesticides. Through popular films such as *Fantastic Fungi*, Stamets has become perhaps the world's leading mushroom advocate with an almost soteriological vision of the power of fungi. A peculiar blend of entrepreneurial businessman and spiritual visionary, Stamets embodies the complex, often ambivalent place of mushrooms in contemporary America.

Chapter 6, "Mushrooms, Mysticism, and Pharmaceuticals," then examines the resurgence of interest in psychedelic mushrooms in the twenty-first century, both in universities and in the pharmaceutical industry. Roland Griffiths's landmark study, "Psilocybin Can Occasion Mystical Experiences," helped inspire tremendous new interest in the clinical use of psychedelics that continues to this day. Over the last seventeen years, there have been dozens of studies of the use of psilocybin for the treatment of a wide range of disorders, ranging from depression and anxiety to OCD and PTSD. Almost all of these studies continue to use a revised form of Pahnke's metric called the Mystical Experience Questionnaire (MEQ), which suggests yet a new variation on the theme of "mysticism without religion"—that is, the claim to predictably generate mystical experience in a highly controlled research setting.

At the same time, not surprisingly, a number of powerful pharmaceutical companies have begun to pour millions of dollars into psilocybin research, hoping to produce a revolutionary new class of drugs with tremendous market potential. While Mazatec healers such as María Sabina were adamant that one should not profit from the mushrooms, biopharmaceutical companies such as atai Life Sciences, Compass Pathways, and others appear to have reached the opposite conclusion. All of this has raised profound concerns about the commercial development not just of *Psilocybe* mushrooms but of other substances with roots in traditional cultures, such as peyote and ayahuasca. While many see this as an opportunity to develop a powerful new group of therapeutic drugs, others regard this as a form of cultural appropriation that erases the complex interrelations between plants, humans, and the divine. This deep tension will likely shape the future development of all these substances in the twenty-first century.

Finally, in the conclusion, "Mushrooms and the Arts of Living and Dying on a Damaged Planet," I reflect on the complex role of fungi in the twenty-first century and argue for some more constructive alternatives to the current push toward corporate pharmaceutical exploitation. While I am by no means as romantically utopian as Paul Stamets, I do think we may have something to learn from mushrooms in the twenty-first century, as we face massive environmental destruction, rapid loss of species, and the devastating effects of climate change. As we saw above, fungi play a variety of different roles in the ecosystem: some are *parasitic*, feeding upon and often killing living trees and plants; some (like *Psilocybe* species) are mainly *saprobic*, breaking down dead trees and plants and recycling them into the greater ecosystem; and others (such as most terrestrial mushrooms) are *mycorrhizal*, existing in symbiotic, mutually beneficial relationships with plants and trees. As such, mushrooms offer us several possible models for our relationship with other species: Shall we be parasites, feeding upon, exploiting, and destroying other species? Or could we be recyclers and symbionts, helping to regenerate our environments and cooperate in a mutually beneficial way with other living systems? Fungi might help us to learn, as Donna Haraway put it, to "become less deadly, more response-able, more attuned, more capable of surprise, more able to practice the arts of living and dying well in multispecies symbiosis."[77]

Perhaps even more so than the psychedelic experience produced by psilocybin itself, the complex networks of mushroom mycelia might provide us with a model for this sort of "multispecies symbiosis." This should apply as much to relations with other humans—such as Indigenous cultures and formerly colonized peoples—as to relations with nonhuman species.

[CHAPTER ONE]

Flesh of the Gods?

Mushrooms in the History of Religions

They had another form of intoxication that made them more cruel, and it was with some fungi or small mushrooms [*hongos o setas pequeñas*]. . . . These mushrooms are called in their language *teunanacatlth*, which means flesh of god [*carne de dios*], or of the demon they worshiped.

Fray Toribio de Benavente o Motolinía, *Memoriales o libro de las cosas de la Nueva España y de los naturales de ella* (sixteenth century)[1]

Every psychoactive substance does not lead to a religion, and every religion does not arise from such a substance.

Fritz Staal, "How a Psychoactive Substance Becomes a Ritual" (2001)[2]

For a relatively unassuming group of fungi, *Psilocybe* and other psychoactive mushrooms have generated intense debate over their possible role in the development of religion and of human culture more broadly. In the eyes of many mushroom enthusiasts—beginning with R. Gordon Wasson, then continuing with Terence McKenna, and resurfacing with more recent authors such as Brian Muraresku—psychedelic fungi lie at the very roots of religion itself, providing the chemical impetus that generated some of the earliest human mystical experiences, spiritual visions, and conceptions of the divine. From Wasson onward, many have identified psychedelic mushrooms as the source of mystical flights to other worlds, of the sacred beverage of the Eleusinian Mysteries, of the Vedic soma ritual, perhaps even of the Christian Eucharist. This idea has given birth to many best-selling books, such as *Persephone's Quest, The Sacred Mushroom and the Cross, Food of the Gods*, and more recently *The Immortality Key*.[3] It has even resurfaced in mainstream magazines such as *Popular Mechanics*, which published an article on how "Magic Mushrooms May Have Shaped Our Consciousness."[4]

More skeptical authors, conversely, have generally regarded these claims for the psychedelic origins of religion as fanciful, amateurish, and flawed. Wasson's, McKenna's, and Muraresku's narratives about the psychedelic origins of religion have all been dismissed or derided by most established scholars. Claims that *A. muscaria* is the source of the Vedic soma and that ergot fungus lay at the origins of the Eleusinian Mysteries are rejected by many if not most Indologists and classicists today.[5]

And yet, there is also a significant body of evidence that suggests that some cultures—particularly but not solely in Mesoamerica—have historically used *Psilocybe* and other mushrooms for religious purposes. At least at the time of the Spanish conquest of Mexico, mushrooms of some variety were clearly used both recreationally and religiously, some version of which may have continued up to the twentieth century when Wasson first encountered María Sabina. This chapter aims to navigate the complex debate over the role of mushrooms in the history of religions, by focusing primarily on *Psilocybe* species and looking closely at the available archaeological, historical, and ethnographic evidence.[6] I begin by tracing the existing historical evidence for their use in Mesoamerica, both in Spanish colonial accounts and in modern anthropological literature. I then briefly examine the evidence for the possible religious use of other mushroom species, such as *A. muscaria* and *Claviceps purpurea*.

The historical evidence, it seems, offers a far more complicated picture than Wasson's narrative of the ancient religious origins of mushroom use and its fortuitous rediscovery in the twentieth century. While some sort of mushrooms were clearly used in Mesoamerica at the time of the Spanish conquest, their identity is by no means clear, and (at least in the highly biased Spanish accounts) they were used as much for recreational as for "spiritual" purposes. The idea that they were a kind of "sacrament" was largely a projection of the Spanish Catholic clergy, who viewed them as a perverted form of the Christian Eucharist. Meanwhile, the idea that there was widespread religious use of *Psilocybe* or other fungi outside of Mesoamerica remains an intriguing yet mostly imaginative speculation. The evidence for a fungal basis for the soma beverage of the Vedas or the *kykeon* of the Eleusinian Mysteries is indeed provocative but still contested by most Indologists and classicists today. None of this, of course, has prevented the idea of the fungal origin of religion from continuing to spread widely in popular culture and on the internet, where it remains a very common trope today.[7]

The Earliest Evidence for Psychedelic Mushroom Use

There is one curious and—I think—significant point about *Psilocybe* mushrooms that we should highlight from the outset of this book. While psychoactive *Psilocybe* species are found in many regions across the globe, including North, Central, and South America, Europe, various parts of Africa, South Asia, East Asia, and Australia,[8] there is surprisingly little evidence that they were actually consumed by many human cultures outside of southern Mexico and a few other regions. As Erik Davis notes, "One of the curiosities about psilocybe mushrooms is that, while they are widely distributed across the planet, very few indigenous societies seemed to have been particularly interested in them."[9] For example, *Psilocybe* species occur throughout North America, particularly on the eastern and western coasts of Canada and the US. But outside of southern Mexico, there is at present no evidence that they were used by any Native Americans in these regions. Indeed, most Native Americans appear to have made little use of *any* mushrooms, even for culinary or medical purposes, apart from a few species such as giant puffballs (*Calvatia gigantea*) and some polypores such as *Haploporus odorus* and *Phellinus igniarius*.[10] This seems surprising, given the general importance of spiritual experiences and vision quests in most North American Indigenous traditions, as well as their use of other substances such as the peyote cactus. As Gastón Guzmán observes in his overview of *Psilocybe* species, "hallucinogenic species of *Psilocybe* occur on all continents. However, only in Mexico and perhaps in New Guinea . . . are they confirmed to be traditionally consumed as visionary 'sacred' mushrooms."[11] Of the more than one hundred species of *Psilocybe* cataloged by Guzmán worldwide, less than a third are known to be ceremonially used, and almost all of these are in the higher elevations of Mexico (above 1,500 meters).[12] A couple of notable exceptions, as we will see below, are some recent reports of *Psilocybe* use in South America, South Africa, and Nepal.[13]

Because of the modern rediscovery of *Psilocybe* use in Mexico during the twentieth century, many authors have looked for earlier historical evidence throughout Mesoamerica. The results are intriguing but ultimately inconclusive. For example, about three hundred stone and pottery mushroom effigies have been uncovered throughout Central America, dating all the way from the second millennium BCE to roughly 600–900 CE. The stones have been found in all parts of highland Guatemala, in El Salvador, and in the Mexican states of Oaxaca, Tabasco, Veracruz, and Chiapas. While many scholars have eagerly pointed to these stones as evidence of ritual use of fungi and the "importance of the mushroom cult among the Mayas,"[14] it is very difficult to say with any certainty what species of mushroom these might have been, much less how they were used. As Letcher acknowledges, "Quite what they were for is uncertain: they have been variously and plausibly interpreted as phallic symbols, boundary markers, seats even, or as being connected in some way to the Mesoamerican 'ball game' . . . beloved of the Aztecs and the civilizations that preceded them."[15]

There has also been much excitement over a statue of Xochipili—the Aztec god of art, games, dance, flowers, and song—which was unearthed in the nineteenth century on the side of the volcano Popocatépetl. Dating to the fifteenth or sixteenth century, the figure is decorated with various flowers, vines, and other natural forms and raises his head skyward in an

FIGURE 1.1. Xochipili statue. Photo by Antony Stanley. CC BY-SA 2.0, https://creativecommons.org/licenses/by-sa/2.0/.

expression of seeming rapture or ecstasy. Wasson and others have suggested that the circular earrings and other shapes on the figure represent the psychedelic *Psilocybe aztecorum*, which is native to the region.[16] However, in the absence of any broader context for the statue, this suggestion seems highly speculative at best. Apart from simply being round, there is nothing that identifies these circles as any kind of mushroom caps, much less *Psilocybe* species.[17] It seems equally likely that they are flowers, various species of which adorn the rest of the figure's body.

Similarly intriguing but unclear evidence can be found in several of the Mesoamerican codices—Indigenous texts written in symbolic picture language—that seem to portray mushrooms in various ways. One of the most interesting of these is the *Codex Vindobonensis*, a fifteenth–sixteenth-century Mixtec work that contains a wide range of vivid illustrations of ritual and mythical figures. As Osiris Gonzáles Romero explains in his analysis of the text, one of the sixty-six folios depicts a series of figures who are adorned with and/or handling mushrooms. These include the deities Lady Eleven Lizard and Lady Four Lizard, who each wear headdresses bearing mushrooms, Lord Seven Flowers, who holds two mushrooms, and several other deities, who

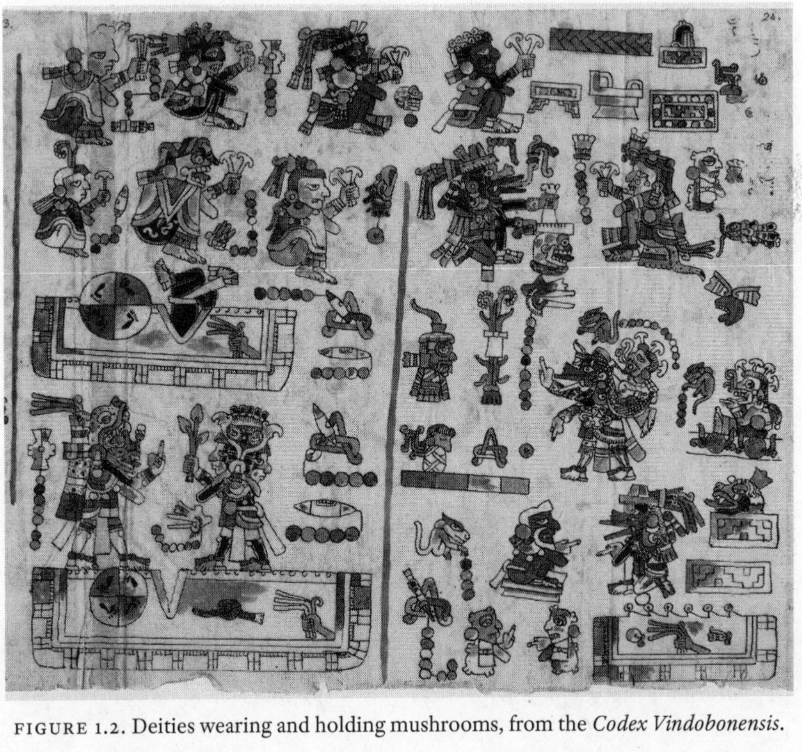

FIGURE 1.2. Deities wearing and holding mushrooms, from the *Codex Vindobonensis*.

FIGURE 1.3. Seated figure with mushrooms, from the *Magliabechiano Codex*.

hold mushrooms and may be participating in some kind of ritual.[18] Another sixteenth-century text, the *Codex Magliabechiano*, depicts a person eating mushrooms, while a masked supernatural figure stands behind him.[19] Wasson and other authors have concluded enthusiastically that these texts offer "full dress recognition of the major place occupied by mushrooms in the culture of the Mixtecs."[20] Yet in the absence of any broader contextual evidence, it is difficult to say what species of mushrooms these were (*Psilocybe* or other) and how exactly they may have been used by the culture at the time (ritually, recreationally, etc.).

"With This Bitter Food They Received Their Cruel God in Communion": Spanish Encounters and Accounts

While we cannot say a great deal with any certainty about the specific uses of mushrooms in ancient Mesoamerica, we do have a good deal of information about the ways in which mushrooms were *perceived* by Europeans when they first explored and conquered this region. The Spanish left numerous accounts of their observations of the Aztecs in the sixteenth century, and they recorded the use of a wide variety of psychoactive plants and fungi.[21] These included not only psychedelic mushrooms but also jimsonweed

(*Datura stramonium*), peyote (*L. williamsii*), and others. Perhaps not surprisingly, the Spanish—and particularly the Catholic clergy they brought with them to convert the Indigenous populations—had an intensely negative view of these substances. The psychoactive mushroom used at the time of these encounters was called *teonanácatl* in the Nahuatl language, which translates as "flesh of the gods." To Catholic priests and missionaries hoping to Christianize these people, this must have sounded like a perverse or even demonic inversion of the Eucharist as Christ's own body and blood—"an appalling simulacrum of the Holy Communion."[22] In the words of the sixteenth-century Franciscan friar Toribio de Benavente, the mushrooms were nothing less than the flesh "of the devil that they worshipped and . . . with this bitter food they received their cruel god in communion."[23]

The earliest and arguably most comprehensive account of mushroom use recorded by the Spanish was written by the Franciscan priest Bernardino de Sahagún (1499–1590) in his *Historia general de las cosas de Nueva España* (*General History of the Things of New Spain*, also known as the *Florentine Codex*).[24] Both a missionary and an ethnographer, Sahagún described the use of small black mushrooms called *teonanácatl* or *nanacatl*,[25] along with various plants, such as tobacco, peyote, and morning glory seeds. It is worth noting that, in his account, the mushrooms were not consumed in any particularly "religious" or "ritual" way by priests, but rather by merchants as part of an elaborate feast. Their main use in this account was for divination, or seeing into the future and determining the individual's fate:

> At the very first mushrooms had been served. . . . They ate no more food, they only drank chocolate during the night. And they ate the mushrooms with honey. When the mushrooms took effect on them, then they danced, then they wept. . . .
>
> One saw in a vision that he would die in battle; one saw in a vision that he would be eaten by wild beasts; one saw in a vision that he would take captives in war . . . one saw in a vision that he would commit adultery—he would be struck by stones . . .
>
> And when the effects of the mushrooms had left them, they consulted among themselves and told one another what they had seen in vision.[26]

Significantly, Sahagún's text also indicates that mushroom consumption was associated with bad behavior and people of ill repute—much like drunkenness and other social evils. When listing good and bad deeds of various members of the society, both noble and common, the texts states that "the bad one of noble lineage [is] a scandalizer, a flatterer—a drinker, besotted drunk. He goes about becoming crazed, he goes about eating *Datura stramonium* [jimsonweed] and mushrooms."[27] Moreover, "The lewd youth is a madman. He goes about drinking crude wine—a drunkard, foolish, dejected; a drunk, a sot. He goes about eating mushrooms. He goes about demented."[28] At least in Sahagún's account, it would seem that mushrooms are subject to both recreational uses and various abuses.

Another early account of mushroom use comes from the Franciscan missionary Toribio de Benavente, also known as Motolinía (d. 1565). In his treatise on Indigenous religious customs, Motolinía described the Aztecs eating bitter mushrooms sweetened with honey. In his detailed but quite critical account, the mushrooms were said to produce both drunkenness and visions, often of a frightening nature:

> They had another form of intoxication that made them more cruel, and it was with some fungi or small mushrooms. . . . But the ones of this land are of such quality that, when eaten raw and because they are bitter, they drink after them or eat a little bees' honey with them; and shortly thereafter, they would see a thousand visions, especially snakes, and as they lost all sense, it seemed to them that their legs and bodies were full of worms eating them alive, and so, half-crazed, they would rush out of the house, wishing someone would kill them; and with this bestial drunkenness . . . it sometimes happened that they hanged themselves. . . . These mushrooms are called in their language *teunanacatlth*, which means flesh of god, or of the demon they worshiped; and in this manner, their cruel god gave them communion with this bitter delicacy.[29]

According to other early accounts, mushrooms were used by members of Aztec society at the highest levels. In his detailed treatise, *Historia de las Indias de Nueva España*, the Dominican friar Diego Durán (d. 1588) described the coronation of the Aztec sovereign, Tizoc, in 1481, where mushrooms were offered to the guests. Significantly, in Durán's account of the coronation, the mushrooms seem to be used mostly recreationally as a pleasant intoxicant rather than as a religious or mystical substance:

> After the dance the nobility came to offer them garlands of flowers delicately arranged and handsomely decorated pipes of tobacco. To make the feast more solemn all ate wild mushrooms [*hongos monteses*] which make a man lose his senses.[30]

In other anecdotes, Durán does describe the use of mushrooms for more religious and divinatory purposes. According to his account, the last great ruler of the Aztec empire, Montezuma II (?–1520), employed a group of priests, whose job it was to consume mushrooms for divination, especially to foresee the outcome of battles.[31] Durán also recounts that Montezuma appeased enemy kings from neighboring states with an annual "Feast of Revelations," which involved a wild celebration with mushrooms. After a grizzly mass sacrifice of war captives, the guests were offered mushrooms that brought both drunkenness and revelatory visions of the future:

> When the sacrifice was finished and the steps and courtyard were bathed with human blood, everyone went to eat raw mushrooms. With this food they went out of their minds and were in a worse state than if they had drunk a great quantity of wine. They became so inebriated and witless that many of them took their lives in their hands. With the strength of these mushrooms they saw visions and had revelations about the future, since the devil spoke to them in their madness.[32]

Obviously, we need to read these Spanish accounts with a certain degree of skepticism and an awareness of their Eurocentric and Christocentric bias. Nonetheless, I think we can see throughout all of them a complex picture of the Indigenous use of mushrooms, which were consumed for many different reasons. By no means exclusively "religious," they had clear recreational uses and seem to have been closely tied to practices of divination.

In the seventeenth century, we also find a handful of references to mushrooms in the accounts of the Spanish Inquisition. As part of their efforts to weed out idolatrous and demonic practices among the Indigenous peoples, several Inquisitors described the use of mushrooms for divinatory and religious practices. Thus in 1630, a man named Gonzalo Pérez was said to have consulted with Indian named Joseph in his attempt to locate his missing wife. Joseph gave him an herb called *nanacate* (mushroom) with which he could see where she was.[33] An even more detailed account comes from Jacinto de la Serna, a seventeenth-century cleric ministering to Indians, in his *Manual de ministros de indios, para el conocimiento de sus idolatrías y extirpacíon de ellas*. Here Jacinto describes an Indian named Juan Chichiton, who officiated at a ceremony that involved a mixture of mushrooms, Indigenous ritual, and elements of Christianity:

> There had come to [the village] an Indian native of the village of Tenango, a great maestro of superstitions, and his name was Juan Chichiton, which means "little dog," and he had brought the red-colored mushrooms that are gathered in the uplands and with them he had committed a great idolatry. . . . Said mushrooms . . . are called in the Mexican language *Quautlannamacatl*. . . . It was the custom for the

> priests and old men deputized as minsters for this kind of humbuggery to go up into the mountain, and they remained almost the whole night in prayer and superstitious entreaties, and at dawn, when there sprang up a certain breeze that they knew then they gathered the mushrooms, attributing divinity to them, possessing as the same effect as *ololiuqui* [*Rivea corymbosa*]. . . . or peyote [*L. williamsii*], because whether eaten or drunk, it intoxicates them and deprives them of their sense, and makes them believe a thousand foolish things. . . . And so this Juan Chichiton, having gathered the mushrooms upon a certain night, in the house where everyone had gathered on the occasion of a saint's feast, the saint was on the altar, and the mushrooms with pulque and a fire beneath the altar, the *teponastli* [a percussion instrument peculiar to the Aztecs] and singing going on the whole night through, after most of the night had passed, said Juan Chichiton, who as the priest for that solemn rite, to all those present at the fiesta gave the mushrooms to eat, after the manner of communion, and gave them pulque to drink, and . . . they all went out of their heads, a shame it was to see.[34]

A few things are worth noting in Jacinto's account. First, it is not entirely clear from the description what species the mushrooms were, since they are described as "red-colored." This does not sound much like a *Psilocybe* species but possibly like *A. muscaria* (discussed below). Second, despite the obviously hostile nature of Jacinto's account, it does appear to show that local mushroom practices had begun to be mixed and blended with elements of Catholicism by the seventeenth century. This hybridization of Indigenous mushroom use and elements of Christianity, we will see, is characteristic of most later practices in southern Mexico.

The Use of *Psilocybe* Species in Modern Mexico

Intensely condemned by the Spanish Catholic Church, the use of mushrooms and other substances appears to have been either eradicated or driven to the margins of society after the sixteenth century. However, some use of psychedelic mushrooms could still be found in a few regions of Mexico up to the twentieth century, primarily in the higher elevations. As Guzmán and others speculate, it is possible that this represents the survival of an older tradition of ritual mushroom use, which was largely destroyed in most parts of Mexico but continued in more remote mountainous regions. Communities that continue the ceremonial use of mushrooms include the Nahuatls in the states of Mexico, Morelos, and Puebla; the Matlatzincas in the state of Mexico; the Totonacs in the state of Veracruz; and the Mazatecs, Mixes, Zapotecs, and Chatinos in the state of Oaxaca.[35] The species of *Psilocybe* used by these groups include *P. aztecorum, P. barrerae, P. caerulescens, P. candidipes, P. cordispora, P. cubensis, P. fagicola, P. hoogshagenii, P. mexicana, P. muliercula, P. subcubensis, P. yungensis,* and *P. zapotecorum.*[36] Among the present-day Nahuatl, *P. caerulescens* is known by the highly poetic name *teotlaquilnanácatl* or "divine mushroom that paints or describes," leading Guzmán to speculate that this may be the same as the ceremonially used *teonanácatl* mushroom cited by Sahagún in the sixteenth century.[37]

It is worth noting, however, that some Mexican communities also use at least two other mushrooms that are *not* psychedelic in their rituals. In addition to *Psilocybe* species, Guzmán observes, the Nahuatl also use *Cordyceps* and *Elaphomyces* species in their rites. These two mushrooms actually grow together, the *Cordyceps* parasitizing and growing out of the *Elaphomyces,* which is a small subterranean fungus also called "false truffle" or "deer truffle." In the Nahuatl ceremony, the non-hallucinogenic *Elaphomyces* holds center stage, occupying an even more important place than the *Psilocybe* itself:

> Nahuatl from the townships of Tenango del Valle and San Pedro Tlanixco . . . use *Psilocybe muliercula,* which they call *siwatsitsintli* or *mujercitas* ("little women"), often in tandem with *Cordyceps capitata* or *C. ophioglossoides,* known as *hombrecitos* ("little men"). In their sacred mushroom ceremonies, some people eat only *mujercitas* and others eat only *hombrecitos* (apparently no one eats both, and the sex of the mushroom eater does not determine the sex of the mushroom they eat). One or more species of *Elaphomyces* (the truffle-like hypogeous mushroom form which the *Cordyceps* grows) typically occupy center stage during the ritual, usually on the altar or a sleeping mat on the ground. At the end of the ceremony everyone partakes of the *gran mundo* ("the great world") as *Elaphomyces* is called.[38]

Guzmán also notes that there are various other hallucinogenic fungi found commonly throughout Mexico—such as *Panaeolus* species—that are *not* used in any way for religious purposes: "in Mexico no *Panaeolus* is used as sacred or divine mushrooms . . . in spite of the fact that the species of *Panaeolus* are very common."[39] All of his suggests two important points that we should keep in mind throughout this book: 1) achieving a "psychedelic experience" is not the only reason to use mushrooms in a religious context (just as getting intoxicated is not the only reason to use alcohol in a religious context); and 2) *non*-hallucinogenic fungi are as important as or sometimes *more* important than those with psychoactive effects (just as non-hallucinogenic substances such as bread, fish, meat, or grains are as important if not more important than hallucinogenic substances in many ritual contexts).

The details of the ceremonial use of mushrooms vary depending on the specific community and region of Mexico. However, as Guzmán notes, there are some common elements found throughout the rituals performed in most communities in southern Mexico. Always held at night, the ceremony takes place under the guidance of a healer or elder, typically in the guide's home in front of a Catholic altar:

> Typically, the mushrooms are placed in a gourd or *jicara* . . . and incensed with *copal* resin. . . . The ceremonies show a mixture of native and Catholic elements; prayers may be in Spanish and/or indigenous tongues. The mushrooms are typically counted out in "male-female" pairs, though only one species of mushroom is used for a given ceremony (except in the Nevado de Toluca region where . . . *Cordyceps* and *Elaphomyces* are used in conjunction with *Psilocybe*). Participants are traditionally offered up to six pairs of mushrooms. . . . It is widely believed that excessive doses (more than 12 mushrooms) can produce mental disorders and that different species of *Psilocybe* should not be mixed.[40]

It also seems important to note here the complex blending of Indigenous and Catholic features in the ceremony. While the Spanish missionaries of the sixteenth century had been intensely hostile to the local use of mushrooms, by the twentieth century, the two traditions had often become inextricably entwined.

Possible Evidence of *Psilocybe* Use in Other Regions

Despite the widespread geographic distribution of *Psilocybe* species around the world, there are only a few known areas outside of Mesoamerica where they may have been used for religious purposes. Guzmán notes that there are some references to the use of *Psilocybe* and other mushrooms in New Guinea, and possibly also some evidence for their use in Columbia, Peru, and Africa—though most of these remain fairly speculative.[41]

Another intriguing site for the possible use of *Psilocybe* species comes from a prehistoric archaeological site in Spain known as Selva Pascuala. Dating to the post-Paleolithic era, the site is a rock shelter that contains numerous cave paintings, including many that appear to depict mushrooms.

A team of scholars led by archaeologist Juan Ruiz, mycologist Gastón Guzmán, and others explored the site and compared the cave images to local species of mushrooms. Based on fungal morphology, they hypothesize that the mushrooms depicted may have been *Psilocybe hispanica*, a dung-loving hallucinogenic species that grows in the region. If their hypothesis is correct, this would be the oldest known site depicting psychedelic mushrooms. However, they emphasize in their conclusions that this identification remains "tentative" and that there is really no material evidence beyond the prehistoric images themselves.[42]

Another possible candidate for a *Psilocybe* site—though with even less material support—is the famous rock art from the cave at Tassili in the Sahara Desert, dating to roughly 7000–5000 BCE. While the original art is highly abstract and difficult to identify with any certainty, a drawing of a figure called the "bee-headed shaman" appeared in Terence McKenna's book *Psilocybin: The Magic Mushroom Grower's Guide*—one of the most influential texts of the psychedelic movement in the 1970s (see below chapter 4).[43] Drawn by McKenna's then-wife, Kat Harrison-McKenna, the figure has multiple mushrooms sprouting from its hands and the outline of its body—though this is quite a bit of an extrapolation from the original rock art. Harrison-McKenna's drawing became an icon of post-1990s psychedelia, widely appearing on T-shirts and coffee mugs; and many enthusiasts point to this as evidence of prehistoric religious use of *Psilocybe* species. However, as Brian Aker notes, her rendition is quite a bit of an artistic leap from the far more obscure cave painting, which—unlike the images from Spain—does not even show mushrooms very clearly.[44] The idea that this is a *Psilocybe* shaman is surely provocative but not supported by anything other than enthusiastic speculation.

More recently, in 2024, some new evidence emerged for the use of *Psilocybe* species in traditional medicine and religious rites in southern Africa. In an article in *Mycologia*, a team of scholars reported the use of a mixture of *P. maluti* with another psychoactive herb for purposes of healing and divination among the Basotho community of Lesotho. This is apparently the first known evidence of the use of *Psilocybe* mushrooms in any sort of ritual context in Africa; however, the authors also acknowledge that their evidence is anecdotal and passed on through oral reports without any empirical confirmation:

> Two kinds of Basotho healers use the *Psilocybe*: linohe, who are the equivalent of a diviner or soothsayer and are able to "foresee the future" using tools such as medicinal plants and the *Psilocybe* described here, and the ngaka-chitja, who have a vast knowledge of herbs and remedies

> but do not possess the ability of divination. . . . The indigenous name for *P. maluti* is given as koae-ea-lekhoaba, and the psychoactive mushroom is used to induce a trance-like state. A brew is made by collecting large quantities of *P. maluti* and steeping the mushrooms in warm water, along with *Boophone disticha* (L.f.) herb., a strong hallucinogenic plant. . . . The *Psilocybe* and *Boophone* extract, referred to as seipone sa koae-ea-lekhoaba, is consumed by the patient, who is then placed in front of a reflective surface and relays the hallucinations/visions seen in the reflection to the healers who interpret these as answers to the patient's spiritual questions. This appears to be the only recorded firsthand report of hallucinogenic mushrooms being used traditionally in Africa and the first mention of hallucinogenic mushroom use in Sub-Saharan Africa.[45]

It is possible, of course, that *Psilocybe* is or has been used more widely in Africa but is not well known because of traditional rules of secrecy in the religions of the region.[46] It is also possible, however, that the use of *Psilocybe* is a more recent import to the region as a result of modernity, globalization, and the spread of psychoactive drugs across the globe. In any case, the possible use of *Psilocybe* more widely in Africa and other parts of the world remains an important area for future research.

Religious Uses of Other Mushrooms: Amanita muscaria

If we examine the broader role of mushrooms in the history of religions, one other important fungus to mention is *A. muscaria*, the "fly agaric." With its bright red cap and its prominent white warts, *A. muscaria* is known throughout the world as the quintessential "toadstool," appearing not only in psychedelic art but in fantasy literature, in children's cartoons such as the *Smurfs*, and on household products such as mushroom-shaped kitchen canisters.[47]

Amanita muscaria contains a number of active agents, including muscimol, which is the primary psychoactive constituent. A powerful agonist of the $GABA_A$ receptor, muscimol produces sedative, depressant, and hallucinogenic effects. Another compound found in the mushroom is ibotenic acid, which also converts to muscimol when the fungus is dried or ingested. Although many texts list *A. muscaria* as deadly, there have actually been few recorded instances of death from ingesting the mushroom; instead, the mushroom produces a wide range of symptoms depending on its habitat, dosage, and the body weight of the individual consuming it. These range

FIGURE 1.4. *Amanita muscaria var. guessowii.* Photo by the author.

from nausea and drowsiness to euphoria and visual and auditory hallucinations, as well as seizures and coma in severe cases.[48]

Amanita muscaria grows throughout the Northern Hemisphere in temperate and boreal regions of North America and Eurasia. However, as Letcher notes, the consumption of *A. muscaria* for either religious or recreational purposes does not appear to be particularly widespread and is mostly limited to a few communities in specific parts of Siberia:

> The mushroom seems to have been ignored or overlooked in all but two comparatively small regions of Siberia: in the west around the tributaries of the Ob river and including the Taimyr peninsula, amongst the Khanty, the Ket, the Forest Nenets, the Nganasan and Mansi peoples; and in the far northeast, roughly to the east of the meridian that passes through the mouth of the Kolyma river . . . amongst the people known as the Even, the Yukagir, the Itelmen, the Inuit, the Chuvanians, the Chukchi, and the Koryak.[49]

The use of *A. muscaria* for both religious and recreational purposes has been documented at least as early as the eighteenth century among tribes such as the Koryak in Kamchatka.[50] As Stepan Krasheninnikov observed in his

Description of Kamchatka Land (1755), the mushroom was consumed in dried form at feasts, where it produced states of intoxication, twitching of the limbs, and the urge to jump up and dance:

> Sometimes for the enjoyment they also use the mukhumor, the well-known mushroom that we ordinarily use for poisoning flies. . . . The first and usual sign by which one can recognize a man under the influence of mukhumor is the shaking the extremities which will follow after an hour or less after which the persons thus intoxicated have hallucinations, as if in a fever; they are subject to various visions, terrifying or felicitous . . . owing to which some jump, some dance, others cry and suffer great terrors. . . . But this applies only to those who overindulge, while those who use a small quantity experience a feeling of extraordinary lightness, joy, courage, and a sense of energetic well-being.[51]

In his Swedish travelogue, *Historico-Geographical Description of the North and Eastern Parts of Europe and Asia* (1736), Philip von Strahlenberg also described the use of mushrooms by some Koryak tribes, who consumed it primarily as a form of intoxication. According to his account, the poorer members of the community would also drink the urine of the wealthier folks, receiving their inebriation by secondhand means:

> The Russians who trade with [the Koryak] carry thither a Kind of Mushroom, called in the Russian tongue Muchumur, which they exchange for Squirrel, Fox, Hermin, Sable and other furs. Those who are rich among them lay up large Provisions of these Mushrooms for the winter. When they make a Feast they pour Water upon some of these Mushrooms and boil them. Then they drink the Liquor, which intoxicates them. The poorer Sort on these occasions post themselves around the Huts of the Rich, and watch for the Opportunity of the Guests coming down to make Water, and they hold a wooden Bowl to receive the Urine, which they drink of greedily . . . and by this Way they also get Drunk.[52]

Throughout these regions, there are accounts of shamans[53] using mushrooms as one form of what Eliade calls a "technology of ecstasy" or a means of entering into states of religious trance and otherworldly experience. However, there is much scholarly debate as to exactly how important the mushrooms were to the religious practices in these regions. While some early authors such as the Hungarian scholar J. Balazs argued that *Amanita* was integral to the trance states achieved by Siberian shamans, others such as Eliade dismissed this as either a late or degenerate addition to shamanic practice.[54] More recently, other scholars such as Z. P. Sokolova have concluded that shamans in these regions do sometimes make use of mushrooms, but that these are by no means the only or even most common of their many spiritual technologies.[55] Altered states of consciousness could be achieved in a variety of ways, including "fasting, abstaining from sexual relations . . . solitude, ritual donning of the shaman dress, and singing of hymns";[56] in short, "the shamans within these regions who employed the mushrooms as a tool to gain access to the spirit realm seem to have been in the minority; it was far from necessary or essential to being a shaman."[57] Moreover, the mushrooms do not seem to have been objects of "religious, ritual veneration" in Eurasia, and they were also clearly not used exclusively by shamans for spiritual reasons but also by ordinary people for simple enjoyment, inebriation, and pleasure.[58]

As the Estonian scholar Maret Saar outlines, there are many different uses for the consumption of *A. muscaria* among the Siberian shamans. These include 1) communication with the souls of the dead; 2) treatment of disease; 3) naming a newborn child; 4) revealing the cause of a dangerous situation and finding ways to overcome it; 5) interpretation of dreams; 6) visiting different worlds and flight over the earth; 7) creation of assistant spirits; 8) increasing the shaman's courage; 9) inspiration to recite songs or epics; 10) increasing bodily resistance to physical strain; and 11) calling forth spirits of high status.[59] Among many communities, the mushrooms are said to invoke particular spirits who can assist the shaman and take him to other worlds. According to the Koryak, for example, the spirits are called wapaq—the same term used to denote the mushroom itself, and they in turn assume the form of a mushroom. Among the Khanty, the spirits are said to be about half as tall as a human and can give answers to the shaman's questions, communicating in the form of a song or narrative. In general, as Nyberg notes, the mushroom spirits are seen as ambivalent and potentially dangerous helpers on the shaman's journey.[60]

Outside of Siberia, there are only scattered references to the use of *A. muscaria* for either religious or recreational purposes. The Lithuanian archaeologist and anthropologist Marija Gimbutas reported to Wasson that the mushroom was mixed with vodka and consumed at wedding feasts in some remote parts of Lithuania. She also claimed that Lithuanians used to export the mushroom to the Sami people for use in shamanic rites.[61] However, apart from this one anecdotal report and some from Nepal, there do not appear to be any other confirmed accounts of *A. muscaria* being consumed in Europe or elsewhere around the globe.[62] This seems noteworthy, considering its widespread presence throughout North America, Europe, and Asia.

Divine Mushroom of Immortality? Soma and Psychedelics

One of the great mysteries in the study of religion centers on the sacred beverage called soma.[63] First appearing in the Vedas—the oldest and foundational sacred texts of all later Hindu traditions, dating back to at least 1500 BCE—soma is both a deity and a beverage that was ritually prepared and consumed during sacrificial rites. As a deity, soma is identified with the moon and is the divine counterpart to Agni, the god of fire and the sun. As a beverage, soma is a central part of Vedic ritual, appearing throughout the Vedic corpus and serving as the central focus of an entire book (*Mandala* IX, containing some 114 hymns) of the *Rigveda* itself. In the latter sense, soma also has a counterpart in the contemporaneous Zoroastrian sacred corpus, the *Avesta*, where the sacred drink was known as *haoma* and played a very similar ritual role.

The Vedic soma ritual (*Somayaga* or *Somayajna*) had many different forms, the most important of which was the *Agnistoma* or "praise of Agni." An elaborate, five-day ritual, the *Agnistoma* required four days of preparations that included, among other acts, the invitation of the priests, the buying of the soma plants, the construction of the ritual altars, and several animal sacrifices. On the final day, the soma was pressed three times, purified, mixed with milk, and offered to the gods before it was drunk by the participants. The ritual concluded with a final ceremonial bath.[64]

In the hymns of the *Rigveda,* the effects of soma are described as primarily euphoric and energizing, characterized by a feeling of intense vitality and life force. Soma is said to bring creative inspiration and poetic imagination, while also making its drinker feel strong, powerful, even immortal. Throughout these texts, soma is also associated with states of *mada/madha* (exhilaration, intoxication, drunkenness, or madness), which John Brough glosses as a kind of "possession by a divinity" that often stimulates poetic creativity.[65] In the words of the Vedic poets,

> I of good wisdom have partaken of the vitality of the sweet drink, which is rich in purpose and excellent at finding wide space,
> which all the gods and mortals, calling it honey, converge upon.
> When you have gone within, you will become Aditi [boundlessness], appeaser of divine wrath . . . We have drunk the soma; we have become immortal; we have gone to the light; we have found the gods.
> What can hostility do to us now, and what the malice of a mortal, o immortal one?[66]

Although most of the soma-related hymns do not appear to reflect a hallucinogenic or psychedelic experience, one of the most often-cited hymns (called the *labasukta*, or "hymn of the lapwing") does describe the soma drinker as being carried up into the skies and experiencing a kind of vast state of expansive being:

> —Have I drunk the soma? Yes!
> The draughts have lifted me up, like horses a chariot.
> —Have I drunk the soma? Yes!
> . . .
> Because both world-halves are not equal to even one wing of mine.
> —Have I drunk the soma? Yes!
> By my greatness I have surmounted heaven and this great earth.
> —Have I drunk the soma? Yes!
> . . .
> Here I am—greater than great, sped upwards to the clouds.
> Have I drunk the soma? Yes![67]

At some point in time, the original soma plant appears to have no longer been accessible in South Asia, and a wide range of substitutes began to be used in its stead.[68] Today in South India, the soma sacrifice is still performed by some Shrauta brahmins, who use a leafless vine called *somalata* (*Sarcostemma acidum*). Recently, the anthropologist Ian Baker has also identified a small group of Tantric practitioners in West Bengal who consume a substance they call soma that is made from sixty-four different substances, including not only *somalata* but also cardamon, cinnamon, and *dhattura* (white thornapple, a species of flowering nightshade whose seeds produce psychoactive effects).[69] However, the original identity of the ancient soma plant remains unclear.

Since the eighteenth century, various scholars have tried to identify the original soma plant and suggested a wide variety of candidates, such as lotus (*Nelumbo nucifera*), Syrian rue (*Peganum harmala*), cannabis (*Cannabis sativa*), and opium poppy (*Papaver somniferum*). One of the most imaginative—and admittedly speculative—theories about the identity of soma is Matthew Clark's recent book *The Tawny One*. Based on his own botanical sleuthing and comparisons with South American practices, Clark suggests that the soma drink may have been based on an analog of ayahuasca that involved a variety of different plants—some of which he claims to have identified. While Clark's theory is intriguing, he acknowledges the limits of his thesis, the weaknesses in his argument, and the need for more research.[70]

The first argument for a fungal source for soma came from R. Gordon Wasson in his 1968 book *Soma: Divine Mushroom of Immortality*. As we will see in more detail in chapter 2, Wasson had become enthralled with mushrooms in the 1950s and recounted his first experience with *Psilocybe* in his famous *Life* magazine article in 1957. He soon began to look for mushrooms everywhere in early human religion and civilization, including ancient Greece and India. To assist in the translation of the Vedic texts (which he could not read), Wasson enlisted the aid of Wendy Doniger, who was then a promising young graduate student at Oxford and soon to become one of the world's leading scholars of Hinduism, mythology, and comparative religions.[71]

Wasson's primary arguments for the identification of soma with *A. muscaria* are the following. First, soma is said to have grown in the mountains, which could indicate a similar habitat as *A. muscaria* and might also explain why it was no longer available in other parts of South Asia. Second, soma is described as having a tawny, golden, and/or reddish-brown color (*hari, aruna, arusha*, or *babhru*) that could refer to the bright red color of the *A. muscaria* cap. Third, soma is said to inspire states of exhilaration and ecstasy. And finally, some hymns could be read as describing the soma juice being "urinated" from on high (and perhaps subsequently drunk, like the *A. muscaria* in some of the Siberian traditions mentioned above).[72]

Wasson's hypothesis generated an intense firestorm of interest as well as strong rebuttals to each of these claims. One of the most detailed critiques of Wasson's mushroom theory came from John Brough, a Scottish Indologist who taught at University of London and Cambridge. Brough rejected most of these arguments, largely based on Wasson's lack of knowledge of Vedic literature, language, or historical context.[73] For example, Wasson relied almost entirely on the hymns of the *Rigveda* and ignored the large amount of other Vedic literature, some of which describes the soma as being pounded intensely with stones to produce juice (which seems completely unnecessary for a mushroom).[74] Brough argued that Wasson mistranslates and misunderstands the verses that seem to indicate urination, suggesting that they more likely compare the pouring out of soma to the fertile rains of heaven pouring down upon the earth. At the same time, Brough observed, ritual texts such as the Vedic hymns often use extremely lofty, mystical, and visionary language when describing their forms of worship—none of which necessarily points to a psychedelic source: "Exalted language is expected in liturgical utterances, and we can hardly suppose that all of these were drug induced."[75] In the end, Brough (and many others) remained unconvinced that the Vedic accounts of soma really describe a psychedelic experience. Apart from the single hymn of the *labasukta* (RV 10.119), most of the hymns describe soma as a stimulant and a source of exhilaration, elation, and strength in battle; they do not seem to reflect the effects of *A. muscaria*, which include convulsions, stupor, and coma. As Brough concluded, *A. muscaria* would seem to be "a plant whose effects are totally unsuitable to stimulate Indra and human warriors for battle."[76] (In passing, we should also note that Wasson himself tried consuming *A. muscaria* in the mid-1960s and found its effects unpleasant and not really comparable to those of *Psilocybe*.[77])

Several decades later, the respected Sanskritist Jan E. M. Houben offered a very even-handed critique of Wasson's soma = mushroom thesis. In his judgment, Wasson was correct to point out that soma is described as producing an intense ecstatic state; but he was mistaken to assume that this must have been caused by a psychedelic substance rather than by more traditional means used throughout South Asian religions such as ritual, meditation, fasting, and various other techniques:

> The attention paid to the nature of the psychophysiological state induced by Soma, most dramatically emphasized by Wasson, is justified. The trap, however, in which Wasson and most scholars defending or attacking him have fallen is to assume that this psychophysiological state must be attributed directly to a psychoactive substance which brings about a similar state in modern Western well-fed . . . subjects. It must be clear that this is a shortsighted, anachronistic presupposition. It is generally forgotten that participants in a Vedic ritual have undergone preparations which include fasting, restraining speech, sleep-deprivation, sensory deprivation by spending the day in a dark hut, etc.[78]

As Houben aptly observes, many religious practitioners—ranging from Native Americans in their vision quests to modern mystics such as William Blake—report intense spiritual experiences without any apparent need for psychedelic plants or fungi: "The human capacity for imagination, vision, and hallucination seems to have been underestimated by Wasson and others. Merely because Apollinaire published the 'visionary poem' Vendémiaire in his collection Alcools we do not put the label 'hallucinogen' on alcohol. There is no reason to assume that Blake's visions . . . were induced by a psychoactive substance."[79] We might also add that hundreds of Christian saints and mystics have reported visions, miracles, and ecstatic encounters with God as a result of consuming the bread and wine of the Eucharist; yet there is no evidence that these were produced by psychedelic drugs.[80]

A few authors have attempted to resuscitate the soma = mushroom hypothesis by suggesting a different fungus, namely, *Psilocybe*. Terence McKenna and various others have argued that *Psilocybe* is a more likely entheogenic candidate than *A. muscaria,* since it grows in South Asia and produces fewer negative effects. While many psychedelic enthusiasts have eagerly latched on to McKenna's suggestion, it remains largely speculative.[81] One of the few possible pieces of evidence for the soma = *Psilocybe* theory comes from a two-thousand-year-old piece of cloth found in a burial chamber in Mongolia. The cloth depicts two figures handling an object with a large, flattened top, which some have interpreted as a mushroom being passed between a king and a priest as part of a religious ceremony—perhaps a Zoroastrian *haoma* ceremony.[82] While this interpretation is intriguing, it too remains quite speculative in the absence of any other corroborating evidence. Moreover, the *Psilocybe* thesis runs into almost all the same problems with *A. muscaria,* with one additional big question: Why isn't *Psilocybe* used in soma sacrifices today, since it is still widely available in South Asia?

In sum, as Clark concludes, the case for a mushroom source for soma (whether *A. muscaria* or *Psilocybe*) seems fairly weak at this point. While it remains possible that it included some sort of entheogen, the means of preparation alone—which involves intense pounding with stones—seem to rule out something as soft as a mushroom. Nonetheless, Wasson's mushroom theory has been remarkably persistent in popular culture; indeed, "Wasson's mushroom theory has been so influential that it is probably still currently the most widely-held general belief about soma, maintained by many people, despite the objections that have been raised, and it periodically reemerges."[83] The soma = mushroom idea still regularly appears in popular publications such as *Yoga Journal* and even in much of the recent scientific literature on psychedelics.

The Many Weird Roads to Eleusis: The Fungus Theory of the Eleusinian Mysteries

Probably the most intense speculation about the fungal origins of religious experience has centered on the ancient Greek Eleusinian Mysteries. Indeed, so much ink has been spilled on this particular debate that I cannot possibly do it justice here; what follows is simply a brief summary of some of the main points relating to the question of mushrooms and religious experience.[84]

Considered the most important of the secret rites in ancient Greece, the Eleusinian Mysteries were based on the myth of Demeter and her daughter Kore or Persephone. According to the narrative, Persephone was abducted by Hades, god of the dead, and taken to his underworld realm. In her distress, Demeter caused a terrible drought, which led to mass suffering and starvation until Zeus intervened and allowed Persephone to return to her mother. The origins of the mysteries probably date back as far as the second half of the fifteenth century BCE. Initially reserved for local citizens of Eleusis, initiation into the mysteries was later extended to all Athenians and eventually to all visitors in the seventh century BCE. The rites had two phases, the lesser and greater rites; the latter took place for nine days in September/October and culminated in the drinking of a sacred beverage called *kykeon* and a dramatic musical performance at the temple of Eleusis. Conducted in absolute secrecy, the mysteries took place during the final two days that the initiates spent in the sanctuary. Disclosing what took place was punishable by death. As the eminent German classicist Walter Burkert summarizes,

> Mysteries were initiation rituals of a voluntary, personal, and secret character that aimed at a change of mind through experience of the sacred. . . . Participation in mysteries was a special form of experience, a *pathos* of the soul, or psyche. . . . in psychological terms, there must have been a change of consciousness moving far beyond what is found in everyday life.[85]

Since the early twentieth century, various authors have speculated that the Eleusinian Mysteries may have had a psychedelic component. As we saw in the introduction, Aleister Crowley staged his own production of the mysteries using a mixture of peyote and alcohol as the sacred beverage; others have suggested that they might have contained opium or even DMT (dimethyltryptamine).[86] The first major thesis for a mushroom basis of the *kykeon* came once again from R. Gordon Wasson, who collaborated with the chemist Albert Hofmann and the classicist Carl A. P. Ruck. In their book *The Road to Eleusis*, they made the case that the *kykeon* was made from grains that had been infected with the ergot fungus (*C. purpurea*). A naturally occurring fungus that grows on particular grasses, *C. purpurea* contains the alkaloid ergonovine, which is "a psychoactive lysergic acid similar in structure to, but far less potent than," LSD.[87]

The ergot thesis became widely disseminated in popular culture and still appears regularly in nonacademic publications and on internet sources such as Wikipedia. However, it was largely dismissed by most serious classicists, who found the idea of widespread use of ergot in the mysteries implausible and lacking credible evidence.[88] Ruck, meanwhile, became something of a persona non grata in the academic world. Removed as chair of the Classics Department at Boston University, Ruck became increasingly marginalized and even shunned by more sober classicists.[89]

Some twenty-two years after the publication of *The Road to Eleusis*, the ergot thesis was resurrected by Brian Muraresku, a lawyer with a keen interest in ancient languages. In his hugely popular book *The Immortality Key*,

Muraresku makes the case that the Wasson-Hofmann-Ruck thesis can now be proven using more recent archaeological evidence and new scientific tools. Much of Muraresku's argument rests on one particular archaeological site—Mas Castellar de Pontós in Emporion, which was an ancient Greek colony founded in the sixth century BCE, which now lies in present-day Catalonia, Spain. Excavated by the archaeologist Enriqueta Pons in the 1990s, the site is believed to contain a sanctuary dedicated to Demeter and Persephone.[90] In 2000, the archaeologist Jordi Tresserras Juan published an article that claimed to find ergot sclerotia embedded between several teeth of a human jawbone as well as in one of the small chalices at the site.[91] For Muraresku, this provides a smoking gun for the ergot-*kykeon* thesis; indeed, he then takes the argument even farther, by suggesting that psychedelics also infused other ancient sacred beverages, such as those used in the Dionysian Mysteries and ultimately even the early Christian Eucharist.[92]

Despite Muraresku's recent arguments, many scholars remain deeply skeptical of the psychedelic theories for the mysteries. While it is true that ancient Greeks were familiar with a variety of psychoactive substances and made use of them in magical rites,[93] the idea that the mysteries were fundamentally inspired by ergot consumption has been a harder sell for most classicists. As Walter Burkert observes, it seems difficult to imagine that ergot could be produced in quantities large enough and consistently enough to supply the large numbers of annual initiates: "Even if the Rharian plane at Eleusis might have been infected with ergot . . . one may wonder about the quantities needed for thousands of participants in order to provide happy visions for all."[94] Michael Cosmopoulos raises a similar practical problem: namely, the huge numbers of initiates at Eleusis were expected to stand patiently in line for long periods of time *after* consuming the *kykeon*, which seems quite implausible if they were in a state of psychedelic ecstasy:

> There are logistical reasons, as well, for which the use of entheogenic agents does not appear a realistic possibility. The mystai drank the kykeon at the end of their fast; then they had to be lined up outside the Propylaea and wait until their names were checked against the priests' lists and their wreaths of myrtle replaced by wreaths of ribbons. . . . Given the numbers of the initiates . . . this would require an interval of several hours between the ingestion of the kykeon and the beginning of the secret part of the ceremony. In turn, this would mean that 2,000 to 3,000 people stood in line for hours, gave their names to the priests at the door of the Telesterion, and then proceeded inside the Telesterion in an orderly fashion, while they were in a state of ecstasy; this is not a reasonable scenario.[95]

Another fundamental problem is that ergot is a toxic fungus in its raw state. Known as "St. Anthony's Fire" in the Middle Ages, ergot poisoning can cause vomiting, diarrhea, convulsions, and even gangrene.[96] Ergot *can* be turned into *ergine*—a less toxic alkaloid that has psychedelic effects—but only with advanced knowledge of chemistry and access to particular chemicals. Some authors such as Daniel M. Perrine have tried to find a way around this last point by suggesting that ancient Greeks might have used other substances such as the ash of burned hardwood, which contains potassium carbonate. Boiled in water to which the ash was added, raw ergot could theoretically be turned into *ergine*.[97] While Perrine's solution to the ergot problem is intriguing, however, it remains quite speculative. As Matthew Clark aptly observes, no scholar seems to have been brave enough to try this particular recipe out to see if it actually works—or, conversely, if it would be catastrophically toxic: "so far as I am aware, no one has yet tried following the chemical protocols described by these authors and simply boiled or soaked raw ergot with wood ashes and wine . . . and then consumed the drink: perhaps for the simple reason that it could be fatal. If it is that easy to make *kykeon* in this way, why has no one ever reported it or tried it?"[98]

Finally, one other basic problem with the ergot thesis—and with *all* psychedelic theories for the mysteries and for Vedic soma—is that these arguments rest upon what Jules Evans calls a kind of "biochemical reductionism." That is, they all assume that any intense visionary experience must be the result of psychedelic drugs, rather than the myriad other means that religious people have used achieve mystical experiences throughout human history, such as ritual, meditation, prayer, or fasting, or of the larger social and cultural contexts in which these experiences occur.[99]

As Cosmopoulos argues, a much simpler explanation for the mysteries is that they may have involved the same sort of spiritual experience that is found in many religious traditions—including modern Greek Orthodox Christianity—which emerges through the power of collective ritual itself, without any need for psychedelics:

> Not only is there no evidence for the use of entheogens, but common sense suggests that the explanation is simple and does not require us to resort to elaborate theories in order to explain the religious experience of the initiates. To modern Greeks, steeped in the Orthodox religious tradition—a tradition filled with deep religious experiences without the use of entheogens—this is self-evident. The darkness broken by light, which the sources mention, does not require any far-fetched explanations: anyone who has attended the solemn-turned-joyous Resurrection service

> of Greek Easter can testify to the depth and intensity of the experience, as the light of the Anastasi breaks the darkness of death.[100]

In sum, much like the identity of soma, the original identity of *kykeon* remains unclear and the subject of ongoing debate. Its possible connection to a fungus remains an intriguing but still quite speculative hypothesis.[101]

Conclusion: Still Seeking the Flesh of the Gods

In keeping with their unpredictable, spontaneous, and quite mysterious way of appearing and disappearing in nature, the presence of psychedelic mushrooms remains elusive in human history and religion. While we can perhaps catch a glimpse of them appearing in early Mesoamerica, we really cannot say for certain what they were. While some were clearly used in Siberian shamanic traditions, that use—both religious and recreational—seems quite different from the ways in which they are used today. And while many authors have made claims for the religious roles of fungi in ancient India and ancient Greece, those claims seem speculative at best. At the same time, we also still have to account for the fact that large swaths of human cultures for long periods of history appear to have ignored the many *Amanitas*, *Psilocybes*, and other psychedelic mushrooms growing all around them (and perhaps even feared and avoided them, as they did the many similar-looking poisonous species they encountered).

Yet despite the scant and elusive nature of the existing evidence, the idea that psychedelic fungi lay at the roots of human religion and culture remains remarkably persistent. As we will see in the chapters that follow, much of this persistence is the result of popular discourses on psilocybin and other psychedelics that spread from the 1950s onward, particularly through the work of people like Wasson, Pahnke, and McKenna. More recently, this idea has been revived in the psychedelic renaissance in books such as *The Immortality Key* and various others. In light of our own current fascination with magic mushrooms and the therapeutic potential of psychedelics in the twenty-first century, we probably have a strong tendency to read the historical evidence through a psychedelic lens, rather than assuming some other, nonpsychedelic basis for religious experience. We probably also have a strong desire to search for ancient sources of authority and legitimation for modern psychedelic use, rather than simply accepting it as "new." As I argue in that chapters that follow, these tendencies probably need to be subjected to some serious reflection and historical critique.

[CHAPTER TWO]

Seeking the Magic Mushroom

R. Gordon Wasson and the Birth of a Global Mushroom Mysticism in the 1950s

Wherever we have studied the story of Early Man, we have discovered entheogenic mushrooms in use, hedged about with awesome beliefs and trappings of the Holy.

R. Gordon Wasson, *The Wondrous Mushroom* (1980)[1]

The late Mr. Wasson is the Abraham of the reborn awareness in Western civilization of the presence of the shamanically empowering mushroom.

Terence McKenna, blurb for *The Wondrous Mushroom* (1980)[2]

The modern revival of interest in psychedelic mushrooms begins with an extremely unlikely character. At the time that he first encountered *Psilocybe* species in the 1950s, R. Gordon Wasson was a vice president for Public Relations at J. P. Morgan & Co., one of the largest banks in the United States. Yet his wealth and comfortable lifestyle appears to have provided him with the resources to pursue an intense interest in mushrooms, which was first inspired by his Russian wife and quickly grew into a lifelong obsession. His encounter with the Mexican healer María Sabina in 1955 is arguably the most important moment in the transmission—or some would say appropriation—of sacred mushrooms from their traditional Indigenous contexts to a modern global and highly commoditized world. As Wendy Doniger eloquently reflected on this odd combination of square, rich banker and 1960s psychedelic icon,

> He was an old-fashioned aristocrat who almost seemed a holdover from the nineteenth century, a great banker who looked and acted the part: elegant and suave; gracious in the special manner of one accustomed to command; fastidious about manners and haberdashery; prudish about four-letter words . . . and almost spartan in his attitude toward food and even more so drink. That this Gordon Wasson should have become a hero

to the hippies and an unwilling guru to the "drug generation" was truly a great irony.[3]

We should note that Wasson was not in fact the "first white man in recorded history," to experience the mushroom ritual, as he would claim.[4] Other anthropologists had already explored and taken part in Mazatec mushroom ceremonies since at least the 1930s.[5] Yet by publishing his

FIGURE 2.1. R. Gordon Wasson with mushroom stone. Photo by Arnold Newman. Courtesy of Arnold Newman Collection, Getty Images.

experiences in *Life* magazine with the provocative title "Seeking the Magic Mushroom" and numerous photographs of the ritual, Wasson suddenly brought massive global attention to the mushrooms and their use.

At the same time, Wasson was perhaps the most important figure in what I call the simultaneous "religionizing" and "de-religionizing" of the mushroom experience. Throughout his vivid and highly romantic accounts, Wasson described the consumption of mushrooms as a kind of "sacrament" or *agape* (clearly modeled on the sacrament of his own Christian upbringing). All of this was despite the fact that María Sabina and other healers clearly used the mushroom not so much as a kind of "sacrament" (since they were Catholics and had the Mass for that) but instead primarily as a source of healing and divination.[6] Going still further in his later works, Wasson also began to imagine a kind of ancient, global mushroom cult, one that extended from Mesoamerica to ancient Greece, South Asia, and Siberia, in which psychedelic mushrooms were the inspirational catalyst for human evolution and civilization itself.[7]

Yet simultaneously, Wasson was a key figure in what we might call the "de-religionization" of mushrooms. Wasson and his family members themselves consumed *Psilocybe* outside of the traditional ritual contexts, and Wasson soon spread their use widely to a modern audience who had no knowledge of or interest in Mazatec traditions. As such, he was one of the most important figures in the modern idea of a kind of "mysticism without religion"—that is, the idea that one can achieve intense spiritual experiences through a substance such as mushrooms without need for religious institutions, rituals, or priestly authority (or, it would seem, ethical concerns). Although he later lamented and criticized the phenomenon, he was arguably the figure most responsible for the massive popularization of recreational use of mushrooms during the 1960s and 1970s, very much helping to "launch the psychedelic revolution in America."[8] He was also in many ways largely responsible for the decimation of Indigenous Mazatec cultural traditions, as hordes of mushroom-seeking tourists and journalists descended upon southern Mexico in the wake of his *Life* magazine article. And yet, even decades after his death, Wasson's work has rarely been subjected to any kind of critical scrutiny—either for its tremendous impact on psychedelic research over the last seventy years or for its deeply problematic scholarly and ethical issues.[9]

This chapter examines Wasson's complex life, work, and legacy, situating him within the broader explosion of interest in both mushrooms and mysticism in the mid-twentieth century. This otherwise rather unassuming banker was arguably the single most important figure not only in the modern psychedelic movement but also in the modern search for a kind of mystical experience outside of traditional religious institutions. At the same time, he was also arguably the most obvious example of the profound ethical problems involved in the study of Indigenous traditions and in the appropriation of cultural knowledge for a modern audience. Wasson's work has left a complex and ambivalent legacy in the twenty-first century, as spiritual seekers, scientific researchers, recreational enthusiasts, and pharmaceutical companies continue to see seek the magic mushroom.

The Context: Mysticism, Drugs, and the Altered Consciousness in the 1950s

While we often think of the 1950s today as an era of straightlaced conformity and the boring precursor to the countercultural 1960s, this decade was in fact something of a watershed moment for interest in both mysticism and psychedelics. A number of classic works on mysticism were published in these years, such as R. C. Zaehner's *Mysticism, Sacred and Profane* (1957), followed just a few years later by W. T. Stace's hugely influential book *Mysticism and Philosophy* (1960). In 1954, Aldous Huxley published *The Doors of Perception*, which recounted his own first encounter with mescaline—the psychoactive alkaloid in the peyote cactus, which had been synthesized in 1919. In the early 1950s, Huxley had learned that the English psychiatrist Dr. Humphrey Osmond was using mescaline to treat patients with schizophrenia and so arranged to meet with him in Los Angeles. On a bright morning in May 1953, Huxley thus had his first mescaline experience, which he compared to the mystical insight of Meister Eckhart and to the pure "Being" of Platonic philosophy. Huxley also made comparisons between the psychedelic experience and state described in Hindu and Buddhist traditions, such as the *sat-chit-ananda* ("Being-Consciousness-Bliss") of Vedanta and the "Dharma Body" of Mahayana Buddhism.[10] A few years later, in an article for *The Saturday Evening Post*, Huxley went still further, suggesting that peyote and other psychedelics "make possible a genuine religious experience" and offer a kind of "everyday mysticism" that is accessible to anyone. As such, they have the potential to both "revive" and perhaps "revolutionize" religion itself.[11] As we will see below, Huxley's and Stace's works would become foundational texts in both the psychedelic revolution of the 1960s and the psychedelic renaissance of the twenty-first century.[12]

At the same time, the 1950s saw intense new interest in lysergic acid diethylamide (LSD), which was first synthesized by Albert Hofmann in 1938 (and then accidentally experienced by the chemist himself in 1943).[13] Throughout the 1950s, numerous clinical trials on LSD took place alongside experiments in the first generation of antipsychotic drugs, with the hope that it might be useful in treating schizophrenia and other disorders. Perhaps inevitably, LSD and other psychoactive drugs also caught the attention of the Central Intelligence Agency, which began funding research into the potential use of these substances in human interrogations. According to one CIA report from this period, "There is no question that drugs are on hand (and new ones being produced) that can destroy integrity and make indiscreet the most dependable individual."[14] In 1951, the CIA even sent a scientist down to Mexico for the purpose of gathering plants with a "high narcotic and toxic value."[15] Not surprisingly, the Soviet Union was also actively pursuing these drugs and purchased fifty million doses of LSD from Sandoz Laboratories, Hofmann's employer. As Don Lattin notes, this helped kick off a "decade of bizarre and sometimes horrific U.S. sponsored research into the use of psychedelics as chemical weapons," resulting in hugely controversial programs such as the CIA's secret MKUltra project.[16]

Active between 1953 and 1973, MKUltra involved the development of procedures that could be used in interrogations through "brainwashing" and psychological torture. Using a variety of "extreme, baroque, and sometimes unquestionably torturous means," subjects were subjected to "sensory deprivation, hypnosis, and strategies of isolation, as well as to a wide range of drugs," including heroin, amphetamine, mescaline, and LSD.[17] When it was uncovered by the Church Commission in 1975, the program was found to have involved heavy use of psychedelics—often administered to unwitting subjects—as part of its experiments in mind control and manipulation. While the exact extent of the project remains unknown, LSD tests run by the army alone may have involved as many as 1,500 individuals; and Hofmann himself later admitted that the army regularly consulted with him in their experiments.[18]

The Saint Children: María Sabina and the Use of Mushrooms in Southern Mexico

At the time that Wasson first arrived in southern Mexico in the 1950s, mushrooms were used by many Mazatec healers as part of ceremonies called *veladas* or night vigils. As Paja Faudree notes, the mushrooms were not traditionally referred to in Mazatec or Spanish in literal terms but rather in euphemisms, such as *ndi*^{1}*xi*^{3}*tjo*^{3} (usually translated as "little ones who spring forth"); *ndi*^{1} *xti*^{3}*santo* ("saint children"); *ndi*^{1}*santo* ("little saints"); and *ndi*^{1}*tso*^{3}*jmi*^{2} ("little things"). Even in Spanish, the phrases used to denote the mushrooms are similar: *niños santos*, *niñitos*, *las cositas*, or *honguitos*.[19]

Their use in the Mazatec *veladas* largely fit the general pattern of the ceremonial use of mushrooms found in communities across southern Mexico, as described in the previous chapter. Held indoors at night, amid candles, incense, and Catholic devotional images, the *veladas* involved chanting, prayer, and singing in Mazatec. As the anthropologist Henry Munn described the ritual in 1973, the primary purpose was to address a particular physical and/or ethical disorder:

> The Mazatec Indians eat the mushrooms only at night at absolute darkness. It is their belief that if you eat them in the daylight you will go mad. . . . Usually several members of a family eat the mushrooms together. . . . The mushrooms themselves are eaten in pairs a couple representing man and woman that symbolizes the dual principle of procreation and creation. Then they sit together in their inner light, dream and realize and converse with each other. . . . The psychedelic experience of the Mazatecs is inseparably connected with the curing of an illness; not only physical illness but spiritual and ethical problems. The mushrooms are eaten when something is wrong.[20]

It is important to note, however, that the use of mushrooms in the *veladas* was not really aimed at achieving a mystical experience or divine vision; rather, it was primarily aimed at more practical goals such as healing, divination, and finding lost objects: "the mushrooms and *veladas* had always worked as a curative; they had never been used simply to 'see God.'"[21]

Called by some "patient zero" for the entry of *Psilocybe* mushrooms into modern culture,[22] María Sabina was born sometime around 1894 in the mountainous area outside the town of Huautla de Jiménez, in the state of Oaxaca. As she later recalled, her father, grandfather, and great-grandfather were all healers who also used the sacred mushrooms and had visions—though she only knew her father, and even he died when she was very young. After his death, her family moved to Huautla de Jiménez to live with her maternal grandparents, and she grew up very poor.[23]

In her later interviews, María Sabina recalled that she first ate the mushrooms as a child, around age six or seven, while sitting on a mountainside and tending the family's goats. She felt herself drawn out of her body into another realm full of golden palaces and temples, where the mushroom spirits were waiting for her. They appeared to her as "children with trumpets, children that sang and danced, children tender like the flesh of flowers"; she recalled speaking with the mushroom children, who answered, saying that "when we needed something, we should go to them, and they would give it."[24]

Her first healing occurred at age eight when her mother's brother fell ill. After none of the other healers were able to help him, she knew that she needed to consult the mushrooms; once again she was taken to their world and instructed how to cure him: "They told me that an evil spirit had entered the blood of my uncle and that to cure him we should give him some herbs. . . . I asked where these herbs could be found, and they took me to a place on the mountain where tall trees grew."[25] Some years later, she had an even more intense visionary experience when her sister María Ana fell ill. After none of the other healers were able to cure the girl, María Sabina decided to consume the mushrooms herself in order to help her sister. Once again, the mushrooms or "Principal Ones" spoke to her, yet this time they revealed a great book of knowledge as a sign that she was no longer a mere apprentice but now a wise woman herself:

> I remember that I had a vision: some people appeared who inspired me with respect. I knew they were the Principal Ones of whom my ancestors spoke. . . . Right away I heard a voice. A voice that was sweet but authoritarian at the same time. Like the voice of a father who loves his children but raises them strictly . . . I understood that the mushrooms were speaking to me. I felt an infinite happiness. On the Principal Ones' table appeared an open book that went on growing until it was the size of a person. In its pages were letters. It was a white book, so white it was resplendent. One of the Principal Ones spoke to me and said "María Sabina, this is the Book of Wisdom. It is the Book of Language. Everything that is written in it is for you." . . .
>
> I had attained perfection. I was no longer a simple apprentice. For that, as a prize . . . the Book had been granted me. . . . The mushrooms are saints, they give wisdom.[26]

From this book she not only learned how to cure her sister but also millions of other things, past and future; she saw her entire life before her, including the murder of her own son.[27]

For María Sabina and other wise men and women, the power of healing was believed to come from the mushrooms themselves, the saint children with whom they form relationships. During the *velada* ceremony, she recalled, she would speak to the saint children before eating them, asking for their favor and the power to heal: "That they bless us, that they teach us the way, the truth, the cure. That they give the power to follow the tracks of evil in order to be done with it."[28] The mushrooms, she said, were always to be consumed raw, never cooked, since that is the way they emerged from the earth: "The little things [mushrooms] are the ones that speak. . . . And they say so because they sprout by themselves. No one sows them. . . . They should be taken just as they are pulled up . . . they should not be boiled or anything."[29]

As Wasson himself acknowledged in his discussion of the use of mushrooms among the Mazatecs, the primary purpose of the *velada* was quite practical, most often for the purpose of diagnosing and curing illness or finding lost people, animals, or objects:

> Someone who wishes to consult the mushrooms about a grave family worry. A husband may be lying sick or injured . . . will he live or die? . . . If he will live, what must he do to recover? . . .
>
> Or again, a donkey has disappeared. Did he fall into a ravine and break his leg? . . . Or again, money hidden in the thatch roof has disappeared. Who took it and where is he now? Or again, a son has gone out into the world . . . his mother worries. Is he alive or dead? . . . The mushroom will tell.[30]

Moreover, María Sabina was also adamant that the mushrooms should only be used for benevolent purposes and never for malevolent ends; the true wise woman is not a sorcerer or witch (*brujo* or *hechicero*), who uses their power for evil. She was equally clear that a true healer should never profit from the mushrooms and that anyone who demands payment is a charlatan or worse:

> A Wise One like me should not charge for her services. She should not profit from her wisdom. The one who charges is a liar. The Wise One is born to cure, not to do business with knowledge. One receives with humility the two or three pesos that are put in one's hand . . . one should not make money from the *little things*.[31]

Finally, it is also important to note that María Sabina's practice as a *sabia* using mushrooms was never understood to be at odds with her life as a good Catholic. As Wasson notes, she was a "church member in good standing. She has belonged to the Asociación del Sagrado Corazón de Jesús or Society of the Sacred Heart of Jesus, a religious institution established for women."[32] Like many Indigenous men and women, she went to Mass regularly and respected all the rites of the church, even as she practiced privately as a healer, typically blending Indigenous and Catholic symbolism in her rites.

From Banker to Psychedelic Explorer: Wasson and the "Discovery" of *Psilocybe*

Born in Great Falls, Montana, in 1898, Wasson was raised in Newark, New Jersey. His father was an Episcopal rector who had actually published a book entitled *Religion and Drink*, which made the case for the appropriate place of alcohol within Christianity—a fact that seems relevant in light of his son's later interpretation of the religious use of mushrooms.[33] After traveling to Europe in 1914, Wasson enlisted in the US military in 1917 and served as a radio operator for the American forces in France during World War I. After the war, he studied at the Columbia School of Journalism and the London of School of Economics and then worked as a writer for several papers, including *The New Haven Register* and *The New York Herald Tribune*. In 1928, he turned from journalism to the world of banking and joined the Guaranty Trust Company of New York. Finally in 1934, he joined J. P. Morgan & Co., where he began as a credit banker and eventually rose as high as vice president in charge of public relations.[34] As part of his work as an eloquent and articulate public relations man for the firm, Wasson published a book on the controversial "Hall Carbine Affair" from the Civil War, in which he largely exonerated company founder J. P. Morgan Sr. of the charges of war-profiteering that had been leveled against him.[35]

In 1926, Wasson married Valentina (Tina) Pavlovna Guercken, who knew much about mushrooms from her homeland in Russia and first sparked his interest in all things mycological.[36] As he later described he and his wife's enthusiasm for the realm of fungi, they admittedly had no academic training but enjoyed the freedom to roam widely across many cultures in search of new mushroom mysteries: "we were amateurs unencumbered by academic inhibitions, and therefore we felt free to range far and wide, disregarding the frontiers that ordinarily separated the learned disciplines."[37]

Wasson's "discovery" of the magic mushroom had a complicated prehistory, one that made him not so much the first white man to encounter the mushroom but rather one of several scholars who had been circling around southern Mexico for over a decade. One of these was Richard E. Schultes, who is often called the "father of ethnobotany" and spent much of his career at Harvard University studying the use of plants by various Indigenous peoples. Schultes acted on information provided by an Austrian physician named Blas Pablo Reko, who had reported that the Mazatec Indians in Huautla de Jiménez used mushrooms in their rites. Together, Schultes and Reko went to Huautla in 1938 and brought back three specimens, which initially were identified as *P. cubensis*, *Panaeolus sphinctrinus*, and a *Deconica* species (though later, the mycologist Gastón Guzmán studied the specimens at Harvard and determined that the one labeled *Deconica* was actually another *Psilocybe* species, *P. caerulescens*).[38] Reko also sent specimens of the mushrooms to the anthropologist, Robert Weitlaner. Inspired by Weitlaner, the American anthropologist Jean Bassett Johnson then made a trip to Huautla de Jiménez in 1939 and became the first Western scientist (as far as we know) to actually observe the mushroom ceremony.[39]

In the early 1950s, these various discussions of sacred mushrooms reached Wasson's ears and immediately piqued his interest. Although he had no training in ethnobotany or anthropology, he had a growing amateur interest in mushrooms. According to his own accounts, Wasson had first become interested in mushrooms through the influence of his wife, Valentina, who introduced him to edible fungi during their honeymoon in the Catskills.[40] In 1952, he received an envelope from the English poet and novelist Robert Graves that contained a clipping about Schultes's work on the ritual use mushrooms in Mexico. Excited by the news, Wasson and his wife made their first of ten trips to Mexico in 1953, hoping to explore the villages of Oaxaca and track down this exotic mushroom cult.[41] Arriving in Huautla de Jiménez, Wasson persuaded a *curandero* named Aurelio Carreras to allow them to participate in a mushroom ceremony. Rather remarkably, Wasson himself acknowledged that he deceived Carreras, giving him an invented reason for needing to consult the sacred mushrooms. Because the mushrooms were often used to help locate a lost loved one, Wasson came up with the pretext that he was trying to get some information about his son, while admitting that this was a pretty lame excuse since they had only just recently left him behind in the US:

> To justify the ministrations of a curandero, the supplicant must represent a specific problem on which he needs the advice of the divinatory mushroom. We had resolved that our problem lay in our anxiety over our 18-year-old son Peter . . . from whom no news had reached us (naturally enough since we had left home a few days before). This was not a good excuse, but it was the best we could conjure up, and it seemed legitimate to our Indian friends.[42]

Significantly, Wasson also recalls that Carreras asked him to keep their participation in the ceremony secret: "Before leaving us he obtained our assurance that we would discuss the matter with no outsiders in Huautla."[43] This was one of many promises that he would fail to keep.

One interesting sidenote in the story of Wasson's early exploration of *Psilocybe* is that the CIA also caught wind of his research. Since all of this took place during the surreal years of MKUltra and other secret psychedelic mind-control programs, the CIA was naturally very interested in *Psilocybe* and, in 1955, had a chemist in its employ named James Moore arrange for Wasson to receive $2,000 to support his subsequent research trips. However, as Siff notes, "declassified CIA documents indicate Wasson was unaware of the true source of the funds."[44]

Wasson first met with María Sabina on June 29, 1955, during his third trip to Mexico in search of the magic mushroom. As he described her at the time, María was "a woman in her fifties, grave in demeanor, with grave smile, short of stature . . . dressed in the Mazatec huipil."[45] It is worth noting that Wasson also commented on how difficult it was for him to communicate with María. Not only was he unable to speak Mazatec, but he was also baffled by her highly poetic use of language. As he wrote in a letter to Richard de Mille:

> María Sabina is a most intelligent person but communicating with her is extraordinarily difficult, even for a Mazatec speaking to her in Mazatec. She lives in a different world. She will talk endlessly and in a kind of poetic phraseology that I fail to understand and that interpreters are unable to put into Spanish.[46]

Paying her fifty pesos a night for her services, Wasson persuaded María not only to allow him to observe the ceremony but to eat the sacred mushrooms and even have his photographer, Allan Richardson, take photos of the ritual. However, María explicitly asked him to "please refrain from showing [the photographs] to any but your closest friends, it would be a betrayal."[47] According to his own account, Wasson also reused the same

FIGURE 2.2. María Sabina. Photographer unknown.

fabricated excuse that he had previously used in his request for the *velada*, claiming to seek information on the whereabouts of his son: "Once again [he] trotted out the question of his son Peter, now in the army. How was he? Alive or dead, or ill, or in good spirits, or in some trouble? This had seemed to her a sufficient justification."[48]

Wasson also took detailed notes about every aspect of the *velada*, noting precisely when each aspect of the ceremony took place and the minutiae of his own subjective experiences. As he recorded in his notebooks,

> Nausea as vision distorted. Touching wall—made the world of visions seem to crumble. Light from above door and below—moon. Table took new forms—creatures, great processional vehicle, architectural patterns of radiant color.[49]

Wasson's experiences with María Sabina in turn became the basis for his hugely popular article in *Life* magazine. *Life*, we should note, was at that time owned by the powerful magazine magnate Henry Luce who happened to have personal knowledge of psychedelics himself. Having been given LSD under a doctor's supervision, he was enthusiastic to publish Wasson's story about the magic mushrooms of Mexico.[50] Appearing as part of *Life*'s "great adventures series," the article portrayed Wasson as a humble New York banker who had bravely traveled to the remote villages of Mexico in search of this strange fungus with "vision-giving powers."[51] Overall, the article presented a narrative that combined tourism, adventure, mystery, and a not-so-subtle hint of neocolonial conquest, featuring an ordinary American banker who journeyed deep into an exotic land to discover secret knowledge and powerful magical substances from ancient, Indigenous peoples. As Wasson himself recounted the story, he and his photographer had managed to penetrate further into these ancient mysteries than even the most experienced anthropologists ever had before:

> We chewed and swallowed the mushrooms, saw visions, and emerged from the experience awestruck. . . . Richardson and I were the first white men in recorded history to eat the divine mushrooms, which for centuries have been a secret of certain Indian peoples living far from the great world in southern Mexico. No anthropologists had ever described the scene that we witnessed.[52]

In his vivid and highly poetic account of the mushroom experience, Wasson combined several older descriptions of drug-induced mystical encounters. We can detect in them, I think, Samuel Taylor Coleridge's opium-infused poetry about the pleasure domes of Kublai Khan, Aldous Huxley's mescaline-induced insights into the Platonic Forms, and various Orientalist accounts of the "mystic East":

> We were never more wide awake, and the visions came whether our eyes were opened or closed. They emerged from the center of our field of vision, opening up as they came, now rushing, now slowly, at the pace that our will chose. They were in vivid color, always harmonious. They began with art motifs, angular such as might decorate carpets or textiles. . . . Then they evolved into palaces with courts, arcades, gardens—resplendent palaces all laid over with semiprecious stones. Then I saw a mythological beast drawing a regal chariot. Later it was as though the walls of our house had dissolved, and my spirit had flown forth, and I was suspended in mid-air viewing landscapes of mountains, with camel caravans dancing slowly across the slopes, the mountains rising tier above tier to the very heavens. Three days later when I repeated the experience . . . instead of mountains I saw river estuaries, pellucid water flowing through an endless expanse of reeds down to a measureless sea, all by the pastel light of a horizontal sun. This time a human figure appeared, a woman in primitive costume, standing and staring across the water, enigmatic, beautiful, a sculpture except that she breathed and was wearing a woven colored garment. It seemed as though I was viewing a world of which I was not a part. . . . There I was, poised in space, a disembodied eye, invisible, incorporeal seeing but not seen.[53]

Like Huxley in his mescaline experience, Wasson suggests that the mushroom provides insight into the Platonic Forms, the divine archetypes that underlay the phenomenal world: "I was seeing the archetypes, the Platonic ideas, that underlie the imperfect images of everyday life. The thought crossed my mind: could the divine mushrooms be the secret that lay behind the ancient Mysteries?"[54] At the same time, almost plagiarizing Ralph Waldo Emerson's language, he describes the mushroom user as a kind of "transparent eyeball," seeing the universal currents of being circle in, through, and around him: "the bemushroomed person is poised in space, a disembodied eye, invisible, incorporeal, seeing not seen. In truth he is the five senses disembodied, all of them keyed to the height of sensitivity and awareness, all of them blending into one another most strangely, until the person, utterly passive, becomes a pure receptor, infinitely delicate, of sensations."[55]

His account is also filled with the highly Orientalist language of a kind of colonial explorer, journeying through an exotic visionary landscape that seemed like "a vast desert seen from afar, with lofty mountains beyond terrace above terrace. Camel caravans were making their way across the mountain slopes"; and ultimately "space was annihilated for us, and we were travelling as far as thought to our visionary worlds."[56] Moreover, he concludes his account by suggesting that his exploration of these exotic lands will continue—both in physical and visionary space—as he plans to seek out other remote villages and in so doing journey back to the primitive origin of civilization and religion:

> What we have already discovered only opens up new vistas for further study. Today we are embarking on our fifth expedition to the Mexican Indian villages again seeking to increase and refine our knowledge of the role played by mushrooms in the lives of the remote peoples. But Mexico is only the beginning. All the evidence relating to the primitive beginnings of our own European cultures must be reviewed to see whether the hallucinogenic mushrooms played a part there, only to be overlooked by posterity.[57]

In sum, Wasson presented himself in the role of the intrepid explorer, journeying both in space and time into exotic regions of the world and the mind. As Timothy Leary later commented, noting the colonial nature of Wasson's explorations, "Wasson had safaried down his cerebellum and had come back, like most khaki-clad nineteenth-century explorers, expecting to stake *the* claim on these undiscovered regions."[58]

Yet perhaps Wasson's greatest gift was his ability to promote his claims about these ancient spiritual mysteries to a modern audience through the power of twentieth-century media. As Siff persuasively argues, Wasson's celebrity sprang not so much from his scholarly contributions but rather from the sensationalism of his claims and his skillful, coordinated, multichannel campaign to promote them. Thus, an advertisement that aired on CBS television highlighted the fact that the "weird and wonderous experience" of the mushroom ritual "was told through the eyes of R. Gordon Wasson, a vice president of JP Morgan," highlighting both his ordinariness and his credibility as a source.[59] Over the next five years, Wasson was featured in many newspaper and magazine stories, including *Fate Magazine, True: The Men's Magazine, Cosmopolitan, Uncensored,* and *Real for Men,* among various others.

Meanwhile, even as Wasson was widely promoting the exotic mysteries of the magic mushroom, *Psilocybe* was being examined by mycologists and chemists. The French mycologist Roger Heim was the first to identify the mushrooms used in the ritual as several species of *Psilocybe,* including *P. mexicana,* which he then supplied to none other than Albert Hofmann. In turn, Hofmann's team of chemists was able to isolate the active indol, which they called psilocybin.[60] Because Hofmann was both the discoverer of LSD and the first to isolate psilocybin, the two drugs quickly became conflated in the popular imagination (along with *mescaline*). This is despite the fact that the two substances have markedly different effects and potencies, not to mention historical and cultural uses. Wasson (and later Leary) only compounded this conflation of the two substances, which has in many ways persisted to the present day.

Hoffman would later make his own trip to Huautla in 1962, where he met with María Sabina and even presented her with a gift of his synthetic psilocybin in the form of a pill. According to Hofmann's account, María then used the psilocybin pill in a *velada* that evening and concluded that it was indeed "the same" as mushrooms and indeed contained the spirit of the *niños santos*. Hofmann proudly declared this to be an authoritative confirmation of the genuineness of his synthetic psilocybin:

> As we took leave of María Sabina and her clan at the crack of dawn, the *curandera* said that the pills had the same power as the mushrooms, that there was no difference. This was a confirmation from the most competent authority that the synthetic psilocybin is identical with natural product. As a parting gift I let María Sabina have a vial of psilocybin pills. She radiantly explained to our interpreter Herlina that she could now give consultations even in the season when no mushrooms grew.[61]

Today, however, more critical observers have expressed skepticism about Hofmann's account, suggesting that it sounds very much like a kind of "authenticating myth" that provides a legitimizing narrative for modern non-Indigenous people to feel comfortable with using psychedelics derived from Indigenous cultures. As Feinberg notes, Hofmann's narrative about María and the gifted pills "apparently functioned as an important authenticating myth for some psychedelic researchers in the tradition of the myths of Pocahontas and La Malinche, in which indigenous women provide legitimacy for future generations of non-Indians to occupy their territory."[62] This authenticating myth, I think, has had a lasting impact on psychedelic research to this day. On the one hand, it seems to provide evidence for the idea that modern psychedelic research is in continuity with the ancient practices of Indigenous peoples; on the other hand, it seems to provide evidence for the idea that a synthesized drug produced in the laboratory is basically "the same" and can inspire "the same" experience as a naturally occurring mushroom. Both of these claims, I think, are highly suspect, and yet they remain widespread in psychedelic discourse today.

Religionizing and De-Religionizing the Magic Mushroom

Apart from his central historical role in popularizing the use of *Psilocybe* mushrooms, Wasson was also critically important for the modern understanding of psychedelics, mysticism, and religion as a whole. Perhaps most significantly, Wasson was engaged in a simultaneous process of both *religionizing* and *de-religionizing* psychedelic mushrooms. By *religionizing* the mushrooms, I mean that he took a form of folk healing and divination that was not in itself particularly "religious" and redescribed it as a religious sacrament, one comparable to the Christian Eucharist. In Wasson's eyes, Sabina herself was nothing less than "religion incarnate. She was the hierophant, the thaumaturge, the psychopompos in which the troubles and aspirations of countless generations of the family of mankind had found . . . their relief."[63] Similarly, Wasson described the mushroom experience in highly Christian (particularly Catholic) terms, recalling that "the night's events unrolled in an atmosphere of simply friendliness that reminded me of the agapé of early Christian times."[64] As he wrote, in his characteristically flowery and poetic style,

> The mushrooms transport one from the nonce to heaven, where all the senses unite in a joyous symphony shot through with an overwhelming feeling of *caritas*, of peace and affection for the fellow communicants.[65]

Tracing its roots back still further, Wasson also suggested that the use of mushrooms by the Aztecs at the time of the Spanish conquest was a similar kind of Eucharistic sacrament. This explains why the Spanish were so horrified by the practice, which struck them as a demonic inversion of the sacred host:

> The *teonanácatl* struck at the heart of the Christian religion. I need hardly remind my readers of the parallel, the designation of Elements in our Eucharist; Take, eat, this My Body. . . . The orthodox Christian must accept on faith the miracle of the conversion of the bread and wine into God's flesh and blood. . . . By contrast the sacred mushroom of the Aztecs carries its own conviction: every communicant will testify to the miracle that he has experienced.[66]

Ironically, however, this does not seem to be the way that María Sabina saw herself or her rituals. As we saw above, she was a devout Catholic and so had the Mass for her Eucharist, and she explicitly stated that the mushrooms were not consumed primarily to "see God" but were used instead primarily for healing and divination.[67] As she told an interviewer some years later: "before Wasson nobody took the mushrooms only to find God. They were always taken for the sick to get well."[68] Wasson himself clearly knew this, since he did not tell María that he was hoping to commune with God but instead concocted the pretense that he was searching for his son.[69] His description of the mushroom ceremony as a kind of "Eucharist" really seems to reflect his own complex relationship with the Christian faith in which he was raised. As Letcher notes, Wasson had been raised in the Episcopal Church by a father who was a minister, and he had read the Bible twice through already by age eleven. As such, he seems to have been eager to interpret the Mexican ritual as a kind of "proto-Christian mysticism, with mushrooms foreshadowing the sacrament of bread and wine and elevating the communicant to a direct encounter with God."[70]

At the same time, ironically, Wasson was also a key figure in what we might call the *de-religionizing* of the mushroom experience. That is to say, he presented the mushroom as a means to achieve an intense visionary state quite apart from its traditional religious or cultural contexts. In one telling passage in the *Life* article, Wasson does acknowledge that the communal and ritual setting of the *velada* is important. But he then immediately goes on to recount that his wife and daughter both consumed the mushroom outside of the ceremonial context had intense visions; and still further, he consumed them by himself in New York and had an even more powerful visionary experience:

> From the many mushroom celebrations that I have now witnessed, nine in all, it is clear to me that at least in the Mixeteco country the congregation is indispensable to the rite. But this does not mean that the mushrooms lose their potency if not eaten communally. My wife and our daughter Masha, 18, joined us a day after the ceremony. . . . In their sleeping bags, they ate the mushrooms while alone with us. They experienced the visions too. They saw the same brilliant colors; my wife saw a ball in the Palace of Versailles with figures in periods costumes dancing to a Mozart minuet. Again on Aug. 12, 1955 . . . I ate them in my bedroom in New York, and I found that if anything they had gained in their hallucinogenic potency.[71]

Indeed, Wasson even held his own sort of American *veladas* at his home in New York, in which he invited his friends to come partake of the divine mushrooms—though now served in the synthesized pill form supplied by Sandoz.[72]

In this sense, Wasson was one of the first and most influential spokesmen for a kind of "mysticism without religion," or the conviction that profound experiences equivalent to those of exotic shamans can be achieved quite apart from the trappings of institutional forms of religion. Through the medium of this humble fungus, one could access the world of the mystics and poets, seeing the Platonic Forms and the visions of William Blake, yet without the need for arduous ritual or asceticism:

> The advantage of mushrooms is that it puts many, if not everyone, within reach of this state without having to suffer the mortifications of Blake. It permits you to see, more clearly than our perishing mortal eyes can see, vistas beyond the horizons of this life, to travel backwards and forwards in time, to enter other planes of existing, even . . . to go there were God is.[73]

Wasson's mysticism without religion was also very much in keeping with the spirit of his age, amid an American culture that was infatuated with the exotic and the primitive but increasingly less interested in traditional religious institutions. As Siff observes, "He told a story about a personal quest that anticipated the spirit of the times, in both its superficial interest in non-Western shamanism and the ultimate conclusion that the trappings of . . . ritual were unnecessary to achieve the same result."[74] This story, we will see, was a central narrative of much of the counterculture of the next several decades.

A Global Mushroom Mysticism

Following the enormous popularity of his *Life* magazine article, Wasson began to explore the possible role of psychedelic fungi in a variety of other historical and religious contexts. His interest in the mushrooms of Russia included the large and colorful *A. muscaria,* which holds a prominent place in Russian folklore and popular culture. As we saw in chapter 1, *A. muscaria* had been used by some communities in Siberia for both recreational and religious purposes, and Wasson began to speculate that it might have been used far more widely throughout Indo-European cultures, including ancient India. During his exploration of this hypothesis, he began to look for a scholar to help him with the translation of Sanskrit texts and was introduced to Wendy Doniger, then a young graduate student. As Wasson later described her, "She was young, stunningly beautiful, smartly dressed, gracious, conversant with Latin, Greek, German, French, Russian to come, and of course at home in Sanskrit."[75]

As Doniger later recalled, Wasson was generally curious about the descriptions in the *Rigveda*; but when she happened to mention that there is some brief possible reference to drinking the urine of someone who has consumed soma, "his eyes lit up," and he became extremely excited. Noting the similarity to accounts of mushroom urine drinking in Siberia, Wasson became convinced that this was the critical link between *A. muscaria* and soma.[76] He then asked Doniger to help with Vedic translations and to write a short history of soma, which became a major part of his book *Soma: Divine Mushroom of Immortality*, published in 1968.[77] Because of its widespread presence in many parts of the world, Wasson speculated that *A. muscaria* was the psychedelic inspiration not only for the Vedic hymns but probably for religious visions in many ancient cultures prior to the development of agriculture:

> Soma . . . was common everywhere in the woodlands of the temperate zone. All in all, Soma was the entheogen of choice, until grains came to be cultivated in prehistory and then ergot emerged as a major alternative. . . . All entheogens inspire awe and reverence and possess power for good.[78]

In a letter to Hofmann in 1965, Wasson confessed that he had not yet tried consuming *A. muscaria* himself, but he was convinced that its effects were the same as those of the *Psilocybe* mushrooms: "The description of those who have eaten it corresponds with what happens when one has eaten our Psilocybe spp."[79]

From there, Wasson expanded his research on psychedelic fungi to ancient Greece. Already in 1956, Wasson began to speculate that the ancient Greek Mystery religions may have been inspired by some form of magic mushrooms; as he wrote in a letter to Robert Graves, "They never mention the mushroom, but it is as though the thing missing, the thing that they admit is missing, the thing they can't explain were our mushroom."[80] Again claiming to unravel a long-standing scholarly enigma, Wasson later argued that the experiences of the Eleusinian Mysteries were most likely inspired by ergot fungus (*C. purpurea*) growing on wheat and barley.[81] Enlisting the aid of both chemist Albert Hofmann and classics scholar Carl Ruck, Wasson claimed to have uncovered the psychedelic origin of the most enigmatic of the Greek Mysteries—the *kykeon* or sacred drink consumed by initiates after their all-night vigil.[82] In 1975, Wasson first asked Hofmann if early peoples in ancient Greece could have found a way to derive a hallucinogen from ergot that would have been comparable to LSD or psilocybin. Two years later, Hofmann concluded that the Greeks could indeed have worked out a mixture from ergot on wheat or barley that would serve as an "LSD-like consciousness-altering drug."[83] In their book *The Road to Eleusis*, Wasson, Hofmann, and Ruck conclude the accounts of the Eleusinian Mysteries resemble "unmistakably the experience induced by a hallucinogen."[84]

While Wasson's fungal argument for the Eleusinian Mysteries has also been largely dismissed by most serious classicists today,[85] it remains remarkably persistent in popular culture and it is still widely cited on internet sources and in nonacademic publications. Probably the most influential recent example of a reworking of the Wasson hypothesis is Brian Muraresku's *Immortality Key*, which basically restates the ergot thesis while adding some more recent archaeological and pharmacological evidence.[86]

Looking beyond ancient Greece and India, Wasson speculated that psychedelic mushrooms may also have been used by many other cultures, including the Dyaks of Borneo, the Mount Hagan natives of New Guinea, various groups in China and Japan, and even by some North American tribes.[87] While there is minimal evidence for these broader claims, Wasson was clearly making the case that mushrooms were used widely all over the world in various cultures and historical periods for the purpose of achieving profound spiritual experiences.[88]

In his later work, such as *Persephone's Quest* (1986), Wasson went further still by suggesting that psychedelic mushrooms and other entheogens lay at the very origins of religion and played a key role in human evolution itself. By opening the mind to new pathways of thought, language, and symbolism, the mushrooms may have helped *Homo sapiens* first conceive of the idea of a spiritual realm beyond the visible one and indeed the very possibility of a God who pervades and yet transcends the natural world:

> In man's evolutionary past . . . there must have come a moment in time when he discovered the secret of the hallucinatory mushrooms. Their effect on him . . . could only have been profound, a detonator to new ideas. For the mushrooms revealed to him worlds beyond the horizons known to him, in space and time, even worlds on a different plane of being, a heaven and perhaps a hell. . . . One is emboldened to the point of asking whether they may not have planted in primitive man the very idea of a God.[89]

In sum, Wasson imagined a kind of global mushroom mysticism that placed psychedelic fungi at the very heart of human evolution, consciousness, and religion. Indeed, he speculated that the mushroom lay at the very center of a religious cult "with perhaps the longest continuous history in the world."[90] For "early Man thought they were miracle plants that spoke to him with the voice of God."[91]

In his later writings, Wasson also articulated a more evolutionary argument about the role of mushrooms that would also be taken up by authors such as Terence and Dennis McKenna (the "stoned ape" hypothesis). In *Persephone's Quest,* he speculated that the consumption of psychedelic mushrooms may have helped facilitate the rapid growth in the *Homo sapiens* brain, which in turn went hand in hand with an expansion in our powers of memory, language, and self-consciousness:

> A prodigious expansion in Man's memory must have been the gift that differentiated mankind from his predecessors, and I surmise that this expansion in memory led to a simultaneous growth in the gift of language; these two powers generating in man that self-consciousness which is the third of the triune traits that alone make man unique. . . . I am asking whether Soma could have possessed the power to spark what I have called these triune traits.[92]

In short, he suggests that psychedelic mushrooms may have played an instrumental role in the development of human evolution and modern human consciousness itself.

Privacy, Publicity, and Betrayal: Wasson and "Mysticism Without Ethics"

While Wasson's work on the magic mushroom was hugely popular in the United States, England, and Europe, helping to spark a massive new interest in psychedelic fungi, its impact on María Sabina and her homeland was in many ways quite catastrophic. Within a very short time of the *Life* magazine publication, huge numbers of journalists, spiritual seekers, and tourists began to descend upon Huautla, yearning for exotic experiences, mystical enlightenment, and/or cheap drugs. All of this coincided with the dawn of the counterculture, the hippie movement, and the burgeoning interest in both exotic religions and psychedelic drugs. Soon, English-language papers in Mexico City began advertising magic mushroom tour packages that would include participation in a "mushroom ceremony," and waves of foreign seekers began to flood this remote region. Allegedly, even musicians and celebrities such as Bob Dylan, John Lennon, and Mick Jagger began to make the trip in hopes of finding the magic mushroom and its ancient portal to other worlds.[93]

As Letcher notes, the values of the hippies were often jarringly at odds with those of the local Oaxacans, who expected the mushrooms to be treated with sanctity, honor, and ritual respect: "For hippies, the mushrooms were psychedelic, which meant that they were bound up with notions of authenticity, freedom, individualism, bohemianism and rebellion. Used to seeing psychedelics as drugs not deities, commodities not conscious entities, many expected to be able to buy and consume mushrooms as they desired, irrespective of local sensibilities."[94] As one young man bluntly put it,

> Look man, You can go for that curandero shit if you like but it's not my bag. I don't need an old hag mumbling in Mazatecan to turn me on. I don't dig this Indian doctor jazz. I turn myself on. It's not my culture. You just score the mushrooms . . . we'll do the rest.[95]

In many ways, this statement is the very epitome of the ideal of "mysticism without religion," or the conviction that profound spiritual experience could be achieved solely through the mushroom and without any of the social, cultural, or ritual trappings that traditionally accompany it. Unfortunately, this aggressively appropriative attitude did not sit well with the Mexican government. Openly smoking pot, squatting in caves, and having sex in open fields, the throngs of hippies became such a problem that the Mexican army eventually had to be brought in to remove them and set up roadblocks to keep them out.[96]

As María Sabina later recalled, she was at once overwhelmed and mystified by these hordes of strange young people. Among other things, she could not understand their desire to "find God" through the mushrooms, when that was not even the primary purpose of the *niños santos*:

> For a time there came young people of one and the other sex, long-haired with strange clothes. They wore shirts of many colors and necklaces. . . . "We come in search of God," they said. It was difficult for me to explain to them that the vigils weren't done from the simple desire to find God, but were done with the sole purpose of curing the sicknesses that our people suffer from.[97]

She was particularly disgusted that these foreigners disrespected the mushrooms by consuming them at any time they pleased in any context, without reverence or ritual: "the young people ate them wherever they liked; it was the same to them if they chewed them up seated in the shade of coffee trees or on a cliff along some trail in the woods. These young people . . . didn't respect out customs. . . . The improper use that the young people made of the little things was scandalous."[98]

Still more tragically, however, she later concluded that this gross disrespect of the mushrooms and flagrant of violation of tradition had ultimately led to the *niños santos* losing their spiritual power. It one of her most cutting remarks, María directly tied this loss of power to Wasson and his betrayal of her trust when he published her photos and the secrets of the mushrooms for a public audience:

> Before Wasson, I felt that the saint children elevated me. I don't feel like that anymore. The force has diminished. If Cayetano hadn't brought the foreigners . . . the *saint children* would have kept their power. . . . From the moment the foreigners arrived, the *saint children* lost their purity. They lost their force; the foreigners spoiled them. From now on they would not be any good.[99]

Because she had opened her doors to Wasson and was the focus of the *Life* article, María Sabina was blamed by many of the local residents for the hippie apocalypse that had descended upon the region. While some people in the area benefited from all the tourist traffic, most were outraged by the influx of disruptive, disrespectful foreigners. By the late 1960s, María Sabina was regularly harassed by the Mexicans authorities, who believed she had been selling drugs to foreigners. Meanwhile, her neighbors ostracized her and ultimately burned down her home.[100]

Years later, Wasson read María Sabina's tragic words about the mushrooms losing their sacred power as a result of the global forces that he had unleashed. While expressing remorse at this sad outcome, he also defended his decision to publicize the mushroom, justifying this as a kind of greater good for humankind since it had made the secrets of the magic mushrooms known to the entire world.

> These words make me wince. I, Gordon Wasson, am held responsible for the end of a religious practice in Mesoamerica that goes back far, for millennia. . . . A practice carried on in secret for centuries has now been aerated and aeration spells the end.
>
> At the time of my first *velada* with María Sabina in 1955 I had to make a choice: suppress my experience or resolve to present it worthily to the world. . . . The sacred mushrooms and the religious feeling concentrated in them had to be made known to the world. . . . at whatever cost to me personally. If I did not do this, consuming the mushroom would go on for a few years longer, but its extinction was inevitable.[101]

Wasson the straightlaced banker clearly despised hippies, and he claimed that would never use the sacred mushrooms simply for "kicks" or "recreation";[102] but in the end, Wasson the self-promoter also wanted to defend his publicization of the mushrooms for the modern world.

Around the same time, Hofmann would make a similar kind of awkward defense of what Wasson and others had done to María Sabina's way of life. As he reasoned, it was surely sad that this ancient tradition had been profaned by both scientific researchers and drug-seeking tourists. But these negative effects were balanced if not outweighed by the larger scientific and cultural benefits that came from the discovery of psilocybin: "Wherever researchers and scientists trace and elucidate the remains of ancient customs that are becoming rarer, their primitiveness is lost. This loss is only more or less counterbalanced when the outcome of the research represents a lasting cultural gain."[103]

Not surprisingly, not all readers today are satisfied with Wasson's and Hofmann's justifications for their treatment of María Sabina and her body of cultural knowledge. As Letcher argues, Wasson was perhaps the most extreme example of precisely what *not* to do when encountering and studying another culture. He failed to learn local languages or customs, his visits were short and superficial, he lied to and betrayed the native informants who kindly assisted him, and his account of the mushroom ceremony was wildly exoticized. At the same time, he was so focused on the psychedelic properties of the mushroom that he failed to really understand the complexities of either the larger ritual context in which it was embedded or of the religious and cultural significance of the mushroom itself—which is a complex organism that consists of far more than just the single agent psilocybin. All of this had profoundly negative effects on the communities he purported to represent:

> The picture of Mazatec religion he presented within the pages of *Life* . . . was slight, superficial, and in many ways inaccurate; and this misleading picture contributed significantly to the flow of people travelling to Huautla. His exploits provide us with a model of how not to go about ethnographic fieldwork: he made lightening visits of only a few weeks at a time. . . . He never learnt the Mazatec language . . . and overlooked or missed many of the subtleties of the Mazatec worldview. His single-minded focus upon the mushrooms meant that he failed . . . to tease out the complex relationships between the famously taciturn Mazatec and their healing plants, many of which have no psychoactive properties but are nonetheless considered powerful healing agents.[104]

Other critics such as Paloma Martinez-Cruz go further still, by arguing that Wasson's encounter with this Indigenous culture falls very much in line with the longer history of the white colonization and domination of this region. Like so many colonial explorers and conquistadors before him, Wasson felt no qualms about deceiving María Sabina, extracting her sacred knowledge from its traditional contexts, and exporting it to an eager audience of North American consumers:

> Following the late nineteenth century, the prevailing colonial logic held that the White man's superior intellectual curiosity gave him the right to explore as he pleased which required neither justification nor restraint: it was this very compulsion to pursue knowledge that set him apart from other races.[105]

As we will see in the following chapters of this book, this concern about the neocolonial implications of the psychedelic renaissance would recur throughout the next seven decades. Still today in the 2020s, there are intense debates over the appropriation of Indigenous practices and sacred technologies for recreational and scientific purposes by modern consumers. From neo-shamanic ayahuasca retreats to the massive investment in psychedelics by major pharmaceutical companies, the concerns over the neocolonial exploitation of these Indigenous knowledge systems is very much still with us today.[106]

Conclusion: Wasson's Complex Legacy in the Psychedelic Renaissance

Despite his ambivalent character and questionable decisions, it would be difficult to overestimate Wasson's influence on the massive flowering of interest in *Psilocybe* and psychedelics more generally that followed in the 1950s, 1960s, and 1970s. As Siff observes, Wasson was the key figure—for better or for worse—in the transmission of Indigenous sacred knowledge about *Psilocybe* species to a modern global audience. He also helped document that critical moment of transmission, describing the complex and often painful ways in which the mushroom was passed from María Sabina to a new world of psychedelic explorers:

> Using his status, personal wealth and personal associations, Wasson managed to coordinate–and document—the remarkable moment when

> the Mazateca's sacred mushroom passed into Western scientists' hands. This transfer was inevitable given the number of researchers conducting fieldwork toward this end. . . . Wasson's genius was in transforming the moment of private discovery into a public spectacle.[107]

As such, his romantic narrative of a heroic exploration of Mexico and its ancient mysteries really "became part of the mythology of mushrooms for North American recreational users."[108]

In the process, Wasson helped spark the psychedelic revolution that quickly exploded in the early 1960s, beginning with researchers at institutions like Harvard and then spreading wildly throughout the popular culture of the next decade. As Letcher concludes, "Thanks to Wasson, people began looking for and eating psilocybin mushrooms in just about every corner of the world. . . . He may have failed in his attempt to prove the existence of an ancient mushrooming cult, but in so doing he gave the world a modern one."[109] Indeed, one might say that he helped create the modern mushroom cult by attempting to ground it an ancient, widespread mushroom religion that lay perhaps at the very origin of human civilization itself. This narrative of the fungal origins of religion and culture is still very much with us today in the twenty-first century.

At the same time, however, Wasson's work also has a darker and more problematic legacy. As various critics point out, he seems to have been much less interested in a careful understanding of María Sabina's cultural practice than in reimagining it as part of his grand vision of an ancient global mushroom religion. His approach to the local community was remarkably transactional, operating more like a banker making a business deal than a scholar doing serious research or a seeker looking for spiritual insight. Indeed, "he went about research rather as if he were conducting a major financial deal. He treated knowledge as a commodity, something that could be brought sold or treated as an investment—quite literally offering money for information."[110]

Finally, Wasson was also the figure most responsible for the rapid decimation of the traditional cultural life of María Sabina and her surrounding community. As mycologist Gastón Guzmán reflected on the aftermath of Wasson's publications, "Now after five decades of contact with recreational drug users and tourists, the mushroom ceremonies have been further changed. Sacred mushrooms are now widely commercialized, and even the ceremonies themselves have become a kind of tourist attraction."[111]

Today, Huautla de Jiménez retains much of its reputation as a place of magic, mystery, and mushrooms. Indeed, it is promoted as the "Pueblo Mágico" by the local tourism office, which even publishes a brochure on mushrooms entitled "El Hongo: Sagrado de la Sierra Mazateca."[112] The small Casa de María Sabina museum prominently features María and her ritual use of the *niños santos,* along with a (probably photoshopped) image of her posing with John Lennon and a great deal of mushroom-themed art. Meanwhile, images of mushrooms and of María herself appear everywhere in the town—on street murals, on shop signs, even on taxis and the banners of motorcycle clubs. The hotel where I stayed in 2024, for example, was adorned with elaborate murals of María Sabina, her songs, and her *niños santos,* all combined with traditional Catholic themes. Meanwhile, other towns in Oaxaca such as San José del Pacifico have built a large tourist industry based largely on *Psilocybe* that caters primarily to foreigners and now far surpasses Huautla in the psychedelic mushroom business.[113] However, the local residents seem to have a deeply ambivalent attitude toward all of this. While they clearly want to reclaim the *niños santos* as a source of local wisdom, tradition, and identity, many remain quite wary of white foreigners, particularly of hippies and those who come solely looking for magic mushrooms.

No doubt some would argue that the forces of globalization and capitalism would have ultimately made their way to Oaxaca with or without Wasson's work; and probably someone else would have eventually discovered and popularized the psychedelic power of *Psilocybe*. Yet it seems hard to deny that Wasson's pattern of deception represents a particularly egregious lack of scholarly, journalistic, or even basic human ethics; and the speed with which María Sabina's way of life was overrun and destroyed was

FIGURE 2.3. La Casa de María Sabina museum, Huautla de Jiménez. Photo by the author.

FIGURE 2.4. Mural of María Sabina, Huautla de Jiménez. Photo by the author.

particularly shocking, even in the context of twentieth-century neoliberalism. In addition to serving as the forefather of a mushroom-based mysticism without religion, we might say that Wasson also practiced a kind of mysticism without ethics, by lying to María Sabina, publishing her photos against her will, and contributing in no small part to the ruin of her life, reputation, and community.

Moreover, we can also look to the example of other scholars who have interacted with Indigenous cultures and psychedelic substances in a far more respectful way. A good counter example to Wasson that comes to mind is James Mooney, the American ethnologist who worked for the Smithsonian and wrote some of the first sympathetic accounts of the ritual use of peyote among Native Americans. Not only did Mooney undertake a deeply respectful and nuanced study of the tradition, he also helped the community organize and become recognized as "the Native American Church," so that its practices might be protected by law.[114] As Aurélien Bouayad writes, Mooney was "convinced that peyotism was uniquely able to provide a source of unity and cultural integrity to the multitude of Native American tribes uprooted from their traditional territories and thrown together on reservations," and he thus came to play an "instrumental role as cultural expert in the legal defense of the entheogenic practice."[115] In short, if Wasson is a poster child for how *not* to study other cultures, there are still many good examples for how to engage in more ethically responsible studies of the ritual use of psychedelics.[116]

Despite—or perhaps because of—his many flaws and failings, Wasson has left a complex legacy with which we still grapple in the twenty-first century. With the dawn of a new psychedelic renaissance, as pharmaceutical companies invest millions of dollars into research on *Psilocybe* and other substances, we face many of the same ethical questions today. As we continue to "seek the magic mushroom," can we do so in an ethically responsible way? Or do we risk repeating the historical processes through which Indigenous cultures and traditional knowledge systems are displaced by recreational usage and by large pharmaceutical industries that hope to turn them into marketable drugs?

[CHAPTER THREE]

High Priests

Walter Pahnke and the Mushroom Counterculture of the 1960s

With these drugs, science stands on an awesome threshold. Some religious leaders would undoubtedly consider it improper for man to tread upon the holy ground of the unconscious, protesting against the exploration of "inner space." . . . But man's apparent destiny is to seek an ever-greater comprehension of the nature of reality that cannot be thwarted or suppressed.

Walter N. Pahnke and William A. Richards, "Implications of LSD and Experimental Mysticism" (1966)[1]

Start your own religion. Drop-out—detach yourself from the external social drama which is as dehydrated and ersatz as TV. Turn-on—Find a Sacrament which returns you to the temple of God, your own body. Go out of your mind. Get high. Tune-in—Be reborn. . . . Actions which are conscious expressions of the turn-on, tune-in, drop-out rhythm are religious.

Timothy Leary, *High Priest* (1968)[2]

Wasson's wide-ranging body of work was both a general influence and a very specific catalyst for the psychedelic revolution that followed in the 1960s. In general terms, his popular writings on *Psilocybe* mushrooms, together with the new research on LSD, helped inspire a widespread belief that psychedelics were the key to mystical states of consciousness that were analogous to, if not identical with, those described by religious figures from ancient India to medieval Europe. As Jeffrey Kripal notes in his study of the Esalen Institute and its broader context in the American counterculture, Wasson's work thus helped unleash a broader, psychedelic-based spiritual movement across the US:

> Although often fantastically overextended and forced . . . Wasson's hypothesis remains an important . . . theory that . . . undoubtedly played a major role in the psychedelic subcultures of the 1960s, including that of Esalen. Whether established or not, Wasson's mycological theory of

> the origin of religion was unquestionably one of the major narratives of the American counterculture, providing one of its most important and lasting structures. By the founding of Esalen in 1962, Wasson's historical and chemical hypothesis . . . had begun to pass over into the realm of religious revelation. . . . America was now witnessing the birth of a religious phenomenon of immense appeal and broad cultural, musical, medical, metaphysical, and political and legal implications.[3]

By the early 1960s, psychedelic mushrooms had also made their way into popular fiction. Thus, Aldous Huxley's 1962 novel *Island* centers on a utopian kingdom near the Andaman Islands called Pala, where the inhabitants use a mushroom-based drug called *moksha*-medicine. Also called "the reality-revealer, the truth-and-beauty-pill," the drug allows anyone, even beginners, to "catch a glimpse of the world as it looks to someone who has been liberated form the bondage to the ego."[4]

More specifically, however, Wasson's writings and the collection of dried mushroom specimens that he deposited at Harvard University helped trigger a more localized interest in *Psilocybe* in the early 1960s that was in many ways the ground zero for the wider psychedelic revolution. Once *Psilocybe* was confirmed as the primary mushroom species used in the Mazatec ceremonies, and once psilocybin was identified as the primary psychedelic compound in these mushrooms (and one that could now be synthesized in a lab), a flurry of research followed. And Harvard became the epicenter.

From 1960 to 1963, a group of researchers began to focus intensely on psilocybin, mescaline, and other psychedelics. Under the working label of the Harvard Psilocybin Project, the group was spearheaded by Timothy Leary and Richard Alpert, and it included on its board none other than Huxley himself.[5] But the Harvard project was only one of many new research initiatives taking off throughout North America, the UK, and Europe. During the 1950s and 1960s, more than a thousand research papers were written on psilocybin and other psychedelics, and more than forty thousand test subjects were given these drugs for the treatment of a wide range of disorders, including depression, alcoholism, and anxiety. Not surprisingly, the use of these substances quickly spread beyond the narrow confines of the research laboratory and began to permeate popular culture as a whole. As Don Lattin notes, "By 1963 the psychedelic genie was out of the bottle, having escaped from the carefully controlled domain of the researcher's laboratory. . . . Millions of baby boomers were coming of age and starting to experiment."[6]

One of the most influential projects to come out of this early psilocybin research was a dissertation written by Walter Pahnke, a minister and psychiatrist who had developed a keen interest in mysticism. A key part of his research was a psilocybin experiment conducted in the basement of Boston University's Marsh Chapel during the Good Friday service in 1962. Pahnke's dissertation and subsequent articles had a massive influence not only on psychedelic research but on the popular culture of the 1960s more broadly. Referring to his work as a kind of "experimental mysticism," Pahnke concluded that psilocybin made it possible to consistently produce mystical experiences in a controlled research setting and so study these states of consciousness as never before.[7] At the same time, he developed a model for "measuring" psychedelic experiences, which eventually became known as the "Mystical Experience Questionnaire" (MEQ).[8] Based largely on the

FIGURE 3.1. Walter Pahnke. Courtesy of Purdue University Libraries, Karnes Archives and Special Collections.

work of philosopher W. T. Stace, this metric has undergone several revisions but is still widely used in psychedelic research today. As we will see in later chapters, this attempt to "quantify" mystical experiences has had a lasting impact on almost all later research and still informs most of the psychedelic work being done today.[9]

Meanwhile, Pahnke's teacher, Timothy Leary, soon emerged as one of the most controversial and polarizing figures of the 1960s. After being dismissed from Harvard, Leary would go on to found his own psychedelic church and call upon every citizen to take these drugs and "start their own religion."[10] Through the work of Leary and others, psilocybin entered fully into popular culture, inspiring everyone from the Beatles to the Grateful Dead and helping to make psychedelics the new sacrament for a kind of countercultural spirituality.

This chapter places Pahnke and others in the context of the early 1960s, at the very dawn of the new revolutions taking place both in popular culture and in brain science. Not only did their exploration of psilocybin help spark the countercultural movement, but it also coincided with the new science of the brain that was emerging in this decade, as scientists first discovered the role of neurotransmitters. Meanwhile, psychedelics also began to be used widely in psychotherapy, as researchers explored their potential for the treatment of depression, alcoholism, anxiety, and various other disorders.[11]

All of this marks a continuation of the trend we discussed in the previous chapter—the simultaneous "religionizing" and "de-religionizing" of the mushroom experience. Through psychedelic trials and new metrics such as the MEQ, Pahnke and others were hoping to reliably stimulate mystical experiences in controlled research settings, without any necessary connection to religious institutions or ritual practices—in effect, dereligionizing them. Yet simultaneously, more ambitious psychedelic explorers such as Leary were trying to create their own religions out of psychedelic experience, legally incorporating new movements such as the League for Spiritual Discovery and reimagining these drugs as "sacraments" in a radical alternative to Christianity. Leary's work helped inspire a wide range of other DIY psychedelic churches, most of which embodied Kripal's idea of the "religion of no-religion."

To conclude, I discuss the backlash against psilocybin research that followed in the later 1960s and 1970s. As these drugs spread widely into popular use, particularly among young people, they generated a powerful reaction from politicians and conservative religious groups. Already by 1966, LSD was banned in California, and by 1970, both LSD and psilocybin were designated Schedule I controlled substances.[12] The fear of psychedelics, we will see, was not simply a cultural or political anxiety, but also an anxiety about *authority* in Bruce Lincoln's sense.[13] If the 1960s counterculture was largely about "questioning authority," then psychedelics lay at its heart, both scientifically and spiritually. The claim that mystical experience could be achieved in a laboratory or in one's home through eating a mushroom radically challenged conventional ideas of who God is, who can access religious experience, and, perhaps most importantly, who can be a religious authority.

The Harvard Psilocybin Project

The historical context in which Pahnke's research emerged—the late 1950s and early 1960s—was a revolutionary period not only in popular culture and music but also in the modern understanding of the human brain, particularly in psychiatry and in the emerging field of neuroscience. As Andew P. Wickens notes in his *History of the Brain: From Stone Age Surgery to Modern Neuroscience*, the recent discovery of chemical neurotransmission resulted in the introduction of the first antipsychotic drugs in the mid-1950s, which radically changed the understanding and treatment of mental illness:

> During the 1950s a revolution would take place in the fields of psychopharmacology and psychiatry with the introduction of psychoactive drugs to treat mental illness. A notable day in this respect would be the 26 March 1954 when the Food and Drug Administration in the US approved the use of chlorpromazine (Thorazine) as a medication for the treatment of schizophrenia. It was the first time a drug had been specifically marketed to treat a mental illness, and within a decade it was to be followed by many others, including antidepressants and anxiolytics.[14]

During the early 1960s, the first academic units devoted to neuroscience were also established at major universities across the US. These included MIT's Neuroscience Research Program in 1962 and Harvard University's Department of Neurobiology in 1966.

The explosion of interest in psilocybin and its effects on the brain occurred in the very midst of this larger psychopharmacological revolution. In August 1960, just a few years after the publication of Wasson's article in *Life* magazine, Timothy Leary had his own first mushroom experience. Having obtained his PhD in clinical psychology from University of California, Berkeley, in 1950, Leary had a successful career as a clinical psychologist, serving as director of clinical research and psychology at the Kaiser Foundation Hospital in Oakland and establishing himself as a "rising star" in the field of behavioral psychology.[15] He then joined Harvard as a lecturer in clinical psychology in 1959.

FIGURE 3.2. Timothy Leary in 1969. Photograph by James Klepitsch.

Leary's first introduction to psychedelic mushrooms came through Anthony Russo, a colleague who had experimented with *P. mexicana* during a trip to Mexico and told Leary about it. At the time, Leary was undergoing a bit of a midlife crisis, having suffered two failed marriages (his first wife committing suicide).[16] In August 1960, Leary accompanied Russo on his next trip to Cuernavaca (just south of Mexico City), where he consumed mushrooms for the first time. As he recalled, he was sitting on a terrace next to a golf course in Cuernavaca, enjoying a candlelit dinner and margaritas with friends before the mushrooms were passed around. "I ate seven of the Sacred Mushrooms of Mexico," he later wrote, "and discovered that beauty, revelation, sensuality, the cellular history of the past, God, the Devil—all lie inside my body, outside my mind."[17] Using poetic language that is heavily reminiscent of Huxley and Wasson, he described visions of "Nile palaces, Hindu temples, Babylonian boudoirs, Bedouin pleasure tents, gem flashery. . . . Here came those Moorish replicas sliding, coiling, tumbling down the drain in the middle of my retina."[18] And like Wasson and Huxley before him, he also saw his psychedelic experience in direct continuity with the divine visions of the mystics from all cultures and historical periods: "I gave way to delight, as mystics have for centuries when they peeked through the curtains and discovered that this world . . . was actually a tiny stage set constructed by the mind."[19] For Leary, this was a transformative and revelatory experience, one that inaugurated his lifelong exploration of the visionary realms opened by psychedelics:

> It was the classic visionary voyage, and I came back a changed man. You are never the same after you've had that one flash glimpse down the cellular time tunnel. You are never the same after you've had the veil withdrawn. In the seven years since eating seven mushrooms in a garden in Mexico I have devoted all of my time and energy to the exploration and description of these strange deep realms.[20]

Back at Harvard, Leary and his colleague Richard Alpert began to engage in a variety of experiments from 1960 to 1962, generally known as the Harvard Psilocybin Project.[21] Having obtained a batch of psilocybin from Sandoz, Inc., the two began their work under the auspices of a "responsible research organization," the Center for Research in Personality.[22] They began by administering psilocybin to thirty-eight individuals, who included none other than Aldous Huxley, Allen Ginsberg, and William S. Burroughs. Rather unusually for a scientific study, Leary and Alpert allowed the subjects to control their own doses, and they themselves typically took the drug along with the subjects. According to their results, 75 percent reported the experience was "very pleasant," and 69 percent "were judged to have attained marked broadening of awareness."[23] More subjects were subsequently tested—167 in all—95 percent of whom allegedly stated that the drug session "had changed their lives for the better."[24]

Encouraged by the results, Leary undertook a more ambitious project known as the Concord Prison Experiment (1961–63), designed to study the potential use of psilocybin to reduce recidivism among inmates. However, rather than simply administering the drugs and observing in a detached scientific way, Leary and his team wanted to experience a more intimate and personal relationship with the subjects, and so again took the psilocybin along with the inmates. As Don Lattin notes,

> What was radical about Leary's research project was not that he was testing dangerous drugs by giving them to prisoners. That had been done many times before. What was revolutionary about Leary's research protocol was that the members of the Harvard team were really getting to know the prisoners. They were treating them like friends, not research subjects. They were not just administered drugs to the prisoners—they were tripping *with* the prisoners. . . . It was the exact opposite of the double-blind, placebo-controlled study.[25]

While many critics have observed that there were serious basic problems with the experiment and its methods of data collection and analysis, Leary would claim that it had been enormously successful, leading to a drastic reduction in recidivism rates. More importantly, however, he believed that the experiment had revealed to all of them—prisoners and researchers alike—that they shared a common humanity and a common divinity: "In the sessions we were all gods, all men at one. We were all two-billion-year-old seed centers pulsing together."[26]

Walter Pahnke and the Good Friday Experiment

One of the most important episodes in the modern history of *Psilocybe* took place on Good Friday, 1962, in the basement of the Marsh Chapel at Boston University. The instigator of the experiment was Walter ("Wally") Pahnke (1931–71), a minister and psychiatrist with a strong interest in mysticism, who hoped to supplement his medical knowledge with a doctorate in religion. Born in Harvey, Illinois, Pahnke graduated from Carleton College in 1952. As his obituary later described him, Pahnke was a man "with intense intellectual curiosity and mind critical yet open to new truth wherever it might be found," who had a keen sense of adventure both in his personal life and in his scholarly pursuits:

> The types of research he engaged in reflected his courage and disdain of work that would bring merely financial rewards. . . . He was contemptuous of facades. He was known for his absolute honesty and integrity as well as for his competence and his energy. With his keen scientific interest and explorative thrust he also possessed a profound religious nature that constituted an important part of his research motivation. He saw his work as unfolding knowledge of the essential nature of man, toward which both science and religion are converging. Another facet of his personality was an urge for high adventure fed by an active imagination.[27]

In addition to his study of religion, psychology, and psychedelics, Pahnke also had a "keen interest in parapsychological phenomena and faith healing." In his research, he would often note paranormal phenomena such as "cases of ESP and out-of-the-body experiences that often characterized subjects under psychedelic drug influences."[28]

After receiving his MD from Harvard Medical School in 1956, Pahnke went on to receive his master of divinity from Harvard Divinity School in 1960, and was then pursuing his PhD from the Harvard Graduate School of

Arts and Sciences.[29] A student of Leary and Alpert, Pahnke also received support for his project from Howard Thurman, dean of Marsh Chapel at Boston University, and from Walter Houston Clark, who taught psychology of religion at Andover Newton Theological Seminary.[30] Clark would later praise Pahnke's Marsh Chapel experiment as nothing less than "the most carefully carried out of any scientific experiment with religious experience ever devised, in which he demonstrated that a psychedelic chemical can release profound mystical experience."[31] It was also Clark who helped Pahnke procure twenty volunteers from his own seminar, while another ten volunteers were recruited to serve as "guides." Among the guides was the eminent scholar of comparative religion, Huston Smith (1919–2006), who had recently published the hugely successful text *The Religions of Man* (1958), and was then teaching at MIT.

A kind of odd combination of religious service and scientific research, the experiment was held during the two-and-a-half-hour Good Friday service, the sound of which was piped down into a small chapel in the basement of the building. From the outset, Pahnke fundamentally blurred the line between "religious space" and "scientific space" (a controversial blurring we will see come up again with more recent research at Johns Hopkins).[32] Broken into five groups of four students each, the volunteers were each

FIGURE 3.3. Marsh Chapel, Boston University. Photograph by John Phelan.

given a capsule of white powder. Ten of the capsules contained psilocybin, while the other ten contained niacin, which produces a kind of face-flushing and a tingling sensation. Significantly, the "guides" in the experiment were subjected to the same conditions as the volunteers, with half given the psilocybin capsules. As Leary later recalled, Pahnke initially balked at this idea, worrying that it would ruin the objectivity of the experiment; but he was eventually persuaded by Leary's insistent argument that "there can be no doctor-patient game going when you use psychedelics. We are all in it together. Shared ignorance . . . Shared risks."[33]

It quickly became evident which students had received psilocybin and which had not; while most of the latter sat quietly in their pews, many of the former wandered around muttering things like "God is everywhere" and "Oh, the Glory!"[34]

> Ten students sat attentively like good worshippers. Facing the altar. Silent. The others were less conventional. Some lay on the benches—one lay on the floor. Some wandered around the chapel murmuring in prayer and wonderment. . . . One sat at the organ bench and played weird, exciting chords.[35]

In all, eight of the ten students who had received the psilocybin reported profound spiritual experiences, while only one in the placebo group did. Pahnke recorded dozens of these experiences in his dissertation, highlighting those that seemed to confirm mystical experiences of oneness or unity as he understood it. For example, as subject QX reported in Pahnke's account,

> I lapsed into a period of complete lostness of self that must have lasted for an hour but seemed very brief. This was a blank sensation, better still, a void. . . . My experience seemed to be dominated by a sense of *oneness, unity and harmony*.[36]

Significantly, despite the fact that the participants were all divinity school students, and despite the fact the session took place during a Good Friday service in a chapel, only a couple of the participants reported experiences with any specifically "Christian" content. Apart from one who "saw Christ carrying his cross" and one who had a feeling of "being with Christ," most of the experiences recorded were markedly absent of Christian language or imagery.[37]

Huston Smith was among the "guides" who received the psilocybin pill. As he later described the experience, he was particularly moved by the music in the service, and the climax for him came when the solo was sung by a soprano whose voice he could only describe as "angelic": "The gestalt transformed a routine musical progression into the most powerful cosmic homecoming I have ever experienced."[38] Ultimately, he claimed to have had his first real and direct encounter with the God he had so long believed in theoretically:

> I had known and firmly believed that God is love and that none of love's nuances could be absent from his infinite nature; but that God loves *me* and I *him,* in the concrete way that human beings love individuals, each most wanting from the other what the other most wants to give . . .—that relation with God I had never before had.[39]

After the study, both Pahnke and Leary expressed tremendous excitement that they had in fact found a way to reliably produce and study mystical experience in a scientific way "under laboratory conditions." As Pahnke wrote in an article in 1966, scientists could now study firsthand the kinds of experiences once only written about by famous mystics of the past:

> Thus, at long last, research into mysticism need no longer be limited to the scholarly scrutiny of various devotional or metaphysical documents left behind by such historical personages as Shankara, Plotinus, Meister Eckhart, William Blake, and Teresa of Avila. Persons can be studied extensively both before and after the experience of mystical consciousness in controlled settings.[40]

Leary, meanwhile, was even more certain that the experiment had finally provided solid proof that mystical experiences were real and that they could be reliably produced in a scientific way. Perhaps most importantly, he believed that these experiences could be produced in essentially *anyone*, yet *without* the need for traditional religious methods, such as prayer, meditation, asceticism, and the like:

> The results were clear-cut and consistent. The men who ate the mushrooms had mystic religious experiences. The control group didn't.
>
> There was proof—scientific, experimental, statistical, objective. The sacred mushrooms, administered in a religious setting to people who were religiously motivated, did produce that rare, deep experience which men have sought for thousands of years through sacraments, through flagellation, prayer, renunciation.[41]

Of course, many readers are now wondering whether the conclusions that Pahnke and Leary reached were really warranted by the evidence provided by this—admittedly problematic—experiment. After all, the volunteers involved were all divinity school students, who presumably already had a strong belief in God, and the experiment took place in a chapel during Good Friday service. In contemporary terms, we would say that the "set and setting" were quite heavily favored to produce a "spiritual" sort of experience. The fact that half of the "guides" were also tripping on psilocybin does little to lend credibility to the experiment. Some years later, Rick Doblin—the founder of the Multidisciplinary Association for Psychedelic Studies (MAPS)—conducted a follow-up study in which he interviewed most of the students who had received the psilocybin during Pahnke's experiment. According to Doblin's findings, Pahnke had really only reported the positive side of the participants' experiences, leaving out many of the quite negative experiences that several recounted under the influence of the drug:

> Most reported that the experience had reshaped their lives and work in profound and enduring ways. However, Doblin also found serious flaws in Pahnke's published account: Pahnke had failed to mention that several subjects had struggled with acute anxiety. . . . One had to be restrained and given an injection of Thorazine, a powerful antipsychotic, after he fled from the chapel and headed down Commonwealth Avenue, convinced he had been chosen to announce the news of the coming of the Messiah.[42]

These sorts of omissions from psychedelic studies, we will see later in this book, continue to pose important questions for much of the recent research on psychedelic drugs, as many critics worry that similar omissions may be occurring in trials conducted today.[43] Nonetheless, despite its various methodological and intellectual flaws, Pahnke's was arguably the most influential psychedelic experiment of the 1960s and has helped shape psychedelic research to this day.

Pahnke and the Mystical Experience Questionnaire: Quantifying the Ineffable

Pahnke's dissertation was completed in 1963, and it made the links between psychedelics and mystical experience explicit even in its very title: "Drugs and Mysticism: An Analysis of the Relationship Between Psychedelic Drugs and the Mystical Consciousness." Among other things, Pahnke's work was hugely important for developing and helping to popularize a numerical scale for measuring spiritual states in these sorts of trials. The scale first emerged in his dissertation as a follow-up questionnaire used to assess whether psilocybin could induce mystical experiences.[44] Eventually dubbed the Mystical Experience Questionnaire (MEQ), this metric has undergone various modifications over the years but is still used in some form in virtually all research on psychedelics carried out in labs to this day.[45]

For his understanding of mysticism, Pahnke relied primarily on a few key authors. Foremost among them were the novelist Aldous Huxley, the scholar of mysticism Evelyn Underhill, and, perhaps most importantly, the British philosopher W. T. Stace. Published just a few years earlier in 1960, Stace's key text, *Mysticism and Philosophy*, was clearly a major influence on Pahnke's work—and, as we will see, on much later psychedelic research. Born in London, Stace had worked in Ceylon (now Sri Lanka) for twenty-two years as part of the British Civil Service before pursuing a degree at Trinity College. Following his service abroad, he was hired by Princeton University and was appointed chair of philosophy in 1935. While his early work had focused on British empiricism, during his final years, Stace began to write widely on the topics of mysticism and religion.[46]

As Karl Baier observes in his discussion of the MEQ, Stace's view of mysticism is at once perennialist and universalist. That is to say, Stace assumes that there is a singular mystical experience at the core of all religion and that this experience is universal and transhistorical, transcending any particular religious or cultural identity.[47] In this regard, Stace is heavily influenced by the modern Hindu philosophical movement known as neo-Vedanta, which was widely in vogue during the first half of the twentieth century. A modern variant of the classical Hindu philosophical school of Vedanta, neo-Vedanta is based on the idea that there is one Ultimate Reality or Truth (*Brahman*) and that all individual religious traditions are simply different manifestations of and paths back to that one divine summit of Truth. This version of Vedanta passed into the English-speaking world through various sources, such as the hugely popular works of Swami Vivekananda (1863–1902) and Swami Prabhavananda (1893–1976), particularly the latter's translations of the *Upanishads*. Neo-Vedantic authors such as Vivekananda and Prabhavananda presented a version of Hinduism that was largely palatable to a "Western" audience, emphasizing the Oneness of God and the harmony of all religions. They also tended to see direct mystical experience—and, specifically, the experience of transcending the individual self and merging with the divine—"as a universal human possibility and the heart of all religion."[48]

This sort of neo-Vedantic version of Hinduism and of mysticism more generally had many admirers in England and the US. Among them was Aldous Huxley, who was not only an early advocate of psychedelics but also active in the Vedanta Society in California. As Jeffrey Breau and Paul

Gillis-Smith note in their study of the MEQ and its legacy, "In the years before he wrote *The Perennial Philosophy* (1945), he was close friends with Swami Prabhavananda, and . . . his philosophical outlook was shaped by his connection to the Vedanta Society."[49]

Stace's work on mysticism also comes out of this larger context of neo-Vedanta and perennial philosophy.[50] Indeed, Pahnke himself later noted that Stace's model of mysticism is a universalistic one that assumes a common core to all mystical experiences regardless of historical or cultural context: "As Stace has emphasized, such categories attempt to describe the core of a universal psychological experience, free from culturally determined philosophical or theological interpretations."[51] In his general model, Stace first distinguishes between two broad types of mystical experience, which he calls the "extrovertive" and the "introvertive." In the extrovertive experience, the mystic feels unity between oneself and the material world, seeing the divine in everything around them. In the more "complete" form of mystical experience, the introvertive, the mystic extends the feeling from differentiated unity with the external world to an undifferentiated unity in which all distinctions between the self, the world, and divine ultimately disappear.[52] Both the extrovertive and introvertive forms of experience, Stace believed, were characterized by seven main features, which varied only slightly. The former includes the qualities of 1) unifying vision or the sense that all things are One; 2) the concrete apprehension of the One as an inner subjectivity or life in all things; 3) a sense of objectivity or reality; 4) a blessedness and peace; 4) a feeling of the holy, sacred, or divine; 6) paradoxicality; and 7) ineffability. The latter or introvertive experience, meanwhile, has most similar though slightly different qualities of 1) a unitary consciousness (the One, the Void, etc.); 2) nonspatiality and nontemporality; 3) a sense of objectivity or reality; 4) blessedness or peace; 5) a feeling of the holy or sacred; 6) paradoxicality; and 7) ineffability.[53]

Pahnke's dissertation largely follows Stace's understanding of mystical experience along with its universalist and perennialist assumptions. As he states from the very outset of his project, he takes as a basic presupposition Stace's conclusion that "in the mystical experience there are certain fundamental characteristics which are universal and are not restricted to any particular religion or culture (although particular cultural, historical, and religious conditions may influence both the interpretation and description of these basic phenomena)."[54] Indeed, "in mystical states there is no difference of religion. All experiences are absolutely identical."[55]

Pahnke essentially adapted and combined Stace's extrovertive/introvertive model and its seven characteristics, creating a nine-point description of mystical experience. These include all of Stace's seven categories with two additional points: 1) unity (subdivided into internal and external); 2) transcendence of time and space; 3) deeply felt positive mood; 4) a sense of sacredness; 5) objectivity and reality; 6) paradoxicality; 7) alleged ineffability; 8) transiency; and 9) persisting positive changes in attitude and behavior.[56] It does seem significant that Pahnke thought it important to add these last two characteristics, particularly the ninth point of persisting positive changes in attitude and behavior. This was perhaps an effort to reinject a sense of "ethics" into the mystical experience, which otherwise seems without any obvious ethical requirement or consequences.

Soon after the Marsh Chapel experiment, the subjects were asked to write up a detailed phenomenological account of their experiences. Within a week, each subject also completed a 147-item questionnaire "designed to measure phenomena of the typology of mystical consciousness on a qualitative, numerical scale." The results of the questionnaire were then used as the basis for ninety-minute tape-recorded interviews with each of them. And finally, six months later, each subject was interviewed again after completion of a follow-up questionnaire that used a similar scale.[57] The nine categories of mystical experience served as the underlying framework for the questions and evaluations, with each of the items in the questionnaire falling under one of the nine. For example, under the first category of "unity," subjects were asked about their experience of "loss of self," "sense of the loss of the multiplicity of all particular sense impressions," "pure awareness with no empirical distinctions," and "sense of unity with ultimate reality." They then rated each of these on a scale of 0–4, ranging from "did not experience at all" (0) to "experienced strongly" (4).[58] This resulted in quite specific sorts of numerical evaluations, such as ".016" for "external unity" or ".001" for "transcendence of time and space."

As Breau and Gillis-Smith observe, Pahnke basically took Stace's universalist model of mystical experience and turned it into a numerical scale that could be used in a laboratory setting—in effect, attempting to "quantify the ineffable" in a controlled, scientific way: "Pahnke turned Stace's typology of mystical experience into a set of psychometric factors that would structure and measure the degree and kind of mystical experience of participants."[59] This sort of attempt to "quantify the unquantifiable" is clearly reminiscent of other attempts to measure ineffable experiences, such as the numerical scales of pain that were also widely developed during this period. As historian Theodore M. Porter observes, this "trust in numbers" or urge to quantify everything has been a central part of the modern rise and success of science; it has also been closely tied to political and social pressures to produce results that are seen to be "objective" and impartial rather than merely subjective.[60] Pahnke's quantitative analysis is clearly part of this larger "trust in numbers," which he believed would provide the scientific authority (and cover) for his research into the spiritual realm. At the same time, Pahnke claimed that his metric had helped prove scientifically that the experiences of those who received psilocybin were not only roughly similar to but in fact "indistinguishable from, if not identical" to classical mystical experiences; and still further, he concludes that other drugs such as LSD and mescaline also produce these same experiences:

> The experimental evidence has strongly suggested that under the conditions described psilocybin can induce states of consciousness which are apparently indistinguishable from, if not identical with, those experienced by the mystics. . . . This conclusion gives support to the claims made by others who have used . . . similar drugs such as LSD or mescaline to aid in the induction of such experiences.[61]

As we will see in more detail in chapter 6, Pahnke's metric underwent several revisions over the next several decades. In the 1970s, Pahnke's collaborator, William Richards, revised the model for use in the study of the psychedelic dipropyltryptamine (DPT).[62] Several decades later, the MEQ was further revised by Roland Griffiths and his team in their landmark study of psilocybin and mystical experience, which added fifty-seven distractor questions to Pahnke's original list of forty-three questions. And then in 2012, the MEQ was revised yet again, with Pahnke's original nine factors now reduced to four, and his evaluation questions now reduced to thirty.[63] Known as the MEQ-30, this latter version is now widely used in psychedelic research, usually alongside the Hood Mysticism Scale (M-scale). Nonetheless, as Breau and Gillis-Smith conclude, most of the universalistic, perennialist, and neo-Vedantic assumptions inherited from W. T. Stace have persisted in the current iteration of the MEQ: "Although the questionnaires have changed over the years, their reliance on the work of Walter Stace is consistent."[64] In particular, Stace's emphasis on the "intense, all-encompassing feeling of unity" continues to be regarded in most current psychedelic research as the "critical definitional feature" of the mystical-type experience.[65]

This heavy reliance on Stace's understanding of mysticism has a number of problematic implications. As Ann Taves pointedly observes, Stace's definition of mysticism and the models that use it (such as the MEQ) have a number of serious weaknesses. Most importantly, these models tend to reaffirm Stace's bias toward one particular kind of mystical experience as the most pure or authentic—namely, the experience of unity, usually described in monistic neo-Vedantic terms (the "all is One," loss of self in the Absolute

Reality). In so doing, they also mask an implicit theological assumption that the experiences of unity and loss of self are not only universal but also inherently positive (rather than terrifying experiences or expressions of psychosis, as they are for some):

> From a scientific perspective, the use of Stace's (1960) definition to operationalize mystical experience has two major drawbacks. First, Stace's definition, by virtue of its perennialist aims, singles out experiences of unity and isolates them from other—potentially related—alterations of the self. Second, his focus on positive experiences of unity has allowed researchers to avoid comparisons with negative experiences that have psychopathological associations. This helped to maintain the idea that mystical experiences are sui generis and undercut research into how and why experiences of unity can acquire both positive and negative valence.[66]

At the same time, Taves argues, scales like the MEQ tend to marginalize or diminish *other* sorts of experiences that do not feature the sense of unity, while also obscuring the role of culture, society, history, and language in shaping all experiences (mystical or otherwise):

> As defined by Stace and operationalized in the scales, the mysticism construct presupposes, on theological grounds, that experiences of undifferentiated unity are inherently positive . . . and that the experience is culturally unmediated (i.e., that the cultural environment does not play a significant role in constituting the positively valued experience as it unfolds). The claim that such experiences are "unmediated" does not consider the possibility that subjective experience is assembled through processes of "mediation" or "interpretation" that take place below the threshold of consciousness.[67]

Many scholars of mysticism—myself included—would argue that factors such as language, history, and cultural context are as important if not more important to understanding mystical experiences than the claim to an unmediated universal core (if anything, I would argue that the historical-cultural context is precisely what makes such experiences *interesting*, rather than simply more examples of monistic absorption into the One).[68] Yet this sort of attention to rich contextual detail is precisely what is lost in Stace's model; and this loss is arguably carried over into Pahnke's metric, which from the outset assumes that all mystical experiences refer to a common core, regardless of their particular religious origin.

As Breau and Gillis-Smith argue, Pahnke's metric also reinforces Stace's universalist view of mysticism in an oddly circular way. By assuming Stace's idea of mystical experience from the outset, it then categorizes and quantifies individual experiences in these same universalist terms and so tends to reproduce the same sorts of experiences it began with: "In this way, the MEQ and the perennialist, Vedantic mystical experience have become mutually reinforcing. . . . What is elided . . . are the origins of those philosophies and theories. . . . Critical philosophical and theoretical aspects of the MEQ are the result of long, complex conversations in the intellectual traditions—in fact, the religious traditions of Hinduism, Vedanta, and perennialism."[69]

Finally, Pahnke's metric suffers most of the same problems shared by other scientific models that attempt to quantify unquantifiable phenomena. For example, pain scales are widely used in hospitals and doctor's offices today, but they are notoriously subjective and unreliable. Not only is every patient's report of pain wildly different, but there are often deep racial, gendered, and other biases buried in the implementation of these scales. As Dr. Daniel Barron wrote in an article for *Scientific American*, "there must be a better way to capture my patient's experience than 'zero to 10.' Such questions leave me feeling like I'm just kicking the tires on a much larger and complex problem."[70] It is difficult not to see scales such as the MEQ as a similar kind of "kicking the tires" on the vast and complex range of experiences that these individuals underwent—and kicking them with perennialist and universalist boots, no less.

Pahnke continued his research on psychedelics throughout the 1960s. In personal documents preserved in the Walter Pahnke collection at Purdue University, he also described his own experimentation with psychedelics, including impressions of his first LSD experience of March 30, 1964. His account, written the following day, contains most of the same themes from Stace's model of mysticism that reappear in his MEQ: the sense of unity, the loss of self, the feeling sacredness and awe, and so on, are all featured prominently in his description:

> The most impressive and intense part of this experience was the WHITE LIGHT of absolute purity and clearness. It was like a glowing and sparkling flame of incandescent whiteness and beauty . . . The associated feelings were those of *absolute* AWE, REVERENCE and SACREDNESS. Just before this experience I had the feeling of going deep within myself to the Self stripped bare of all pretense and falseness. This was the point where a man could stand firm with absolute integrity . . . The white light was of *supreme importance*—absolutely validating and something worth staking your whole life on and putting our trust in. . . .

> Later I again went deep within myself, and I had the image of going down deep into a dark silent pool. Then I had a vision of absolute DIVINE love. It was like a flowing spring of silvery white liquid overflowing upward and was very beautiful to watch and feel. The feeling was of love and compassion toward the Divine and toward all men.[71]

Indeed, Pahnke's words highlighted in capital letters and underlined here clearly reaffirm many of the basic categories of Stace's definition and of his own MEQ.

In 1967, Pahnke joined the Maryland Psychiatric Research Center in Baltimore, where he conducted numerous therapy sessions with LSD and related drugs. He continued to publish on the topic of psychedelics and spirituality, such as his 1969 article "Psychedelic Mystical Experience in the Human Encounter with Death," which foreshadowed some of the more recent research on psychedelics and terminal illness.[72] In 1971, his work was unexpectedly cut short when he died in a scuba diving accident in Maine. However, both his general model of mystical experience and a version of his MEQ remain widely influential today, more than fifty years later. As we will see in chapter 6, many of the problems with Pahnke's metric also persist in much of the current psychedelic research, which continues to rely on these same perennialist assumptions and lack of attention to historical or cultural context.

"Start Your Own Religion": Leary and the Psychedelic Religions of the 1960s

While Pahnke saw the Marsh Chapel experiment as clear evidence that psychedelic drugs can occasion genuine mystical experiences, his mentor Timothy Leary believed the experiment to have much greater implications. For Leary, this was a sign that the time was ripe for a far more radical and ambitious spiritual movement, one that would leave the old institutions behind altogether and inaugurate a new kind of religion based on experimentation and direct experience of the sacred. In place of the one God of the Abrahamic religions, we could now celebrate a kind of radical polytheism through psychedelic rites:

> We had run up against the Judeo-Christian commitment to one God, one religion, one reality that had cursed Europe for centuries. . . . Drugs that open the mind to multiple realities inevitably lead to a polytheistic view of the universe. We sensed that the time for a new humanist religion based on intelligent good-natured pluralism and scientific paganism had arrived.[73]

In this sense, Leary saw himself and his fellow psychedelic explorers as not simply drug researchers but as spiritual seekers in the same great lineage as other mystics and holy men, such as the "Tantrics, Sufis, Bauls, Gnostics, Hermetics [and] Sivaites." They are all part of an "ancient underground society of alchemists, artists, mystics, alienated visionaries, dropouts and the disenchanted young," united in the "quest for eternal freedom, for the elixir of life, for the draught of immortality."[74]

For Leary, psychedelic drugs are the means to achieving a genuine religious experience, one that is essentially non-different from the enlightenment experience of the Buddha under the bodhi tree or the after-death experiences described in the *Tibetan Book of the Dead* (*Bardo Thödel*). Following Huxley, he describes drugs not as the source of the mystical experience but more as a kind of "key" that opens the door to transcendental awareness:

> A psychedelic experience is a journey to new realms of consciousness. The scope and content of the experience is limitless, but its characteristic features are the transcendence of verbal concepts, of space-time dimensions, and of the ego or identity. Such experiences of enlarged consciousness can occur in a variety of ways: sensory deprivation, yoga exercises, disciplined meditation, religious or aesthetic ecstasies, or spontaneously. Most recently, they have been made available to anyone through the ingestion of psychedelic drugs such as LSD, psilocybin, mescaline, DMT, etc.
>
> Of course, the drug does not produce the transcendent experience. It merely acts as a chemical key—it opens the mind.[75]

We should note in passing that Leary's psychedelic interpretation of the *Tibetan Book of the Dead* had massive cultural implications. Perhaps most famously, it helped inspire the Beatles song "Tomorrow Never Knows," which appeared as the final track on their hugely popular and landmark album *Revolver* in 1966. Amid hypnotic drum and bass lines and a swirl of psychedelic sounds and backward effects, John Lennon intones the lines from Leary's version of the *Bardo Thödel*, "turn off your mind, relax, and float downstream." After Wasson's 1957 *Life* magazine article, the recording of this song was perhaps the most powerful and influential moment when the psychedelic interpretation of religious experience entered directly into mainstream mass culture for general consumption.

Like many in the 1960s who began to embrace aspects of Buddhism and other Asian traditions, Leary had a largely negative view of most mainstream religious institutions of twentieth-century America. The Judeo-Christian worldview, in Leary's opinion, is based on an enormous gulf between divinity (which is "up there") and the self ("down here");[76] but psychedelics quickly cross over that gulf and allow us to find God here and now within ourselves. And because these drugs transgress the boundaries of both conventional social norms and outdated religious dogma, they now require their own kind of new spiritual belief system and spiritual practices: "Like all sacraments, the psychedelic drugs threaten society and that part of your own mind that is attached to the current social taboos. Like all new sacraments, the psychedelics require a new religion."[77] Most importantly, Leary concluded, psychedelics fundamentally reveal to each one of us that we are in fact already divine—indeed, we are all God. Therefore, we must each create our *own* religion in order to realize and celebrate our personal divinity: "To drop-out you must form your own religion."[78] Going still further, "You must start your own religion. You are GOD—but only you can discover and nurture your divinity. No one can start your religion for you."[79] "Your new religion can be formed only by you. Do not wait for a Messiah. Do it yourself. Now."[80]

In this sense, Leary saw psychedelics as a powerful means to a kind of radical democratization of mystical experience. No longer limited to a few holy men meditating in caves, profound religious experience could be achieved quickly and easily by literally anyone: "You can be a convict or a college professor. You'll still have a mystical, transcendental experience that may change your life."[81]

In 1962, Leary and Alpert set up a grassroots nonprofit called the International Federation for International Freedom (IFIF) in order to carry out studies of the religious use of psychedelics.[82] The organization was later renamed the Castalia Foundation (after the intellectual colony in Herman Hesse's novel *The Glass Bead Game*) and took the form of a small communal group at the Hitchcock Estate in Millbrook, New York. The group published a small journal called the *Psychedelic Review* and hosted weekend retreats for yoga, meditation, and group therapy. Eventually, this evolved into a formally incorporated "religion" dubbed the "League for Spiritual Discovery," which was dedicated to the cultivation and realization of the divinity in each person, particularly through the use of psilocybin, LSD, and other psychedelics. As Leary explained in his 1968 book *High Priest*,

> The League of Spiritual Discovery is a legally incorporated religion dedicated to the ancient sacred scripture of turning-on, tuning-in, and dropping out. Its aim is to help recreate every man as God and every woman as Goddess. This book is the first of a four-volume biblical account of the birth, structural growth, exile, return, persecution, redemption, and flowering of the LSD religious cult.[83]

Knowing that modern religions must also deal with the modern legal system, Leary turned his idea over to lawyers and had papers filed with the secretary of state. As he explained—with a certain amount of prescience about our own situation in the twenty-first century (see below)—he suggests that psychedelic law will be an important emerging field in the coming decades:

> Don't be surprised at the idea of having a lawyer to handle your psychedelic affairs. Psychedelic lawyers will be the most numerous and popular segment of the legal profession in fifteen years. For a small amount of money, you can have on-going legal protection for your religion. You'd have it for your business, wouldn't you?[84]

The legal process in Leary's case was initially fairly painless. Within ten days, he recounts, his new religion was legally incorporated and so put forward its own set of bylaws. The League for Spiritual Discovery was said to have three main purposes:

> a) individual worship of the Supreme Energy—God; b) communal worship of the Supreme Energy—God; and c) public worship of the Supreme Energy—God. These three forms of worship based on revelation and empirically validated methods for spiritual discovery.[85]

While most of this book examines the theme of a psychedelic-based "mysticism without religion," Leary was one of the first of many examples of attempts to create a new kind of "religion" based on psychedelic mysticism. Yet even here, this idea of a new religion is wildly idiosyncratic, anti-institutional and radically individualistic. It really seems much closer to what Kripal calls the modern American "religion of no religion" or what the Indian guru Osho-Rajneesh called a kind of "religionless religion" than any sort of formal institutional tradition.[86]

A number of other groups followed Leary's suggestion of creating their own religion. One of the first and most entrepreneurial was the Brotherhood of Eternal Love, started by John Griggs and friends after reading Leary's work.[87] The leader of a motorcycle gang from Anaheim, Griggs's unique spiritual journey began when he robbed a Hollywood producer and stole his stash of Sandoz LSD. After dropping the acid in Joshua Tree National Park, he had a profound revelation, began a new life, and took up Leary's suggestion that he start his own religion. The Brotherhood was established as a tax-exempt entity in 1966—ironically just ten days after LSD was made illegal in the state of California. According to their articles of incorporation, the Brotherhood's mission was primarily

> to bring the world to a greater awareness of God through the teachings of Jesus Christ, Buddha, Ramakrishna, Babaji, Paramahamsa Yogananda, Mahatma Gandhi, and all true prophets of God, and to spread the love and wisdom of these great teachers to all men. . . . We believe this church to be the earthly instrument of God's will. We believe in the sacred right of each individual to commune with God in spirit and in truth as it is empirically revealed to him.[88]

Very quickly, the Brotherhood embarked on an ambitious project that combined a kind of psychedelic missionary zeal with an array of illegal activities. While it clearly believed that LSD was the "solution to man's inhumanity to man and all other problems," the Brotherhood also became a hugely profitable and often criminal business enterprise.[89] As Lee and Shlain describe the group and its remarkable history,

> The saga of the Brotherhood of Eternal Love is a bizarre mélange of evangelical, starry-eyed hippie dealers, mystic alchemists, and fast-money bankers. Federal investigators described them as a "hippie Mafia" of approximately seven hundred fifty people that allegedly grossed $200,000,000, . . . They were fired with idealism, committed to changing the world by disseminating large quantities of psychedelics.[90]

As Leary recalls, the Brotherhood was quite an operation, opening a popular store on the Pacific Coast Highway called Mystic Arts World, which was known as "the ultimate head shop, a veritable LL Bean Supermarket of hippy gear." The shop's bookstore stocked all the latest titles in Eastern religions, mysticism, psychology, magic, and science, while its clothing boutique offered South Asian garments, sandals, and local tie-dyed apparel. At the same time, the shop had a more practical business function as a major hub in the underground circulation of drugs and drug money: "Mystic Arts World . . . served to launder funds raised by dealing hashish, marijuana, and LSD. Here we observed the birth of a new American agro-business: the cannabis trade."[91] Dubbed "the most famous cult of dope dealers in the world," the Brotherhood not only drove cannabis across the border from Mexico, they also smuggled people as part of their business model.[92] As we will see below, this complex mixture of religion and business has been a recurring theme in many modern psychedelic churches, such as the controversial Church of Ambrosia in the Bay Area today.

However, perhaps the most famous of the mid-1960s psychedelic religions was the Neo-American Church. Founded in 1965, the church was the brainchild of Arthur Kelps, who had been a participant in Leary's circle at Millbrook. Mixing serious legal arguments with a kind of absurdist sense of humor, the Neo-American Church claimed LSD as its sacrament while also dubbing its clergy "Boo Hoos" and its sacred the text the *Boo Hoo Bible*. Its religious hymns included "Puff the Magic Dragon" and "Row, Row, Row Your Boat," among others. While making a more sober legal case that they were a legitimate religious entity with a genuine "sacrament" comparable to the Native American Church with its use of peyote, the Neo-American Church also eschewed the formal trappings of conventional religion and instead openly employed silliness, satire, and "massive doses of absurdity" in its spiritual teachings:

> We do not employ set rituals, make conditions for membership other than agreement with our principles, or regulate the frequency or intensity of the sacramental experience. Many of our members are damned fools and miserable sinners; membership in the church is no guarantee of . . . spiritual wisdom; it may even be possible that one or two of our Boo Hoos are opportunistic charlatans.[93]

While the Neo-American Church was easily able to incorporate in the state of New York as a nonprofit religious organization, it soon faced legal challenges due to its open use of various illegal substances.[94] The church eventually made its case before the US Supreme Court after one of its ministers, Judith Kuch, was arrested and put on federal trial for narcotics charges in 1968. Among the church's main arguments was that their use of LSD was no different than the sacramental use of peyote by Native Americans—a point that had recently been argued successfully in many courts.[95] However, the Supreme Court in this case found Kuch's arguments unpersuasive, concluding that the Neo-American Church was more of a joke than a serious religion and that there was no evidence of "a religious discipline, a ritual, or tenets to guide one's daily existence" in the group. Moreover, the court ruled that LSD was a harmful substance and that there was compelling state interest to regulate such drugs:

> There is also a clear and compelling interest in the regulation of the transfer and possession of LSD. The drug is more harmful than marihuana and defendant's religious interest in its ingestion does not outweigh the threat to the public health and safety which LSD presents. The free exercise clause of the First Amendment does not prohibit the prosecution of this defendant under either Act. The practice of her beliefs, if beliefs they be, must give way to the public good.[96]

Ultimately, the court determined that the Neo-American Church was not a serious religion but merely a pretext for using drugs. It is clear, the court ruled, that "the desire to use drugs and to enjoy drugs for their own sake, regardless of religious experience, [was] the coagulant of this organization and the reason for its existence."

Although it may seem like a frivolous case today, the Kuch decision has had complex implications for religious law and drug law for last fifty years. On the one hand, it arguably complicated the case for Native Americans to make their own case for the religious use of peyote—which was actually denied by the US Supreme Court in the landmark Oregon v. Smith decision in 1990.[97] On the other hand, it has also made it more challenging for newly emerging psychedelic groups, such as the Church of Ambrosia in California, among many others.

Conclusion: Pahnke's Legacy and the Question(ing) of Authority

If Wasson was the most influential figure in the early popularization of mushrooms in the 1950s, Pahnke was arguably the most important figure in giving psilocybin both a *religious* and a *scientific* sort of credibility. His Marsh Chapel experiment made the claim that psilocybin could reliably inspire mystical experiences and that these experiences could now be reproduced and studied in a controlled scientific setting. This helped set the stage for virtually all the psychedelic research that followed in the 1960s and for the psychedelic renaissance of the twenty-first century. Perhaps most importantly, Pahnke's metric would serve as the basis for the MEQ, one of the most widely used tools to quantify mystical experience, still employed in various forms to this day. The MEQ has helped solidify the broader scientific "trust in numbers" even when applied to the most ineffable and seemingly unquantifiable phenomena such as mystical experience.[98] In the process, it has also helped provide psychedelic research with a twofold kind of authority—the seemingly objective authority of science and the seemingly transcendent authority of spirituality. This paradoxical mix of scientific and spiritual authority continues to inform (though some would say muddle and confuse) psychedelic research to this day.[99] At the same time, Pahnke's metric also imported a profound element of universalism and perennialism, largely based on Stace's view of mysticism, which also continues to inform (and/or muddle) most research in the twenty-first century.

Leary, meanwhile, left many controversial legacies. Perhaps the most significant one for the purposes of this book was his assertion that we can each "create our own religion" based on psychedelic experience—that is, that we should reject all institutional forms of religion (particularly Jewish and Christian forms) and embrace our own spiritual worldview based on the direct experience offered by psilocybin, LSD, and other substances. Although this idea has been modified and moderated in various ways over the last several decades, I think it is a foundational element in the broader "spiritual but not religious" view that circulates widely today.

Of course, it was not long before the psychedelic research launched by Pahnke, Leary, and others faced a powerful backlash. Leary was infamously dismissed from his position at Harvard in 1963 amid rumors of "orgies, naked poets, junkies, and homosexuality" flying around campus.[100] He would eventually be arrested numerous times and sentenced to twenty years in prison in 1970; even some of his psychedelic friends grew tired of his antics and declined to come to his aid. When Huston Smith wrote to Wasson in 1971, asking for financial help with Leary's bail, Wasson replied rather curtly: "I am unwilling to help bail Timothy Leary out. For upwards of 10 years he has been skirting the edge of the law. I like him. I think he is utterly sincere. He writes effectively. But when a man shows as bad judgment as he has done consistently, he should take the consequences."[101]

Meanwhile, both *Psilocybe* mushrooms and the far more powerful psychedelic LSD had inevitably leaked beyond the ivory tower walls of institutions such as Harvard and circulated promiscuously in popular culture. As mainstream publications such as *Cosmopolitan* reported in 1963,

> Suddenly LSD has become the sophisticated "fun thing" to try around the smart set, the fast set, and the best set. . . . If you haven't got a buddy who runs down to his friendly neighborhood LSD bootlegger and buys an ampule of these little pills, you are simply not *in*, my friend.[102]

By the mid-1960s, *Psilocybe* mushrooms and LSD had entered fully into the counterculture, championed by musicians, artists, filmmakers, and, increasingly, by middle-class suburban young people. Once seen as revolutionary new drugs that might treat mental illness and even inspire mystical experience, by the late 1960s, they were widely accused of creating profound psychological, social, and spiritual disorders, particularly among the American youth. Richard Nixon would make the question of drug abuse a central part of his "law-and-order campaign" during in the 1968 election, declaring LSD public enemy number one and dubbing Leary "the most dangerous man in America."[103] While psilocybin is of course a fundamentally different and far less powerful drug than LSD, it was basically equated with other "hard drugs" and classified as a Schedule I controlled substance under the 1971 United Nations Convention on Psychotropic Substances. By 1975, the National Institute of Mental Health stopped funding LSD research, and most scientific studies of psilocybin and other psychedelics ceased for the next two decades.

The intense backlash against psychedelics, I would argue, was not simply a matter of public safety concerns or anxieties over the well-being of America's youth. Another larger anxiety was a profound question of authority, in Bruce Lincoln's sense.[104] This was in many ways similar to the crisis of authority that emerged during the late Middle Ages, when many mystics—particularly female mystics—began to make spiritual claims that seemed to stray outside of or defy the authority of the Catholic Church. The claim to mystical experience, as Grace Jantzen persuasively argues, is inevitably tied to relations of power and authority; and many mystics who made claims that challenged or defied the church were branded heretics, witches, or worse. Some such as Meister Eckhart were tried for heresy, while others such as Marguerite Porete were burned at the stake for their radical claims.[105]

With the advent of psychedelics and the claim to instant access to mystical experience, this crisis of authority was amplified exponentially. After all, if anyone could achieve profound mystical experience or even "see God" simply by consuming a mushroom or a pill, what need was there for the hierarchy of any church or formal religious institution? If the Protestant Reformation of the sixteenth century represented a profound crisis of authority based on the idea of personal access to the Bible,[106] then the psychedelic revolution of the 1960s represented a far more profound crisis of authority, in which anyone with a mushroom could claim direct access to the divine. As we see in the epigraph at the beginning of this chapter, Pahnke himself was clearly aware that his psilocybin research would pose exactly this challenge to religious authorities; and Leary gleefully embraced this challenge with revolutionary fervor, calling on everyone to reject all traditions and create their own religions. At the same time, perhaps more fundamentally and subversively, the psychedelic movement of the 1960s was also challenging the authority of capitalism itself. Here was a simple mushroom that could be foraged or grown at home, and here was a drug that could be mixed up in a kitchen and sold inexpensively; and both could potentially reshape one's religious, cultural, and political worldview, including one's attachment to a capitalist system based on production, accumulation, and consumption. As Don Lattin observes,

> What is it about the nature of . . . psychedelics—as opposed to more addictive and deadly drugs like heroin, methamphetamine, and cocaine—that the government finds so dangerous? . . . What is so threatening to

> the powers that be about psychedelic plants and drugs are the ideas and insights they inspire. In the counterculture of the 1960s, they compelled many to question the consumerism and materialism that form the foundation of our capitalist economy.[107]

In retrospect, the backlash against the work of Pahnke and Leary in the late 1960s and 1970s was not particularly surprising. If the psychedelic counterculture was largely about "questioning authority" through different ways of perceiving reality, the self, the universe—and perhaps most radically, the marketplace—then no wonder the political establishment found this all deeply threatening.

[CHAPTER FOUR]

Neo-Shamans

Terence McKenna and the Explosion of Mushroom Mysticism in the 1970s and 1980s

> This mushroom is a trans-dimensional doorway which sly faeries have left slightly ajar for anyone to enter into who can find the key and who wishes to use this power—the power of vision—to explore this peculiar and naturally occurring psychoactive complex.
>
> Terence McKenna, *True Hallucinations* (1993)[1]

> In the end, all McKenna is asking anyone to do is to become a shaman, journey to the numinous, and draw their own conclusions.
>
> Mark Pesce, interview in "Terence McKenna's Last Trip" (2000)[2]

> The new western shamanism represents a self-conscious, counter-cultural reversal of attitudes dominant in western societies since those societies first encountered Siberian shamans. Instead of seeking to remove tribal magicians from the world as devil-worshippers, charlatans, maniacs, or fanatics, it seems to imitate some of their methods in order to serve the needs of a society which is increasingly seeking direct and personal experience of spirit-worlds and of divinity outside of institutional and dogmatic frameworks.
>
> Ronald Hutton, *Shamans* (2001)[3]

In 1971, Terence McKenna and his brother Dennis made a trip to the Columbian Amazon in search of locally used plant preparations that contained the powerful psychedelic DMT (dimethyltryptamine).[4] Originally from a Catholic family in western Colorado, McKenna had read the work of Aldous Huxley and encountered a variety of psychedelic drugs, including LSD and DMT, during his time in San Francisco during the 1960s. While searching for DMT in the Amazon, he and his brother stumbled upon a large amount of *P. cubensis*, and he recorded his various visionary experiences with the mushrooms in his hugely influential book *The Invisible Landscape* (1975). Describing the mushroom not simply as a hallucinogen but as a kind of "shamanic ally" and even an "intelligent entity—not of earth,"[5] McKenna helped craft a new kind of fungal mysticism that built upon the work of 1960s psychonauts but also took it in some strange, surprising, and often surreal new directions.[6]

In this chapter, I situate McKenna and his writings on psilocybin in the decade of the 1970s, discussing the ways in which he continued many of the themes in Wasson's global mushroom mysticism and helped pave the way for the mushroom renaissance that we see today. As Erik Davis suggests in his insightful study of spirituality in the 1970s, this was in many ways "the uncanny decade, the undecade," that fell between the countercultural utopianism of the 1960s and the conservative backlash that followed in the 1980s, with its reactionary turn to Reaganomics, the New Christian Right, and the "war on drugs." By the early 1970s, the 1960s' dreams of mass transformation had largely deflated, along with all faith in government amid the Vietnam War, Watergate, and the surreal revelations about MKUltra. All of this left many young people profoundly disillusioned with

FIGURE 4.1. Terence McKenna. Photograph by Lea Suzuki. Courtesy of Hearst Newspapers / Getty Images.

the idea of collective political transformation and instead seeking more personal sorts of transformations—in music, art, and spirituality. This was, in short, a kind of "liminal" or "betwixt and between" decade, to use Victor Turner's phrase:

> Things were particularly weird in these years, which remain shrouded in America's cultural memory, as if by a kind of smog. One reason for the haze is the period's elusive placement between the highly overdetermined sixties . . . and the more garish icons that came to the fore later in the seventies, like disco and Punk, Pong and *Star Wars*. . . . Indeed, *liminality* is a key characteristic of the early seventies. Radical and transformative forces unleashed in the sixties mutated and dissipated into much broader segments of culture. . . . Thresholds were everywhere.[7]

But in addition to being a liminal period of music, film, and religious movements, the 1970s were a decade when interest in psychedelic mushrooms exploded. In the wake of the drug revolution of the 1960s, many seekers began to discover that active *Psilocybe* species grew widely all over the United States. Throughout fields, forests, and suburbs, waves of enthusiastic mushroom hunters began to scour the countryside for these blue-staining fungi. As Paul Stamets later recalled,

> Beginning in the mid-seventies, a new subculture evolved from the fabric of the counterculture movement of the sixties. In the northwestern and southeastern United States, hunting the *Psilocybes* approached the status of a national sport. . . . The wave of interest soon became an invasion—a pandemic and a cause célèbre of an entire generation.[8]

Through his numerous books, talks, and interviews, McKenna quickly became the most influential psychedelic thinker since Wasson and Leary. As a kind of "post-religious visionary,"[9] McKenna articulated a form of modern shamanism in which mushrooms were nothing less than "transdimensional doorways" that opened onto other worlds of experience and knowledge.[10] In this sense, he was also a clear reflection of the romantic fascination with "primitives," the "archaic," and "shamanism" that ran throughout Western culture of the twentieth century.[11] As Marianna Torgovnick observes in her work on modern primitivism, "the West seems to need the primitive as a precondition and supplement to its sense of self: it always creates heightened versions of the primitive as nightmare or pleasant dream."[12] Throughout the twentieth century, the primitive was a source of both fear and allure, in some cases denigrated as a dangerous threat to rational civilization, and in other cases romanticized as an exotic noble savage, deeply in touch with nature and the sacred. McKenna's mushroom-inspired shamanism and his call for an "archaic revival" clearly reflects the latter sort of romanticization of the primitive. Indeed, we could say that McKenna was one of the most important figures in the modern reimagining of "shamanism" as a new kind of psychedelic mysticism without religion.

However, perhaps McKenna's most lasting contribution was to develop a reliable technique for actually growing mushrooms, which he described in step-by-step instructions in his widely read book *Psilocybin: Magic Mushroom Grower's Guide* (first published in 1976). This short text, probably more than anything else, made McKenna the single most influential figure in the explosion of interest in magic mushrooms from the 1970s onward. In a mere eighty pages, he showed any reader the basic way to grow *P. cubensis* in their own home and become their own shamanic explorer of other worlds.

But beyond inspiring a new generation of home cultivation, McKenna also combined his shamanic exploration of mushrooms with a wide range of other alternative beliefs and New Age ideas circulating in the 1970s.[13] These included an enthusiastic belief in UFOs and alien life, the use of Asian divinatory tools such as the *I Ching*, and a utopian vision of a coming global transformation that would radically change human consciousness. "The McKennas," Davis observes, "were baby boomers who came of age in the bloom of the counterculture . . . their accounts provide crucial insights into that peculiar moment when esoteric and psychoactive experience was woven into an emancipatory politics with radical Promethean overtones."[14] With the apparent power to speak with and through McKenna himself, mushrooms served as the mycelial network connecting all these ideas in a new kind of psychedelic spirituality that was oddly well-suited to this highly weird decade.

Mushrooms, Shamans, and Con Artists in the Late 1960s: The Strange Case of Carlos Castaneda

McKenna was not the first to develop the idea of a kind of neo-shamanism based on the use of psychedelic mushrooms. The fascination with shamanism spread widely in the English-speaking world following the translation of Mircea Eliade's seminal text, *Shamanism: Archaic Techniques of Ecstasy*, in 1964, inspiring many new imaginings of the "shaman."[15] Perhaps the most infamous of these in the late 1960s was the hugely popular—though probably largely fictional—work of Carlos Castaneda (1925–98). Often called the "godfather of the New Age," Castaneda claimed to have met a Yaqui shaman named don Juan while conducting his master's thesis research as an anthropology student at UCLA.[16] First published in 1968 as *The Teachings of Don Juan* and continuing in a series of books over the next two decades, Castaneda's work was a hugely influential force in the psychedelic revolution, spurring a generation of young people to explore *Psilocybe* and various other hallucinogens. As Jay Fikes observes, Castaneda's vivid accounts of the mercurial figure of don Juan and his psychedelic adventures in other worlds helped pave the way for the much broader "marketing of shamans" in the 1970s.[17]

It is worth noting that Castaneda had also been in correspondence with Wasson as early as 1962, and the two exchanged numerous letters on the topics of shamanism and the Indigenous use of psychedelic substances, including *Psilocybe* mushrooms. As Castaneda wrote in a letter to Wasson in 1968, he was not 100 percent certain what species the mushrooms were, but he claimed that "I have gathered the mushrooms myself. I have held perhaps hundreds of specimens in my hands. Don Juan and I made yearly trips to collect them in the mountains southwest and northwest of the Vallé Nacional in the state of Oaxaca."[18] Wasson would later write quite positive reviews of Castaneda's first several books, which seemed to confirm his own work on the Indigenous use of psychedelic mushrooms.[19]

Overall, Castaneda's books painted a vivid picture of an Indigenous shaman who used mushrooms and various other substances to open a secret portal to another world. As Walter Goldschmidt wrote in his forward to *The Teachings of Don Juan*,

> Carlos Castaneda, under the tutelage of don Juan, takes us through that moment of twilight, through the crack in the universe between daylight and dark into a world not merely other than our own, but of an entirely different order of reality. To reach it he had the aid of *mescalito, yerba del diablo*, and *humito*—peyote, datura, and mushrooms.[20]

In his account of don Juan's various shamanic techniques, Castaneda provided a description of these three substances in particular, which he identified as the cactus *L. williamsii* (peyote), the plant *Datura stramonium* (jimsonweed), and the mushroom *P. mexicana* (one of many species of *Psilocybe* used by Mexican *curanderas* and *sabias*). For teachers such as don Juan, these were not mere plants but shamanic "allies" that could be used for a wide range of spiritual and magical purposes. But most importantly, they were used to enter ecstatic states of altered consciousness and altered reality:

> Since before their contact with Europeans, American Indians have known the hallucinogenic properties of these three plants . . . the plants have been widely enjoyed for pleasure, for curing, for witchcraft, and for attaining a state of ecstasy. In the specific context of his teachings, don Juan related the use of *Datura inoxia* and *Psilocybe mexicana* to the acquisition of power, a power he called an "ally." . . . The importance of the plants was, for don Juan, their capacity to produce stages of peculiar perception in a human being. . . . I have called them "states of nonordinary reality"[21]

As don Juan explained to Castaneda in the first volume of the series, mushrooms are in many ways the most important and most dangerous of these substances. Easily mistaken for toxic species, the mushrooms require the most knowledge in collection and the most skill in use:

> The real secret of the mixture lies in the mushrooms. . . . They are the most difficult to collect. The trip to the place where they grow is long and dangerous, and to select the right variety is even more perilous. There are other kinds of mushrooms growing alongside which are of no use. . . . It takes time to know the mushrooms well in order not to make a mistake. Serious harm will result from using the wrong kind. . . . I know of men who have dropped dead from the foul smoke.[22]

In the early years after their publication, the tales of don Juan received many glowing reviews and positive responses. The books were featured prominently in major publications such as *Time Magazine*, *The New York Times*, and *Los Angeles Times*, which praised their "extraordinary narrative" and the remarkable, almost legendary character of don Juan himself. Almost immediately, however, the books also aroused intense suspicion from more critical academic readers. Anthropologist such as Weston LaBarre and Edmund Leach raised serious questions about Castaneda's knowledge of Yaqui culture, language, and religious life; Wasson himself even wrote to Castaneda, asking how it was possible that a Yaqui like don Juan could have learned how to use the psychedelic mushrooms, which only grow in the wetter portion of southern Mexico.[23] Other scholars such as Jay Fikes concluded that Castaneda's work was ultimately little more than "vulgar pseudo-ethnography" based not on actual research but on his own personal fantasy and blatant copying from other sources:

> Castaneda failed to distinguish the most elementary aspects of peyote meetings he described, including the purpose of such meetings and

> the ritual leader's identity. Having done no routine ethnographic research presumably disposed Castaneda toward taking elements or emotions derived from his personal life . . . as well as taking anecdotes without attribution (plagiarizing) from diverse sources he had read or heard about.[24]

One of the most aggressive critiques of Castaneda's work came from Richard de Mille, who pointed out numerous inconsistencies in the books and over forty pages of apparent plagiarism. In a letter to Wasson, de Mille described Castaneda as a "talented" but fraudulent "cult figure" who was "tragically caught in his own web of power," while don Juan was essentially a fictional character.[25] Indeed, de Mille suggests that the real inspiration for Castaneda's don Juan was none other than Wasson's own work—and specifically, Wasson's descriptions of María Sabina and don Aurelio.[26]

Regardless of their veracity, however, Castaneda's books had a massive impact on alternative spirituality, the counterculture, and the popular interest in psychedelics from the late 1960s onward. Perhaps even more so than Wasson's article in *Life* magazine, his books inspired a whole new generation of young people to begin exploring Indigenous cultures and experimenting with all manner of psychedelics. In fact, I read all the don Juan books as a teenager in central Pennsylvania back in the 1980s, and they were definitely among the most important influences that led me to explore mushrooms and LSD, which I eagerly imagined to be the key to my own "shamanic journey." Unfortunately, like Wasson's *Life* magazine publication, Castaneda's books had a significant—and, many would say, largely negative—impact on the Indigenous peoples of Mexico. Now yet another wave of hippies, tourists, and journalists began to descend on local communities in search of mushrooms, peyote, and other substances that might offer access to otherworldly shamanic journeys. As Fikes laments, "tour operators began guiding . . . shaman-seekers to Huichol villages. In recent years, peyote tourists have invaded the sacred land where Huichol venerate the peyote spirit. The rising tide of tourists in that area is rapidly depleting peyote and has stimulated Mexican authorities to incarcerate Huichol peyote hunters."[27]

"True Hallucinations": McKenna's First Encounter with Mushrooms

Born in Paonia, Colorado, in 1946, Terence McKenna grew up very much in the wake of Wasson's and Castaneda's popular writings on psychedelic shamanism. The son of a salesman for an industrial electrical equipment company, McKenna described the county he grew up in as a poor and "hard-scrabble environment."[28] According to his brother Dennis's recollections, Terence first read about magic mushrooms in Wasson's *Life* magazine when he was ten years old. Dennis, who was then six, remembered his older brother "trailing our mother as she did her housework, waving the magazine demanding to know more. But, of course, she had nothing to add."[29]

After relocating to California for high school, McKenna encountered the newly emerging counterculture and psychedelic movement of the 1960s, exploring its most radical dimensions both spiritually and politically. He first read Huxley's *Doors of Perception* in the spring of 1963 and began experimenting with morning glories and other substances. In 1965, he entered the University of California, Berkeley, and was accepted into the Tussman Experimental College—a short-lived program that eschewed exams and grades and allowed students to pursue big ideas. This proved to be an ideal environment for McKenna, allowing him to pursue his interests in history and shamanism.[30] He later reflected that this early study of shamanism as a general phenomenon (heavily influenced by the work of Mircea Eliade) led him to his later studies of shamanic-type phenomena in other cultures.[31] His time at Berkeley seems to have stimulated him both psychedelically and politically; he had his first experience with LSD in these years and also became active in the anti-Vietnam and free speech movements, quickly finding himself fighting police at the barricades.[32] He would also participate in the Human Be-In and rolling orgies of the Summer of Love in 1967, as well as the massive student-led strikes at San Francisco State University in 1968.[33]

Inspired by his interest in Tantric Buddhist art, McKenna then traveled to Nepal in 1968, seeking out Bön shamans and studying Tibetan language. As he later recalled, he was attempting to "integrate the psychedelic experience into a Buddhist model," making sense of LSD encounters through the lens of Tibetan Buddhism and shamanism.[34] Following the global hippie circuit of the era, he worked for a time as a hashish smuggler and then traveled throughout Southeast Asia, exploring religious sites and even briefly working as a butterfly collector in Indonesia.[35] When he returned to Berkeley, he actually finished his degree through the Department of Conservation of Natural Resources—though he would later describe his program of study as a kind of "a self-organized major in shamanism."[36]

After his mother's death from cancer in 1970, Terence traveled to the Columbian Amazon and then returned a year later with his brother Dennis and three friends. The primary inspiration for the trip was an article by the anthropologist Richard Schultes that described a plant preparation called *oo-koo-hé* used by Indigenous Witito communities. Derived from *Virola theiodora* trees, *oo-koo-hé* contained a unique form of DMT that could be ingested orally rather than smoked, thus producing a less extreme and more extended psychedelic experience.[37]

During their search for *oo-koo-hé*, the brothers stumbled unexpectedly upon huge fields of *P. cubensis* growing in cow dung and soon engaged in a series of complex spiritual, psychological, and physiological experiments that would profoundly change both themselves and the course of the modern psychedelic movement. In many ways, these experiments marked "a turning point in American psychedelic culture."[38] As McKenna later recalled, "I had never had psilocybin before and was amazed at the contrast with LSD, which seemed more abrasively psychoanalytic and personal. In contrast, the mushrooms seemed so full of merry elfin energy that casting off into a visionary trance was all the more enticing."[39] The brothers decided that they would engage in a kind of spiritual-alchemical-genetic experiment that would somehow bond plant-based *harmine* DNA with their own human neural DNA through consumption of the mushrooms, combined with the use of specific vocal techniques. "We were," he recalls, "operating in a world where scientific method, ritual, and participation mystique were inseparably intertwined."[40] Their belief was that this would give them access to the collective memory of the human species and ultimately manifest the fabled alchemical "Philosopher's Stone," which they interpreted as a hyperdimensional union of spirit and matter. As Dennis later recalled, their aim was to "create an artifact that was a visible exteriorization of our own consciousness that we could see and would basically be able to do anything."[41]

Beginning on March 4 at La Chorrera, Columbia, the experiments involved a complex series of operations that mixed a number of different magical, occult, and mystical traditions. Creating a circle on the floor of their hut, they marked the four directions and set drawings of the *I Ching* hexagons at each cardinal point. In the center, they placed a large fresh mushroom, and nearby they hung the chrysalis of a blue morpho butterfly as a symbol of metamorphosis.[42] The brothers ate mushrooms, brewed ayahuasca, and prepared for what they thought could be the "eschaton" or "outbreak of the millennium."[43]

The experiment, the brothers believed, had in fact been successful, at least in some sense. While they did not produce an actual "Philosopher's Stone," they did have a mutual vision of the central mushroom of the ritual assuming a cosmic form with the entire earth on its cap.[44] As Dennis later recalled, the brothers underwent a kind of simultaneous shamanic initiation, in which they felt themselves to be radically "spread across spacetime" and completely one with the "Cosmic Mind."[45] And while Dennis seemed to become disengaged from reality, uttering gibberish and nonsense for days,[46] Terence believed that he had come into contact with the *Logos* itself—the divine voice or Word—which he also called the ancient spirit of the mushroom: "Alien presences and translinguistic elves bent near to me in those trances. The mushroom stressed its age, its vast knowledge of the ebb and flow of historical forces in many civilizations through the millennia. Images of the past and future abounded."[47] Indeed, McKenna believed that he had himself become the mouthpiece for the mushroom voice, which could now speak and write through him:

> Aided by my devotion to psilocybin and the experiment at La Chorrera . . . I had apparently evolved into a sort of mouthpiece for the incarnate Logos. I could talk to small groups of people with what appeared to be electrifying effect about the peculiarly transcendental matters.[48]

Ultimately, McKenna believed that the experience had implications not simply as a personal vision but as a kind of global eschatological revelation, one that had the potential to "awaken all the residents of planet Earth to a new reality of transdimensional galactic citizenship."[49]

DIY Mysticism: McKenna's Psilocybin Magic Mushroom Grower's Guide

Perhaps McKenna's most influential and lasting contribution to the world of psychedelics was his 1976 book *Psilocybin: Magic Mushroom Grower's Guide*. Having brought spores of *P. cubensis* back home from South America, McKenna became an expert and prosperous mushroom grower: "He could turn out 70 pounds of them every six weeks, like clockwork. The trade financed the middle-class existence of a relatively settled man."[50] And he made it his mission to offer the same basic technical knowledge for home-growing to everyone who was willing to listen. As Davis observes, this book more than any other "transformed the culture of hallucinogenic mushroom use in the developed world by providing a relatively simple method of cultivating Psilocybe cubensis."[51]

Published under the pseudonyms O. T. Oss and O. N. Oeric, this short, simple, step-by-step text promised to make growing psychedelic mushrooms as easy and foolproof as canning homemade jam.[52] In his 1985 preface to the second edition, McKenna reflected on the fact that the book had quickly sold thousands of copies, creating a massive wave of psychedelic mushroom cultivation worldwide and inspiring more spiritual seekers to explore psilocybin than perhaps ever before in human history:

> This book, first published in 1976, opened a new phase in the rebirth of the mushroom religion by placing the knowledge of cultivation into the body of publicly available information. . . . This means there are now many thousands of mushroom cultivators in the world. It is reasonable to suppose that more people are now actively involved in a religious quest using psilocybin than ever before in history. This is a complete rebirth of a religious mystery, and it has taken place in less than a decade![53]

Perhaps most provocatively, McKenna leaves the reader with a question, which is still relevant today and in many ways at the heart of this book: "What are the implications of this emergence of a pagan mystery in the banal world of modernity?"[54] In many ways, we are very much grappling with the implications of that very question in the twenty-first century, amid a massive new psychedelic renaissance: What are the implications of making such powerful psychedelic drugs so widely available, and who stands to profit or suffer from such mass distribution of psychedelic mysteries?

Neo-Shamanism and Heroic Doses

Not only did McKenna provide ordinary readers with the knowledge to grow their own mushrooms, but he also promised them the possibility of becoming spiritual explorers of other realms that lie beyond ordinary consciousness. These simple brown mushrooms—cultivated by anyone in their home—could open gateways to new worlds and offer the possibility of transforming both the individual and the human species itself. By consuming what he called "heroic doses" (five grams or more of mushrooms), the psychedelic seeker could embark on an inward voyage and so become a kind of "Magellan in his own mind":[55]

> Psilocybin is a light shedding illumination on a landscape both within and without the mind and body of human beings and previously invisible to them. The exploration of this vast region by persons whose mental equipment is that of the modern West has only begun. . . . You are a pioneer in a world whose future is undetermined and whose living organisms are full of singularities and surreal transforming promise.[56]

By engaging in these heroic practices, McKenna believes, those who pursue the mushroom experience are following in the footsteps of shamans and healers who have explored these realms through psychedelics plants and fungi for millennia. Largely influenced by the work of Mircea Eliade, McKenna defines shamanism as "the use of the archaic techniques of ecstasy that were developed independent of any religious philosophy," while ecstasy is simply "the contemplation of wholeness."[57] However, McKenna also gives his image of the shaman a notably 1960s/1970s countercultural spin, by describing this archaic religious figure as a kind of Indigenous rebel or trickster, one who is always integral to and yet ultimately outside of traditional religious institutions. As he and his brother wrote in an unpublished manuscript on "Shamanic Investigations" from 1972,

> The shaman is something of a maverick among religious practitioners; while shamanism occurs in virtually every culture on the planet, manifesting itself in religious traditions both ancient and modern . . . the shaman remains yet eminently individualistic, idiosyncratic, and enigmatic, standing even apart from organized ecclesiastical institutions while still performing important functions for the psychic and religious life of the culture.[58]

One of the few points on which McKenna seriously disagreed with Eliade's account of shamanism, however, was on the role of psychoactive plants and fungi. Whereas Eliade had largely dismissed the use of *A. muscaria* and other hallucinogens as a kind of degradation of authentic shamanic practice, McKenna argues that they are in fact widespread, common, and often integral to shamanic experiences of other worlds:

> While Eliade asserts that the use of narcotic substances as an aid to ecstasy invariably indicates a decadence or vulgarization of the shamanic tradition, there is reason to doubt this. On the contrary, the use of narcotic plants as an adjunct to shamanism is widespread and occurs in every region of the globe.[59]

Indeed, in McKenna's opinion, the use of sacred plants or "botanical shamanism" is perhaps the oldest and most profound form of shamanic practice, one that makes use of "God's own given psychedelics," such as fungi, cactus, and various plants.

> Of the techniques used by the shaman to induce ecstasy and visionary voyaging—fasting, prolonged drumming, breath control, and visionary

voyaging—I now feel confident that the use of hallucinogenic plants is the most effective, dependable, and powerful.[60]

In the twentieth century, McKenna suggests, psychedelic plants also offer the most practical and effective means for modern Western individuals to achieve a kind of neo-shamanic experience. While modern humans may have lost much of their contact with the archaic world, they still have this natural technology that offers them a portal into or even a vehicle transporting one into the ecstatic other realms of the ancient shamans:

> If you take mushrooms, you know, you're climbing on board a starship manned by every shaman whoever did it in front of you, and this is quite a crew, and they've really pulled some stunts over the millennia, and it's all there, the tapes, to be played.[61]

More than just traveling through sacred space into other worlds, then, psychedelics offer modern neo-shamans the possibility of traveling through time back to the world of the ancient shamans themselves. Once again echoing Eliade, he sees this botanical shamanism as the most effective means for modern humans to return to the primordial time of the sacred and so perhaps radically transform modern society itself:

> The modern enthusiasm for shamanism and . . . psychedelics is actually an intuitive feeling-back-toward this state of non-neurotic empathy that characterized archaic time. And that is what has specifically been lost by the descent into the historical process. And this notion: that there is . . . that something was lost which is tangible, then allows us to set a radical reconstructive agenda for society.[62]

A modern neo-shamanism, therefore, would not simply look backward into an ancient past but would also look forward into the human future on Earth and beyond: "We can redeem the ideal of shamanism from pretechnological social stasis and actually project it, perfect it, and travel with it out to the stars."[63]

If psychedelics could in some cases lead to frightening psychological breakdowns or even psychotic episodes, such as Dennis's mental disintegration following their first experiment, this too was part of the shamanic process. Heavily influenced by Julian Silverman's 1967 article "Shamans and Acute Schizophrenia," McKenna saw the shaman's path as a kind of hero's journey, which involves a kind of descent into psychological chaos before spiritual rebirth: "Transposed to drugs, the recuperation of psychosis suggested that even the scariest and most insane aspects of psychedelic experience—aka 'tripping balls'—could be redeemed within a narrative of psychological development and integration, if not spiritual growth."[64]

In this sense, McKenna believed that his archaic revival represented something far more ambitious in scale and scope than what was popularly known as "New Age" spirituality at the time. While the New Age is in his view a kind of eclectic grab bag of Eastern spirituality, crystals, and astrology that looks forward to a coming era of peace and light, the "archaic revival" digs much deeper into the origins of human evolution and the emergence of human consciousness itself:

> The New Age is essentially humanistic psychology '80s-style, with the addition of . . . channeling, crystal and herbal-healing. The archaic revival is a much larger, more global phenomenon that assumes that we are recovering the social forms of the late neolithic. It reaches far back in twentieth century to Freud, to surrealism, to abstract expressionism, even to a phenomenon like National Socialism which is a negative force. But the stress on ritual, or organized activity, on race/ancestor consciousness—these are the themes that have been worked out throughout the twentieth century, and the archaic revival is an expression of that.[65]

In all of this, McKenna clearly reflects what Marianna Torgovnick has aptly called the "primitive passions" of modern developed societies. Longing to escape the chaos of modern civilization, many Americans and Europeans of the twentieth and twenty-first centuries have tried to "go primitive" in the hope of discovering some more intimate connection to nature and the sacred, which their archaic ancestors had perhaps once possessed. Our continuing fascination with Native Americans, Indigenous religions, and shamans, she suggests, reflects our deep "hunger for the exotic Other"—our simultaneous fear of the dangerous savage and our romantic attractive to the unspoiled premodern, who is still imagined to be pure and in touch with the cosmos. This ideal of the primitive, Torgovnick suggests, is particularly attractive to those who feel disillusioned with mainstream religion but still yearn for some deep connection to spirituality and mysticism: "The primitive can be a channel for spirituality outside of organized religion; the primitive can be one route in the quest for ecstatic contact with the essence of life."[66] Similarly, as Partridge observes, this fascination with shamans and primitives seems to reflect a deeper anxiety about what damage the modern Western world has wrought upon the world—both natural and human—one "driven by the Romantic utopian eco-idealism of getting back to the garden."[67]

But McKenna was not simply a reflection of this modern fascination with shamanism and the primitive; he was perhaps one of the most important figures in helping to reimagine shamanism as a spiritual path that is no longer reserved for a few elders in Siberia but effectively open to anyone willing to consume psychedelics. As Hutton notes, the idea of a neo-shamanism that emerged in the 1970s was a kind of popularization of the figure of the shaman as a role now essentially open to anyone: "In many ways it represents a democratization and liberalization of Eliade's concept. In place of his secretly trained and initiated elite of spiritual warriors, pitted against essential evil for the common good, shamans can be anybody willing to learn the core set of practices."[68] McKenna simply took this democratized ideal a step further by presenting psychedelics as the simplest, most direct means to a kind of DIY shamanism.

Stoned Apes and the Birth of Human Consciousness

Like Wasson, McKenna saw *Psilocybe* as playing a key role not simply in the development of religion but in the very evolution of human consciousness itself. Perhaps the most famous advocate of the "stoned ape" theory, McKenna speculated that the shift from *Homo erectus* to *Homo sapiens* was caused by a profound cognitive revolution that resulted from the consumption of *Psilocybe* around one hundred thousand years ago. As he explained the theory in an interview with *High Times* magazine, the psychedelic experience brought with it a number of effects that enhanced our evolutionary development, such as heightened visual acuity and increased sexual arousal:

> The presence of psychedelic substances in the diet of early human beings created a number of changes in our evolutionary situation. When a person takes small amounts of psilocybin their visual acuity improves. They can actually see slightly better, and this means that animals allowing psilocybin into their food chain would have increased hunting success, which means increased food supply, which means increased reproductive success, which is the name of the game in evolution. It is the organism that manages to propagate itself numerically that is successful. The presence of psilocybin in the diet of early pack-hunting primates caused the individuals that were ingesting the psilocybin to have increased visual acuity. At slightly higher doses of psilocybin there is sexual arousal, erection, and everything that goes under the term arousal of the central nervous system. Again, a factor which would increase reproductive success is reinforced.[69]

Perhaps most importantly, according to McKenna's theory, psychedelic mushrooms enhanced our capacity for language and symbolic communication, which are the key features that distinguishes *Homo sapiens* from other animals. The development of language created a kind of self-reflexive feedback loop that gave rise to the unique form of self-consciousness that humans possess.[70] In turn, McKenna believes, the capacities for language, symbolism, and self-reflection that emerged from mushroom consumption are also closely tied to our capacity for shamanic-type religious experiences. As he explained in 1987,

> A property of the mushrooms . . . is that they seem to activate or stimulate the language forming center of the brain, whether that's a physical location or simply a name for a set of functions. It seems clear that *psilocybin* by its ability to inspire glossolalia, inner voices, spontaneous shamanic singing, etc. operates on the symbolic processing parts of the brain. These were pack hunting animals which had already evolved a complex set of signals arising first out of their arboreal existence and then transferred into this pack hunting mode. So it's reasonable I think to suggest that *psilocybin* can be seen in that situation as a catalyst for language. It is a catalyst for greater visual acuity and enhanced hunting. . . . It's through a greater facility for the processing of symbols at a still higher level. This gives way of course to the shamanic experience that we associate with *psilocybin*.[71]

In sum, the mushrooms gave our ancestors "access to realms of supernatural power, catalyzed the emergence of human self-reflection" and so "brought us out of the animal mind and into the world of articulated speech and imagination."[72]

Different versions of McKenna's "stoned ape" theory have circulated widely over the past several decades and are still a central part of much of the psychedelic literature to this day.[73]

Interplanetary Mushrooms and Citizens of the Star Swarm

While McKenna's claim that *Psilocybe* lay at the origin of human culture is ambitious enough in itself, he would also imagine an even greater—indeed, cosmic—role for mushrooms in the universe. Mushrooms, he suggests, are not only far older than *Homo sapiens*; they are perhaps older than Earth and are part of a vast mycelial network that extends both far into space and far into the distant past. Indeed, they embody a kind of ancient "galactic intelligence" that has touched millions of worlds and thousands of civilizations,[74] and one with whom we have only just begun to learn to communicate:

> The *Stropharia cubensis* mushroom is a memory bank of galactic history. Alien, but full of promise, it throws open a potential for understanding that will sweep away the petty concerns of earth and history-bound humanity.[75]

Here McKenna is developing a more radical version of the "panspermia" idea suggested by scientists such as Francis Crick—the idea that life was "seeded" throughout the universe either by interplanetary objects such as asteroids and meteoroids or by intelligent beings from another planet.[76] In McKenna's iteration of this theory, psychedelic fungi and plants may have been "seeded" (or rather "spored") on Earth by some extraterrestrial intelligence in order to spread the ancient wisdom that they bear: "I think that it is possible that certain of these compounds could be 'seeded genes' injected into the planetary ecology eons ago by an automated space-probe arriving here from a civilization somewhere else in the galaxy."[77] Indeed, in his one of his weirder texts, *True Hallucinations*, McKenna channels the voice of the mushroom itself, who tells us Earth-dwellers about its long cosmic journey to our world from its original home in the "collective hypermind":

> I am old, older than thought in your species. . . . Though I have been on earth for ages, I am from the stars. My home is no one planet, for many worlds scattered through the shining disk of the galaxy have conditions which allow my spores an opportunity for life. The mushroom which you see is the part of my body given to sex thrills and sunbathing. My true body is a fine network of fibers growing through the soil. These networks may cover acres and may have far more sections than the number in the human brain. My mycelial network is immortal. . . . By means impossible to explain because of certain misperceptions in your model of reality all my mycelial networks in the galaxy are in hyperlight communication across space and time. The mycelial body is as fragile as a spider's web, but the collective hypermind and memory is a huge historical archive of the career of evolving intelligence on many worlds in our spiral star swarm. Space, you see, is a vast ocean to those hardy life forms that have the ability to reproduce from spores. . . . Across the aeons of time and space drift many spore-forming life-forms in suspended animation for millions of years until contact is made with a suitable environment.[78]

This mushroom intelligence is calling out specifically to *Homo sapiens*, since we are a species with the unique ability to hear its message, use our opposable thumbs, and become mycelial partners with this ancient being from across the universe: "A mycelial network has no organs to move the world, no hands, but higher animals with manipulative abilities can become partners with the star knowledge within me and if they act in good faith, return both themselves and their humble mushroom teacher to the million worlds to which all citizens of our star swarm are heir."[79] If we partner with this ancient organism, joining symbiotically with its mycelial network, we can help usher in a new era of individual and collective transformation, a kind of "planet-saving global shift in consciousness."[80] In the words of the mushroom, "You as an individual and Homos sapiens as a species are on the brink of the formation of a symbiotic relationship with my genetic material that will eventually carry humanity and earth into the galactic mainstream of the higher civilizations."[81]

The increasing confusion and chaos of modern society, McKenna believes, is actually a sign that we are about to experience a radical—indeed, eschatological—evolutionary transformation of human consciousness. All of this is anticipated by the transformation of consciousness brought about *Psilocybe* and other psychedelics; we are on the brink of a primal crisis—not unlike the shamanic "descent into chaos"—that will be followed by an eschatological transformation:

> I'm talking about a shockwave which precedes eschatology and is modern times, basically. It has been increasing throughout history but as we grow closer to this moment where the human mind will evolve into hyperspace—ah, the confusion, the amount of contradiction . . . just the amount of vibration in the system is increasing to the point where it seems that the system is about to fly to pieces. This signals to me that the onset of the primal crisis that when we have gone through it, we will then live in this realm of altered understanding that psilocybin and these drugs anticipate. And, it isn't a coincidence that they anticipate them. It is, in fact, what eschatological time is is what they reveal. That's why the cultures that we find using them are eschatological and historical coaches.[82]

Yet out of this eschatological crisis, he believes, we have the potential to reemerge radically transformed and ready to move on to the next great stage of human evolution:

> Today we stand on the threshold of the stars. Slowly it is emerging in mass consciousness that the next evolutionary step forward will so transform

> humanity that all that has gone before will seem but a prelude. We stand at the edge of history ready to accelerate our human experience out into the vast chasm of night which engulfs our planet. . . . We are about to embark on the greatest adventure we have ever known, one that will change our very notion of what it is to be human.[83]

Later in life, after reflecting on the computer revolution taking place in the 1990s, McKenna began to speculate that the real planetary transformation might be taking place not simply through psychedelics but also through the power of the internet. Many of the early pioneers in computer technology, the internet, and artificial intelligence, we should note, were also avid explorers of psychedelics. From Steve Jobs to Mike Pesce, there was a great deal of overlap between interest in psychedelic space and cyberspace.[84] After all, both phenomena center primarily on the idea of interconnectivity, networks, and complex "webs" of information and experience. As McKenna explained in his final interview with Erik Davis in 1999, the internet has the potential to unleash a truly liberating power through the global dissemination of knowledge:

> Everything I require of the alchemical quintessence, the Internet provides, except physicality—which I didn't require. . . . In my internal story about what's supposed to happen, everything is happening right on time, right on schedule. I mean, this is the thing that, if you believe knowledge is power—which I certainly do—then the Internet is the dispensation. The angels have landed, the aliens have unfurled their banner on this planet. And now let's see if information can liberate. That's why I don't want to do something stupid like die and miss the whole unfoldment of this proposition that knowledge is power, information will liberate. And it will be settled in the next ten or fifteen years. Either they'll get a handle on it—whoever "they" are, whatever "a handle" means—or it will slip from their control, and it will be clear that some kind of dialogue is now going on between individual human beings and the sum-total of human knowledge, and that nothing can stop it. That some kind of Renaissance, some kind of total new relationship to knowledge and possibility is put in place.[85]

Eventually, McKenna determined that the most likely date for the coming eschatological transformation would be 2012. This date, of course, coincided with the end date of the Mesoamerican long-count calendar, which had a 5,126-year cycle ending on December 21, 2012, and inspired many other New Age ideas about a coming global transformation. In McKenna's view, all of this was confirmed by the dramatic changes taking place in science, technology, and psychedelics, which were breaking down old systems of thought on all sides:

> The purpose of existence is novelty-generation, and our culture is generating novelty at an accelerating rate. The internet, nanotechnology, pharmacology, superstring theory, genetic engineering, artificial intelligence are shattering our old paradigms and bearing us toward some fantastic, psychedelic future. And according to his calculations on December 21, 2012, something big would happen, something apocalyptic, that would bring about "the end of life as we know it."[86]

Unfortunately, McKenna would not live to see the date for this radical transformation himself. In 1999, he was diagnosed with glioblastoma multiforme, an extremely aggressive form of brain cancer, and would die the following year. Oddly enough, the doctor who gave him the diagnosis described the tumor as a kind of "'fruiting body' that sent 'mycelia' throughout the surrounding tissue—mycological lingo straight out of the *Magic Mushroom Grower's Guide* that McKenna had published in 1975."[87]

Conclusion: Primitive Passions in the Postmodern World

While much weirder and wilder than Wasson's mushroom speculations, McKenna's work has arguably had a broader impact on popular culture and attitudes toward psychedelics. As Paul Stamets reflected in an interview in 2017, McKenna's writings were so ambitious and far-reaching that even if most of them were nonsensical rambling, they would still be worth reading: "Even if ten percent of what Terence said is true, it's frickin' amazing."[88] Perhaps the most valuable aspect of McKenna's odd body of work is that—much like psychedelic drugs—it forces us to think differently about the world and our place within it. As Christopher Partridge aptly put it, "Like mushrooms and science fiction the value of [McKenna's] work is perhaps best gauged by its subversive ability to introduce new ways of thinking about and responding to the world."[89] McKenna himself basically said as much when he later reflected on the paradoxical and sometimes contradictory ways in which psychedelic mushrooms had spoken to him, suggesting all sorts of fantastic ideas but often creating more confusion than clarity in the process:

> On these matters of specific fact—like is the mushroom an extraterrestrial and that sort of the thing?—I haven't the faintest idea. The mushroom

> itself is such a mercurial, elusive, Zen sort of personality that I never believe a word it says. I simply entertain its notions and try and sort through them, and I found that to be the most enriching approach to it. . . . As to what is really going on, uh, the mushroom assures me that I haven't got even the faintest, uh, grip on what is really going on, but something is going on![90]

Among other things, McKenna was one of the most important figures in the modern imagining of a kind of psychedelic spirituality, very much helping to pave the way for the renaissance of psychedelic mysticism that we see today. For McKenna, the use of psychedelic plants raises some of the most important legal and philosophical questions of our time. If, as he argues, psychedelics lie at the very origin of human culture and religion, inspiring both language and spirituality, then the legality of psychedelics is also a fundamental question of religious freedom—indeed, perhaps the most fundamental and original religious freedom of all:

> Religious use of psychedelic plants is a civil rights issue; its restriction is the repression of a legitimate religious sensibility. In fact, it is not a religious sensibility that is being repressed, but *the* religious sensibility, an experience of *religio* based on the plant-human relationships that were in place long before the advent of history.[91]

At the same time, McKenna was a central figure in the modern reimagining of "shamanism" as something that is no longer the province of a few elite holy men or tribal elders but instead something that anyone could experience simply by being brave enough to take heroic doses of mushrooms. Particularly in the wake of McKenna's DIY guide to *Psilocybe* cultivation, shamanic experiences to other worlds were now said to lie in the hands of anyone willing to pick up the book, grow some mushrooms, and embark on the fungal journey to other realms. In this sense, McKenna was arguably one of the most important catalysts for what Hutton calls the "democratization" and "liberalization" of shamanism that took place from the 1960s onward in the wake of Eliade's and Castaneda's work.[92] He thus put an important new spin on the idea of "mysticism without religion," by offering a form of psychedelic neo-shamanism that would "abandon belief systems for direct experience."[93]

Like his underground best-selling guide to DIY mushroom cultivation, his DIY guides to shamanic experience remain among the most popular and influential writings in the psychedelic counterculture to this day. Not only has his work fundamentally informed the whole idea of "mysticism without religion" that lies at the heart of this book, it has also helped shape much of the current wave of interest in psilocybin that now flows wildly through Silicon Valley and the larger tech industry, where cyberspace and psychedelic space frequently converge.[94] As *Wired* magazine wrote in an article on McKenna's work, "Steve Jobs is on record calling his first LSD experience 'wonderful.' Mitch Kapor credits 'recreational chemicals' with inspiring crucial programming insights. 'Psychedelics have infiltrated the computer industry,' says McKenna, 'because psychedelic use is a response to the environment that's been found to actually work.'"[95] While McKenna may have been mistaken in his prediction for the precise date of the global eschaton, he does seem to have been mostly correct in his ideas about the increasing convergence of computer technology, psychedelics, and spirituality.

[CHAPTER FIVE]

How Mushrooms Can Save the World

Paul Stamets and Myco-Evangelism in the 1980s and 1990s

> I am not religious, but I'm spiritual. Who could not be spiritual looking at astronomy, looking at the stars?
>
> Paul Stamets, "How Psilocybin Mushrooms Can Save the World" (2023)[1]

> Psilocybin mushrooms carry with them a message from nature about the health of the planet. At a time of planetary crisis brought on by human abuse, the earth calls out through these mushrooms—sacraments that lead directly to a deeper ecological consciousness and motivate people to take action.
>
> Paul Stamets, *Psilocybin Mushrooms of the World* (1996)[2]

While McKenna's hopes for a planetary transformation probably seem a bit far-fetched to most readers, other mushroom enthusiasts have suggested more practical—though perhaps no less utopian—plans for a mycological renewal of the earth. Arguably the most influential driving force behind the modern renewal of interest in "fantastic fungi" has been Paul Stamets (b. 1955), whose books, research articles, websites, TED Talks, and films have helped spark a broad popular interest in the mysterious world of mushrooms generally and of *Psilocybe* in particular. As Merlin Sheldrake observes, "It is no exaggeration to say that Stamets has done more than anyone else to popularize fungal topics outside university biology departments."[3]

Stamets's enthusiastic work followed in the wake of McKenna's hugely popular writings on *Psilocybe*—both figuratively and quite literally. As the practice of DIY mushroom cultivation became increasingly popular throughout the United States, and as more and more home growers began using McKenna's simple techniques, *Psilocybe* species quickly naturalized and spread wildly. This was particularly true in urban and suburban zones on the West Coast, where *Psilocybe* spores and mycelia found a happy home in wood chips, gardens, and strip malls across the country. As Stamets

FIGURE 5.1. Paul Stamets. Photograph by Nicola Gell. Courtesy of Getty Images Entertainment / Getty Images.

recalls, "In the mid-eighties, whole cities were overrun with *Psilocybes*—from Vancouver BC to San Francisco. The growth of suburbia was expanding the zones of colonization. In particular, the marketing of wood chips . . . from landscaping continues to drive a *Psilocybe* revolution."[4]

Stamets is perhaps not nearly as weird and radical as McKenna in his claims about mushrooms and their interstellar origins, but he is in many ways even more assertive about their transformative potential. In Stamets's opinion, mushrooms have the power to literally "save the world." They can boost immune systems, treat cancer, remediate toxic soil, combat insect infestation, and ultimately transform human consciousness for a more environmentally sustainable future.[5] As he put it, "I contend that the planet's health actually depends on our respect for fungi. . . . You can help save the world using mushrooms."[6] And his quasi-messianic claims about the power of mushrooms to "save the planet" have been echoed by many other fungal enthusiasts over the last decade.[7]

Raised by a mother who was a charismatic Christian but finding his own spirituality more in the forest than in the church, Stamets is also a very good example of the "mysticism without religion" theme that lies at the heart of this book. Like McKenna, Stamets has a lot to say about the connections between mushrooms and spiritual experience; but he is also quite critical of institutional forms of religion, particularly monotheistic traditions, which, in his view, set up gatekeepers and economic barriers between human beings and the sacred. Overall, he describes himself as not at all religious but as "deeply spiritual" and credits his *Psilocybe* experience as a key part of his spiritual view of the universe.[8] Stamets's worldview thus seems to fit pretty well with the broader trend that has been dubbed the religious "nones"—those who adhere to no institutional religion but often claim to be spiritual—which increased rapidly from the 1980s and 1990s onward. As the Pew Research Center recently reported, "Most 'nones' believe in God or another higher power. But very few go to religious services regularly. Most say religion does some harm, but many also think it does some good. . . . They express more positive views of science than religiously affiliated Americans do."[9]

At the same time, Stamets is also much more of a successful businessman than McKenna or almost any other modern mushroom advocate. While McKenna published a simple DIY book for mushroom cultivation, Stamets has built an entire company—Fungi Perfecti—that offers an impressive line of mushroom products, such as his "Host Defense" supplements that are now sold in every Whole Foods and most other major health food stores in North America.[10] In this sense, Stamets is a good example of the ways in which many spiritual ideas that were once considered radical in the 1960s quickly entered into popular culture and the larger American marketplace during the 1970s and 1980s. In what some have called the "Hippie Inc." or "hippie capitalist" era, many previously countercultural products went quite mainstream.[11] Along with yoga, Tantra, meditation, Reiki, crystals, and various other formerly "exotic" practices, psychedelic mushrooms became a major part of the alternative spiritual landscape that emerged in the latter half of the twentieth century. As such, they also became an important feature of what Kimberly Lau calls "New Age capitalism," which has exploded over the last several decades with the massive growth of the wellness industry and a vast array of alternative herbal, mineral, and fungal dietary supplements.[12] If neoliberalism is best defined as the "commodification of everything," then it is perhaps not surprising that even small brown fungi—not to the mention psychedelic experiences they claim to generate—should become part of the ever-expanding global consumer marketplace.[13]

As such, Stamets is also a striking example of the "cultural contradictions of capitalism"[14] in the psychedelic age. Deeply committed to his belief that mushrooms really can save the world, he strives to make his business as environmentally friendly as possible. By no means a simple crystal-selling neo-shaman out to make a buck in the New Age marketplace, Stamets hopes to use his financial success to fund an array of new programs aimed at sustainability and conservation. Thus, his company boasts that they offset 110 percent of their carbon emissions and engage in a variety of environmental initiatives, such as "BeeFriendly," which promotes programs that support the health of bees and other pollinators.[15] He has also created a nonprofit Center for Ecological Consciousness that supports a wide range of environmental projects, from biodiversity to mycoforestry.[16] Yet at the same time, he has also been accused of "union avoidance" or discouraging his Fungi Perfecti employees from unionizing in order to secure better pay and more consistent health benefits. While he denies the charge of "union busting," he has employed a law firm that is known for discouraging unions among employees.[17] In this sense, Stamets lies at the complex intersection between environmentalism and big business, between alternative spirituality and commercial marketing, between the utopian dream of saving the planet and the real-world practicalities of running a viable company in the age of neoliberal capitalism.

Coming of Age in the Era of Magic Mushrooms: Stamets's Background

Born in Salem, Ohio, in 1955, Stamets was the youngest of five children. As he recounts in numerous interviews and TED Talks, his mother was an extremely devout charismatic Christian who resisted modern medicine, even when confronted with very advanced cancer later in life.[18] His father, meanwhile, was an industrialist who had a laboratory in the basement, which inspired both Paul and his older brother to take an interest in science from a very early age.[19] When he was twelve, his father's engineering company failed, which led to his dad drinking heavily and the family ultimately splitting up. "My mother went into religion; my dad went into alcohol," he later recalled. "They both were self-medicating in a sense with those two avenues."[20] His mother first moved him and his twin brother to a small apartment in Columbiana, Ohio, and then to a home near Seattle. He later recalled that it was there, in the beauty of the Pacific Northwest, that he first began to admire mushrooms, sensing that they were not just fascinating organisms but somehow representative of a deeper connection to the natural environment:

> An awakening began within me, one undoubtedly repeated for millennia. Mushrooms symbolized the bridge between life and death, between myself and the woodlands in which I lived. I sensed that they were guardians of the sacred forest—conscious and watchful of my presence.

> Mushroom spirits soon enveloped my daily life, convincing me that they could be vehicles for greater good.[21]

For three years, Stamets worked as a logger in Washington state, living the life of a hippie in the woods. After three of his crew buddies died in logging accidents, however, Stamets decided to return to school and enrolled in Evergreen State College in Olympia with the hope of becoming a mycologist. In order to support his family and try to go on to graduate school, he created his own scientific supply company focused on mycology; and then in 1980, he formed Fungi Perfecti, which has emerged as one of the most successful outlets for mushroom products, cultivation supplies, and various other fungi-related merchandise.[22] But he also complains that his success was initially very slow and hard-won. For years, he recalls, most conservative mycologists either ignored or rejected him, dismissing him as a dropout hippie who was only interested in psychedelics:

> When I first went to the North American Mycological Association Conference, I met Gary Lincoff; it was like I had a force-field of repulsion. I'd walk into a crowd, and people would just be pushed away; they didn't want to be seen with me because I was a long-haired hippie, and [I] must be into magic mushrooms, and it was a forbidden subject. It's really interesting to me that it was so disturbing and unsettling to the status quo.[23]

Despite his initial rejection, Stamets has emerged over the last forty years as probably the most well-known and recognizable mushroom advocate, publishing six books and numerous academic articles, as well as appearing widely in films, TED Talks, YouTube interviews, and podcasts.

As he recalls in one interview, Stamets's first interest in psychedelic mushrooms came from his oldest brother, John. A scientist and student at Yale University, John had traveled to Mexico and South America and came home with amazing tales of his vacation eating magic mushrooms in these exotic places. Paul, who always idolized older brother, was enthralled with these fantastic stories of eating magic mushrooms in the mountains of Mesoamerica.[24] Between the ages of sixteen and twenty-four, he began experimenting with mushrooms on his own, which he has described as a personal sort of spiritual "coming of age ceremony."[25]

Stamets has recounted his own first experience with *Psilocybe* in numerous interviews and often refers to it as one of the most formative moments of his entire life. At the time, he recalls, he suffered from a serious congenital stuttering habit, a problem with which he had struggled for his entire life, even after six years of speech therapy. Then one day at around age seventeen or eighteen, he bought a large bag of *Psilocybe* mushrooms. He doesn't recall exactly how many mushrooms were in there but has estimated that it was something like twenty grams (which is a huge amount, well beyond McKenna's "heroic dose" of five grams). He went out into the woods, ate the giant bag of mushrooms, and climbed a tall tree. As he sat there in the tree, quickly getting higher and higher, black boiling clouds appeared on the horizon, and a huge summer lightning storm swept in. "I grabbed the tree and held onto the tree, and it became my *axis mundi* into the earth, and then the lightning started coming closer," he recalls.[26] He saw the tree as the "tree of life itself," "expanding into the sky and connecting me to the universe. And then it hits me: I'm going to be struck by lightning! . . . On the verge of enlightenment, I'm going to be electrocuted. It's my destiny!"[27] As the lightning began to strike, he had an incredibly powerful experience of oneness not only with the tree but with the entire cosmos:

> The lightning would hit, and I saw fractals for the first time. The atmosphere became liquid. I saw this liquid wave of these multidimensional geometrical patterns everywhere, and the sparks of lightning would just create this amazing crescendo of secondary, tertiary fractals all around me. It was amazing. . . . I felt in touch with Gaya, the universe. My heart opened up. I felt one with all. . . . It was an incredibly spiritual and wonderful experience, but I also had the fear . . . this comes with the hero's journey; you always have the dark side, not just the light side . . . I realized, oh gosh I could die up here.[28]

Finally, as he sat pondering the meaning of existence and his own possible death, he began to think about what he might learn from this experience. He decided that he should finally address the terrible stuttering problem that had plagued him throughout his life: "If I don't die what are your issues? Let's get something out of this experience. I said this stuttering habit is ridiculous. I'm not stupid. So I said to myself, 'stop stuttering now, stop stuttering now.' I said that dozens and hundreds of times, over and over."[29] And he claims that the experience essentially resolved his stuttering from that day onward. At the same time, Stamets also believes the experience changed his basic perception of himself. It allowed him to see himself for the first time as the fundamentally good person that he was rather than always judging himself through others' eyes:

> The other message that I got is that I'm a good person, I really am a good person. I looked at my soul and I realized, you are okay, Paul. You know,

> love yourself. And knowing that it doesn't matter what people think of you, it matters what you think of yourself.[30]

A second powerful *Psilocybe* experience occurred in the winter of 1975, when Stamets claims that his life was radically changed by "an event that challenged my concept of time and space and called into question my notion of reality."[31] Under the influence of another large dose of mushrooms, he had a vision of "unfolding geometric patterns . . . in wave after wave of beauty and complexity. My thoughts centered on God, evolution, the living earth, the infinite universe, the forces of good and evil, the mystery of death, and paradox of time."[32] He then drifted off into a dream that seemed to have a powerful sense of urgency: he found himself in a broad valley that had undergone a devastating flood, in which the bodies of hundreds and hundreds of cows floated dead and bloated in the frigid sunlight. Two weeks later, he claims, an unusual temperature inversion swept over western Washington, and, as temperatures suddenly soared, the snowpack melted and caused tremendous flooding across the region. When he rushed back to his cabin to try to save his books, he saw the valley just as in his mushroom dream, now actually flooded and filled with hundreds of drowned cattle. All of this persuaded him that the *Psilocybe* experience can actually "facilitate precognition of the future," which is why he believes that the Mazatecs and Aztecs also saw them as divinatory.[33]

Fungally Spiritual but Not Institutionally Religious: Stamets's Mushroom-Based Mysticism Without Religion

In various interviews and public talks, Stamets has been quite open about the fact that his mother (whom he clearly loved very much) was deeply religious but that he himself is not. In one interview, in fact, he was asked about what he thinks is really preventing human beings today from acting in a more environmentally responsible way, preventing us from protecting nature rather than destroying it. He first paused to note that his mother is a charismatic Christian and that she would probably see the interview. After saying a quick "Hi, mom," he went to offer his own brief narrative of the history of religions, which began with humans worshipping nature and ended with oppressive domination of monotheism and the politicization of religion:

> We were forest people, and we worshiped in the woods, and we relished a celebrated nature. We all have a sense of our own mortality, and the idea of an afterlife is something that most cultures share in common. So with the rise of monotheism, the belief in one God and other gods are evil,

> and this materialistic system of churches requiring parishioners to give money to the church so the church can build bigger buildings and bigger congregations, and then the politicization of the religious movement by the right, is really causing a lot of harm.[34]

In other interviews, Stamets observes that religious elites tend to control access to the sacred, acting as the divine gatekeepers and often requiring the laity to pay to access the sacred. This is particularly a problem, in his view, in monotheistic religions, which demand allegiance to one God rather than to many:

> At times when fables and parables and religious rites were controlled by the *cognoscente*, and they were the gatekeepers of knowledge that was too powerful for the general population to understand or appreciate, and so they protected that knowledge. That's the rule of most religions, the inner circle controls the keys to the kingdom. And what's happened to orthodox religions is they create institutions where you have to pay tithings in order to have a gatekeeper in order to have contact with God, and I think that is the problem with monotheism as opposed to polytheism.[35]

However, Stamets's most incisive criticisms of religion came in the wake of the 2016 election of Donald Trump and the four years of his presidency that followed. Shocked by what he saw as the blatant hypocrisy of self-professed Christians who supported Trump and his policies, he decried this as the final dying gasp of an outdated view of human life, gender, and society that had reared its ugly head one last time before being consigned to the dustbin of history:

> How can these Christians who espouse the Golden Rule—do unto others as you wish them to do to you, to be kind, to have forgiveness—how can we have a leader who is supported by the Christian movement? It is totally hypocritical. It is antithetical to the basic beliefs. . . . I feel like this is the last gasp . . . a Hail Mary pass of the sexist, misogynistic, white male dominated society that was fearful of change, fearful of the technological revolution, the revolution in gay rights, the revolution in recognizing the importance of ethnic diversity and the respect for all peoples.[36]

Despite his overall critique of organized religion—particularly of monotheism—Stamets has repeatedly described himself as "deeply spiritual." That is, he sees himself and all living beings as intimately connected to the vast oneness that is the universe in all its amazing, interconnected complexity. As he put it in a TED Talk from 2009, he sees nature itself as his sacred space, particularly the old growth forests of the Pacific Northwest, with their complex networks of plant, animal, and fungal life: "Dusty and I, we like to say, on Sunday this is where we go to church. I'm in love with the old growth forest, and I'm a patriotic American because we have those."[37] And he claims that psilocybin has been perhaps the most important tool that has helped him realize this deep sense of interconnectivity with all things. It is, in short, a "sacrament" whose personal use is a "private spiritual matter."[38] As he put in an interview in 2021,

> There is no doubt in my mind that these are spiritual medicines. . . . I see a convergence of science and spirituality. I am not religious, but I am deeply spiritual. Who could not be spiritual looking at the extent of the galaxies and the universe and the billions of stars and planets. The more that we study nature, the more that we realize how vast it is, and that you and I are just temporarily a molecular configuration of stardust that has come together in this form, and we're speaking now, but we're going to disambiguate. We're going to fall apart, our molecules are going to stream back into the abyss from which we sprang. I think that's not a bad thing. I think that's the way of nature and the way of existence.[39]

Through his various experiments with psilocybin, he has come to believe that there is a larger consciousness—a "super-consciousness, which some people call God,"[40] and of which we are each a small part. Although it exceeds our capacity for language or comprehension, this consciousness, he believes, is fundamentally good and filled with profound knowledge that we can learn from:

> There's a unity with one giant consciousness. You realize that you're part of this enormous oneness, and it's greeting you with open arms. It has enormous wisdom and knowledge. It's based on the power of goodness and kindness. I believe the universe is kind, and our existence is part of this one unanimity of consciousness. . . . We don't have the word skills, the language, to be able to explain this. It's beyond our ability to communicate the vastness of the idea that we enter into, and when you enter into the Mycoverse . . . you enter this giant landscape that you realize is all around us all the time and that we all exist vibrantly together. It's just that we reassimilate in different forms.[41]

In his opinion, this insight into our profound connection with the universe is perhaps the primary inspiration for all religion—the essential realization of our deep connection with the cosmos and with one another: "Clearly mushrooms have inspired religion, . . . I don't care if you're Muslim or Christian or Hindu . . . these mushrooms [make] you feel the spiritual universe, more spiritually connected."[42]

As such, the mushroom experience appears to have helped Stamets to reconcile two seemingly conflicting parts of his own background—the intense religiosity of his beloved mother, on one side, and his deep commitment to science, on the other. If mushrooms can reveal that nature itself is divine and that a benevolent Consciousness permeates all things, then there can be no contradiction between spirituality and science, or between the idea of God and the scientific understanding of evolution.

> I had this epiphany, it makes perfect sense: evolution is God's intelligent design. There's two things that we can accept, that most religions all accept. We are incapable of comprehending the enormity of the concept of God. Whatever it is, we know that we are incomplete and can't even imagine the enormity of the concept. And two, we have evolved and are born from nature. And if we claim that we are intelligent, how can nature not be intelligent? And yet if we acknowledge that our intelligence is inadequate to the concept of God, then we are still children in the ecosystem.[43]

At the same time, Stamets believes that mushrooms can help with some of the most fundamental of all spiritual questions—particularly end of life questions. These are questions that we all face, whether we happen to be religious or not, and psilocybin offers one of the most powerful means of coming to terms with the fact of our mortality:

> We all die. And yet, are we capable of comprehending the meaning of being? Some find religion as a solution to these age-old questions. Others see religion as someone else's rodeo. Although I am not religious, I am spiritual. Ultimately, it is your destiny, your consciousness, that seeks to come to peace with the mortality we all share.
>
> We all have a right to our own consciousness and how we come to terms with our death.
>
> This is why the safe use of psilocybin mushrooms for end of life is—or should be—an inalienable right of passage. Hopefully we have evolved to respect each other's choice. This is why I support the legalization of psilocybin for end-of-life, a first step on the long path for full legalization.[44]

Overall, Stamets's mushroom-based spirituality is one of the clearest articulations of the "mysticism without religion" attitude that we have been exploring in this book. While religious institutions have in his view led to hierarchies of power and the manipulation of spirituality for monetary gain, *Psilocybe* mushrooms offer the possibility of a direct encounter with the oneness of the universe, without any need for religious gatekeepers.

Fungal Evolution and Nature's Internet

Although he is much more grounded in science and research than either Wasson or McKenna, Stamets accepts many of their basic mushroom theories. Indeed, we might say that Stamets has been one of the most important figures in helping to solidify many of Wasson's and McKenna's ideas in the popular imagination of the late twentieth and early twenty-first century. For example, he accepts Wasson's highly controversial theory about the fungal origin of the Eleusinian Mysteries;[45] he more or less accepts the idea that psychedelic mushrooms were revered in ancient India; and he largely agrees with both Wasson and McKenna that *Psilocybe* species were probably "pivotal in human evolution."[46]

Yet Stamets also pushes many of these ideas further still, by suggesting that mushrooms are essential not only to human evolution but to the very fabric of the entire natural environment. Through their complex and omnipresent networks of mycelia, Stamets argues, mushrooms serve as the ecological fabric and structure that underlie most ecosystems: "Fungi are the grand molecular disassemblers in nature, they're the interface organisms between life and death. . . . The entire food web in nature is based on these fungal filaments, the mycelial network that infuses all land masses in the world is a supportive membrane upon which life proliferates and further diversifies."[47]

Going further still, Stamets cites recent research that suggests that fungal mycelia also help to connect trees and plants, allowing them to transfer nutrients to one another through these complex subterranean networks. Some research even suggests that mycelia may allow trees to communicate information to one another, such as warnings about pests or other environmental threats. In short, he regards mycelia as "nature's internet" or the "wood-wide web," linking trees, connecting roots, and circulating resources throughout the forest:

> I believe that mycelium is the neurological network of nature. Interlacing mosaics of mycelium infuse habitats with information-sharing membranes. These membranes are aware, react to change, and collectively have the long-term health of the host environment in mind.[48]
>
> Like a matrix, a biomolecular superhighway, the mycelium is in constant dialogue with its environment, reacting to and governing the flow of essential nutrients cycling through its food chain.[49]

Ultimately, in some of his most ambitious speculations, Stamets argues that these complex mycelial networks represent a kind of sophisticated intelligence and even a form of environmental consciousness.[50] Indeed, he imagines that we might even one day be able to communicate with such an intelligence, transferring information to it much as mycelia do between trees in the ecosystem:

> I believe the mycelium operates at a level of complexity that exceeds the computational powers of our most advanced super computers. I see the mycelium as Earth's natural Internet, a consciousness with which we might be able to communicate. Through cross-species interfacing, we may one day exchange information with these sentient cellular networks.[51]

In a sense, Stamets suggests, we already have been communicating with these mycelia for millennia through the consumption of psychedelic mushrooms. Like McKenna, he believes that many of our advances in cognition, language, art, technology, and even religion have been inspired—and will continue to be inspired—by mushrooms such as *P. cubensis*:

> The species and its relatives can be helpful for sparking creativity in artists, philosophers, theologians, mathematicians, physicists, astronomers, computer programmers, psychologists, and other intellectual leaders. I personally believe that the computer and Internet industries and astrophysics have been inspired through use of this fungus, which has stimulated the imagination and fields of vision of scientists and shamans with complex fractals, hyperlinking of thoughts and mental tools for complex systems analysis. Many users over thousands of years have elevated this and other Psilocybe species to the level of a religious sacrament.[52]

Future communication with these fungi depends on our willingness to listen to nature and learn to work with rather than against its complex networks of life forms.

Saving the World (and Ourselves) with Mushrooms

Although he claims not to be religious, Stamets does ultimately have a kind of eschatological and perhaps even messianic vision for the potential role of fungi in human history. We are now at a point, he believes, where our destruction of the natural environment poses a threat not only to all other species on Earth but to ourselves, as well. If we keep going at the current pace of environmental devastation, we will likely precipitate a global ecological collapse, which will affect *Homo sapiens* as well as every other organism. As he put it in a public talk in 2016,

> I've often thought that if there was a united organization of organisms—otherwise known as "U-O-O" [pronounced "uh-oh"]—and every organism had a vote, would we be voted off the planet? I think there is a chorus of voices from the microbial world and from the natural world that is voting right now.
>
> If you look in the crystal ball of this planet, we may well have a future that looks like Mars and as the ecosystems collapse because of our disrespect, not being a responsible citizen of this biological community on this planet, then the ecosystem can unravel. What we don't know is at what point as we lose biodiversity the system will start to fall apart.[53]

We are now at a crucial global and historical tipping point—an existential choice between environmental self-destruction and environmental salvation. And at this critical inflection point, mushrooms present the most powerful model for moving forward, both biologically and psychedelically. Biologically, the complex networks of mushroom mycelia offer a model of interconnectivity and symbiosis between life forms that is critical for our survival as a species living in complex relationships with myriad other species on Earth. We can, he thinks, learn from the mycelial model of symbiosis and forge mutually beneficial rather than parasitic and destructive relationships with the world around us.

Psilocybe mushrooms, in particular, can serve as the most powerful tools in this search for a more symbiotic environmental relationship. Precisely because they inspire profound experiences of interconnectivity and oneness with all of existence, *Psilocybe* mushrooms are for Stamets the most obvious and direct means to help guide us toward a healthier relationship with the world all around us: "Psilocybin mushrooms carry with them a message from nature about the health of the planet. At a time of planetary crisis brought on by human abuse, the earth calls out through these mushrooms—sacraments that leads directly to a deeper ecological consciousness and motivate people to take action."[54] Most importantly, he thinks, these mushrooms reveal to us that we are not simply isolated individual beings but are in fact radically interconnected with all other things in a far more complex matrix of life that far exceeds our own personal timeline on Earth.

> Mushrooms have taught me the interconnectedness of all life-forms and the molecular matrix that we share. . . . I no longer feel that I am in this envelope of a human life called Paul Stamets. I am part of the stream of molecules that

> are flowing through nature. I am given a voice, given consciousness for a time, but I feel that I am part of this continuum of stardust into which I am born and to which I will return at the end of this life.[55]

But these mushrooms, Stamets believes, also give us a new kind of hope and purpose, an understanding that we are not only connected with all other things but therefore have a responsibility to care for all other things:

> Plants and mushrooms have intelligence, and they want us to take care of the environment, and so they communicate that to us in a way we can understand. . . . We humans are the most populous bipedal organisms walking around, so some plants and fungi are especially interested in enlisting our support. I think they have a consciousness and are constantly trying to direct our evolution by speaking out to us biochemically. We just need to be better listeners. . . . I think *Psilocybes* have given me new insights that may allow me to help steer and speed fungal evolution so that we can find solutions to our problems.[56]

In this sense, Stamets suggest, mushrooms can actually make us better people. Through the vision of interconnectivity that they offer, mushrooms can teach us to nurture our relationships with all other beings, and ultimately even rewire our own brains to think in a more positive symbiotic way with the world around us. Indeed, "Psilocybin can morph a person into a better, more compassionate, more intelligent being. . . . They can fundamentally change your mind."[57] In a sense, "*Psilocybin* is the medicine for our time. . . . *Psilocybin* makes nicer people . . . more cooperative, more collaborative."[58] Through the psilocybin experience, we are forced to ask ourselves difficult questions that may very well lead to profound personal transformation:

> Are you a person that you admire? Can you be a better person? Can you raise your expectations to be a more generous, kinder, intelligent, compassionate person? If you know that every time you move that goal post, you get closer to that new goal post to be a better person, then that elevates you literally into a higher state of consciousness.[59]

Stamets himself acknowledges that all this talk of interconnectivity and planetary transformation may sound a bit hokey and flaky, like the worst sort of 1960s hippie-dippy fantasy. But he insists that we are now at a severe ecological and historical tipping point—one that requires that we either accept our radical interconnectivity with and responsibility toward all beings or we die together in an ecological catastrophe of our own making:

> Five or ten years ago, the idea that "everything is connected" sounded like New Age nonsense. Now it is less controversial, but we still need to develop more ways to show that this interconnectedness is real and that anyone can participate in a solution. . . . Like it or not we're actively involved in our evolution; the challenge is that we have to evolve faster because the problems we're creating are eclipsing our ability to adapt. And if we don't adapt and get ahead of this curve, we will lose the race and our species will instead simply race toward extinction . . . it will require a different mindset, a paradigm shift in consciousness, that looks at everything holistically.
>
> When you consider the webs of dark matter showing up in hi-tech scans of the universe, the webs of mycelium branching out through the planetary biosphere, the webs of capillaries in our bodies, and the neural structure in our brains, these to me are this new paradigm. It's all connected, it's all co-evolving. Networks are the rule of nature, not the exception.[60]

In this sense, Stamets does echo much of the rhetoric of the "New Age" that he seems to deride. The idea that we are at a global tipping point between either a catastrophic environmental apocalypse or a new green utopia is central to what Marilyn Ferguson long ago dubbed the "Aquarian conspiracy."[61] Stamets's unique spin on this theme is to suggest that mushroom mycelia are the key to understanding our profound interconnection with one another and all other beings: "Making peace with mushrooms and psilocybin gets into that cellular network of knowledge, because all mycelial membranes are listening and acting. . . . Nature is sentient and aware. . . . Nature is our mother and nature is watching us. . . . Anything that we do that hurts this community ultimately hurts ourself."[62] Like other New Age enthusiasts, Stamets does believe that we are potentially on the brink of a kind of planetary shift in consciousness in which we will realize our profound mycelial interconnectedness with all other things. But unlike many New Agers, Stamets is also much more sober about the possibility that we may very well destroy ourselves and the planet before we ever get that far.

Fungi Perfecti and Host Defense: The Cultural Contradictions of Hippie Capitalism

In addition to serving as perhaps the world's most outspoken "myco-evangelist," Stamets is also one of the most successful mycological entrepreneurs, who has built a large and flourishing business based almost entirely on mushroom products. If many idealists emerging from the 1960s counterculture hoped to build a new kind of "hippie capitalism,"[63] Stamets is one of the few who has actually done so successfully and profitably. In an interview in 2021, he recounted the story of Fungi Perfecti, which he described as a "model for a lot of entrepreneurs to follow" and a possible formula for success for others.[64] While at Evergreen State College, he became a teaching assistant for Professor Michael Beug, a respected mycologist. Given his expertise in the taxonomy of *Psilocybe* species and in mushroom cultivation, Stamets was later hired as an adjunct professor to teach courses on growing gourmet mushrooms. Frustrated with the bureaucracy of obtaining lab equipment through the college, he began buying his own petri dishes and other supplies wholesale for his classes and also began selling preorders for the mushroom cultivation book that emerged from his teaching. Eventually, this developed into a mail order business for mushroom cultivation equipment that also served to promote his book and his classes:

> I created a triangle of literally robbing Peter to pay Paul, because I was borrowing—I got about $5000 in pre-orders from my students [for the book I was writing] that allowed me to print the catalogue that allowed me to send the catalogue out to have more people order pre-publication copies of the book and order the equipment and also advertise the classes. So I started spinning this little permaculture profit people faster and faster, and it worked sort of.[65]

Nonetheless, it took many years of struggle and persistence before he was actually able to pay his bills and create a successful business. "It was never to me about money," he recalls, "it was about science, it was about knowledge, exploring this underground universe of mycelium and mushrooms."[66] Nonetheless, by 1984, he was able to purchase a twenty-acre farm on Kamliche Point, northwest of Olympia.[67]

Today, Fungi Perfecti is a large and successful business, which offers a wide array of mushroom products. Its "Host Defense" products are advertised as the "#1 best-selling mushrooms supplement in the U.S."[68]—a claim that seems to be borne-out by the fact they are prominently featured on the shelves of most Whole Foods, health stores, and alternative medicine shops throughout North America, as well as widely available online. Host Defense offers an array of mushroom products, ranging from "Mycobotanicals Brain" capsules to support mental function to "MyCommunity" supplements for comprehensive immune support. In keeping with his philosophical and spiritual belief in the power of mycelia, Stamets emphasizes that his supplements primarily use mushroom mycelia (rather than just the fruiting bodies), since that is where he strongly believes the healing and protective potential of the fungus lies. Meanwhile, Fungi Perfecti also offers a range of other mushroom-themed merchandise, including cups, T-shirts, hoodies, hats, posters, knives, books, "brushrooms," and even tick-removers.[69]

While Stamets has managed to build a successful for-profit company in Fungi Perfecti, he also wants to balance this with other, more charitable works. Thus, he has created the nonprofit Center for Ecological Consciousness (CEC), whose stated aims are fighting for a more sustainable world, strengthening ecological sustainability, protecting biodiversity, mycoforestry, and protecting bees. He readily admits that he profits from Fungi Perfecti, but he argues that he can only fund his other more charitable environmental projects if he has the adequate funds to do so:

> This is where I hope my financial assets will mostly go, so we can help other eco-warriors as they pursue these dreams. But we must be practical. We must be profitable to afford to be charitable so that charity is sustainable. I think and act on this constantly. I am constantly trying to be a better Earth citizen. I think science and spirituality are intimately intertwined. This gives me strength to move forward.[70]

In the end, Stamets seems to believe quite firmly that a commercial business can be both successful and environmentally positive. After creating a Sustainability Committee and making efforts to minimize the company's impact, Stamets claims that Fungi Perfecti is now not only climate neutral but in fact "110% climate positive." In addition to using 100 percent recycled paper and cardboard and 100 percent PCR plastics in its products, the company also supports carbon offset projects around the world, making it in his estimate an overall net good for the planet.[71] This sort of work is not only important but urgent, in his opinion, as we now face a massive environmental catastrophe with very little time left to address it:

> Time is of the essence, too. There needs to be a threshold of mass in a very short period of time in order to have a positive effect. We're currently in the sixth major extinction event known to this planet. It's the first extinction event caused by an organism, us. . . . So we're all ending up in this giant cesspool of a planet, and I'm afraid the tipping point has been passed. Unless we make a dramatically positive impact in a very short period of time, future generations are going to look back and think we lost the golden opportunity.[72]

In this sense, Stamets is a very clear example of the sort of "countercultural capitalism" or "hippie capitalism" that emerged out of the 1960s and developed throughout the 1970s and 1980s.[73] While rooted in many countercultural values, and often selling countercultural products such as drug paraphernalia or equipment to grow cannabis or mushrooms, many hippie capitalists also found ways to flourish in the mainstream commercial marketplace. As Joshua Clark Davis argues in his study of the business of headshops during these decades, these kinds of hippie capitalists were often more than simply sellouts trying to make a buck by marketing the counterculture; rather, many of these hippie entrepreneurs remained deeply committed to their larger social and political ideas and were instrumental in real-world causes such as the movement to legalize cannabis.[74] Similarly, Stamets hopes to combine the success of his business endeavors with a larger environmental politics that hopes to turn the profitability of the former to the aid of the latter.

Perhaps inevitably, however, Stamets has also been mired in some of the less admirable aspects of the business world. Despite the utopian rhetoric on his companies' websites, some of Stamets's employees appear to have a less favorable view of the enterprise. In early 2024, employees at Fungi Perfecti began efforts to unionize with the Laborers' International Union of North America (LiUNA) Local 252. Among other requests, the workers were seeking higher pay and more consistent healthcare coverage; one of their chief complaints was that the company had switched health insurance providers five times in the past six years, making it difficult to get adequate coverage. As *Double Blind* magazine reported, their push to unionize could have much broader implications beyond Fungi Perfecti and perhaps "set higher standards for working conditions in psychedelics and wellness industries."[75]

In response to their efforts, some workers claim that they have faced a strong "union avoidance" campaign—a term coined in the 1950s and 1960s to refer to strategies used to thwart unionization.[76] In April 2024, Fungi Perfecti hired the consulting firm American Labor Group (ALG). Critics charge that ALG has a known "history of deterring workers from organizing" and has held several meetings for employees to discuss "the pitfalls of unions."[77] In 2019, we should note, Fungi Perfecti had also hired the law firm Littler Mendelson PC, which specializes in labor and employment law and has represented major companies such as Apple, Starbucks, and Amazon during workers' unionization efforts. Sources within the Fungi Perfecti steering committee told *Double Blind* that Stamets openly stated that he does not support the union. "He made his position very clear that he doesn't support us," said one employee, speaking on condition of anonymity.[78]

Stamets, for his part, denies all of these accusations. Fungi Perfecti, he argues, provides employees with better healthcare coverage than anything they could get through LiUNA; moreover, the company offers competitive pay, as well as paid sick leave, vacation time, bonuses, and 401(k) benefits. He also claims that he and the company have not engaged in union avoidance but "stand strongly in support of employees' rights to vote on a union, and think the better informed they are, the better the outcome for all." He opted to hire ALG, he says, "in order to gain guidance on how to best help inform employees of the unionization process and their legal rights throughout."[79]

Clearly, not everyone has found Stamets's arguments persuasive. Indeed, some students at his own alma mater, Evergreen College, even circulated a petition to have him removed as the 2024 commencement speaker, accusing him of "actively and illegally squashing his workers' efforts to organize at his company."[80]

In short, if Stamets embodies a kind of "hippie capitalism," he has also become perhaps inevitably mired in what Daniel Bell long ago called the "cultural contradictions of capitalism." Writing in 1972, in the wake of the 1960s counterculture, Bell described what he saw as the deep tension within modern capitalist societies—namely, the tension between the capitalist demands for "efficiency, least cost, maximization, optimization, and functional rationality" and the desire for freedom, experimentation, and ecstatic experience that emerged out of the 1960s counterculture and psychedelic revolution.[81] In Stamets's Fungi Perfecti and many other of these sorts of countercultural businesses, we can see a similar tension between a kind of utopian communitarian idealism and the harsh necessities of survival and profitability in a ruthlessly unforgiving capitalist marketplace.[82] This is perhaps the inevitable "cultural contradiction of hippie capitalism," as businesses try to embody the values of freedom, experimentation, and egalitarianism advocated by the 1960s counterculture while still struggling to survive in the cut-throat world of twenty-first-century capitalism.

Conclusion: Saving the World in Capitalist Ruins

Overall, Stamets is a remarkable example of the many new forms of alternative spirituality—and alternative capitalism—that emerged in the United States from the 1980s onward. With his deep personal faith in the transformative power of mushrooms, he is clearly continuing in the tradition of the 1960s counterculture and its utopian view of psychedelics. Like Leary, McKenna, and many others, he has a profound belief that psychedelic experiences will lead to a more harmonious, integrated, and peaceful view of human existence and the natural environment. As Brian Pace and Neşe

Devenot observe, this belief in the inherently positive cultural and political impact of psychedelics is one of the most influential legacies of the 1960s counterculture:

> The notion that psychedelic experiences can result in individual dispositional change has its roots in their association with the cultural and political upheavals of the late 1960's and 1970's. Because this specific time witnessed an explosion in countercultural fascination with widely available classical psychedelics like LSD, psilocybin, and mescaline, psychedelics have often been conflated with the progressive and radical politics of the moment.[83]

Stamets's form of myco-evangelism comes directly out of this countercultural worldview and its psychedelic politics.

Yet at the same time, Stamets also reflects much of the darker side of the Aquarian Age—its fear of impending environmental catastrophe, its profound distrust of politicians and bureaucrats, and its sense that self-induced apocalypse may well be as likely a future for human civilization as peace-and-love utopia. Like Anna Tsing, he seems well aware that his fantastic fungi are struggling to survive in "capitalist ruins."[84] And his faith in mushrooms' ability to "save the world" is tempered by a sober acknowledgment that humans may very well destroy the world anyway.

In this sense, Stamets seems to embody many of the tensions and paradoxes that emerged amid the new spiritual currents of the 1980s and 1990s more broadly. As Marilyn Ferguson observed in her classic book on the New Age movement, *The Aquarian Conspiracy*, these include the tensions between magic and science, between an ideal of interdependence and a sense of individuality, between the nostalgic yearning for something very old and the utopian hope for something radically new. As Ferguson put it,

> The spirit of our age is fraught with paradox. It is at the same time pragmatic and transcendental. It values both enlightenment and mystery . . . power and humanity . . . interdependence and individuality. It is simultaneously political and apolitical. . . . Within recent history "it" has infected medicine, education, social science, hard science, even government. . . . It is characterized by fluid organizations reluctant to create hierarchical structures, averse to dogma. It operates on the principle that change can only be facilitated not decreed. . . . It seems to speak to something very old. And perhaps, by integrating magic and science, art and technology, it will succeed where all the king's horses and all the king's men failed.[85]

To these various tensions, I would also add the tension between spirituality and capitalism, between the ideal of otherworldly transcendence and the harsh reality of this-worldly business in a global marketplace. Stamets is a particularly clear example of someone who is genuinely trying to thread the needle between a utopian vision of saving the environment and the everyday necessities of running a profitable business that will give him the funds to do so. His recent feud with employees over unionization is just one of many examples of this tension playing out across many contemporary businesses, including many in the "hippie capitalist" or "counterculture capitalist" model. And more deeply, this is perhaps a question that lies at the very heart of our entire global economic system. Can we save the world from the devastating impact of capitalism by using the very tools of capitalism—that is, undo the catastrophic environmental damage reaped by current corporate enterprises by engaging in kinder, friendlier forms of Stamets-style eco-capitalism (in projects such as Fungi Perfecti, BeeFriendly, etc.)? Is it possible to reimagine a kind of "green capitalism" or "climate capitalism"?[86] Or is capitalism—at least in its current global configuration—a system so inherently based on profit, consumption, and destruction that it cannot possibly be reconciled with an ethic based on environmental sustainability and human well-being?[87] Is the very quest for a kind of green capitalism simply a comforting "illusion," a form of "wishful thinking," or even a "God that failed," which cannot seriously address the massive impact on both the environment and human well-being wrought by this global economic juggernaut?[88] As Hartmut Burgoff and Adam Rome summarize this debate,

> To radical critics of capitalism, the corporate environmental initiatives of the last generation are trivial. . . . The dream of greening capitalism is a delusion. . . . It can't lead to a sustainable economy. . . .
>
> The green boosters see capitalism in much more flexible terms. They take for granted that the profit motive ultimately is compatible with many kinds of enterprise. . . . Their hope is to encourage business leaders to be proactive—to make the transition to sustainability smoother and faster.[89]

This is arguably among the most pressing debates of the twenty-first century, and Stamets is a living example of the complex tensions that lie at its very heart.

[CHAPTER SIX]

Mushrooms, Mysticism, and Pharmaceuticals

Roland Griffiths and the Rebirth of Psilocybin Research

Psilocybin can occasion, in most people studied, mystical and insightful experiences virtually identical to those that occur naturally.

Roland R. Griffiths, "Psilocybin and Mystical Experience" (2020)[1]

A specter is haunting planetary culture—the specter of drugs. . . . Previously obscure forms of chemical use now freely compete in a largely unregulated global marketplace.

Terence McKenna, *Food of the Gods* (1993)[2]

Psychedelics are suddenly awash in money.

Andrew Jacobs, "The Psychedelic Revolution is Coming" (2021)[3]

In 2000, more than two decades after the last government-funded research into LSD and other substances had ended, a group of researchers at Johns Hopkins University obtained approval to reinitiate research into psychedelics. Dubbed the Johns Hopkins Center for Psychedelic and Consciousness Research, the group was spearheaded by Roland R. Griffiths, a professor in the Departments of Psychiatry and Neurosciences. While his early research had focused on caffeine addiction and withdrawal syndrome, in 1999, Griffiths began to turn his attention to the study of psychedelic drugs—a move that he described as profound and "career changing."[4] Perhaps the most important event in the modern renaissance of psychedelic research was the publication of Griffiths's article "Psilocybin Can Occasion Mystical-Type Experiences Having Substantial and Sustained Personal Meaning and Spiritual Significance." Appearing in the journal *Psychopharmacology* in 2006, this was one of the first rigorously designed, double-blind, placebo-controlled clinical studies to take place in four decades.[5] As its title indicates, moreover, Griffiths's work claimed to reveal the potential for psilocybin to generate profound experiences with "mystical" and "spiritual" implications. This and other publications helped spark a massive explosion of psychedelic research that continues to this day, exploring not only the potential of these drugs to occasion "mystical" experiences but also to be used in the treatment of depression, anxiety, PTSD, and myriad other disorders. Upon his death in 2024, Griffiths was even eulogized as the "psychedelic evangelist" in The *New York Times*.[6]

In their evaluation of the psychedelic experience, Griffiths and virtually all subsequent researchers have used a modified version of the Mystical Experience Questionnaire (MEQ), typically in combination with another metric called the Hood Mysticism Scale (M-scale), developed by psychologist Ralph Hood in 1975.[7] As we saw in chapter 3 above, the MEQ is not without its intellectual and methodological problems, and most of these are also shared by the Hood scale. Not only are both rooted in a very specific understanding of mysticism, largely based on W. T. Stace's heavily Vedantic and perennialist definition; they also begin from the rather odd assumption that mystical experiences can be quantified on a numerical scale and then scientifically evaluated by researchers who are trained neither in theology nor religious studies.[8] These problems arguably persist with virtually all current studies using the MEQ and Hood scale today. Indeed, some critics wonder if Griffiths and other psychedelic researchers have not only imported many of these theological assumptions into their

FIGURE 6.1. Roland R. Griffiths. Courtesy of The Washington Post / Getty Images.

scientific research but may also be creating a new kind of "psychedelic religion of mystical consciousness."[9]

At the same time, the studies led by Griffiths and many others have helped open the floodgates to massive new interest in psychedelics from major pharmaceutical companies. Particularly in the last decade, companies such as atai Life Sciences have begun pouring millions of dollars into research on psilocybin and other substances in the hopes of discovering the next big class of breakthrough drugs that might redefine mental health in the twenty-first century.[10]

This chapter traces the rebirth of psilocybin research in the twenty-first century, as it reentered the scientific laboratory and the corporate domain. While there is now tremendous excitement about the potential for psilocybin and other psychedelics to revolutionize the mental health care industry and offer new treatments for an array of disorders, this also raises profound philosophical and ethical questions. Some critics worry that this new pharmaceutical interest risks obscuring the traditional cultures from which *Psilocybe* mushrooms (as well as other substances such as peyote and ayahuasca) originated, along with the religious, ritual, and social contexts in which they were used. Are we simply continuing the legacy of colonialism, by appropriating the sacred technologies of Indigenous cultures, uprooting them from their religious contexts, and turning them into marketable commodities?[11] Others, meanwhile, worry that this reinforces the general biological reductionism that is pervasive in American health care today—the assumption that all mental health concerns (and indeed, spiritual concerns) are reducible to brain chemistry and that the key to well-being lies in developing ever newer and more powerful drugs.[12]

How we navigate these complex ethical questions will likely become one of the defining problems for both the study of psychedelics and the study of religion in the decades ahead.

The Psychedelic Renaissance: *Psilocybe* Research After the 1970s

The Johns Hopkins Center was not the only group to continue psychedelic research in the post-1970s era. During the 1980s and 1990s, there was a slow shift in attitudes toward psychedelics among government agencies, which opened small spaces for research.[13] After years of lobbying, the psychiatrist Rick Strassman was allowed to conduct a study of DMT using human subjects, which helped inform books such as *DMT: The Spirit Molecule*.[14] Other pioneers in the field during this liminal period include the private groups,

Multidisciplinary Association for Psychedelic Studies (MAPS), founded in 1986, and the Heffter Research Institute, founded in 1993. As Nicolas Langlitz observes in his history of the psychedelic renaissance, it is no accident that this new wave of research coincided with President George H. W. Bush's announcement of the "Decade of the Brain" in 1990, as a great deal of new attention and money was suddenly being devoted to neuroscience and the study of consciousness.[15]

However, for researchers such as Rick Doblin—the founder and executive director of MAPS—psychedelic experience is far more than simply an interesting facet of human consciousness or a tool of self-exploration. In his view, it is the key to human and planetary survival. In an age in which we are literally on the brink of destroying ourselves, psychedelics offer a powerful vision of the interconnectedness of all human beings and all living things. As he put it in a podcast in 2002, psychedelics offer a much-needed spiritual alternative to both destructive politics and destructive religious fundamentalisms of all forms:

> I would say that the key challenge going forward with the psychedelic renaissance and also with the survival of humanity, is that we have to really help fundamentalists of all the different religions move to a more mystical orientation. . . . Psychedelics can help with that, to see that . . . what people take literally are metaphors and are symbols. . . . So I think back to America now where we got the Christian fundamentalists . . . as a major force: how do we help them see that there is a deeper spirituality that they can have a richer life by surrendering some—And it's not just Christian fundamentalists, it's Orthodox Jews who are crazy in their own way too. And . . . orthodox Muslims.[16]

In 2000, the research group at Johns Hopkins was the first team at an American academic institution to obtain regulatory approval to reinitiate research with psychedelics.[17] Led by Griffiths and his colleagues, the Johns Hopkins group published a series of landmark studies of psilocybin in the early 2000s, including several on the mystical and spiritual implications of the drug. However, long before his research on psychedelics, Griffiths had an interest in the workings of the mind and the practice of meditation. He first tried meditation as a graduate student in the early 1970s but said that he quickly gave up in frustration after failing to quiet his busy mind. Two decades later, after studying psychology and pharmacology and becoming a professor at Johns Hopkins, he gave meditation another try in 1994 through the Siddha Yoga movement. A modern form of Hindu meditation spread by Swami Muktananda (1908–82) and his disciples in the mid- to late twentieth century, Siddha Yoga combines elements of Vedanta and the philosophy of Kashmir Shaivism (the movement has also, we should note, had its share of scandals, mostly involving accusations of sexual assault by its founder).[18] After employing the Siddha Yoga style of meditation, Griffiths claims to have had a "funny kind of awakening"—a sort of mystical experience that was "something way, way beyond a material worldview that I can't really talk with my colleagues about."[19] Siddha Yoga allowed him to explore the "fantastically interesting" process by which thoughts arise in our consciousness. "We tend to believe that we are the voice in our heads," he said in an interview in 2017: "There's an ongoing dialogue, and very often we think that the dialogue is in the mind. But if you sit with the mind, you realize the voice is saying all kinds of stuff and you may or may not agree with everything it says."[20] Beyond that voice of interior dialogue, however, he said that he discovered something else—namely, "a sense of clarity and wonder and observational power," which is the observing consciousness that transcends the internal flow of thoughts. He would go on to compare psilocybin to a kind of "crash course" in the nature of the mind, allowing one to quickly experience these profound insights into the nature of consciousness; but it is also potentially hazardous if not done with the proper precautions. As such, it's "literally a crash course because it can go off the rails."[21] Yet for Griffiths, this was a practice that "profoundly shifted [his] worldview."[22]

Griffiths's interest in the study of consciousness took another profound turn when he began to explore psychedelics drugs, and specifically psilocybin. His 2006 article "Psilocybin Can Occasion Mystical-Type Experiences" was not only a pivotal moment in his own research but arguably one of the most important texts that helped spark the current psychedelic renaissance. As he summarized the implications of his work on psilocybin, this represents a profound breakthrough in our understanding of the human mind and our potential to bring about life-changing psychological insights: "As a scientific phenomenon, if you can create a condition in which 70 percent of people will say they had had one of the most meaningful experiences of their lives . . . well, as a scientist that's just incredible."[23]

Although he is not trained in theology or religious studies, Griffiths has made quite bold pronouncements about the similarity if not complete "identity" between psilocybin-induced experiences and the mystical experiences reported by religious figures throughout history. "Under some conditions classic hallucinogens like psilocybin could occasion mystical experiences that look very much like those that occur naturally and have been reported by mystics throughout the ages."[24] Elsewhere, Griffiths and his collaborators make even more confident claims that their studies have shown classic psychedelics can occasion in the majority of people studied "complete mystical experiences"[25] and in many cases even "God encounters" similar to "personal encounters with God, gods or emissaries of God" that have been "documented for centuries."[26]

Griffiths's research was also praised by some scholars of religion, including Huston Smith, who had participated in the Marsh Chapel experiment some forty-five years before. As Smith suggests, the new Johns Hopkins research can not only help re-enchant a demystified modern world, but it can now do so using the authority of science itself. As he wrote in a letter to Bob Jesse in 2006:

> The Johns Hopkins experiment shows promise that under controlled experimental conditions, psilocybin can occasion genuine mystical experiences. It uses science, which modernity trusts, to undermine modernity's secularism. In so doing, it offers a hope of nothing less than a resacralization of the natural and social world, a spiritual revival that is our best defense against not only soullessness but against religious fanaticism.[27]

Griffiths's 2006 study was soon followed by a steady stream of other articles on the uses of psilocybin not only to occasion mystical experiences but also to help in the treatment of a wide range of psychological disorders. In 2016, for example, two landmark studies were published on the use of psilocybin in treating anxiety and depression in patients with life-threatening cancer.[28] Since then, research has been explored on the possible use of psilocybin for everything from smoking cessation to anorexia nervosa, obsessive-compulsive disorder, and a variety of other disorders.

The MEQ-30 and the M-Scale

Throughout this renaissance of psychedelic research, virtually all recent studies continue to rely on some version of the MEQ, whose origins date to Pahnke's dissertation research back in 1962. As we saw in chapter 3, the MEQ was revised several times over the years, though much of its basic structure and underlying assumptions have remained constant. The original metric was revised in the 1970s in collaboration with William Richards and used in his research on the psychedelic DPT. Three decades later, the questionnaire was revised again when it was used in the Johns Hopkins psilocybin study that helped inaugurate the modern rebirth of psychedelic research. The current version of the MEQ emerged in 2012. In this

"MEQ-30," the original eight factors and forty-three evaluatory questions in Pahnke's model were reduced to four factors and just thirty of the original questions.

In its current form, the items in the MEQ are rated using a six-point scale that ranges from 0 (meaning none or not at all) to 5 (meaning extreme or more than any other time in my life). It includes four subscales, which are largely derived from Stace's and Pahnke's work: Mysticality, Positive Mood, Transcendence of Time and Space, and Ineffability, which are expressed in MEQ items such as "'Experience of unity with ultimate reality,' 'Experience of ecstasy,' 'Loss of your usual sense of time,' and 'Sense that the experience cannot be described adequately in words,' respectively."[29] A score greater than 60 percent on all subscales is classified as a "Complete Mystical Experience" (CME). For example, the following are some typical narratives from a trial with their CME classification and MEQ score:

> The trip was mostly concerned with the love pertaining to the different relations in my life, but also the love that exists between human beings in general, to the planet and to the universe.
>
> Report 3, female, CME, MEQ total 3.9

> The light of love brings clarity to everything. I get a deep feeling of purity and feel that everything is beautiful, and that love is what makes up the world and the universe and connects everything like a network of roots.
>
> Report 22, female, CME, MEQ total 3.9

> I have the answer to the riddle of the universe, but I'm forced to look into a TV-screen.
>
> Report 31, male, CME, MEQ total 4.2[30]

As Breau and Gillis-Smith argue, the influence of W. T. Stace and his perennialist assumptions has remained largely unchanged in the more recent iterations of Pahnke's metric: "Although the questionnaires have changed over the years, their reliance on the work of Walter Stace is consistent."[31] Much of the current psychedelic research continues to identify the intense, all-encompassing feeling of unity as a "critical definitional feature" of the mystical experience, while most of the other characteristics of Stace's model are also preserved in the current MEQ. As Barrett and Griffiths put it in an article from 2018, "mystical experiences have not been restricted to any particular path, canon, or dogmatic viewpoint."[32] In the process, much of the research has also largely absorbed—often unknowingly—the neo-Vedantic metaphysical assumptions that underlie Stace's understanding of mysticism:

> Concepts and the very language of modern Vedantic thinkers have embedded themselves . . . in this research through mysticism scales. These religious understandings of mysticism are inherited not only through the use of the MEQ itself but in psychedelic researchers' basic theoretical approach to mystical experience. . . . In this way, the MEQ and the perennialist, Vedantic mystical experience have become mutually reinforcing . . .
>
> What is elided . . . are the origins of those philosophies and theories. . . . Critical philosophical and theoretical aspects of the MEQ are the result of long, complex conversations in the intellectual traditions—in fact, the religious traditions—of Hinduism, Vedanta, and perennialism.[33]

At the same time, as Ann Taves persuasively argues, one of the most problematic consequences of this ongoing reliance on the MEQ is that it glosses over the social, historical, and personal contexts in which these experiences occur. By assuming a universal, transhistorical core of all mysticism, it erases the cultural environments in which individuals perceive, interpret, and articulate these experiences.[34]

The second metric that is most often used in conjunction with the MEQ-30 today is the Hood Mysticism Scale (M-Scale). A professor of religious studies at the University of Tennessee at Chattanooga, Ralph W. Hood, first developed his scale in 1975.[35] Like Pahnke, Hood based his model directly on the work of Stace. Using Stace's eight factors of mystical experience, the scale employs thirty-two items (four for each of the eight factors) and asks the subject to rate them on a scale of −2 to +2. The items include statements such as "I have had an experience which was both timeless and spaceless"; "I have had an experience in which something greater than myself seemed to absorb me"; and so on. And much like Stace, Hood believes that his scale is able demonstrate that there are indeed universal mystical experiences that transcend particular religious traditions or cultural and historical contexts:

> [The] scale has shown that you can identify mystical experiences across religious traditions—among Buddhists, Hindus, Catholics, Protestants, Jews, Muslims, and people who have no religious beliefs. And you can identify that same experience with people in deep meditative prayer; people who have it occur spontaneously; people who practice the presence of God with a kind of contemplative prayer; and among people

> who take drugs. . . . So not one of those things [exclusively] produces the experience. There are occasions.[36]

Hood also believes that his scale has been one of the key tools that has allowed psychedelic research to be taken seriously. By creating a clear and standardized metric, it gave researchers "the ability to go to quality journals," and so "became the most widely used measure. . . . It's been translated into over 20 different languages."[37] Again, this is a metric that has lent psychedelic research an aura of "authority," in Bruce Lincoln's sense.

However, more critical scholars have raised many of the same questions about the Hood scale as they have about the MEQ. As Taves incisively argues, the questions used in the scale do not simply objectively reflect the subject's experiences; they actively help shape them and in so doing reinforce many of the same universalist and perennialist ideas about "the" mystical experience: "Hood's questionnaire . . . doesn't just influence the volunteer into seeing the experience as a positive one, it also suggests and reinforces their *assumption* that the mystical experience is a distinct or *sui generis* one."[38] At the same time, Taves argues, the Hood scale blurs the line between empirically verifiable scientific evidence and theological claims to nonverifiable mystical experiences. The claim that all mystical experiences (psychedelic or religious) share a common core, for example, cannot possibly be proven by any scientific method; and yet this claim remains a basic assumption in much of the current psychedelic research:

> If scientists fail to make a clear distinction between scientific claims based on empirical evidence and theological claims based on revelation or tradition, they risk setting mystical experiences apart from other similar experiences on theological rather than scientific grounds. They have no scientific basis for making theological claims regarding the common core of all religions or the presence of an ultimate reality that unites them.[39]

As we will see below, this blurring of the line between science and theology remains a troubling problem for many more critical observers of the modern psychedelic renaissance.

The Psychedelic Session as Ritual Process and Sacred Space

Another example of this complex tension between science and theology is the structure and space of the psychedelic session itself. As scholars of science and technology studies have long noted, the ostensibly "secular" spaces of laboratories and research trials often have far more in common with "religious" spaces than most scientists like to acknowledge; likewise, the practices and protocols of scientific research often have a surprising amount in common with religious practices. As Bruno Latour and Steve Woolgar put it in their study *Laboratory Life*, "Whereas we have fairly detailed knowledge of the myths and circumcision rituals of exotic tribes, we remain relatively ignorant of the details of equivalent activity among tribes of scientists."[40] Many scholars have compared the complex rules and behavior of science to religion, suggesting that the analytical frameworks of ritual theory could also apply to the practice of science. For example, in an article on "laboratory ritual," Robert M. Geraci suggests that

> technical achievement in laboratories requires millennia-old ritual formulations; the methodological expectations and presuppositions of scientists stem not only from investigations of the last three centuries but also from the ritual knowledge-making that has governed human religion. Laboratory research is a form of human ritual open to interpretation in the manner of religious ritual. The experiments of the laboratory are fact-gathering ventures, but the integration of that knowledge into our general understanding of a universe of information networks is the process of knowledge-making, and it is the highest achievement of all rituals, be they religious or scientific. Ritual theory offers insight into the nature of scientific experimentation.[41]

In passing, we should also note that Timothy Leary himself made the comparison between religious ritual, psychedelic experimentation, and scientific experimentation way back in 1969: "Ritual is to the science of consciousness what experiment is to external science."[42]

The room used for the Johns Hopkins sessions clearly blurred the line between "secular" and "sacred" space. For the most part, the space was designed as a kind of "aesthetic living room–like environment," with sofas, chairs, soft lighting, and attractive artwork on the walls.[43] Yet at the same time, as *Johns Hopkins Magazine* reported, Griffiths also obtained support from the Council on Spiritual Practices to create the space, which included clearly "spiritual" sorts of decorations including a mandala and a Buddha image, along with a sort of general Orientalist decor. Meanwhile, the psilocybin pill itself was administered on a "chalice" obtained from none other than Huautla de Jiménez, the key site where Wasson first sat in a *velada* with María Sabina:

> They used funds from the Council on Spiritual Practices to transform a section of Griffiths' lab into what looks rather like a hip therapist's

> office. The focal point is a long white couch, where participants recline during the sessions. The guides sit in a pair of leather chairs. Relics from various cultures and faith traditions decorate the room—a blue-and-gold mandala, a statue of the Buddha, a brightly beaded mask. On one table sits an earthenware chalice that [Robert] Jesse brought back from Huautla de Jiménez. . . . Participants pluck a capsule of psilocybin from this chalice and the session begins.[44]

If the "set and setting" are integral if not formative in the psychedelic session, then these sorts of details surely helped to create a particular kind of experience.

Probably even more so than universities such as Johns Hopkins, many of the private centers that offer psychedelic sessions also blur this line between religious and secular space. In the summer of 2024, I visited Life Trek in Albany, Oregon, one of several licensed centers in the state where *Psilocybe* mushrooms are legal under strict regulation. As I observed when I toured the facility, the Life Trek center offers four rooms for their *Psilocybe* sessions, each modeled on a slight variation of the four traditional elements (earth, water, space, and desert). As we read in their description of the "space" room:

> Welcome to the Space Room, where relaxation transcends earthly bounds and reaches for the stars. Step into a realm of cosmic serenity, where the mysteries of the universe unfold in a symphony of light and color. The walls are painted in deep, velvety shades of midnight blue and shimmering silver, evoking the vast expanse of the cosmos. Plush recliners are arranged. Sink into the embrace of celestial-themed pillows and mattresses, designed to cradle you in comfort as you drift among the stars. The room is filled with ethereal music and ambient sounds inspired by the cosmos, transporting you to a realm of peace and tranquility beyond earthly concerns. Let the infinite expanse of space envelop you in a sense of wonder and awe, as you embark on a journey of inner exploration and relaxation.[45]

In this description, we can clearly see an attempt to walk the fine line between plainly "secular" sorts of language and overtly "religious" sorts of language. We definitely see key spiritual terms such as "transcends," "mysteries," "cosmos," "celestial," "ethereal," "peace," "tranquility," and "inner exploration"; but nowhere do we find any explicit reference to particular religious traditions. This is very much the "mysticism without religion" idea that lies at the heart of this book.

Marsh Chapel 2.0

One of the most striking recent psychedelic experiments—and one that still further blurs the religion-science boundary—was undertaken from 2015 to 2020 by researchers at Johns Hopkins School of Medicine in Baltimore and NYU Langone Health in Manhattan.[46] In a sort of "Marsh Chapel 2.0," a dozen religious professionals participated in a psilocybin study. Consisting of rabbis, priests, and seminary professors, the members of the group were all "psychedelically naïve," that is, inexperienced with this class of drugs. Moreover, as Episcopal reverend Roger Joslin noted, many had never had a "mystical" experience, either—hence one of the reasons for wanting to participate in such experiments: "It's surprising how many clergy have never had a mystical experience. . . . How are you going to incorporate mystery into the life of your congregation if you don't know what that's like yourself?"[47] Rather significantly, most of the participants reported meaningful and often deeply spiritual sorts of experiences; yet few of them reported experiences that were unique to any particular religions. For example, James Lindberg, pastor in the Evangelical Lutheran Church, described a classic sort of experience of oneness much like those recounted in the first Marsh Chapel experiment:

> It was a unitive experience. . . . A loss of self and boundaries and identifying roles—male, pastor, husband—becoming singular in my experience of me rather than my roles. . . . It felt like a soul journey. . . . It was like getting into a little boat and going out into the cosmic ocean.[48]

Yet when asked if there was anything specifically "Christian" about his experience, he replied, "not anything, really."[49] Similarly, Reverend Rita Powell found herself wondering after the experiment why she hadn't encountered Christ on her journey: "I entered a space of nothing. There was no space to enter. I saw no one. I was nowhere. . . . There was no form, nor its absence. There was no fear. There was not joy. There was not revelation. There was nothing."[50]

One of the few participants who did recount a more specifically "Christian" experience was Reverend Hunt Priest. While he identified as Episcopalian at the time, he described his trip as a sort of Pentecostal feeling of the Holy Spirit flowing through his entire being: "I had a very Pentecostal experience the first time—feeling my body, speaking in tongues. I felt a force of energy blow through my body. . . . Now I see that spiritual healing is real. . . . This was in my body. . . . I *did* experience the Holy Spirit. . . . I felt like my journey at Hopkins was a second ordination."[51] In the end, Hunt concluded that psychedelics were as important for the understanding of religion as religion was for the understanding of psychedelics: "Institutional religion has a lot to learn from psychedelics. . . . And the psychedelic community has a lot to learn from organized religion."[52] Interestingly enough, however, Priest would actually leave his parish at St. Peter's Episcopal Church in Savannah in order to start a new Christian psychedelic society called "Ligare" (meaning to join, link, or unite). As Priest describes his own experience and reasons for founding Ligare,

> My encounters with psilocybin opened me to the healing and consciousness-raising power of sacred plants and fungi and their connection to my own Christian practice. The epiphanies forever changed the trajectory of my work.
>
> Through Ligare, I want the healing power of these sacred plants to be in the toolkits of all who are healers of bodies, minds, and souls. Part of this entails actively collaborating to bridge the knowledge gap between psychedelic research and religious and spiritual communities. The other part is providing a network and community of like-minded people who have had such positive experiences and wish to have continued fellowship together.[53]

All these experiences, of course, raise many of the same questions that were raised by Pahnke's original Marsh Chapel experiment. After all, one might expect religious professionals such as rabbis and priests to have some predisposition toward experiences that they would describe as mystical or spiritual. And, as we have seen above, the use of metrics such as the MEQ-30 and M-scale tends to shape the ways in which subjects narrate their experiences and the ways in which researchers interpret them. Are these studies measuring unique encounters with the divine, or are they amplifying and reinforcing preexisting spiritual inclinations, particularly among those who would want to participate in such studies? One might also wonder why the study did not include professionals from non-Christian or non-Jewish religions, such as Hindu priests or Native American elders? And what about professionals in traditions that prohibit the use of drugs, such as Muslims or most Buddhists? In the end, this study, like most others of its kind, raises many more questions than it answers (which is also perhaps not a bad thing).

Criticisms of the New Psychedelic Research

This explosion of new research on mushrooms and other psychedelics is surely not without its critics. A variety of skeptical authors have raised alarm bells about this rapidly growing current of research, particularly the claim that psychedelics can generate actual "mystical" experiences. One of the most incisive critiques comes from Rick Strassman, a professor of psychiatry who has also published widely on the effects of DMT and other psychedelics. As Strassman wrote in his review of William Richards's book *Sacred Knowledge*, scientific researchers should be very cautious in making claims about the mystical quality of psychedelic drug experiences, since they risk crossing over from the realm of serious scientific inquiry into the domain of religious faith:

> Clinical research with psychedelics must remain within the mainstream. Over-reaching into theology and religion, most obviously exemplified by the loose use of "mystical" to describe particular drug effects, is certain to generate backlash from bona fide religions. No religious tradition is going to simply accept the proposition that their foundational spiritual experience is "mystical consciousness" that most people can reach with several hours of psychotherapy and a psychedelic drug.[54]

In effect, Strassman argues, the research at Johns Hopkins looks less like traditional science than the flowering of a new kind of "psychedelic religion of mystical consciousness" with psilocybin as its new sacrament and initiation ceremony: "It's a messianic movement. . . . They want to bring about a utopia, and in this case, the messiah is the mushroom."[55] In Strassman's opinion, psychedelics such as psilocybin do not in themselves have any inherent spiritual effects; those effects are largely caused by set and setting, by specific musical playlists, by sensory isolation, and by filtering the results through questionnaires such as the MEQ and M-Scale. All these together begin to create a sort of feedback loop that makes it seem as though psychedelic and mystical experience are the same and can be easily reproduced:

> The current psychedelic movement . . . is essentially the emergence of a new mystico-scientific religion—"camouflaged by scientific studies and statistical firepower"—with its own Moses (William James) and cult vocabulary (psychedelics "occasion" effects; adverse effects are now "challenging"; flashbacks are "reactivations"); and if you read the articles, they all start to borrow the same language.[56]

Griffiths himself, meanwhile, is often revered as kind of a guru or a saint by many psychedelic enthusiasts. For example, renowned psychedelic artist Alex Grey memorialized Griffiths with a portrait of him holding a trippy model of the psilocybin molecule surrounded by images of María Sabina and key terms from the MEQ such as "Ineffable, Spirit, Ultimate Reality,

Ecstasy, Transcendence of Space and Time, Numinous," and so on. Griffiths's himself signed the back of the painting.[57]

Even some of Griffiths's former colleagues grew critical of the increasingly "religious" nature of his psychedelic research. Dr. Matthew Johnson, a professor of psychiatry and behavioral sciences, who worked with Griffiths for nearly twenty years, even filed an ethics complaint to Johns Hopkins in 2023. In his opinion, "Dr. Griffiths has run his psychedelic studies more like a 'new-age' retreat center, for lack of a better term, than a clinical research laboratory."[58] In his article "Consciousness, Religion and Gurus: Pitfalls of Psychedelic Medicine," Johnson warns of the dangers of scientists imposing their own personal beliefs and spiritual ideas onto their research. He notes that much of the current psychedelic work seems to be based on a kind of vague mixture of mystical ideas drawn from multiple traditions—a "loosely held eclectic collection of various beliefs drawn piecemeal from mystical traditions, Eastern religions, and indigenous cultures perhaps best described by the term 'new age.'"[59] Johnson warned in particular about a pervasive tendency for researchers (such as Griffiths) to impose their own personal religious and spiritual beliefs onto the practices of psychedelic medicine.[60] As Joanna Kempner from Rutgers University observes, all of this reflects a broader debate within the psychedelic field over the potential for "blurring the lines between empirical research and spiritual practice."[61]

Other critics have argued that the very use of the category of "mysticism" in psychedelic research is inherently problematic due to its theological (rather than scientific, empirical) basis. As James W. Sanders and Josjan Zijlmans argue in a recent article, the concept of mysticism is loaded with theological, metaphysical, and cultural assumptions that only muddle and undermine the scientific study of psychedelics. In their view, serious research on psychedelics should be based on empirically verifiable claims, not on appeals to nonempirical categories such as mysticism: "The current blend of mysticism and science in psychedelic research risks damaging the credibility and potential of psychedelic science. A theoretical shift is needed to clarify the division between psychedelic science and supernatural or nonempirical belief systems."[62] Other scholars have argued that researchers should simply abandon the terminology of mysticism and instead adopt "alternative 'non-mystical' conceptualizations of psychedelic effects, still with attention to operationalizing these alternative concepts in culturally sensitive and properly historicized ways."[63]

Griffiths himself, we should note, did not seem to be particularly bothered by this mingling of science and spirituality in his psychedelic research. As Michael Pollan recounts, "I asked him if he agreed with E. O. Wilson, who has written that all of us must ultimately choose either the path of science or the path of spirituality. But Griffiths doesn't see the two ways of knowing as mutually exclusive and has little patience for the absolutists on either side of the supposed divide."[64] However, even Griffiths in his later years did acknowledge some of the potential dangers and pitfalls of psychedelic research. Noting the tremendous enthusiasm surrounding this research in recent years, he added a word of caution about the possible downsides and negative effects of these very powerful drugs, which do not always produce beneficial experiences in every subject:

> We are in a disconcerting psychedelic bubble right now in which people have unbridled enthusiasm for the potential of psychedelics to cure everything. They minimize the risk and make it sound like psychedelics are completely harmless. Psychedelics are not harmless. People are going to die. People are going to become psychotic. . . . We need to get realistic as to what this program is about.[65]

In short, as Travis Kitchens aptly observes, we might do well to learn from the hard lessons of other new and aggressively marketed drugs that turned out to be problematic: "The truth is that the effects of psychedelics are far from predictable. We have been here before: The opioid crisis began with uncritical enthusiasm for drugs whose real effects were only later recognized."[66]

Faith and Doubt in the Drug Lab: A Harvard Divinity School Student's Experiences

Some of the most thoughtful and complex accounts of the psilocybin trials at Johns Hopkins have come from Rachael Petersen, a writer, scholar, and graduate student at Harvard Divinity School. In a series of articles based on her own experiences, she critically examines both the positive implications and negative potential of this research. In 2018, Petersen was suffering from severe depression and not finding much relief in other forms of therapy or medication. At the suggestion of a friend, she decided to enroll in a psilocybin trial at Johns Hopkins and published her reflections on the experience in 2019. As she recalls, she was an atheist at the time, having sworn off the Catholic Church when she was twelve years old. Yet to her surprise, the profound experience she had during the psilocybin trial forced her to fundamentally reconsider her belief in an Ultimate Reality—almost against her will:

> at the peak of my experience, my sense of self dissolved and I unified with an abiding force that permeated all existence—something that felt

> conscious, vast, benevolent, eternal, peaceful, and furiously important. After sitting up on the couch six hours later, covered in snot and tears, I struggled to put words to an encounter that felt more real than everyday reality—a mind-bendy paradox characteristic of many mystical experiences.[67]

At least for the first several months after the trial, Petersen's experience also seems to have had continuing and generally very positive effects. As she recalls, her depression was replaced by a sense of well-being and compassion, with greater love both for herself and others:

> in a few blessed months after the trial, I glided through life on a cloud of equanimity and intensely present joy. When I awoke each day, the soft light of morning felt like a sweet drink I had never tasted, but one that I suddenly knew I deserved. I told everyone I loved that I loved them, two times over. Walking to work I was content to exist in the radiant suchness of all things, felt myself a purposeful part of existence, a rightful creature among creatures. My coworkers asked me if I had joined a cult. "You're so zen," they marveled.[68]

As Petersen later explained to Jeffrey Kripal, the psilocybin experience did not exactly "cure" her depression. Rather, it was more like she was able to see her life in a broader perspective, in which her depression was just one part of herself that did not determine her whole being: "she now knew—really knew—that her body-brain and sense of self was just one room in a much, much larger house. And it was this new ontological recontextualization, this new scale, that made life worth living again."[69]

Yet even with these overall positive effects, Petersen still had a number of troubling questions about the nature of these psilocybin experiments and the larger ethical, philosophical, and religious issues they raise. Isn't it a bit problematic, she wondered, to offer individuals treatment for depression and then present them with an encounter with Ultimate Reality or God, something that might radically change their worldview? "In choosing this treatment," she wrote, "I wonder if patients will grasp that they could be choosing an entirely new ontology?" This seems to her like an odd kind of metaphysical bait and switch:

> Encountering what I feel most comfortable calling "Ultimate Reality" during an experimental depression trial sometimes feels like a profound spiritual bait-and-switch. Why couldn't they just treat my illness without screwing with my worldview? But exploding one's worldview

> is the whole point of these treatments; in fact, the trial protocol—the doses, a welcoming environment, guides, preparation, laying down with eyeshades while listening to a carefully-selected musical playlist—is optimized to increase the likelihood of profound experiences.[70]

As Petersen observes quite astutely in this account, the entire context of the trial was clearly designed to help *induce* precisely this kind of experience. Following scholars of mysticism such as Robert Gimello, we might say that the set and setting of the trial not only *influenced* the experience but, in many ways, helped *shape* and *construct* it. As Gimello put it, these kinds of structures "are of the essence of mystical experiences. They engender it. They inform its identity."[71]

At the same time, she was also disturbed by the fact that these profound encounters with Ultimate Reality were being treated in an almost utilitarian way, as mere means to the practical end of treating mental health problems:

> When I asked Griffiths about the practical implications of his latest study, he emphasized the therapeutic potential of these experiences for increased well-being and greater mental health. Reducing "God-encounters" to their therapeutic potential feels like a breathtakingly transactional approach to the divine. But it's one in keeping with our times.[72]

Finally, Petersen was also concerned by what she saw as a kind of "medicalization of mysticism"—that is the "bottling and marketing" of powerful substances such as psilocybin as "more drugs for those who can afford them" and yet another way to line the pockets of pharmaceutical companies.[73]

These concerns became even more acute when Petersen had her second encounter with psilocybin a couple of years later. This time her experience of the mushroom was radically different and far more negative, unleashing feelings not of joy and well-being but of generalized fear and sorrow. As she recounted in her second trip report:

> These feelings persist well into the evening, and I can't sleep. I sit in bed meditating, beholding this sadness and anxiety. I feel as though something is unresolved in me but am unsure what. The night after my first session, I stayed with a friend in Baltimore, sobbing on her futon, restless throughout the night. When writing this piece, I reached out to her about how she had perceived me. "Shaken," she said. "Intensely shaken."
>
> . . . Admittedly, I was less depressed than before the trial, but also more anxious. I slept less and less, clutching my pounding chest at night

> and praying that whatever wanted to bang down the door I had slammed shut between me and oblivion didn't break through. . . .
>
> My anxiety became nonreferential, totalizing. I could not consciously locate the object I feared.[74]

In addition to her concerns about the ways in which psilocybin is being used and marketed in these trials, Petersen also became more critical of the ways in which researchers were describing these experiences. Negative experiences like her second trip, she fears, are being minimized or glossed over amid the eagerness (and probably academic and financial pressure) to present positive results in these trials:

> The effort to medicalize psychedelics has focused on a narrow subset of experiences that are positive and therapeutic. Variations are dismissed as statistical outliers, flukes resulting from flaws in set and setting or vulnerabilities in the patient. . . . a full account of what psychedelics are, how they are, and—most vexingly—why they are, is as beholden to the harrowing as it is to the heavenly, to abject terror and to unbearable bliss.[75]

Ultimately, she worries that as psychedelics are increasingly used as therapeutic and medical interventions "people will be harmed. How many, how, and why, we don't yet know, in part because so few are given voice to share their stories, and little research exists."[76]

Petersen's concerns in this case are probably not unwarranted. As we saw in the case of the Good Friday Experiment discussed in chapter 3, there is a precedent for researchers glossing over negative experiences in these trials. Moreover, this tendency to emphasize the positive results in these sorts of trials is a common problem across many scientific (and other academic) fields. According to a study from the University of Edinburgh, there is a "growing pressure to report only positive results" in scientific papers, due to the intensely competitive nature of grant funding and academic tenure and promotion. The study also found that the problem of overreporting positive results was worse in the US than in Europe, probably due to the more intense competition in this country.[77] Authors such as Neşe Devenot, Trey Conner, and Richard Doyle worry that this sort of bias may well be at work in the realm of psychedelic research, as well: "Standards can often slacken as the portfolio grows. . . . Negative results may not be what massively funded new university research programs are looking to including in their weekly MailChimp PR as they report their role in the 'new psychedelic science.'"[78]

Finally, one other concern that Petersen raises is that many in the psychedelic movement seem to want to replace traditional religious institutions with psilocybin-based mysticism based on intense individual spiritual experience; yet they often fail to address many of the other basic roles that religions typically play. As we have seen above, psychedelic experiences do not necessarily lead to clear moral positions or ethical guidelines; nor do they necessarily play a role in building community and fostering a sense of social cohesion, which is arguably central to most religions:

> I do sometimes worry that the psychedelic movement is cashing in with collective glee on the failing of religion. "Religion is dying. It's not giving people what they need. We're going to give them what they need." . . . Some in the psychedelic community have this premise that religion has lost touch with its true purpose, and its true purpose is to connect people with the transcendent. But that's not what modern religion thinks its role is. It is teaching people how to behave in an ethical way. Community is something it cares about.[79]

As a divinity school student, Petersen surely has some bias here; but her larger point about the lack of ethical and social commitment in much of the current psychedelic movement should be taken seriously.

Corporadelia: Fungi, Big Pharma, and Corporate Profit

Given the intense new interest in the potential for psilocybin to provide dramatic mental health benefits for a wide range of disorders, it is not surprising that many large pharmaceutical companies have begun to explore the market potential of these drugs. As *Chemical & Engineering News* reported in 2022, more than eighty companies are now devoted to developing or administering psychedelic compounds, while "investors expect demand for psychedelic therapies to mushroom in the coming years."[80] Suddenly, it seems, "psychedelics are suddenly awash in money,"[81] as a number of companies have waded boldly into the rising psychedelic market, including the UK's Compass Pathways, the US's CaaMTech, and M2BIO, which is a division of Chinese-owned biotech company MJ MedTech:

> As the profile of psilocybin has grown, so too has a cluster of for-profit firms. . . . All are eyeing the size of the psilocybin market since the global market for conventional antidepressants alone was valued at $13.7 billion in 2016, and is projected to grow to $15.9 billion by 2023.[82]

As Kitchens, notes, many psychedelic research labs are now teaming up with venture capitalists to "make the world a happier place" by developing what Compass Pathways calls the mental health care clinic of the future.[83]

Compass Pathways and similar companies are now actively exploring psilocybin and other psychedelics for the possible treatment of a wide range of disorders, including addiction, anxiety disorders, cluster headaches, depression, obsessive compulsive disorder, and others.[84] And many see this as a market with huge growth potential. Thus in 2023, *Business News Daily* published an article that asked "Are Magic Mushrooms the Next Cannabis Industry?" and concluded with tips on "how to prepare for psilocybin business opportunities."[85] Many entrepreneurs such as Ronan Levy, the executive chair of the company Field Trips, seemed eager to pursue the many psychedelic business opportunities now opening amid the $240 billion that Americans spend each year on mental health services: "We are riding the forefront of what I think is going to be a significant cultural and business wave."[86]

In 2022, Compass Pathways also raised some legal eyebrows when it tried to patent its own form of synthetic psilocybin called Comp 360. The patent was immediately challenged by the group Freedom to Operate, which argued that Comp 360 was not a novel invention but simply a repackaging of a drug that had already long been in the public domain. As *Psychedelic Spotlight News* reported, the Patent Trial and Appeal Board ultimately decided in Compass Pathway's favor in this case.

> Ever since Compass Pathways (Nasdaq: CMPS) first entered the public eye, there has been a debate raging on whether their version of psilocybin, Comp 360, is deserving of a patent. The crux of the debate came down to whether Comp 360 is a unique compound that has never been created before, or whether the synthetic psilocybin had previously existed in the public domain. Now it seems—at least in the eyes of the law—this debate has been settled, and Compass Pathways has emerged victorious.[87]

All of this has raised complex questions about psilocybin and intellectual property rights. Could a company like Compass Pathways claim IP rights to *all* synthetic psilocybin, or only to specific versions such as Comp 360? In a potential market of billions of dollars, these are loaded questions indeed.

One of the most aggressive companies in the new psychedelic business is atai Life Sciences, which was valued at $3.2 billion as of 2022.[88] Founded by the eccentric German billionaire Christian Angermayer of Apeiron Investment Group along with CEO Florian Brand and CSO Srinivas Rao, atai's goal is to become a global biotech platform and company builder with "paradigm-shifting interventions" in the mental health space.[89] Atai owns a 21 percent stake in Compass Pathways, one of the major companies investing heavily in psilocybin research, including some of the largest trials of a psychedelic compound to date.[90] As Angermayer said on CNBC's Squawk Box: "The world we're building is a bad place for our brain, so mental health issues will go up. But I do think we have some real shots in our portfolio to end the mental health crisis."[91] Still more ambitiously, Angermayer claims that he hopes to "extend human life by a century and put psychedelics into the hands (and mouths) of the 'more than one billion' people suffering from crippling depression around the world" and eventually treat "collective mental health issues" and diseases that "we don't even have a name for yet."[92]

Another prominent investor in atai Life Sciences and Compass Pathways is American tech billionaire Peter Thiel. A cofounder of PayPal and an early investor in Facebook, Thiel had an estimated worth of $11.2 billion as of July 2024. While he has not explicitly acknowledged use of psychedelics, he has invested at least $12 million in atai Life Sciences. In striking contrast to the radical leftist politics of countercultural figures of the 1960s, Thiel is much better known for his aggressively capitalist and arguably authoritarian politics. He has described his preferred business strategy as monopolization (since "competition is for losers"[93]); he has expressed open support for South African apartheid as a "sound economic system";[94] he has been a strong supporter of and donor to politicians such as President Donald Trump and Senator Ted Cruz; and, in a rather infamous article for the libertarian think-tank *Cato Unbound*, he concluded that "I no longer believe that freedom and democracy are compatible."[95] In short, the recent wave of psychedelic investment suggests that these drugs are no longer solely the province of left-wing idealists but have also been embraced by those on the far-right end of the political spectrum.[96]

For many enthusiasts, mushrooms offer the possibility not simply of addressing mental health problems, but of enhancing productivity and success in the business world. Psychedelics have been widely embraced by many in Silicon Valley and the tech industry, who see them as ways of thinking outside the box and discovering new kinds of business innovation. As Brian Pace observes, "Corporadelic actors are currently folding psychedelics into a corporate ethos predicated on novelty and cognitive labor: from microdosing coders to ayahuasca business coaches, psychedelics are seen as shortcuts to divergent market insight in a globalized neoliberal marketplace."[97]

Some more critical observers worry, however, that this corporate rush toward the development of psilocybin and other psychedelics may have some disturbing side effects. Among other things, it risks obfuscating or even completely erasing the Indigenous cultures who have used these substances for centuries or even millennia, ignoring the vast body of local knowledge and ritual technologies that have accompanied them as part of more complex relationships between humans and the natural environment. As Devenot, Conner, and Doyle argue,

> When contemporary psychedelic medicine "discovers" the efficacy of psychedelic plants, they "erase" the long lineages and diverse knowledges that have curated, tended, and ultimate the human relationships to these plants. . . . Indigenous and countercultural knowledges are repackaged, intensified, and sold back to an underinsured public.[98]

We have already seen the very real and quite tragic effects of this sort of erasure in the case of María Sabina, whose life and community were radically impacted by Wasson's *Seeking the Magic Mushroom*.

Similar concerns have also been raised about other natural psychedelics, such as mescaline, the psychoactive alkaloid in the peyote cactus. Used for thousands of years by tribes such as the Huichol in Mexico and now a sacrament in the pan-Indian Native American Church, peyote recently caught the attention of the pharmaceutical industry as part of the larger interest in psychedelics. As with *Psilocybe*, many pharmaceutical ventures are eager to explore mescaline or the cactus for market potential. Hugh Rogers, the CEO of XPhyto Therapeutics Corp. (now BioNxt Solutions), stated in an interview with *Forbes*: "What we see in mescaline, is an opportunity to enter the market—at least participate in the market—by being a wholesaler of mescaline for R&D, for clinical research, for clinical use. That's the opportunity."[99] Not surprisingly, this corporate interest in peyote has alarmed many Native American communities who see this as a dangerous co-optation of traditional practices and of a plant that is already endangered. As *The Guardian* reported in 2023, many see this as fundamentally at odds with the traditional understanding of the cactus, which is part of wholistic worldview based on a deep relationship of interconnectedness between humans, the natural environment, and the divine:

> For Indigenous Americans, the boom has a dark side that rarely comes up in venture capital pitches. Many Diné tribal members are describing this moment as a "peyote crisis" that threatens to appropriate and commodify their sacred way of life.
>
> Decriminalizing peyote could fuel poaching and a black market for the slow-growing cactus, whose limited habitat is already threatened by climate change and development. A sudden surge in demand might completely wipe out peyote from its natural environment. . . .

> Then there are the deeper concerns about turning peyote and mescaline into an on-demand drug. Members of the Native American church of North America . . . are alarmed by pharmaceutical ventures seeking to create mescaline in a lab, in much the same way opium from the poppy flower was synthesized to create fentanyl. . . .
>
> At its core, the push to medicalize and mass-produce peyote and mescaline goes against the Indigenous American worldview of interconnectedness. There are no English words that describe how the spiritual character of peyote is inextricably intertwined with its hallucinogenic properties, the land where it grows and the Indigenous Americans who consume it.[100]

Others, meanwhile, worry that the mass production of pharmaceutical psychedelics will only continue and intensify the general drug dependency—the "drugs for life" attitude—that characterizes much of modern American society.[101] As Jules Evans observes, this is perhaps simply the next wave of our drug-reliant lifestyle, which sees drugs as the solution to every problem—even spiritual ones—and regards no life complete without some pharmaceutical intervention:

> The psychedelic renaissance could actually exacerbate what Theodore Roszak called "our disastrously drug-dependent" culture, and our belief that we are somehow less than human without a pharmaceutical boost. The big pharma companies are already lining up to turn us on—Johnson & Johnson has launched its ketamine nasal spray, Sprovato, for $5000 a month.
>
> We're in a psychedelic boom, with psychedelic companies getting billion-dollar valuations. We can expect as much hype for psychedelic therapies as there was for Prozac.[102]

At the same time, all of this seems to reinforce the "biological reductionism" that has arguably become the dominant paradigm in modern mental health—that is, the belief that all mental health problems are the result of chemical imbalances, and therefore that the key to optimal well-being must also lie in some chemical treatment.[103]

Even some figures who were instrumental in the development of modern psychedelic studies are deeply uncomfortable with the current wave of pharmaceutically driven and profit-driven research. As Ralph Hood himself explained in an interview, he felt that the new research had lost sight of the spiritual origins and cultural roots of substances such as *Psilocybe* mushrooms, turning them into just more marketable drugs for the pharmaceutical industry to keep us all buying:

> Academic institutions such as Johns Hopkins, Hood says, are focusing too much attention on the medical application of psychedelics, at the expense of their potential as agents of spiritual transformation. . . . The thing that drives medical research is pharmaceutical companies, and they are happy to find any condition for which they can have a patented drug that you have to take for the rest of your life. So that model is drastically wrong.[104]

Finally, it is worth noting that many legal scholars have also begun to examine the complex intersection between the work of psychedelic researchers and the interests of large pharmaceutical companies. In 2022, the Petrie-Flom Center for Health Law Policy, Biotechnology, and Bioethics at Harvard Law School hosted a panel on "Conflicts of Interest in the Psychedelics Ecosystem." As we read in the summary of the panel's concerns:

> In recent years, a growing number of observers have raised concerns about conflicts of interests in the growing psychedelics industry. . . .
>
> [T]his panel will explore questions about the ways in which conflict of interest can influence psychedelics research, policy, and practice standards. How might the influx of investor funding influence the type of research that is done on psychedelics? What should we make of the fact that a relatively small group of organizations, often with financial ties to for-profit entities, are influencing regulations and norms for many facets of the psychedelic landscape?[105]

As was the case with Wasson and his "mysticism without ethics," we have to wonder about the ethical implications of this new wave of psychedelic research and its spiritual consequences.

Conclusion: The Potential and the Peril of the Psychedelic Renaissance

The seemingly magical power of mushrooms, as we have seen throughout this book, has long been associated with both benevolent and malevolent sorts of possibilities. As "poisons and panaceas," mushrooms have been imagined as both visionary portals to other realms and bearers of corruption and decay, as both vehicles of otherworldly beings and sources of delusion and death. This ambivalent nature of the mushroom is no less evident in the current psychedelic renaissance.

There does now seem to be a good deal of evidence that a controlled use of *Psilocybe* mushrooms and the drug psilocybin may be beneficial in treating a wide range of psychological disorders, ranging from anxiety and depression to PTSD. Arguably some of the most interesting research has been on the use of psilocybin in palliative care—for example, in treating depression in patients with life-threatening cancer.[106] Despite their methodological problems and the use of questionable metrics such as the MEQ-30 and M-scale, the numerous studies over the last twenty years make a compelling case that psilocybin does have some therapeutic value, at least in certain contexts.

Yet at the same time, the increasingly widespread use of psilocybin in both scientific and recreational settings has raised a number of troubling questions that remain largely unresolved. To summarize what we have discussed in this chapter, three of these questions seem most relevant today. From the perspective of this book, the first and most important question concerns the largely uncritical use of the term "mysticism" and the simplistic equation of psychedelic and religious experience. As several critics have pointed out, the very use of the terms "mystical" and "mysticism" in this context is problematic, since these categories have such a long and complex history of theological uses that arguably muddle rather than illuminate what is happening with psychedelic experiences.

While many participants in psilocybin trials do indeed report profound and meaningful experiences, the assertion made by Griffiths and others that these are "virtually identical" to religious mystical experiences throughout history is ultimately unverifiable. How could we possibly know if Meister Eckhart's or Shankara's or the Buddha's experiences were the same as a psychedelic experience in a laboratory? This assertion also involves a highly reductionistic assumption that a single compound such as psilocybin can be isolated from the mushroom (which contains many other compounds) and extracted from its larger cultural and ritual settings, yet still produce "the same" experience as that of María Sabina in her *velada*, or a Siberian shaman in his trance, or a Vedic priest in the *somayaga*. The assertion that they are "virtually identical" is ultimately not a scientific claim at all but a *theological* claim, and one with deep perennialist assumptions.

Second, many critics have raised concerns about cultural appropriation and the uprooting of traditional knowledge practices from their historical contexts and local meaning systems. Amid all the excitement over the therapeutic power and pharmaceutical possibilities of *Psilocybe* mushrooms, some worry that their cultural and religious histories have largely been erased. Is this yet another example of modern researchers taking the sacred knowledge of other cultures and transforming it into a marketable drug? Is it a new form of colonial extraction, yet on a much grander late capitalist scale? As Travis Kitchens observes in his discussion of the recent enthusiasm for psychedelics by billionaire investors such as Christian Angermayer, "Once seen as 'deconditioning agents' (Timothy Leary's pet phrase) or a route to hidden knowledge, psychedelics are now viewed as critical to the future of industrial capitalism."[107]

Finally, and most practically, many have raised questions about the safety of psilocybin and other psychedelics. Some like Petersen worry that the darker side of these experiences has not been taken seriously enough amid the enthusiasm of the psychedelic renaissance, where "bad trips" tend to be either downplayed or explained away. And even Griffiths himself raised concerns about the rapid explosion of psychedelic research, predicting that without clearer regulation and adequate safeguards people could become psychotic or even die.

Yet in this sense, as in so many others, psychedelic mushrooms are really a reflection of much larger questions and anxieties of twenty-first-century American culture. They embody both a deep faith in science and a persistent yearning for some form of transcendent spiritual experience outside the domain of materialist science. They express both a desire to connect our contemporary experiences to ancient, Indigenous cultures and the fear of erasing those same cultures in the process. And they reflect both a hope for immediate pharmacological solutions to all our spiritual woes and the threat of mass commercial exploitation. To borrow Huxley's phrase, they are perhaps the "appropriate drugs" for our time.

[CONCLUSION]

Mushrooms and the Arts of Living and Dying on a Damaged Planet

What we don't know about psychoactive mushrooms far exceeds what we do know.

Michael Pollan (2019)[1]

The decisions and transformations so urgent in our times for learning again, or for the first time, how to become less deadly, more response-able, more attuned, more capable of surprise, more able to practice the arts of living and dying well in multispecies symbiosis, sympoiesis, and symanimagenesis on a damaged planet, must be made without guarantees or the expectation of harmony with those who are not oneself—and not safely other, either. Neither One nor Other, that is who we all are and always have been.

Donna Haraway, *Staying with the Trouble* (2016)[2]

[We] have never been individuals. . . . We are all lichens.

Scott F. Gilbert, Jan Sapp, and Alfred Tauber, "A Symbiotic View of Life" (2012)[3]

In the course of its long mycelial journey from central Mexico to the twenty-first-century American laboratory, the magic mushroom has undergone a number of striking transformations. As part of its complex genealogy over the last century, the story of *Psilocybe* has involved a variety of what Michel Foucault calls "accidents, minute deviations, complete reversals, errors, false appraisals, and faulty calculations."[4] Once the highly private domain of a few wise men and women working in night vigils in the mountains of Oaxaca, the mushroom burst prominently into popular culture in the 1950s, exploded in the psychedelic revolution of the 1960s, became the target of intense government opposition in the 1970s, circulated underground as a DIY home-grown product in the 1980s, reemerged as a potential world savior in the 1990s, and is now being promoted as an exciting new drug for a wide range of psychological disorders in the twenty-first century. In all this complex genealogy, the mushroom has served as a key node or "hyphal knot"[5] amid some of our most intense cultural and spiritual concerns. As a kind of myco-cosm, it lies at the critical intersection between the ongoing desire for intense mystical experience and the increasing rejection of mainstream religions; between the yearning to ground these experiences in the ancient past and the obsession with the latest technology; between the desperation to save the earth from catastrophic environmental destruction and the no less desperate clinging to capitalism and economic development. For a relatively small and unassuming little fungus, the magic mushroom has come to embody a tremendous range of modern hopes, fears, anxieties, and desires.

Perhaps most importantly, the story of magic mushrooms reveals the complex ways in which the very categories of "mysticism" and "religion" have been transformed and reimagined over the last seventy years. This reimagining, I think, is at least threefold. First, the idea of mystical experience has been largely "de-religionized," that is, separated from any necessary connection to institutional religious structures, ritual practices, or hierarchies of authority. We saw this trend beginning with Wasson's dissemination of *Psilocybe* in the 1950s, and it has only expanded and merged with the larger "spiritual but not religious" current of the last several decades. Second, mystical experience has been largely "de-ethicized," that is, largely disconnected from any particular moral or ethical commitments. Today, psilocybin can be taken as easily by CEOs hoping to maximize profits as by spiritual seekers hoping for enlightenment or a glimpse of ultimate reality. And finally, the concept of mysticism has undergone an odd sort of quantification and commodification. We now have many licensed facilitation centers such as Odyssey PBC in Oregon, where mystical experiences can be calibrated with precise doses of psilocybin (from 25 to 40 mg) with corresponding fees (from $2,400 to $4,500).[6] And we now have metrics such as the MEQ and M-Scale that claim to show us our precise quotient of mystical experience. All of this, I think, reflects a deeper sort of "religious faith" that circulates in twenty-first-century America—namely, a deep faith in science and the authority of numbers, a deep faith in capitalism and the ever-expanding power of the market, and a deep faith in drugs to address any and all physical, psychic, or spiritual woes.

Surely, the brief genealogy traced in this book is not exhaustive, and there are myriad other mycelial threads that we could have pursued, from the many *Psilocybe*-based churches now proliferating around the world to the widespread influence of psychedelic mushrooms in Silicon Valley and the software industry. Yet even from this short history, I think we can see that the ongoing fascination with magic mushrooms is far from a fringe or marginal phenomenon; rather, it runs like a hidden thread or subterranean mycelial network beneath the landscape of the twenty-first century.

To conclude, I would just like to reflect on some of the broader implications of this mycological genealogy for life and spirituality amid the "capitalist ruins" that we inhabit today.[7]

Mysticism With and Without Religion

In February 2024, I was contacted by lawyers from Terrapin Legal, a law firm based in Spokane, Washington, that specializes in psychedelics. Terrapin was at that time working with a group in the Bay Area called the Church of Ambrosia, which uses *Psilocybe* mushrooms and *Cannabis* as its primary sacraments. Founded by David Hodges in 2019, the Church of Ambrosia is just one of many psychedelic churches now spreading across the country. However, it has also become one of the most controversial and the subject of intense scrutiny because of its large membership and its practice of dispensing *Psilocybe* mushrooms (currently illegal in California) to its many adherents. Indeed, the church claims to be the "largest mega-church" in the US with over one hundred thousand members, thus surpassing (at least on paper) other huge mega-churches such as Joel Osteen's.[8] The lawyers representing Hodges were seeking scholars such as myself to help the church make the case that it is in fact a bona fide "religion" and that its sacramental use of *Psilocybe* mushrooms should be protected as a matter of religious freedom, analogous to exemptions for peyote use by the Native American Church. In the eyes of many critics, however, the church operates more as a for-profit drug dispensary than a religious organization.[9]

In August 2020, the Oakland Police Department raided the Zide Door Church of Entheogenic Plants, an assembly of the Church of Ambrosia, seizing roughly $200,000 worth of mushrooms, *Cannabis*, and cash.[10] While Hodges himself was not charged with any crime, he continues to worry about possible government interference and harassment from law enforcement. As such, the case of the Church of Ambrosia raises profound questions about what is and isn't "religion," what counts as a valid "mystical experience," and where is the line (if any) between a religious organization and a commercial enterprise.

In various public talks and interviews, Hodges has recounted his own mystical experiences, which led him to founding this new church. As he explained in a talk in 2022, one of his most profound revelations occurred during a high dose of twenty grams of mushrooms, when he claims to have experienced the consciousness of God and witnessed the unfolding of the universe itself:

> I was dragged through every dimension, heaven and hell, and ended in a space of pure light. There was nothing that existed. I didn't exist. There was but one consciousness, and I consider that the consciousness of God. . . . Out of that experience the message I got was actually a question, which is if you were God, what would you ask yourself? If you were the creator of everything, the knower of everything, what would you ask yourself? The only thing you might not know is: what am I? And that's where I experienced the creation of the universe and space and time, everything that exists. We are the answer to God's question: what am I? So, God is a space, a consciousness, it's not an old man with a beard that's dictating your life. . . .
>
> All of consciousness [is] God experiencing itself.[11]

Elsewhere, Hodges describes another revelatory experience that he had while taking a high dose of mushrooms in 2019. On this occasion, he recalls, he encountered a group of "mushroom gods" who gave him the specific mission of spreading the sacramental use of *Psilocybe* and *Cannabis* to the entire world:

> The ceremony ended with three bright, shining golden beings who identified themselves as the oldest of the mushroom gods, sitting down with me and telling me why I went through everything in my life, and what they needed me for and what I'm supposed to do. And they told me what I need to do was make sure that people have access to these sacraments and spread the knowledge.[12]

Hodges's Church of Ambrosia is fairly minimalist when it comes to its specific beliefs and practices. One of its core ideas, however, is a sort of variant of McKenna's "stoned ape" theory, which Hodges calls the "Religious Evolution Doctrine." Expanding on McKenna's ideas, this doctrine suggests that mushrooms not only helped foster the kinds of symbolic thinking and language that led to the modern human consciousness; they also gave us the ability to communicate with and then conceptualize the gods, spirits, and transcendent ideas that constitute "religion" itself:

> Magic Mushrooms catalyzed both the evolution of human communication and the emergence of religion itself. Our ancestral apes, having experienced these otherworldly entities, endeavored to convey their experiences, trying to explain concepts as profound as spirits and God to each other. . . . Mushrooms have the potential to facilitate a deep connection with our true selves and what exists beyond our ordinary realm.[13]

Because mushrooms lie at the origins of religion, they are also the most important sacrament used in the church today. Like Leary, McKenna, and others, Hodges believes that "mushrooms sparked the first mystical and religious experiences and are a uniting force that can bring individuals closer to their God, their own soul, and their truest understanding of faith."[14] As such, he argues that consumption of the mushroom should be considered a "ceremony" and "approached with deep reverence for the spiritual and transcendental power of the Sacrament." However, Hodges also recommends doses of *Psilocybe* that go much further than even McKenna's large "heroic doses" of five grams. Indeed, the church's website has recommendations for *very* high doses of *Psilocybe*, including what they call "breakthrough doses" of six to ten grams or more. In these superhigh-dose circumstances, they recommend not only that one have a sitter on hand, but that one should be "in a bedroom with a bathroom and shower nearby"; they also suggest "wearing Depends and having a mattress cover" in order to be prepared for a possible "system purge." They emphasize firmly (in capital letters) that "YOU MUST BE COMFORTABLE WITH YOUR SITTER. THEY WILL PROBABLY SEE YOU NAKED, AND MIGHT EVEN HAVE TO CLEAN UP YOUR VOMIT, ETC."[15] But they also suggest that these high-dose heroic journeys may open the door to exceptionally profound shamanic experiences of other realities:

> What you might experience: leaving your body; inner knowledge of your body; Visions of other realms; meeting creatures, gods, aliens, things that cannot be described with words . . . visions of god, space, the inside of your body and/or things that cannot be described with words.[16]

The police raid on the Oakland church in 2020 was apparently triggered by a tip from the Alameda County Health Department, which alleged that the pot smoke issuing from the facility was "creating respiratory health issues" for children nearby.[17] However, a larger issue is that the church seems to be operating as an illegal dispensary, selling *Cannabis* (which is legal in California but only for licensed facilities) and *Psilocybe* (which is illegal in the state). In response, the church has made two separate arguments. One is that it is not actually "selling" *Cannabis* or *Psilocybe*, since all members "sign an agreement which means they own everything within the church, including the sacrament. Therefore . . . there is no transfer of ownership."[18] In other words, members technically already "own" the *Cannabis* and *Psilocybe* and are simply making donations to the church. Second, Hodges argues that *Psilocybe* should be given in an exemption for religious use, in much the same way that peyote is given an exemption for use by the

Native American Church and *Cannabis* is given an exemption for use by Rastafarians.[19]

It was primarily on this latter point that Hodges and his lawyers were seeking assistance from scholars of religion such as myself. It seemed fairly clear from Hodges's statements and those of his lawyers that the main reason for seeking recognition as a religion was simply to get law enforcement off their backs (a motivation, we should note, that was also shared by other controversial groups historically such as the Native American Church and the Church of Scientology).[20] While I ultimately declined to work on this case for a variety of reasons, I do think it raises important questions about law, religious freedom, the First Amendment, and the very definition of religion that are central to this book, including, among others, What is the line (if any) between something that is considered to be deeply meaningful, spiritual, or mystical and something that is recognized legally to be "religious" in the eyes of courts, law enforcement, and the IRS? And what is the line (if any) between a for-profit "business" and a bona fide "religion"? After all, we can think of countless examples of groups that are generally accepted as religions that also make quite a lot of money (Joel Osteen Ministries, World Harvest Church, the Church of Scientology, and countless others)[21].

Ironically, the search for a "mysticism without religion" has led back to a desire to "re-religionize" the mushroom experience in order to receive the same sorts of protections and benefits as other recognized "religions." Yet it has raised many of the same tensions and questions that we have seen throughout this book—tensions between religious freedom and the law, between spirituality and capitalism, between the yearning for otherworldly transcendence and the messiness of this-worldly politics and economics.[22]

The Dark Side of the Shroom: The Complex Politics of Mycological Mysticism

From the time of Timothy Leary down to more recent psychedelic visionaries such as David Hodges, it has often been assumed that mushrooms—and psychedelics more generally—will naturally lead to a progressive vision of environmentalism, social justice, antiracism, LGBTQ+ rights, and other left-leaning political ideals. For much of the 1960s and 1970s, this was indeed often the case, as most of those using psychedelics were themselves activists in the social and political movements of the counterculture. However, as more critical scholars such as Brian Pace and Neşe Devenot have observed, the link between psychedelics and left-leaning politics is far from a necessary or universal one. On the contrary, they argue, "Members of reactionary and right-wing authoritarian political movements make their own uses of psychedelics," and they provide numerous examples of the use of psychedelics to reinforce far-right and even openly racist, homophobic, and fascist ideologies.[23] While psychedelics have surely been used by utopian visionaries with egalitarian politics, they have also been used by manipulative and violent groups such as the Manson family and Aum Shinrikyo.[24] More recently, members of Neo-Nazi groups such as the Base, white supremacists who post on websites such as Stormfront, and others involved in far-right-wing politics have made their own use of psychedelics, which often reinforce rather than challenge ideals of social hierarchy and racial superiority.

Psychedelics, Pace and Devenot argue, are not naturally aligned with any particular social or political ideology but are instead more like "non-specific amplifiers of political set and setting." That is to say, they tend to enhance one's suggestibility and so can intensify whatever social-political ideology one happens to have or be surrounded by in the particular circumstance in which they are taken.[25] Hence during the 1960s, in the context of the civil rights movement and the counterculture, psychedelics tended to enhance far-left politics, while in the twenty-first century, in a very different cultural context, they can serve to amplify any number of different political ideas. While some enthusiasts such as Paul Stamets might see them as the key to a vision of interconnectivity and harmony between humans and the environment, others see them as an affirmation of their own ideas of hierarchy, power, and sometimes violence. As we saw in chapter 6, some of the greatest enthusiasts of magic mushrooms and other psychedelics today are tech billionaires like Christian Angermayer and Peter Thiel, who seem to be more interested in corporate profit than in a unifying vision of global harmony.

A similar argument has been made by Ralph Metzner, an early psychedelic pioneer and former student of Leary and Alpert. As Metzner put it, psychedelics "do not in themselves show you a way to live. There is nothing inherently good in these chemicals.... Charles Manson can use LSD and do what he did."[26] In this sense, he argues,

> Psychedelic drugs function as amplifiers of whatever we are already thinking or feeling, whether consciously or unconsciously. They do not change the underlying ways our minds work unless they are done in conjunction with some kind of serious meditation practice, spiritual discipline, therapeutic regime, or shamanic oversight.[27]

Hence, the idea that mushrooms by themselves can "save the world" does not appear to be very well supported by the historical record. While psilocybin and other psychedelics can surely have a profound impact on consciousness and lead to radically different ways of seeing the world, the claim that they inherently lead to a planet-saving vision of unity seems tenuous at best.[28]

Parasites, Saprobes, and Symbionts: "We Are All Lichens"

So, if we have to leave behind the 1960s utopian ideal of mushrooms as our psychedelic saviors, where does that leave us today? Are we doomed to a world of neoliberal despair, in which corporations inevitably co-opt everything—even mysticism and fungi—into profitable goods as part of the larger "commodification of everything"?[29] Or should we retreat into a kind of romantic nostalgia for a premodern world—a world of María Sabina before Wasson—when mushrooms were still respected as sacred beings and not yet reduced to the soulless chemicals of the pharmaceutical industry?

Paul Stamets's missionary zeal probably strikes many readers as too utopian and romantic to be very practical in an age of rampant capitalism, advanced climate change, and a general assault on the natural environment. The sheer magnitude of the ecological challenges we now face makes the idea of simply eating mushrooms and seeing that "we are all one" probably seem a bit quaint to most readers sitting in a twenty-first-century context of rising temperatures, devastating floods, severe droughts, and other self-inflicted disasters. Nonetheless, I do think there is an important kernel of truth in his suggestion that mushrooms could still offer us some glimmer of hope for life in the Anthropocene age. While mushrooms might not necessarily "save" the world, they might at least help us learn to *survive* and *coexist* upon the severely damaged planet that we inhabit today.

My suggestions here are thus less utopian and romantic than realist and pragmatic. I advocate something closer to Donna Haraway's argument that we need to learn as a species to "become less deadly, more response-able, more attuned, more capable of surprise, more able to practice the arts of living and dying well in multispecies symbiosis."[30] We need, in short, to acquire some survival skills "in the urgent times called the Anthropocene, when the arts for living on a damaged planet demand sympoietic thinking and action."[31] Haraway cites a number of fascinating examples that reveal how radically interconnected humans and all animals are with other life forms, exploring the ways in which we are not so much bounded, autonomous "individuals" but rather far more porous sorts of assemblages that are profoundly dependent upon other species in complex symbiotic ways.[32] Among other examples, Haraway cites the remarkable article "A Symbiotic

View of Life: We Have Never Been Individuals," by Scott F. Gilbert, Jan Sapp, and Alfred I. Tauber. Using a range of evidence from anatomy, physiology, genetics, evolution, and immunology, the authors show the many complex ways in which almost all life is bound up in delicate symbiotic relations with other organisms. From the "duality of lichens" to the "fungi living in the roots of orchids and forest trees," to the "algae living inside the cells of translucent cnidarians," symbiosis seems to be more the norm than the exception in nature. Indeed, they argue persuasively that even most animals (including *Homo sapiens*) are not so much neatly bounded individuals but rather complex amalgams of myriad diverse organisms. From the bacteria that inhabit our guts to the billions of microorganisms that crawl across our skin, we are very much heterogeneous assemblages made up of countless different life forms:

> Microbial symbiosis also has been demonstrated in vertebrate physiology. Lipid metabolism, the detoxification of xenobiotics, regulation of colonic pH, vitamin synthesis, and intestinal permeability are each biological functions provided to the holobiont by bacteria. . . . The role of symbiotic microbes in mammalian disease prevention is well recognized today. . . . The common gut symbiont *Bacteroides thetaiotaomicron* induces angiogenin-4 gene expression in the intestinal Paneth cell. This protein functions to produce new blood vessels. But it is also a bacteriocidal factor against *Listeria*, the major competitor of *Bacteroides* and a gut pathogen. From these examples, we may conclude that on classical physiological grounds, animals are not individuals.

In sum, they conclude, we "have never been individuals. . . . We are all lichens."[33]

Although Haraway does not cite the example of mushrooms directly, the realm of fungi seems to provide ample evidence for precisely this sort of complex, de-individualized, and interconnected view of life. As we saw in the introduction, mushrooms play a variety of different—and often simultaneous—roles in their ecosystems. Some, such as the honey mushrooms (*Desarmillaria caespitosa*) that grow in my backyard in Ohio are notorious parasites, whose thick, ropey mycelia strangle and kill most of the trees they encounter. Others such as the *Psilocybe* species at the heart of this book are saprobic, breaking down organic matter such as wood chips, leaf litter, or animal feces, and recycling it back into the ecosystem. As Sheldrake observes in *Entangled Life*, "Fungi are metabolic wizards and can explore, scavenge, and salvage ingeniously, their abilities rivaled only by bacteria. Using cocktails of potent enzymes and acids, fungi can break down some of the most stubborn substances on the planets, from lignin, wood's toughest component, to rock, crude oil, polyurethane plastics and the explosive TNT."[34]

And still other mushrooms—including most terrestrial fungi such as *A. muscaria* and thousands of others—are *mycorrhizal* or symbiotic, forming complex and mutually beneficial relationships with various plants and trees. Growing around their roots, mycorrhizal fungi take up sugars or lipids from plants and trees, which they in turn supply with water and mineral nutrients from the soil. As Sheldrake explains, these mycorrhizal associations have in fact been a key part of the development of life on Earth as we know it: "This ancient association gave rise to all recognizable life on land, the future of which depends on the continued ability of plants and fungi to form healthy relationships."[35] In short, life itself is unimaginable without these elaborate webs of interconnection and symbiosis:

> More than ninety percent of all plant species depend on mycorrhizal fungi. They are the rule, not the exception: a more fundamental part of planthood than fruit, flowers, leaves, wood, or even roots. Out

FIGURE C.1. *Mycorrhizal* fungi on beech tree roots. Steven Morris / Alamy.

> of this intimate partnership—complete with cooperation, conflict, and competition—plants and mycorrhizal fungi enact a collective flourishing that underpins our past, present and future. We are unthinkable without them.[36]

In this sense, fungi provide us with several possible examples of how we have related to other species in the past and how we might think about relating to other species in the future. If we look at the history of human civilization over just the last two hundred years, it would be difficult to see our relationship to other species as anything other than exploitative and destructive, if not actually "parasitic." Since the beginning of the Industrial Revolution, we have unleashed catastrophic climate change and either caused or threatened the extinction of millions of species, ushering in an Anthropocene age (or what Haraway calls the "Chthulucene age") with devastating and increasingly unpredictable consequences for all life on Earth. According to the Center for Biological Diversity, more than one million species are on track for extinction in the coming decades, largely due to human activity. This shocking list includes roughly one-third of all amphibians; 12 percent of birds; 21 percent of fish; 30 percent of invertebrates (from butterflies to mollusks, earthworms, and corals); one-fifth of mammals, including 50 percent of primates; 68 percent of plants; and 21 percent of reptiles.[37] As Elizabeth Kolbert writes in *The Sixth Extinction*, "No creature has ever altered life on the planet in this way before," comparing our impact to five previous catastrophic extinction events when the diversity of life on Earth dramatically plummeted.[38] The fact that we have done so much damage in so short a time is simply staggering. It also lends support to those who argue that *Homo sapiens* has become the most aggressively invasive species and the most destructive parasite the earth has ever seen.[39]

Perhaps one thing we can still learn from our fungal allies is that parasitism and endless cycles of consumption and destruction are not the only way that a species—including our own—can relate to other forms of life. As Sheldrake suggests, fungi offer us numerous, powerful, and fascinating examples of multispecies collaboration and survival, even in periods of intense ecological crisis: "Fungi are survivors of ecological disruption. Their ability to cling on—and even flourish—through periods of catastrophic change is one of their defining characteristics. They are inventive, flexible and collaborative. With much of life on Earth threatened by human activity, are there ways we can partner with fungi to help us adapt?"[40] Learning to exist in more symbiotic and sympoietic relationships, as Haraway argues, might be our only hope of surviving in the increasingly chaotic and unpredictable world that we inhabit today. And mushrooms offer at least one hopeful model of this sort of symbiotic relationship—a way of thinking of ourselves not as separate "individuals" detached from the world around us but instead as radically decentralized assemblages that are intimately entangled with bacteria, plants, animals, fungi, and all sorts of other weird and wonderful stuff swirling around us all the time. They provide a powerful example of Haraway's sympoietic vision of a "compostable" future:

> We are compost, not posthuman; we inhabit the humusities, not the humanities. . . . Critters—human and not—become-with each other, compose and decompose each other, in every scale and register of time and stuff in sympoietic tangling, in ecological evolutionary developmental earthly worlding and unworlding.[41]

Like mushrooms, we already exist in multiple, complex relationships with our environment and with other organisms. We have clearly proven to be very good parasites and destroyers of other life; now in the twenty-first century, our survival may well depend upon learning to be better symbionts and saprobes. Such a more symbiotic, *mycorrhizal* form of relating might apply not only to other plant, animal, and fungal species, but also to other humans—including the various Indigenous communities who have so long borne the brunt of our drive for colonial expansion and commercial conquest. As we saw in chapter 6, one of the dangers of the new corporate push to develop psychedelics as marketable drugs is that they tend to "erase the long lineages and diverse knowledges that have curated, tended, and cultivated the human relationships to these plants," effectively repackaging Indigenous knowledge in order to sell drugs back to an underinformed public.[42] In contrast, authors such as Neşe Devenot, Trey Conner, and Richard Doyle suggest an alternative to this parasitic attitude, one that acknowledges the complex, entangled relationships between humans, plants, fungi, and cultural practices:

> We look forward to a culture that makes these medicines available in a safe and affordable way that respects the lineages of the knowledges that are essentially and not accidentally bundled with these plants—Indigenous and counterculture wisdoms for whom these medicines were never "fringe," but always foundational. In place of corporadelia's pursuit of standardization, we emphasize the care and wisdom of the Indigenous and countercultural teachings—traditions that have made psychedelics available to the emerging corporate/research partnership in the first place.[43]

Mushrooms may not necessarily or directly lead us to a utopian vision of global unity, care for the environment, or concern for other cultures;

but with their complex subterranean networks of mycelial webs, running silently yet vitally throughout the soil under our feet, even *non*psychedelic fungi present us with truly mind-boggling evidence of the radical interconnectivity, interdependence, and symbiosis that is already at work all around, beneath, and within us.[44] And with their remarkable ability to grow and thrive in degraded environments, they offer some hope of rediscovering a sense of beauty, awe, wonder, and "enchantment," even in the most fraught and frightening conditions of this damaged Earth that we now inhabit.[45] They remind us that we are all inextricably entangled and inherently symbiotic, whether we like it or not.

It does not necessarily require a heroic dose of psilocybin to recognize this profound and quite humbling sense of interdependence. In fact, it might only take a thoughtful walk in the woods, an intimate encounter with other cultures, or even just a careful attending to the weirdly, wildly sympoietic nature of our own bodies.

Maybe that's magical enough.

Notes

PREFACE

1. See Anna Tsing, *The Mushroom at the End of World: On the Possibility of Life in Capitalist Ruins* (Princeton, NJ: Princeton University Press, 2015), viii–ix.

2. See Hugh B. Urban, *Tantra: Sex, Secrecy, Politics, and Power in the Study of Religion* (Berkeley: University of California Press, 2003); Urban, *The Church of Scientology: A History of a New Religion* (Princeton, NJ: Princeton University Press, 2011); Urban, *New Age, Neopagan and New Religious Movements: Alternative Spirituality in Contemporary America* (Berkeley: University of California Press, 2015); Urban, *Secrecy: Silence, Power, and Religion* (Chicago: University of Chicago Press, 2021); Urban, *The Path of Desire: Living Tantra in Northeast India* (Chicago: University of Chicago Press, 2024).

INTRODUCTION

1. Rolfe and Rolfe, *The Romance of the Fungus World: An Account of Fungus Life in Its Numerous Guises, Both Real and Legendary* (London: Chapman and Hall, 1925), 17.

2. McKenna, *Food of the Gods: The Search for the Original Tree of Knowledge* (New York: Bantam Books, 1992), 273.

3. Petersen, "Taking Mushrooms for Depression Cured Me of My Atheism," *The Outline*, April 29, 2019, https://theoutline.com/post/7367/taking-mushrooms-for-depression-cured-me-of-my-atheism.

4. Wasson, "Seeking the Magic Mushroom," *Life*, May 13, 1957, 100–102, 109–20. At the time of the publication of the *Life* article, Wasson was vice president of public relations at J. P. Morgan & Co., where he had previously been a credit banker. He had also worked at Guaranty Trust Company of New York. See Thomas J. Riedlinger, ed., *The Sacred Mushroom Seeker: Essays for R. Gordon Wasson* (Portland: Dioscorides Press, 1990); Stephen I. Siff, "R. Gordon Wasson and the Publicity Campaign to Introduce Magic Mushrooms to Mid-Century America," *Revue française d'études américaines* 156, no. 3 (2018): 91–104; Jan R. Irvin, "R. Gordon Wasson: The Man, the Legend, the Myth," in *Entheogens and the Development of Culture*, ed. John Rush (Berkeley, CA: North Atlantic Books, 2013), 565–619.

5. See R. Gordon Wasson, Stella Kramrisch, Jonathan Ott, and Carl A. P. Ruck, *Persephone's Quest: Entheogens and the Origins of Religion* (New Haven, CT: Yale University Press, 1986); Brian C. Muraresku, *The Immortality Key: The Secret History of the Religion with No Name* (New York: St. Martin's Press, 2020); Jeffrey J. Kripal, *Esalen: America and the Religion of No Religion* (Chicago: University of Chicago Press,

2008), 115; Manasee Wagh, "Magic Mushrooms May Have Shaped Our Consciousness," *Popular Mechanics*, July 23, 2024, https://www.popularmechanics.com/science/a61678397/magic-mushrooms-psilocybin-human-consciousness/.

6. On Wasson and his interactions with María Sabina, see Andy Letcher, *Shroom: The Cultural History of the Magic Mushroom* (New York: Harper Collins, 2007), 100–112; Alvaro Estrada, *María Sabina: Her Life and Chants* (Santa Barbara, CA: Ross-Erikson, 1981); R. Gordon Wasson, George Cowan, Florence Cowan, and Willard Rhodes, *María Sabina and Her Mazatec Mushroom Velada* (New York: Harcourt Brace Jovanovich, 1974); Joan Halifax, *Shamanic Voices: A Survey of Visionary Narratives* (Harmondsworth: Arkana, 1979); Paloma Martinez-Cruz, "María Sabina as Vanishing Indian: Writing Mazatec Culture Out of Mushroom Medicine," in *Human Rights on the Move*, ed. Wendy S. Hesford, Momar K. Nduaye, and Amy Shuman (Columbus: Ohio State University Press, 2024), 177–93.

7. Wasson, in Estrada, *María Sabina*, 20.

8. See Don Lattin, *Changing Our Minds: Psychedelic Sacraments and the New Psychotherapy* (Santa Fe, NM: Synergetic Press, 2017), 67.

9. Roland R. Griffiths, Matthew W. Johnson, William A. Richards, Brian D. Richards, Robert Jesse, Katherine A. MacLean, Frederick S. Barrett, Mary P. Cosimano, and Maggie A. Klinedinst, "Psilocybin-Occasioned Mystical-Type Experience in Combination with Meditation and Other Spiritual Practices Produces Enduring Positive Changes in Psychological Functioning and in Trait Measures of Prosocial Attitudes and Behaviors," *Journal of Psychopharmacology* 32, no. 1 (2018): 49–69. See also Nicolas Langlitz, *Neuropsychedelia: The Revival of Hallucinogen Research Since the Decade of the Brain* (Berkeley: University of California Press, 2012).

10. See Andrew Jacobs, "With Promise of Legalization, Psychedelic Companies Joust over Future Profits," *The New York Times*, October 25, 2022, https://www.nytimes.com/2022/10/25/health/psychedelic-drug-therapy-patents.html; Bethany Halford, "Drug Companies Are Investing Big in Psychedelics," *Chemical and Engineering News*, March 6, 2022, https://cen.acs.org/pharmaceuticals/drug-development/Drug-companies-investing-big-psychedelics/100/i9.

11. See Letcher, *Shroom*; Lattin, *Changing Our Minds*; Christopher Partridge, *High Culture: Drugs, Mysticism, and the Pursuit of Transcendence in the Modern World* (New York: Oxford University Press, 2018); Erik Davis, *High Weirdness: Drugs, Esoterica, and Visionary Experience in the Seventies* (Cambridge, MA: MIT Press, 2019); William Richards, *Sacred Knowledge: Psychedelics and Religious Experiences* (New York: Columbia University Press, 2016); Don Lattin, *God on Psychedelics: Tripping Across the Rubble of Old-Time Religion* (Hannacroix, NY: Apocryphile Press, 2023).

12. See Letcher, *Shroom*, 5. "The history of magic mushrooms is much more than a good old tripper's tale. It is intertwined with and inseparable from the social, cultural, scientific and technological changes that have occurred since the industrial revolution, the forces that have wrought the modern western world." On the ubiquitous role of pharmaceutics in modern life, see Joseph Dumit, *Drugs for Life: How Pharmaceutical Companies Define Our Life* (Durham, NC: Duke University Press, 2012).

13. As Foucault uses the term (adapting it from Friedrich Nietzsche), genealogy does not attempt to trace a smooth linear history from past to present; instead, it seeks to "identify the accidents, the minute deviations—or conversely the complete reversals—the errors, the false appraisals, and the faulty calculations that gave birth to those things that continue to exist and have value for us" ("Nietzsche, Genealogy,

History," in *Language, Counter-Memory, and Practice*, ed. D. F. Bouchard [Ithaca, NY: Cornell University Press, 1977], 146). For a similar genealogical method, see Hugh B. Urban, *Tantra: Sex, Secrecy, Politics and Power in the Study of Religion* (Berkeley: University of California Press, 2003).

14. On the complex role of mycelia in ecosystems, see Paul Stamets, *Mycelium Running* (Berkeley, CA: Ten Speed Press, 2005); Merlin Sheldrake, *Entangled Life: How Fungi Make Our Worlds, Change Our Minds and Shape Our Future* (New York: Random House, 2020); Suzanne Simard, "Listening to the Mother Trees," *To the Best of Our Knowledge*, May 5, 2011, https://www.ttbook.org/interview/listening-mother-trees. See also Tsing, *Mushroom at the End of the World*; Eduardo Kohn, *How Forests Think: Toward an Anthropology Beyond the Human* (Berkeley: University of California Press, 2013).

15. See Jason Josephson-Storm, *The Myth of Disenchantment: Magic, Modernity and the Birth of the Human Sciences* (Chicago: University of Chicago Press, 2017); Christopher Partridge, *The Re-Enchantment of the West*, vol. 1, *Alternative Spiritualities, Sacralization, Popular Culture, and Occulture* (London: T&T Clark, 2005); Egil Asprem, *The Problem of Disenchantment: Scientific Naturalism and Esoteric Discourse, 1900–1939* (Albany, NY: SUNY Press, 2018); Sabina Magliocco and Sadie Rittman, "Faeries, Environmental Justice, and Re-Enchantment in Modern Pagan Narratives," *Journal for the Study of Religion, Nature, and Culture* 17, no. 3–4 (2023): 1–20.

16. Sara Lyons, "The Disenchantment/Re-Enchantment of the World: Aesthetics, Secularization, and the Gods of Greece from Friedrich Schiller to Walter Pater," *The Modern Language Review* 109, no. 44 (2017): 873–95. See Eugene McCarraher, "We Have Never Been Disenchanted," *Hedgehog Review*, Fall 2015, https://hedgehogreview.com/issues/re-enchantment/articles/we-have-never-been-disenchanted. Weber used the phrase in his "Science as Vocation," republished in *From Max Weber: Essays in Sociology*, ed. H. H. Gerth and C. Wright Mills (New York: Routledge, 2009), 155. See also Charles Taylor, *A Secular Age* (Cambridge, MA: Harvard University Press, 2007), 539–93.

17. Josephson-Storm, *Myth of Disenchantment*, 25, citing polling data from David Moore, "Three in Four Americans Believe in Paranormal," Gallup News Service, June 16, 2005; and Linda Lyons, "Paranormal Beliefs Come (Super) Naturally to Some," Gallup News Service, November 1, 2005. See also Magliocco and Rittman, "Faeries, Environmental Justice, and Re-Enchantment."

18. Josephson-Storm, *Myth of Disenchantment*, 3. See also Partridge, *Re-Enchantment of the West.*

19. Shelley, "The Sensitive Plant," in *The Complete Poetical Works of Percy Byshe Shelley*, ed. Thomas Hutchison (New York: Oxford University Press, 1914), 589.

20. See Greg A. Marley, *Chanterelle Dreams, Amanita Nightmares: The Love, Lore and Mystique of Mushrooms* (White River Junction, VT: Chelsea Green Publishing, 2010), 7: "Whether depicted as benign or malevolent, Baba Yaga often appeared with mushrooms."

21. Rolfe and Rolfe, *Romance of the Fungus World*, 17.

22. See Richard King, *Orientalism and Religion: Postcolonial Theory, India, and "the Mystic East"* (New York: Routledge, 1999), 14–15; William Parsons, ed., *Teaching Mysticism* (New York: Oxford University Press, 2011), 3–5; Louis Dupré, "Mysticism," in *The Encyclopedia of Religion*, ed. Lindsay Jones (New York: MacMillan, 2005), 9:6341.

There are, of course, many different definitions of mysticism. Peter Moore offers one of the more useful or at least less problematic definitions: "the term mysticism relates to traditions affirming direct knowledge of or communion with the source of ground of ultimate reality, as variously experienced in visionary, ecstatic, contemplative, or unitive states of consciousness and as diversely embodied in doctrines and practices expressing a unitary and compassionate view of the cosmos and human existence" ("Mysticism: Further Considerations," in *The Encyclopedia of Religion*, ed. Lindsay Jones [New York: MacMillan, 2005], 9:6355).

23. See Louis Bouyer, *The Christian Mystery: From Pagan Myth to Christian Mysticism* (Edinburgh: T&T Clark, 1990); Bernard McGinn, *The Foundations of Mysticism* (New York: Crossroad, 1991).

24. As Moore notes, "Given its persistently Christian associations and the fact that the term has no real counterpart in other traditions, it is not surprising that suitability of mysticism as a neutral, global term has been questioned by some scholars" ("Mysticism: Further Considerations," 6355). See also Hugh B. Urban, "Teaching 'Hindu Mysticism,'" in *Teaching Mysticism*, ed. William Parsons (New York: Oxford University Press, 2011), 11–13; David B. Gray, "The Mystical Dimensions of Buddhism," in *Teaching Mysticism*, ed. William Parsons (New York: Oxford University Press, 2011), 69; Lee Irwin, "Chosen by Spirits: Visionary Ecology and Indigenous Wisdom," in *Teaching Mysticism*, ed. William Parsons (New York: Oxford University Press, 2011), 123.

25. King, *Orientalism*, 33; see Urban, "Teaching 'Hindu Mysticism,'" 11–13.

26. Grace Jantzen, *Power, Gender, and Christian Mysticism* (Cambridge: Cambridge University Press, 1997), 12: "The current philosophical construction of mysticism is . . . only one in a series of social constructions of mysticism; and, like the others, is implicitly bound up with issues of authority and gender." On the concept of authority in general and religious authority in particular, see Bruce Lincoln, *Authority: Construction and Corrosion* (Chicago: University of Chicago Press, 1994).

27. On this point, see Kripal, *Esalen*.

28. Grim, *This Is Your Country on Drugs: The Secret History of Getting High in America* (Hoboken, NJ: John Wiley & Sons, 2009), 4. See also Dumit, *Drugs for Life*.

29. William James, *Varieties of Religious Experience: A Study in Human Nature* (New York: Modern Library 1902), 371–72. On James's work, see David B. Yaden and Andrew B. Newburg, *The Varieties of Spiritual Experience: Twenty-First Century Research and Perspectives* (New York: Oxford University Press, 2022); Karl Baier, "High Mysticism—On the Interplay Between the Psychedelic Movement and Academic Study of Mysticism," in *Constructions of Mysticism as a Universal: Roots and Interactions Across Borders*, ed. Annette Wilke, Robert Stephanus, and Robert Suckro (Wiesbaden: Harrassowitz Verlag, 2021), 365–66; Partridge, *High Culture*, 125–90.

30. James, *Varieties*, 385.

31. Emerson, *Nature, as Natural History and as Human History* (Boston: Beacon Press, 1985), 12–14.

32. James, *Varieties*, 377–78.

33. James, *Varieties*, 378. On nitrous oxide, see Partridge, *High Culture*, 62–87.

34. James, *Varieties*, 380, 382.

35. See Hugh B. Urban, *Scientology: The History of a New Religion* (Princeton, NJ: Princeton University Press, 2010), 37–39. The Indian guru Bhagwan Shree (aka Osho) was also said to have been a user of nitrous oxide, particularly during his time in Oregon in the 1980s. See Urban, *Zorba the Buddha: Sex, Spirituality, and Capitalism in the Global Osho Movement* (Berkeley: University of California Press, 2016).

36. Partridge, *High Culture*, 125–90.

37. On peyote, see Omer Stewart, *Peyote Religion: A History* (Norman: University of Oklahoma Press, 1993); Thomas Maroukis, *The Peyote Religion: Religious Freedom and the Native American Church* (Norman: University of Oklahoma Press, 2012).

38. Christopher Partridge, "Aleister Crowley on Drugs," *International Journal for the Study of New Religions* 7, no. 2 (2016): 125–51. See also Partridge, "Psychedelia Sub Rosa: The Eleusinian Mysteries and the Psychedelic Imagination," in *The Routledge Handbook of Religion and Secrecy*, ed. Hugh B. Urban and Paul Christopher Johnson (New York: Routledge, 2022), 60–61.

39. Crowley in Symonds, *The Great Beast: The Life and Magick of Aleister Crowley* (London: Hamilton & Co., 1971), 236.

40. Crowley, *The Rites of Eleusis* (privately printed, 1910), 9; cited in Partridge, "Psychedelia Sub Rosa," 61.

41. Huxley, *Doors of Perception* (New York: Harper & Row, 1954), 4.

42. Huxley, *Doors of Perception*, 4.

43. Huxley, *Doors of Perception*, 4–5. See also Kripal, *Comparing Religions: Coming to Terms* (Malden, MA, and Oxford: John Wiley & Sons, 2014), 381.

44. Huxley, *Moksha: Aldous Huxley's Classic Writings on Psychedelics and the Visionary Experience* (Rochester, VT: Park Street Press, 1999), 81. As he said of his second mescaline experience, "What came through the closed door was the realization . . . direct, total awareness, from inside, so to say, of Love as the primary and fundamental cosmic fact" (81). See also Baier, "High Mysticism," 370.

45. "Religion" has of course been defined in a countless ways and continues to be a contested category. However, for the purposes of this book, I largely follow Bruce Lincoln's four-part definition: 1) a discourse whose concerns transcend the human, temporal, and contingent; 2) a set of practices whose goal is to produce a proper social world and/or proper human subjects; 3) a community whose members construct their identity with reference to a religious discourse and its practices; 4) an institution that explains and regulates religious discourse, practice, and community (Lincoln, *Holy Terrors: Thinking About Religion After September 11* [Chicago: University of Chicago Press, 2003], 5–7). Following Lincoln's definition, experiences claiming to "mysticism without religion" would generally lack the third and fourth and sometimes even the second of these components.

46. Robert Gimello, "Mysticism in its Contexts," in *Mysticism and Religious Traditions*, ed. Steven T. Katz (New York: Oxford University Press, 1983), 86.

47. Richards, *Sacred Knowledge*, xxi.

48. Pollan, *How to Change Your Mind: What the New Science of Psychedelics Teaches Us About Consciousness, Dying, Addiction, Depression, and Transcendence* (New York: Penguin, 2018), 2–3. See also Kripal, *Esalen*, 115: "America was now witnessing the birth of a religious phenomenon of immense appeal and broad cultural, musical, medical, metaphysical and political and legal implications."

49. Lattin, *God on Psychedelics*, 3.

50. On this point see also Josephson-Storm, *Myth of Disenchantment*.

51. Fuller and Parsons, "Understanding Spiritual but Not Religious: An Introduction," in *Being Spiritual but Not Religious: Past, Present, Future(s)*, ed. William B. Parsons (New York: Routledge, 2020), 17. See also Yaden and Newburg, *Varieties of Spiritual Experience*.

52. Lattin, *God on Psychedelics*, xiii.

53. Muraresku, *Immortality Key*, 8–9.

54. Lattin, *God on Psychedelics*, x–xi. See also Langlitz, *Neuropsychedelia*, 48–49: "In contemporary neurotheology, an experience-centered spirituality and the heuristic individualism of cognitive neuroscience meet in the abstraction of experience from its social and cultural context. Mysticism is narrowed down to peak experiences and isolated neural events. Thereby it is also stripped of cultural difference and antagonism."

55. Lester Black, "Magic Mushroom Pastor Is Willing to Go to Jail for His New San Francisco Church," *San Francisco Gate*, April 12, 2023, https://www.sfgate.com/cannabis/article/oakland-magic-mushroom-church-sf-17885505.php.

56. McKenna, *Food of the Gods*, 273.

57. O. T. Oss and O. N. Oeric, *Psilocybin: Magic Mushroom Grower's Guide* (Berkeley, CA: Lux Natura, 1986), 7–8.

58. Dominique Strauss, Soumya Ghosh, Zurika Murray, and Marieka Gyrzenhout, "An Overview of the Taxonomy, Phylogenetics, and Ecology of the Psychedelic Genera of *Psilocybe, Panaeolus, Pluteus* and *Gymnopilus*," *Frontiers in Forests and Global Change* 5 (2022), https://www.frontiersin.org/articles/10.3389/ffgc.2022.813998/full.

59. Stamets, *Psilocybin Mushrooms of the World: An Identification Guide* (Berkeley, CA: Ten Speed Press, 1996), 16.

60. Stamets, *Psilocybin Mushrooms of the World*, 16.

61. Gastón Guzmán, "Hallucinogenic Mushrooms in Mexico: An Overview," *Economic Botany* 62, no. 3 (2008): 408. See Guzmán, *The Genus Psilocybe: A Systematic Revision of the Known Species Including the History, Distribution and Chemistry of the Hallucinogenic Species* (Vaduz: J. Cramer 1983); Stamets, *Psilocybin Mushrooms*.

Prior to 2007, the genus *Psilocybe* was thought to include both blue-staining (psychoactive) and non-blue-staining (nonpsychoactive) species; however, in keeping with the general reclassification and relabeling of many fungi that has taken place in the twenty-first century, the non-blue-stainers were transferred to the genus *Deconica*. See Scott A. Redhead, Jean-Marc Moncalvo, Rytas Vilgalys, P. Brandon Matheny, Laura Guzmán-Dávalos, and Gastón Guzmán, "Propose to Conserve the Name *Psilocybe* (*Basidiomycota*) with a Conserved Type," *Taxon* 56, no. 1 (2007): 255–57.

62. Strauss, Ghosh, Murray, and Gyrzenhout, "An Overview of the Taxonomy." Other genera with species containing psilocybin include *Agrocybe, Conocybe, Copelandia, Hypholoma, Inocybe, Psathyrella*, and *Stropharia*. See Christer Andersson, Jakob Kristinsson, and Jorn Gry, *Occurrence and Use of Hallucinogenic Mushrooms Containing Psilocybin Alkaloids* (Copenhagen, Denmark: Nordic Council of Ministers, 2009).

63. Matthew Meyer and Jason Slot, "The Evolution and Ecology of Psilocybin in Nature," *Fungal Genetics and Biology* 167 (2023), https://doi.org/10.1016/j.fgb.2023.103812: "It is possible that, like many other fungal specialized metabolites, psilocybin evolved as a defense against antagonistic organisms such as fungivores and resource competition. However, given its neuroactive properties, psilocybin may increase spore dispersal distance by altering the behavior of animals visiting the mushroom and expanding their travel radius." See also Peter Spiteller, "Chemical Defense Strategies of Higher Fungi," *Chemistry: A European Journal* 14, no. 30 (2008), https://doi.org/10.1002/chem.200800292; Karin Heineman, "The Not-So-Trippy Reason Mushrooms Are Psychedelic," *Inside Science*, October 4, 2018, https://ww2.aip.org/inside-science/the-not-so-trippy-reason-mushrooms-are-psychedelic.

64. Letcher, *Shroom*, 17.

65. Letcher, *Shroom*, 18–20.

66. See McKenna, *The Archaic Revival: Speculations on Psychedelic Mushrooms, the Amazon, Virtual Reality, UFOs, Evolution, Shamanism, the Rebirth of the Goddess, and the End of History* (San Francisco: HarperSanFrancisco, 1991).

67. Michael Pollan, quoted in "Psychedelics: The Scientific Renaissance of Mind-Altering Drugs," *Big Think*, 2021, https://www.youtube.com/watch?v=5T0LmbWROKY.

68. Johnson, "How Psychedelics Work, Explained in Under 6 Minutes," *Big Think*, 2022, https://www.youtube.com/watch?v=yS9FBB19Ws0. See also Rebecca Smausz, Joanna Neill, and John Gigg, "Neural Mechanisms Underlying Psilocybin's Therapeutic Potential—The Need for Preclinical in vivo Electrophysiology," *Journal of Psychopharmacology* 36, no. 7 (2022): 781–93.

69. Robin L. Carhart-Harris, David Erritzoe, Tim Williams, James M. Stone, Laurence J. Reed, Alessandro Colasanti, Robin J. Tyacke, Robert Leech, Andrea L. Malizia, Kevin Murphy, Peter Hobden, John Evans, Amanda Feilding, Richard G. Wise, and David J. Nutt, "Neural Correlates of the Psychedelic State as Determined by fMRI Studies with Psilocybin," *Proceedings of the National Academy of Science* 109, no. 6 (2012), https://doi.org/10.1073/pnas.1119598109; Robin L. Carhart-Harris, Suresh Muthukumaraswamy, Leor Roseman, Mendel Kaelen, Wouter Droog, Kevin Murphy, Enzo Tagliazucchi, Eduardo E. Schenberg, Timothy Nest, Csaba Orban, Robert Leech, Luke T. Williams, Tim M. Williams, Mark Bolstridge, Ben Sessa, John McGonigle, Martin I. Sereno, David Nichols, Peter J. Hellyer, Peter Hobden, John Evans, Krish D. Singh, Richard G. Wise, H. Valerie Curran, Amanda Feilding, and David J. Nutt, "Neural Correlates of the LSD Experience Revealed by Multimodal Neuroimaging," *Proceedings of the National Academy of Science* 113, no. 17 (2016), https://doi.org/10.1073/pnas.1518377113; Robin L. Carhart-Harris, "How Do Psychedelics Work?," *Current Opinion in Psychiatry* 32, no. 1 (2019), https://doi.org/10.1097/YCO.0000000000000467.

70. Pollan, *How to Change*, 302.

71. James J. Gattuso, Daniel Perkins, Simon Ruffell, Andrew J. Lawrence, Daniel Hoyer, Laura H. Jacobson, Christopher Timmermann, David Castle, Susan L. Rossell, Luke A Downey, Broc A. Pagni, Nicole L. Galvão-Coelho, David Nutt, and Jerome Sarris, "Default Mode Network Modulation by Psychedelics: A Systematic Review," *International Journal of Neuropsychopharmacology* 26, no. 3 (2023), https://doi.org/10.1093/ijnp/pyac074.

72. Pollan, *How to Change*, 307.

73. Pace and Devenot, "Right-Wing Psychedelia: Case Studies in Cultural Plasticity and Political Pluripotency," *Frontiers in Psychology* 12 (2021), https://doi.org/10.3389/fpsyg.2021.733185.

On this point see also Sam Woolfe, *Altered States: Critical Essays on Psychedelic Consciousness* (Iff Books, 2025); Shayla Love, "The False Promise of Psychedelic Utopia," *Vice*, November 1, 2021, https://www.vice.com/en/article/the-false-promise-of-psychedelic-utopia/.

On Aum Shrinrikyo's use of LSD, see Mark Juergensmeyer, *Terror in the Mind of God: The Global Rise of Religious Violence* (Berkeley: University of California Press, 2017), chap. 6. On the Manson family and LSD, see Jeff Guinn, *Manson: The Life and Times of Charles Manson* (New York: Simon and Schuster, 2013). See also

Rick Strassman, "The Psychedelic Religion of Mystical Consciousness," *Journal of Psychedelic Studies* 2, no. (2018): 4: "It is important to refrain from glorifying the psychedelic drug state. Simply look at how Charles Manson used LSD's meaning-enhancing effects in those similarly predisposed to particular goals and aspirations."

74. Pace and Devenot, "Right Wing Psychedelia." See also Love, "The Case Against Psychedelic Utopianism"; David Dupuis and Samuel Veissière, "Culture, Context and Ethics in the Therapeutic Use of Hallucinogens: Psychedelics as Active Super-Placebos?," *Transcultural Psychiatry* 59, no. 5 (2022), https://doi.org/10.1177/1363461522113146.

75. For example, Ido Hartogsohn argues that the complex religious, ritual, and cultural "set and setting" of Santo Daime produces a unique experience that is unlikely to be replicated outside of that context: "Drinking daime is much more than just drinking ayahuasca. The effects of ayahuasca are profoundly mediated through complex layers of intentions, expectations, visual, auditory, and symbolic environments, social and cultural systems, etc. . . . Such contextual factors produce a distinct form of experience, that is often markedly different form the experiences produced by other contextual environments, e.g., those of neo-shamanic ayahuasca rituals" ("Set and Setting in Santo Daime," *Frontiers in Pharmacology* 12 (2021), https://doi.org/10.3389/fphar.2021.651037). See also Alexandre Augusto de Deus Pontual, Luís Fernando Tófoli, Clarissa Mendonça Corradi-Webster, Kim Van Oorsouw, Alicia Raquel Osuna Delgado, and Johannes G. Ramaekers, "The Influence of Ceremonial Settings on Mystical and Challenging Experiences Occasioned by Ayahuasca: A Survey Among Ritualistic and Religious Ayahuasca Users," *Frontiers in Psychology* 13 (2022), https://doi.org/10.3389/fpsyg.2022.857372.

76. Guzmán, "Hallucinogenic Mushrooms," 404.

77. Haraway, *Staying with the Trouble: Making Kin in the Chthulucene* (Durham, NC: Duke University Press, 2016), 98. As Haraway suggests, "Perhaps as sensual molecular curiosity and definitely as insatiable hunger, irresistible attraction toward enfolding each other is the vital motor of living and dying on earth. Critters interpenetrate one another, loop around and through one another, eat each another, get indigestion, and partially digest and partially assimilate one another, and thereby establish sympoietic arrangements that are otherwise known as cells, organisms, and ecological assemblages" (58).

CHAPTER ONE

1. Fray Toribio de Benavente o Motolinía, *Memoriales o libro de las cosas de la Nueva España y de los naturales de ella* (Mexico City: Universidad Nacional Autónoma de México, 1971), 32. There is some debate as to whether the best translation here is "flesh of god" or "divine flesh" or "meat of gods"; see Jaime Lara, "A Meaty Incarnation: Making Sense of Divine Flesh," in *Image and Incarnation: The Early Modern Doctrine of the Pictorial Image*, ed. Walter Melion and Lee Palmer Wandel (Leiden: Brill, 2013), 109–36.

2. Staal, "How a Psychoactive Substance Becomes a Ritual: The Case of Soma," *Social Research* 68, no. 3 (2001): 772.

3. See R. Gordon Wasson, Stella Kramrisch, Jonathan Ott, and Carl A. P. Ruck, *Persephone's Quest: Entheogens and the Origins of Religion* (New Haven, CT: Yale University Press, 1986); Allegro, *The Sacred Mushroom and the Cross: A Study of the*

Nature and Origins of Christianity Within the Fertility Cults of the Ancient Near East (New York: Bantam, 1971); McKenna, *Food of the Gods: The Search for the Original Tree of Knowledge* (New York: Bantam Books, 1992); Muraresku, *The Immortality Key: The Secret History of the Religion with No Name* (New York: St. Martin's Press, 2020).

4. Manasee Wagh, "Magic Mushrooms May Have Shaped Our Consciousness," *Popular Mechanics*, July 23, 2024, https://www.popularmechanics.com/science/a61678397/magic-mushrooms-psilocybin-human-consciousness/.

5. On the *Amanita*/soma debate, see John Brough, "Soma and *Amanita muscaria*," *Bulletin of the School of Oriental and African Studies* 34, no. 2 (1971): 331–62; Harry Falk, "Soma I and II," *Bulletin of the School of Oriental and African Studies* 52, no. 1 (1989): 77–90; Jan E. M. Houben, "The Soma-Haoma Problem: Introductory Overview and Observations on the Discussion," *Electronic Journal of Vedic Studies* 9, no. 1 (2003): 3–44; Matthew Clark, *The Tawny One: Soma, Haoma, and Ayahuasca* (London: Muswell Hill Press, 2017); James McHugh, "Soma, Ancient Drugs and Modern Scholars," in *An Unholy Brew: Alcohol in Indian History and Religions*, ed. James McHugh (New York: Oxford University Press, 2021), 289–97.

On the ergot/Mysteries debate, see Walter Burkert, *Ancient Mystery Cults* (Cambridge, MA: Harvard University Press, 1989), 108; Michael B. Cosmopoulos, *Bronze Age Eleusis and the Origins of the Eleusinian Mysteries* (Cambridge: Cambridge University Press, 2015), chap. 2; Sharday Mosurinjohn and Richard Ascough, "Psychedelics, Eleusis, and the Invention of Religious Experience," *Psychedelic Medicine* (2025), https://doi.org/10.1177/28314425251361835.

6. For a good bibliographic overview, see Nicholas Spiers, Beatriz Caiuby Labate, Anna O. Ermakova, Patrick Farrell, Osiris Sinuhé Gonzáles Romero, Ibrahim Gabriell, and Nidia Olivera, "Indigenous Psilocybin Mushroom Practices: An Annotated Bibliography," *Journal of Psychedelic Studies* 8, no. 1 (2024): 3–25.

7. See Wagh, "Magic Mushrooms May Have Shaped Our Consciousness."

8. Gastón Guzmán, *The Genus Psilocybe: A Systematic Revision of the Known Species Including the History, Distribution and Chemistry of the Hallucinogenic Species* (Berlin: J. Cramer, 1983); Paul Stamets, *Psilocybin Mushrooms of the World: An Identification Guide* (Berkeley, CA: Ten Speed Press, 1996).

9. Davis, *High Weirdness*, 108. On this point, see also Graham Harvey and Robert J. Wallis, eds., *Historical Dictionary of Shamanism* (Lanham, MD: Rowman and Littlefield, 2007), 142: "While entheogen use is often perceived to be prevalent in shamanism worldwide, few indigenous shamans have made mushrooms an important part of their practice. Most of these are located in Central America and South America. . . . One major reason for the overemphasis on mushrooms is that the mycologist Gordon Wasson suggested fly agaric was the Vedic 'Soma' and that 'magic mushrooms' more generally produced the religious impulse in humans."

10. See David R. Benjamin, *Mushrooms: Poisons and Panaceas* (New York: W. H. Freeman and Company, 1995), 17: "Despite the wide availability of fungi across North America continent, Native Americans have never used mushrooms as an important food source. Most ethnobotanical surveys failed to mention mushrooms as a significant or even occasional, component of the diet." See also "Mushrooms as Sacred Objects in North America," *Cornell Mushroom Blog*, 2010, https://blog.mycology.cornell.edu/2010/01/06/mushrooms-as-sacred-objects-in-north-america/#:~:text=Because%20of%20its%20strong%20fragrance,objects%20and%20a%20healing%20tool.

11. Guzmán, "Hallucinogenic Mushrooms in Mexico: An Overview," *Economic Botany* 62, no. 3 (2008): 404–12.

12. Guzmán documents use of *Psilocybe* by the Nahuatls in the states of Mexico, Morelos, and Puebla; the Matlatzincas in state of Mexico; the Totonacs in state of Veracruz; and the Mazatecs, Mixes, Zapotecs, and Chatinos in Oaxaca. The species used include *P. aztecorum, P. barrerae, P. caerulescens, P. cubensis, P. fagicola, P. mexicana, P. zapotecorum*, and *P. subcubensis*, among others ("Hallucinogenic Mushrooms," 408).

13. On possible *Psilocybe* use in South America, see Peter Trutmann, *The Forgotten Mushrooms of Ancient Peru* (Lima: Global Mountain Action, 2012); Constantino M. Torres, "The Use of Psychoactive Plants by Ancient Indigenous Populations of the North Andes," *Journal of Psychedelic Studies* 3, no. 2 (2019): 198–211; J. M. Rodríguez Arce, and M. A. Arce Cerdas, "Ritual Consumption of Psychoactive Fungi and Plants in Ancestral Costa Rica," *Journal of Psychedelic Studies* 3, no. 2 (2019): 179–97.

On possible *Psilocybe* use in Africa, see B. van der Merwe, A. Rockefeller, A Kilian, C. Clark, M. Sethathi, T. Moult, and K. Jacobs, "A Description of Two Novel Psilocybe Species from Southern Africa and Some Notes on Traditional African Mushroom Use," *Mycologia* 116, no. 5 (2024), https://doi.org/10.1080/00275514.2024.2363137; Norman Zimunda Nyazema and Jonathan Tinotenda Chanyandura, "The Use and Potential Abuse of Psychoactive Plants in Southern Africa: An Overview of Evidence and Future Potential," *Frontiers in Pharmacology* 14 (2024), https://doi.org/10.3389/fphar.2024.1269247; Gastón Guzmán, Stuart C. Nixon, Florencia Ramírez-Guillén, and Alonso Cortés-Pérez, "Psilocybe s. Str. (Agaricales, Strophariaceae) in Africa with Description of a New Species from the Congo," *Sydowia* 66, no. 1 (2014): 43–53.

Some reference to hallucinogenic mushrooms is also found in China and Japan, though the evidence is scant. See Yoshihiro Matsushima, Fumio Eguchi, Tadahiro Kikukawa, and Takahide Matsuda, "Historical Overview of Psychoactive Mushrooms," *Inflammation and Regeneration*, 29, no. 1 (2009): 47–58; Hui-lin Li, "Hallucinogenic Plants in Chinese Herbals," *Journal of Psychedelic Drugs* 10, no. 1 (1978): 17–26.

There are a few recent accounts of *Psilocybe* mushrooms being used by Nepalese shamans. Thus, one shaman described the use of a *Psilocybe* species that grows on cow dung: "These small mushrooms can be used as amrita. For this, they are roasted with some salt. Through them the shamans receive a heavenly feeling. To achieve this they take a handful of the fresh mushrooms" (Claudia Müller-Ebeling, Christian Rätsch, and Surendra Bahadur Shahi, *Shamanism and Tantra in the Himalayas* [Rochester, VT: Inner Traditions, 2002], 169). However, it should be noted that this account was recorded long after Nepal had become inundated with tourists and psychedelic travelers in the 1960s and 1970s. The same text notes that "Freak Street" in Kathmandu during the 1970s was flooded with psychedelic tourism and many "mushroom motifs." So in the absence of older ethnographic accounts, it is difficult to know whether the use of *Psilocybe* predates the 1960s here.

14. Harri Nyberg, "Religious Use of Hallucinogenic Fungi: A Comparison Between Siberian and Mesoamerican Cultures," *Karstenia* 32 (1992): 76. As Wasson enthusiastically put it, "The so-called mushroom stones . . . were the symbol of a religion, like the cross in the Christian religion or the star of Judea" (Wasson, *Hallucinogenic Fungi of Mexico*, quoted in Leary, *High Priest*, 12).

15. Letcher, *Shroom*, 77. See also Giorgio Samorini, "Mushroom Effigies in Archaeology: A Methodological Approach," in *Fly Agaric: A Compendium of History, Pharmacology, Mythology and Exploration*, ed. Kevin Feeney (Ellensburg, WA: Fly Agaric Press, 2020), 269–96.

16. Wasson, "The Role of Flowers in the Nahuatl Culture: A Suggested Interpretation," *Botanical Museum Leaflets* 25, no. 8 (1978): 305–24.

17. For a critique of Wasson's interpretation, see Jose Alejandro Renteria, "Xochipilli: Unveiling the Spirit of a Nahua Deity," MA thesis, San Diego State University, 2018.

18. Osiris Gonzáles Romero, "Ritual and Religious Uses of Psilocybe Mushrooms in Mesoamerica," *Center for the Study of World Religions*, October 9, 2024, https://cswr.hds.harvard.edu/news/2024/10/ritual-and-religious-uses-psilocybe-mushrooms-mesoamerica. See also Otto Adelhofer, ed., *Codex Vindobonensis Mexicanus 1: vollständige faksimile ausgabe im original format* (Graz: Akademische Druck- und Verlagsanstalt, 1974); Jill Leslie Furst, *Codex Vindobonensis Mexicanus I: A Commentary* (Albany: State University of New York, 1978), 203–6; Alfonso Caso, "Representaciones de hongos en los codices," *Estudios de Cultura Náhuatl* 4 (1963): 27–36.

As Romero explains the image, "The God of Wind carries on his back a deity named Lady Eleven Lizard, who holds four mushrooms on her headdress. Behind the two is Lady Four Lizard, who also has four mushrooms on her headdress. Both figures represent the female spirit of the sacred mushrooms. . . . The God of Wind, Lady Eleven Lizard, and Lady four Lizard are moving to the left, toward the God of Rain and Thunderbolts. . . . Above them, the god Nine-Wind sings while making music. . . . Lord Seven-Flower is in front of Nine-Wind. . . . The Lord holds two mushrooms. To their left, deities participating in the ritual each carry two mushrooms in their hands" ("Ritual and Religious Uses").

19. See Zelia Nuttall, *The Book of the Life of the Ancient Mexicans, Containing an Account of Their Rites and Superstitions* (Berkeley: University of California Press, 1903), 78; Elizabeth Hill Boone, *The Codex Magliabechiano and the Lost Prototype of the Magliabechiano Group* (Berkeley: University of California Press, 1983); Guzmán, "Hallucinogenic Mushrooms in Mexico," 404–12.

20. Wasson, *Wonderous Mushroom* 106–7.

21. Letcher, *Shroom*, 73.

22. Wasson, *Wonderous Mushroom*, xviii. See Pollan, *How to Change*, 109.

23. Motolinía, *Memoriales o libro de las cosas de la Nueva España*, 32. See Lara, "A Meaty Incarnation: Making Sense of Divine Flesh," 109–36.

24. Fray Bernardino de Sahagún, *The Florentine Codex: General History of the Things in New Spain*, trans. A .J. O. Anderson and C. E. Dibble (Salt Lake City: University of Utah Press, 1950–63). The text discusses mushrooms in book 9, 38–39; book 10, 12, 20, 37, 49, 55, 88, 173; and book 11, 120, 129, 130.

25. Guzmán, "Hallucinogenic Mushrooms, 404–12. See Guzman, *The Genus Psilocybe*.

26. Sahagún, *Florentine Codex*, book 9, 38–39.

27. Sahagún, *Florentine Codex*, book 10, 20.

28. Sahagún, *Florentine Codex*, book 10, 37.

29. Motolinía, *Memoriales o libro de las cosas de la Nueva España*, 32.

30. Fray Diego Durán, *The History of the Indies of New Spain*, trans. Ignacio Bernal (New York: Orion Press, 1964), 180. Similarly at the coronation of King Ahuitzotl, it is said that guests were offered "wild mushrooms" and then "became excited, filled with pleasure and lost their senses" (189).

31. Letcher, *Shroom*, 74–75.

32. Durán, *History of the Indies of New Spain*, 225. Another Spanish account that mentions mushroom consumption is Francisco Hernández, *Historia de las plantas de Nueva España*, vols. 1–3 (Mexico City: Imprenta Universitaria Mexico, 1942–46). Hernández mentions three types of hallucinogenic fungi.

33. Wasson, *Wondrous Mushroom*, 211.

34. Quoted in Wasson and Wasson, *Mushrooms, Russia, and History*, 226–27.

35. Guzmán, "Hallucinogenic Mushrooms," 408; Guzmán, *Genus Psilocybe*, 34; Brian P. Akers, ed., *The Sacred Mushrooms of Mexico: Assorted Texts* (Lanham, MD: University Press of America, 2006).

36. Guzmán, "Hallucinogenic Mushrooms," 404–10.

37. Guzmán, "Hallucinogenic Mushrooms," 404.

38. Guzmán, "Hallucinogenic Mushrooms," 408–9; Guzmán, *Genus Psilocybe*, 41.

39. Guzmán, *Genus Psilocybe*, 41.

40. Guzmán, "Hallucinogenic Mushrooms," 409–10. See Jean Bassett Johnson, "The Elements of Mazatec Witchcraft," *Ethnological Studies* 9 (1939): 128–50; Paloma Martinez-Cruz, *Women and Knowledge in Mesoamerica: From East L.A. to Anahuac* (Tucson: University of Arizona Press, 2011), 106–10.

41. See Gastón Guzmán, Florencia Ramírez-Guillén, and Constaino M. Torres, "The Hallucinogenic Species of Psilocybe in Columbia," *International Journal of Medicinal Mushrooms* 6, no. 1 (2004), https://doi.org/10.1615/IntJMedMushr.v6.i1.90; Trutmann, *Forgotten Mushrooms of Ancient Peru*; Torres, "Use of Psychoactive Plants."

Jesuit accounts report that Yurimagua Indians of the Amazon in Peru consumed a beverage prepared from a "tree fungus." Schultes speculates that it could have been *P. yugensis*, but there is no surviving evidence of this practice. See Richard Evans Schultes and Albert Hofmann, *The Botany and Chemistry of Hallucinogens* (Springfield, IL: Charles C. Thomas, 1980), 66.

42. Brian Akers, Juan Francisco Ruiz, Alan Piper, and Carl A. P. Ruck, "A Prehistoric Mural Depicting Neurotropic Mushrooms?," *Economic Botany* 65, no. 2 (2011): 121–28; Brian Akers, "A Cave in Spain Contains the Earliest Known Depictions of Mushrooms," *Mushroom: The Journal of Wild Mushrooming*, https://www.mushroomthejournal.com/a-cave-in-spain-contains-the-earliest-known-depictions-of-mushrooms/; Samorini, "Mushroom Effigies," 282–84.

43. Oss and Oeric, *Psilocybin*, 71. The original cave image on which the drawing is based can be found in Jean-Dominique Lajoux, *The Rock Paintings of Tassili* (New York: World Publishing, 1963), 71.

44. Akers, "A Cave in Spain."

45. Van der Merwe, Rockefeller, Kilian, Clark, Sethathi, Moult, and Jacobs, "A Description of Two Novel Psilocybe Species."

46. See Nyazema and Chanyandura, "The Use and Potential Abuse of Psychoactive Plants": "Because of the legal status of mushroom use, coupled with continued secrecy surrounding some traditional medical practices, it was difficult to obtain information on how *P. cubensis* is actually employed in culturally sanctioned visionary experiences in ritual or religious contexts."

47. *Amanita muscaria* has several variant species. *A. muscaria var. muscaria* is native to Europe, Asia, and Alaska. The species found in North America include *A. muscaria var. flavivolvata*, *A. muscaria var. guessowii*, *A. muscaria var. persicina*, and *A. muscaria var. alba*. For a thorough overview of *A. muscaria* from a range of scientific and

cultural perspectives, see Kevin M. Feeney, ed., *Fly Agaric: A Compendium of History, Pharmacology, Mythology, and Exploration* (Ellensburg, WA: Fly Agaric Press, 2021).

48. L. Satora, D. Pach, B. Butryn, P. Hydzik, and B. Balicka-Slusarczyk, "Fly agaric (*Amanita muscaria*) Poisoning, Case Report and Review," *Toxicon* 45, no. 7 (2005): 941–43.

49. Letcher, *Shroom*, 133. See Hutton, *Shamans*, 100–102; Nyberg "Religious Use," 71–80.

50. According to John Ramsbottom, the Koryak have a mythology surrounding the mushroom. In this narrative, the deity Vajiyinin ("Existence") spat on to the earth; his spittle became the wapaq mushroom, and his saliva became the warts. Raven then experienced the power of wapaq and was so exhilarated that he told it to grow forever on earth so the people could learn from it (*Mushrooms and Toadstools* [New York: Collins, 1953], 45).

51. Krasheninnikov, *Description of the Kamchatka Land* (St. Petersburg, 1755), quoted in Benjamin, *Mushrooms*, 297–98. See Letcher, *Shroom*, 122; Nyberg, "Religious Use"; M. Saar, "Ethnomycological Data from Siberia and Northeast Asia on the Effect of Amanita muscaria," *Journal of Ethnopharmacology* 31 (1991): 157–73; P. T. Furst, *Hallucinogens and Culture* (Novato, CA: Chandler & Sharp, 1976); W. Bogoras, *The Chukchee: The Jesup North Pacific Exploration* (New York: G. E. Stechert, 1904–9).

52. Von Strahlenburg, *An Historic-Geographic Description of the North and Eastern Parts of Europe and Asia* (Stockholm, 1780), quoted in Benjamin, *Mushrooms*, 297. A similar account appears in Karl von Ditmar, *Reise und Aufenhalt in Kamtschatka in der Jahren 1851–1855* (St. Petersburg, 1900): "Mukhumor eaters describe the narcosis as most beautiful and splendid. The most wondrous images, such as they never see in their lives otherwise, pass before their eyes and lull them into a state of the most intense enjoyment."

53. The category of "shamanism" is notoriously problematic and has a complex history. As Ronald Hutton explains, the term "shaman" was first circulated in Russian literature on Siberian religions in the seventeenth century, and the general term "shamanism" was coined much later to refer to a wide range of phenomena found in many Indigenous cultures: "The word 'shaman' was apparently first printed in the memoirs of the Russian churchman Avvakum, in 1672, and seems to have reached Western and Central European scholarship twenty years later in the word of Nicholas Witsen. . . . 'Shamanism,' by contrast is . . . a scholarly construct, used to group together beliefs and activities across the world which have some apparent relationship with those observed in Siberia. It is also generally admitted that no commonly agreed definition has ever been ascribed to the term, and that the recent boom in studies associated with it have only worsened the confusion and diversity in its use" (*Shamans*, vii).

54. See Balazs, "The Hungarian Shaman's Technique of Trance Induction," in *Popular Beliefs and Folklore Tradition in Siberia*, ed. Vilmos Diószegi (Bloomington: University of Indiana Press, 1968), 53–75; Eliade, *Shamanism*, 221. For a good overview of this debate, see Hutton, *Shamans*, 100–102.

55. Sokolova, "A Survey of the Ob-Ugrian Shamanism," in *Shamanism Past and Present*, ed. Mihály Hoppál and Otto von Sadovszky (Los Angeles: Hungarian Academy of Arts and Sciences, 1989), 155–64.

56. Nyberg, "Religious Use." See Anna-Leena Siikala, *The Rite Technique of the Siberian Shaman* (Suomalainen tiedeakatemia: Akateeminen kirjakauppa [jakaja], 1978), 1–385.

57. Letcher, *Shroom*, 133. On this point, see Hutton, *Shamans*, 102; Sokolova, "A Survey."

58. Nyberg, "Religious Use," 71.

59. Saar, "Ethnomycological Data from Siberia and Northeast Asia on the Effect of Amanita muscaria," *Journal of Ethnopharmacology* 31 (1991): 157–73; Nyberg, "Religious Use," 75.

60. Nyberg, "Religious Use," 75. See Saar, "Ethnomycological Data."

61. Wasson, *Wondrous Mushroom*, 43–44.

62. There are a few accounts of Kirati shamans in Nepal using *A. muscaria*: "The Kirati shamans use the fly agaric not more than ten times per year to travel and fly. They also use the roasted fly agaric as medicine for their patients" (Müller-Ebeling, Rätsch, and Shahi, *Shamanism and Tantra*, 177). Again, however, these accounts postdate the 1960s–1970s psychedelic heyday in Nepal, so it is difficult to know whether the use of these mushrooms existed earlier in this region.

The historian Carlo Ginzburg briefly discussed the idea of whether *A. muscaria* might have contributed to accounts of ecstatic experience in the narratives surrounding the witches' sabbath in Europe; but he too believes that the evidence is inconclusive (*Ecstasies: Deciphering the Witches' Sabbath* [New York: Penguin, 1992], 305–7).

63. The literature on soma and its possible identity is vast. See for starters Brough, "Soma and Amanita Muscaria"; Staal, "How a Psychoactive Substance Becomes a Ritual"; Falk, "Soma I and II"; McHugh, "Soma, Ancient Drugs and Modern Scholars"; George Thompson, "Soma and Ecstasy in the *Rg Veda*," *Electronic Journal of Vedic Studies* 9, no. 1 (2003), http://dx.doi.org/10.11588/ejvs.2003.1.788.

64. See Jan Gonda, *A History of Indian Literature: Vedic Literature* (Wiesbaden: Otto Harrassowitz, 1978), 328; Natalia Lidova, *Drama and Ritual of Early Hinduism* (New Delhi: Motilal Banarsidass, 1994), 38; Stephanie W. Jamison and Joel P. Brereton, trans., *The Rigveda: The Earliest Religious Poetry of India*, vol. 1 (New York: Oxford University Press, 2014), 42–43; Clark, *The Tawny One*, 11–13.

65. Brough, "Soma and Amanita Muscaria," 339.

66. *Rigveda*, 8.48.1–3; translated by Jamison and Brereton, *Rigveda*, 2:1128.

67. *Rigveda*, 10.119.2–3, 7–9, 12; translated by Jamison and Brereton, *Rigveda*, 3:1590.

68. See Clark, *Tawny One*, 37–47.

69. Ian A. Baker, "Nectar of the Blue Goddess: A Living Tradition of Soma Consumption in West Bengal," in *Expanding Mindscapes: A Global History of Psychedelics*, ed. Erika Dyck and Chris Elcock (Cambridge, MA: MIT Press, 2023), 23–50.

70. Clark, *Tawny One*, 205–14.

71. See Doniger's recollections in "'Somatic' Memories of R. Gordon Wasson," in *The Sacred Mushroom Seeker: Essays for R. Gordon Wasson*, ed. T. J. Riedlinger (Portland: Dioscorides Press, 1990), 55–59.

72. Wasson, *Soma: Divine Mushroom of Immortality* (New York: Harcourt Brace Jovanovich, 1971), 29–39. On the urination question, see Jamison and Brereton's translation: "The embodied cloud is milked of ghee and milk. The navel of truth, the immortal [drink] is born. United, possessed of good drops, they please him. The swollen men piss down the one propelled" (*Rigveda*, 9.18.4).

73. Brough, "Soma and Amanita Muscaria," 331–62.

74. Brough, "Soma and Amanita Muscaria," 338. The pounding is described, for example, in *Shatapatha Brahmana*, 3.9.4.19 and 4.1.1.8, and in *Katyayana Shrautasutra*,

9.4.14–15. See Clark, *Tawny One*, 124: "Wasson's textual evidence is almost entirely from passages in the *Rigveda*, and he ignores detailed descriptions, particularly in the *Yajurveda* and *Shatapatha Brahmana*, of the elaborate pounding with stones of the soma plant . . . the pounding of the soma stalks with stones seems to rule out the use of fly agaric."

75. Brough, "Soma and Amanita Muscaria," 341.

76. Brough, "Soma and Amanita Muscaria," 360. On soma and warrior virility, see also McHugh, "Soma, Ancient Drugs, and Modern Scholars"; Jarrod Whitaker, *Strong Arms and Drinking Strength: Masculinity, Violence, and the Body in Ancient India* (New York: Oxford University Press, 2011), 151–52.

Some authors have tried to get around this point by suggesting that the method of straining soma after pressing and/or mixing it with milk could have reduced the toxic effects. See Kevin Feeney, "Revisiting Wasson's Soma: Exploring the Effects of Preparation on the Chemistry of *Amanita muscaria*," *Journal of Psychoactive Drugs* 42, no. 4 (2000): 499–506; Kevin Feeney and Trent Austin, "Soma's Third Filter: New Findings Supporting the Identification of Amanita muscaria as the Ancient Sacrament of the Vedas," in *Fly Agaric: A Compendium of History, Pharmacology, Mythology and Exploration*, ed. Kevin Feeney (Ellensburg, WA: Fly Agaric Press, 2020): 51–62.

77. Wasson consumed *A. muscaria* with some coworkers in the mid-1960s, and all of them "felt universally nauseous and several became ill. They fell into deep slumbers and could not be aroused easily. According to Wasson, 'When in this state, I once had vivid dreams, but nothing like what happened when I took Psilocybe mushrooms in Mexico, where I did not sleep at all'" (Marley, *Chanterelle Dreams*, 155).

78. Houben, "Soma-Haoma Problem," 3–44.

79. Houben, "Soma-Haoma Problem," 23.

80. See Georgia Frank, "Taste and See: The Eucharist and the Eyes of Faith in the Fourth Century," *Church History* 70, no. 4 (2001): 619–43; Caroline Walker Bynum, "Women Mystic and Eucharistic Devotion in the Thirteenth Century," in *Beyond the Body Proper: Reading the Anthropology of Material Life*, ed. Judith Farquhar and Margaret M. Lock (Durham, NC: Duke University Press, 2007), 202–12.

81. McKenna, *Food of the Gods*, 118–20.

82. "We Drank Soma, We Became Immortal," *Science First Hand*, August 30, 2010, https://scfh.ru/en/papers/we-drank-soma-we-became-immortal-/.

83. Clark, *Tawny One*, 125–26.

84. See Burkert, *Ancient Mystery Cults*, 108; Michael Cosmopoulos, *Greek Mysteries* (New York: Routledge, 2002).

85. Burkert, *Ancient Mystery Cults*, 11. See Cosmopoulos, *Greek Mysteries*.

86. See Clark, *Tawny One*, 193.

87. Peter Webster, "Mixing the *Kykeon*, Part 1," *Eleusis: Journal of Psychoactive Plants and Compounds* 4 (2000): 2.

88. See Burkert, *Ancient Mystery Cults*, 108.

89. See Muraresku, *Immortality Key*, 6.

90. Enriqueta Pons et al., *Mas Castellar de Pontós (Alt Empordà): Un complex arqueològic d'època ibèrica (Excavacions 1990–1998)* (Girona: Museu d'Arqueologia de Catalunya, 2002), 550.

91. Jordi Juan-Tresserras, "La arqueología de las drogas en la península Ibérica: una síntesis de las recientes investigaciones arqueobotánicas," *Complutum* 11 (2000): 261–74. See Jordi Juan-Tresserras and Jaume Matamala, "Estudio de residuos microscópicos

y compuestos orgánicos en utillaje de molido y de contenido de las vasijas," in *El Dolmen de Azután (Toledo): Áreas de habitación y áreas funerarias en la cuenca interior del Tajo*, ed. Primitiva Bueno, Rodrigro de Balbín Berhmann, and Rosa Barroso Barmejo (Alcalá de Henares: Universidad de Alcalá de Henares, 2005), 235–41.

92. Muraresku, *Immortality Key*, 144–45. For critical reviews of Muraresku's book, see Mosurinjohn and Ascough, "Psychedelics, Eleusis, and the Invention of Religious Experience"; Jerry B. Brown, "The Immortality Key: The Secret History of the Religion with No Name," *Journal of Psychedelic Studies* 5, no. 1 (2021), DOI:10.1556/2054.2021.00170.

93. In his major work on ancient Greek and Roman magic, Georg Luck includes an appendix on "Psychoactive Substances in Religion and Magic," which describes the use of opium, frankincense, myrrh, and other substances that have mind-altering effects: "Psychoactive substances reached the brains of believers in many different ways: in food and drink, in oil rubbed into the skin, in smoke inhaled. . . . A quick survey of the magical papyri shows how often special incense and aromatic oils were applied. Some of the ingredients are well-known psychoactive substances" (*Arcana Mundi: Magic and the Occult in the Greek and Roman Worlds* [Baltimore: Johns Hopkins University Press, 2006], 479).

94. Burkert, *Ancient Mystery Cults*, 108.

95. Cosmopoulos, *Bronze Age Eleusis*, chap. 2.

96. See Alessandra Foscati, ed., *Saint Anthony's Fire from Antiquity to the Eighteenth Century* (Amsterdam: University of Amsterdam Press, 2019), 15–16; Ginzburg, *Ecstasies*, 303–4.

97. Daniel Perrine, "Mixing the Kykeon, Part 2," *Eleusis: Journal of Psychoactive Plants and Compounds* 4 (2000): 14.

98. Clark, *Tawny One*, 195.

99. Jules Evans, "The Immortality Key," *Medium*, October 16, 2020, https://julesevans.medium.com/the-immortality-key-f66fef6e650f. On this point, see also Julien Tempone-Wiltshire and Floren Matthews, "Evaluating the Role of Psychedelic Psychotherapy in Addressing Societal Alienation," *Journal of Psychedelic Studies* 7, no. 3 (2023), https://akjournals.com/view/journals/2054/7/3/article-p238.xml. As Tempone-Wiltshire and Matthews put it, "biochemical reductionism excludes the fact that the efficacy of these ethnomedicines is dependent upon the heavily ritualised and culturally-embedded containers in which they are utilised."

100. Cosmopoulos, *Bronze Age Eleusis*, chap. 2.

101. In his work on the witches' sabbath, Ginzburg also raises the question of whether ergot might have contributed to the narratives of ecstatic and shamanic experiences found in European accounts. He too suggests that the evidence is intriguing but inconclusive (*Ecstasies*, 303–5).

CHAPTER TWO

1. Wasson, *The Wondrous Mushroom: Mycolatry in Mesoamerica* (New York: McGraw-Hill, 1980), xvi.

2. McKenna, blurb for Wasson, *The Wondrous Mushroom*, back cover.

3. Doniger "'Somatic' Memories," 55; see Riedlinger, ed., *Sacred Mushroom Seeker*, 19–24.

4. Wasson, "Seeking the Magic Mushroom," 100. Wasson also made this claim in a letter to Robert Graves, August 8, 1955. Tina and R. Gordon Wasson Ethnomycological

Collection, Botany Libraries, Harvard University, Cambridge, MA, Series, I 255. On this point, see also Martinez-Cruz, "María Sabina," 183–85.

5. See Jean Bassett Johnson, "The Elements of Mazatec Witchcraft," *Ethnological Studies* 9 (1939): 128–50; Guzmán, "Hallucinogenic Mushrooms," 404–12.

6. See Letcher, *Shroom*; Pollan, *How to Change*, 112.

7. Siff, "R. Gordon Wasson," 92.

8. Pollan, *How to Change*, 103. See Stamets, *Psilocybin Mushrooms of the World*, 1.

9. Letcher, *Shroom*, 87. On the tourism issue, see Saraí Piña Alcántara, "Turismo y chamanismo, dos mundos imbricados: el caso de Huautla de Jiménez, Oaxaca," *Cuicuilco Revista de Ciencias Antropológicas* 26, no. 75 (2019): 43–66.

10. Huxley, *Doors of Perception*, 5. See also Jay C. Fikes, *Carlos Castaneda: Academic Opportunism and the Psychedelic Sixties* (Victoria, BC: Millennia Press, 1993), 15.

11. Huxley, "Drugs That Shape Men's Minds," *The Saturday Evening Post*, October 18, 1958. Huxley goes on to say: "Thus a person who takes LSD or mescaline may suddenly understand—not only intellectually but organically, experientially—the meaning of such tremendous religious affirmations as 'God is love.' . . . That famous 'revival of religion,' about which so many people have been talking for so long, will not come about as the result of evangelistic mass meetings. . . . It will come about as the result of biochemical discoveries that will make it possible for large numbers of men and women to achieve a radical self-transcendence and a deeper understanding of the nature of things. And this revival of religion will be at the same time a revolution."

12. Huxley, *Doors of Perception*; Zaehner, *Mysticism Sacred and Profane: An Inquiry into Some Varieties of Praeter-Natural Experience* (Oxford: Clarendon, 1957); Stace, *Mysticism and Philosophy* (London: MacMillan, 1960). On Stace's influence on recent psychedelic research, see Jeffrey Breau and Paul Gillis-Smith. "Psychometric *Brahman*, Psychedelic Science: Walter Stace, Transnational Vedanta and the Mystical Experience Questionnaire," *Interdisciplinary Science Reviews* (2023), https://doi.org/10.1080/03080188.2023.2266322.

13. For the story of LSD, see Albert Hofmann, *LSD, My Problem Child* (Los Angeles: J. P. Tarcher, 1983), 15–17; Nicolas Langlitz, *Neuropsychedelia: The Revival of Hallucinogen Research Since the Decade of the Brain* (Berkeley: University of California Press, 2012), 24–25; Martin A. Lee and Bruce Shlain, *Acid Dreams: The Complete Social History of LSD* (New York: Grove Press, 1992).

14. Quoted in Lee and Shlain, *Acid Dreams*, 13–14.

15. Siff, "R. Gordon Wasson," 93.

16. Lattin, *Changing Our Minds*, 3.

17. Davis, *High Weirdness*, 51. See Alfred McCoy, *A Question of Torture: CIA Interrogation from the Cold War to the War on Terror* (New York: MacMillan, 2006). As Lee and Shlain explain, MKUltra was a super secret program that was largely the brainchild of Richard Helms, a member of the Clandestine Services; it was operated by a small unit within the CIA called the Technical Services Staff. The chemist who directed the program was Dr. Sidney Gottlieb, who approved a plan to give LSD to unwitting American citizens to test its potential use in covert operations (*Acid Dreams*, 27–28).

18. Fikes, *Carlos Castenada*, 20–21.

19. Faudree, *Singing for the Dead: The Politics of Indigenous Revival in Mexico* (Durham, NC: Duke University Press, 2013), 82.

20. Henry Munn, "The Mushrooms of Language," in *Hallucinogens and Shamanism*, ed. Michael J. Harner (New York: Oxford University Press, 1973), 86. See also Guzmán, "Hallucinogenic Mushrooms," 409–10; Wasson, Cowan, and Rhodes, *María Sabina and Her Mazatec Mushroom Velada*, 93–97; Martinez-Cruz, *Women and Knowledge*, 106–10.

21. Alvaro Estrada, *María Sabina: Her Life and Chants* (Santa Barbara, CA: Ross-Erikson, 1981), 73.

22. Martinez-Cruz, "María Sabina," 180.

23. María Sabina, *Selections*, ed. Jerome Rothenberg (Berkeley: University of California Press, 2003), 3–8. Other works on Sabina include Estrada, *María Sabina*; Wasson, Cowan, and Rhodes, *María Sabina and Her Mazatec Mushroom Velada*; Halifax, *Shamanic Voices*; Martinez-Cruz, *Women and Knowledge*; Benjamin Feinberg, *The Devil's Book of Culture: History, Mushrooms, and Caves in Southern Mexico* (Austin: University of Texas Press, 2010), 148–82; Alberto Ongaro, Interview with María Sabina, *L'Europeo* (November 29, 1971).

24. Sabina in Halifax, *Shamanic Voices*, 131. "There is a world beyond ours, a world that is far away, nearby and invisible. And there it is where God lives, where the dead live, the spirits and saints, a world where everything has already happened and everything is known. The world talks. It has a language of its own. I report what it says. The mushroom takes me by the hand and brings me to the world where everything is known. It is they, the sacred mushrooms, that speak in a way that I can understand" (in *Shamanic Voices*, 130).

25. Sabina in Halifax, *Shamanic Voices*, 131–32.

26. Estrada, *María Sabina*, 47.

27. Sabina in Halifax, *Shamanic Voices*, 134.

28. Sabina in Nyberg, "Religious Use," 78.

29. Sabina in Estrada, *La Vida de María Sabina*, 82–83.

30. Wasson, *Wondrous Mushroom*, 32–33.

31. Estrada, *María Sabina*, 62.

32. Wasson, *Wondrous Mushroom*, xxii.

33. Edmund Atwill Wasson, *Religion and Drink* (New York: Burr Printing House, 1914).

34. Riedlinger, *Mushroom Seeker*, 210.

35. Wasson, *The Hall Carbine Affair: A Study in Contemporary Folklore* (New York: Pandick Press, 1941). As Irvin argues, "Documents uncovered at Yale University in the Andrews archives reveal that Wasson had been telling the Civil War historian Allan Nevins what to write about J. P. Morgan and the carbine affair, and then Wasson would turn and cite Nevins as an appeal to authority in his own arguments on the matter" ("R. Gordon Wasson," 590).

36. Donald H. Pfister, "R. Gordon Wasson: 1898–1986," *Mycologia* 80, no. 1 (1988): 11–13. See also Siff, "R. Gordon Wasson"; Riedlinger, ed., *Sacred Mushroom Seeker*, 19–24.

37. Wasson, "The Hallucinogenic Fungi of Mexico," *Botanical Museum Leaflets* 19 (1961): 140.

38. Guzmán, "Hallucinogenic Mushrooms," 406. See also Letcher, *Shroom*, 79.

39. Guzmán, "Hallucinogenic Mushrooms," 405. See Richard E. Schultes, "Plantae Mexicanae II: The Identification of Teonanácatl, a Narcotic Basidiomycete of the Aztecs," *Botanical Museum Leaflets, Harvard University* 7 (1939): 37–56; Richard E. Schultes, "Teonanácatl: The Narcotic Mushroom of the Aztecs," *American Anthropologist* 42 (1940): 429–43.

40. R. Gordon Wasson, Stella Kramrisch, Jonathan Ott, and Carl A. P. Ruck, *Persephone's Quest: Entheogens and the Origins of Religion* (New Haven, CT: Yale University Press, 1986).

41. Wasson, Kramrisch, Ott, and Ruck, *Persephone's Quest*, 21. See the correspondence between Wasson and Graves from 1949 to 1952. Tina and R. Gordon Wasson Ethnomycological Collection, Botany Libraries, Harvard University, Cambridge, MA, Series I, 250–53.

42. R. Gordon Wasson and Valentina Pavlovna Wasson, *Mushrooms, Russia, and History* (New York: Pantheon, 1957), 255.

43. Wasson and Wasson, *Mushrooms, Russia, and History*, 256.

44. Siff, "R. Gordon Wasson," 93.

45. Wasson, *Wondrous Mushroom*, 7–8.

46. Wasson, letter to DeMille, January 10, 1976, Tina and R. Gordon Wasson Ethnomycological Collection, Botany Libraries, Harvard University, Cambridge, MA, Series I, 149.

47. Wasson and Wasson, *Mushrooms, Russia, and History*, 304.

48. Wasson and Wasson, *Mushrooms, Russia, and History*, 296.

49. Field Notebooks, Huautla, June 28–July 10, 1955, Tina and R. Gordon Wasson Ethnomycological Collection, Botany Libraries, Harvard University, Cambridge, MA. Wasson also described his experiences in a letter to Robert Graves: "I can testify of my own knowledge that their effects . . . are breathtaking . . . we retained our full presence of mind, our ability to speak to each other . . . while having visual hallucinations, in colors of the richest splendor. . . . We saw distant lands and great palaces" (Letter to Graves, August 8, 1955, Tina and R. Gordon Wasson Ethnomycological Collection, Botany Libraries, Harvard University, Cambridge, MA, Series, I 255).

50. Pollan, *How to Change*, 104.

51. Wasson, "Seeking," 100.

52. Wasson, "Seeking," 100.

53. Wasson, "Seeking," 102–9. See Wasson, *Wondrous Mushroom*, 15: "As first we saw geometric patterns, angular not circular, in richest colors, such as might adorn textiles or carpets. Then the patterns grew into architectural structures, with colonnades and architraves, patios of regal splendor, the stone work all in brilliant colors, gold and onyx and ebony, all harmoniously and ingeniously contrived, in richest magnificence extending beyond the reach of sight. . . . These architectural visions seemed oriental. . . . They were neither Japanese nor Chinese nor Indian nor Moslem. They seemed to belong rather to the imaginary architecture described by the visionaries of the Bible."

54. Wasson, "Seeking," 109. See Wasson, *Wondrous Mushroom*, 16: "They seemed the very archetypes of beautiful form and color. We felt ourselves in the presence of the Ideas that Plato had talked about. . . . What we were seeing was, we knew, the only reality, of which the counterparts of everyday are mere imperfect adumbrations."

55. Wasson, *Wondrous Mushroom*, 17.

56. Wasson, "Seeking," 17–18.

57. Wasson, "Seeking," 120.

58. Leary, *Flashbacks: An Autobiography* (Los Angeles: J. P. Tarcher, 1983), 93. See Budd Schulberg's account in 1961, which describes Wasson as an explorer who "navigated these voyages to the end of the mind" ("The Night We Ate Magic Mushrooms," *Esquire*, December 1961, 129–30, 312–16). See also Faudree, *Singing for the Dead*, 84.

59. Siff, "R. Gordon Wasson," 99–100.

60. Guzmán, "Hallucinogenic Mushrooms," 404–12.

61. Hofmann, *LSD*, 142. In a letter of November 3, 1962, Hofmann also asserts that the effects of synthetic psilocybin in pill form are "identical with those which have been depicted numerous times as the consequence of taking magic mushrooms" (Tina and R. Gordon Wasson Ethnomycological Collection, Botany Libraries, Harvard University, Cambridge, MA, Series I, 357).

62. Ben Feinberg, "Undiscovering the Pueblo Mágico: Lessons from Huautla for the Psychedelic Renaissance," in *Plant Medicine, Healing and Psychedelic Science*, ed. Beatriz Caiuby Labate and Clancy Clavnar (Cham, Switzerland: Springer, 2018), 52.

63. Wasson, *Wondrous Mushroom*, 28.

64. Wasson, *Wondrous Mushroom*, 10.

65. Wasson, *Wondrous Mushroom*, xvii.

66. Wasson, *Wondrous Mushroom*, xviii.

67. Letcher, *Shroom*, 104.

68. Estrada, *María Sabina*, 73. See Letcher *Shroom*, 102–3: "the veladas were not religious ceremonies. . . . though each was framed within a unique and adaptive blend of Christian and pagan ritual actions . . . they were not performed as an act of worship or to induce mystical experiences of God; they were done for serious and pragmatic purposes of healing."

69. Pollan, *How to Change*, 112.

70. Letcher, *Shroom*, 102.

71. Wasson, "Seeking," 110.

72. Letcher, *Shroom*, 100.

73. Wasson, *Wondrous Mushroom*, 28. See Siff, "R. Gordon Wasson," 98.

74. Siff, "R. Gordon Wasson," 94.

75. Wasson, Kramrisch, Ott, and Ruck, *Persephone's Quest*, 26.

76. Personal conversation with Doniger, June 18, 2023. See also Doniger, "'Somatic' Memories," 55–59.

77. Wasson, *Soma*. See Wasson, *Persephone's Quest*, 26.

78. Wasson, *Persephone's Quest*, 30.

79. Wasson, Letter to Hofmann, July 2, 1965, Tina and R. Gordon Wasson Ethnomycological Collection, Botany Libraries, Harvard University, Cambridge, MA, Series I, 360. In another letter to Hofmann, Wasson suggested that mushrooms, peyote, and morning glory all produce the same essential experience, since they all share a "kindred molecular structure and they are all related to lysergic acid diethylamide (LSD). . . . Taken in appropriate doses, the effects on the human psyche are identical, so far as the scientists can determine" (Letter to Hofmann, June 14, 1971, Tina and R. Gordon Wasson Ethnomycological Collection, Botany Libraries, Harvard University, Cambridge, MA, Series I, 361).

80. Letter to Graves, December 14, 1956, Tina and R. Gordon Wasson Ethnomycological Collection, Botany Libraries, Harvard University, Cambridge, MA, Series I, 257.

81. R. Gordon Wasson, Albert Hofmann, and Carl A. P. Ruck, *The Road to Eleusis: Unveiling the Secret of the Mysteries* (New York: Harcourt Brace Jovanovich, 1978).

82. Wasson, Kramrisch, Ott, and Ruck, *Persephone's Quest*, 28–33.

83. Hofmann, "The Message of the Eleusinian Mysteries for Today's World," in *Entheogens and the Future of Religion*, ed. Robert Forte (San Francisco Park Street Press, 1997), 35.

84. Wasson, Hofmann, and Ruck, *Road to Eleusis*, 61.

85. For critiques of the psychedelic theory of the Mysteries, see Burkert, *Ancient Mystery Cults*, 108; Cosmopoulos, *Bronze Age Eleusis*, chap. 2.

86. Muraresku, *The Immortality Key*. For a critique of Muraresku's work, see Evans, "Immortality Key."

87. Wasson claimed in the 1970s that he had evidence of a Native American shaman who used *A. muscaria*. His evidence was an Ojibway herbalist named Keewaydinoquay Kee Peschel, who lived on an island in Lake Michigan and used the mushroom called *miskwedo*. However, Kee later admitted that other members of tribe opposed the use of the mushroom. It also turned out that Kee and Wasson were lovers, and it seems likely that she adapted her story to fit Wasson's expectations (Letcher, *Shroom*, 149).

88. Wasson, "Seeking," 114. As he wrote in a letter to Robert Graves on August 8, 1955: "I believe we are dealing here with a most ancient belief that we can triangulate back into the past to the time, millennia ago, when the ancestors of all these peoples . . . were first formulating their explanation of a rather hostile and most wondrous world. . . . In Middle America, the Divine Thunderbolt is asked to procreate the Divine Mushrooms that translate the eater into the Divine Presence. We think the original belief, based on hallucinatory mushrooms, survives in our Zapotec informant, Aristeo Matias" (Tina and R. Gordon Wasson Ethnomycological Collection, Botany Libraries, Harvard University, Cambridge, MA, Series, I 255).

89. Wasson, in Pollan, *How to Change*, 111–12.

90. Wasson, *Hallucinogenic Fungi of Mexico*, quoted in Timothy Leary, *High Priest* (New York: World Publishing Group, 1968), 13.

91. Wasson, *Wondrous Mushroom*, xxiii. See Wasson, Kramrisch, Ott, and Ruck, *Persephone's Quest*, 18: "This religious role of *A. muscaria* is accompanied by a startling identity of vocabulary, of religious observances, that bespeak a trait going back for tens of thousands of years, when the virtue of the sacred fungus was first discovered, somewhere in Eurasia."

92. Wasson, Kramrisch, Ott, and Ruck, *Persephone's Quest*, 80.

93. Siff, "R. Gordon Wasson," 101–2. See Alcántara, "Turismo y chamanismo, dos mundos imbricados." On the rumors that John Lennon visited María Sabina, see Feinberg, *Devil's Book of Culture*, 153, 177–78, 232–33. Although many locals repeat the story, there is no solid evidence that he ever visited.

94. Letcher, *Shroom*, 97.

95. Quoted in Nat Finkelstein, "Honghi, Meester?," *Psychedelic Review* 10 (1969): 55.

96. Benjamin Feinberg, "Huautla Pilgrims: The Shapeshifting of Tourism," Planeta .com, July 2003, https://www.planeta.com/huautla-pilgrims/. See Feinberg, *Devil's Book of Culture*.

97. Estrada, *María Sabina*, 86.

98. Estrada, *María Sabina*, 86.

99. Estrada, *María Sabina*, 90–91.

100. Siff, "R. Gordon Wasson"; Alcántara, "Turismo y chamanismo."

101. Wasson, in Estrada, *María Sabina*, 20. See also Wasson, "Drugs: The Sacred Mushroom," *The New York Times*, September 26, 1970: "Huautla, when I first knew it as a humble out-of-the-way Indian village, has become a true mecca for hippies, psychopaths, adventurers, pseudo-research workers, the miscellaneous crew of society's drop-outs. The old ways are dead, and I fear that my responsibility is heavy. . . . Yet what I have done gives me nightmares: I have unleashed on lovely Huautla a

torrent of commercial exploitation of the vilest kind. Now the mushrooms are for sale everywhere—in every marketplace, in every village doorway. Everyone offers his services as a 'priest 'of the rite, even the politicos" (29).

102. Wasson, *Wonderous Mushroom*, xvi.

103. Hofmann, *LSD*, 143.

104. Letcher, *Shroom*, 101. "The anthropological heresy that Wasson committed . . . was that he forced these complex indigenous healing practices into his own preconceptions rather than attempt the more difficult task of trying to understand them on their own terms" (Letcher, *Shroom*, 104).

105. Martinez-Cruz, "María Sabina," 183.

106. See Mark Hay, "The Colonization of the Ayahuasca Experience," *JSTOR Daily*, November 4, 2020, https://daily.jstor.org/the-colonization-of-the-ayahuasca-experience/.

107. Siff, "R. Gordon Wasson," 102.

108. Siff, "R. Gordon Wasson," 94. See Kripal, *Esalen*, 115.

109. Letcher, *Shroom*, 113.

110. Letcher, *Shroom*, 111.

111. Guzmán, "Hallucinogenic Mushrooms," 409.

112. Dirección de Turismo, "El Hongo: Sagrado de la Sierra Mazateca" (Huautla de Jiménez, Oaxaca: Dirección de Turismo, n.d.). See also Faudree, *Singing for the Dead*, 77–90; Martinez-Cruz, *Women and Knowledge*, 101–19.

113. Julien Casanova, "San José de Pacifico: Magic Mushrooms and Mountains," *Oaxaca Travel Tips*, March 30, 2023. https://oaxacatraveltips.com/san-jose-del-pacifico/.

114. Mooney, "Eating the Mescal," *The Augusta Chronicle*, January 24 (1982): 11; Mooney, "The Mescal Plant and Ceremony," *Therapeutic Gazette* 12 (1896): 7–11.

115. Bouayad, "The Cactus and the Anthropologist: The Evolution of Cultural Expertise on the Entheogenic Use of Peyote in the United States," *Laws* 8, no. 2 (2019): 12.

116. See Jay C. Fikes, *Reuben Snake: Your Humble Serpent: Indian Visionary and Activist* (Santa Fe, NM: Clear Light Publishers, 1996); Thomas C. Maroukis, *The Peyote Road: Religious Freedom and the Native American Church* (Norman: University of Oklahoma Press, 2012).

CHAPTER THREE

1. Pahnke and Richards, "Implications of LSD and Experimental Mysticism," *Journal of Religion and Health* 5, no. 3 (1966): 206.

2. Leary, *High Priest* (New York: World Publishing Group, 1968), 320.

3. Kripal, *Esalen*, 115.

4. Huxley, *Island* (New York: Harper & Brothers, 1962), 166. On this text, see also Langlitz, *Neuropsychedelia*, 5.

5. See the Harvard Psilocybin Project Records, 1961–62, MSP 98, Purdue University Libraries and School of Information Studies, Purdue, IN; Don Lattin, *The Harvard Psychedelic Club: How Timothy Leary, Ram Dass, Huston Smith and Andrew Weil Killed the Fifties and Ushered in a New Age for America* (New York: HarperOne, 2010),

6. Lattin, *Changing Our Minds*, 3.

7. Pahnke and Richards, "Implications of LSD," 193.

8. See Walter N. Pahnke, "Drugs and Mysticism: An Analysis of the Relationship Between Psychedelic Drugs and the Mystical Consciousness," PhD diss., Harvard University, 1963, 276–82.

9. On the MEQ and its complex history, see Ann Taves, "Mystical and Other Alterations in Sense of Self: An Expanded Framework for Studying Nonordinary Experiences," *Perspectives on Psychological Science* 15, no. 3 (2020): 669–90; Jeffrey Breau and Paul Gillis-Smith, "Psychometric *Brahman*, Psychedelic Science: Walter Stace, Transnational Vedanta and the Mystical Experience Questionnaire," *Interdisciplinary Science Reviews* (2023), https://doi.org/10.1080/03080188.2023.2266322.

10. Leary, *Start Your Own Religion* (Lexington, KY: Forgotten Books, 2012).

11. Pollan, *How to Change Your Mind*, 2–3; see also Andrew Wickens, *A History of the Brain: From Stone Age Surgery of Modern Neuroscience* (New York: Psychology Press, 2014), 310–11.

12. Lattin, *Changing Our Minds*, 4.

13. See Bruce Lincoln, *Authority: Construction and Corrosion* (Chicago: University of Chicago Press, 1994).

14. Wickens, *History of the Brain*, 310–11. See also Dumit, *Drugs for Life*; Jeremy A. Greene, Flurin Condrau, and Elizabeth Siegal Watkins, eds., *Therapeutic Revolutions: Pharmaceuticals and Social Change in the Twentieth Century* (Chicago: University of Chicago Press, 2016); Martin Halliwell, *Therapeutic Revolutions: Medicine, Psychiatry and Cultural Change, 1945–1970* (New Brunswick, NJ: Rutgers University Press, 2013).

15. Lee and Shlain, *Acid Dreams*, 12.

16. Lee and Shlain, *Acid Dreams*, 73.

17. Leary, *High Priest*, 12.

18. Leary, *Flashbacks*, 32.

19. Leary, *Flashbacks*, 32.

20. Leary, *High Priest*, 34.

21. See the Harvard Psilocybin Project Records, 1961–1962; Lattin, *Harvard Psychedelic Club*.

22. Andrew T. Weil, "The Strange Case of the Harvard Drug Scandal," *Look Magazine*, November 8, 1963, 43, 38, 43–44, 46, 48. See Harvard Psilocybin Project Records, 1961–1962.

23. As Lee and Shlain note, "Huxley brought into the project, first as an adviser and then as a participant in a psilocybin experiment. He and Leary took the drug together and after the session they spoke about what to do within this 'philosopher's stone'" (*Acid Dreams*, 75).

24. Weil, "The Strange Case," 44.

25. Lattin, *Changing Our Minds*, 171–72.

26. Leary, *High Priest*, 211.

27. Walter Houston Clark, "Walter Norman Pahnke, B.D., M.D., PH.D., 1931–1971," *Parapsychology Review* (November/December, 1971): 27.

28. Clark, "Walter Norman Pahnke."

29. "William Richards Collection on Walter Pahnke," Purdue University Archives and Special Collections, 2024, https://archives.lib.purdue.edu/repositories/2/resources/42.

30. Huston Smith, "The Good Friday Experiment," in *Hallucinations: A Reader*, ed. Charles S. Grob (New York: J. P. Tarcher, 2002), 64–65.

31. Clark, "Walter Norman Pahnke."

32. See Travis Kitchens, "The Psychedelic Evangelist," *The New York Times*, March 21, 2024; Matthew W. Johnson, "Consciousness, Religion, and Gurus: Pitfalls of Psychedelic Medicine," *ACS Pharmacology and Translational Science* 4, no. 2 (2021): 580.

33. Leary, *High Priest*, 304.

34. Pollan, *How to Change*, 45.

35. Leary, *High Priest*, 311.

36. Pahnke, "Drugs and Mysticism," 131.

37. Subject GP and subject MC in Pahnke, "Drugs and Mysticism," 164–65.

38. Smith, "The Good Friday Experiment," 67.

39. Smith, "The Good Friday Experiment," 70.

40. Pahnke, "Implications of LSD," 193.

41. Leary, *High Priest*, 314–15. See Leary, *Flashbacks*, 108: "Our administration of the sacred mushrooms . . . provided a scientific demonstration that spiritual ecstasy, religious revelation, and union with God were now directly accessible. Mystical experience could be produced for and by those who sought it."

42. Pollan, *How to Change*, 46. See Rick Doblin, "Pahnke's Good Friday Experiment: A Long-Term Follow-Up and Methodological Critique," *The Journal of Transpersonal Psychology* 23, no. 1 (1991): 1–28.

43. See Will Stone, "Transformation or Trouble," NPR.org, May 13, 2024, https://www.npr.org/sections/health-shots/2024/05/13/1250580932/ecstasy-mdma-ptsd-fda-approval.

44. Pahnke, "Drugs and Mysticism," 276–82.

45. See Breau and Gillis-Smith, "Psychometric *Brahman*."

46. See Stace, *Mysticism and Philosophy* (London: MacMillan, 1960); Stace, *Man Against Darkness* (Pittsburgh: University of Pittsburgh Press, 1967).

47. Karl Baier, "High Mysticism—On the Interplay Between the Psychedelic Movement and Academic Study of Mysticism," in *Constructions of Mysticism as a Universal: Roots and Interactions Across Borders*, ed. by Annette Wilke, Robert Stephanus, and Robert Suckro (Wiesbaden: Harrassowitz Verlag, 2021), 366–70. As Baier defines it, perennialism refers to "approaches to mysticism that suppose the existence of a transhistorical, transcontextual mystic experience." It also typically assumes that the mystical experience is the core of all religion ("High Mysticism," 367). See Taves, "Mystical and Other Alterations," 669–70.

For other critiques of Stace, see Peter G. Moore, "Recent Studies of Mysticism: A Critical Survey," *Religion* 3, no. 2 (1973): 146–56; J. Moussaieff Masson and T. C. Masson, "The Study of Mysticism: A Criticism of W. T. Stace," *Journal of Indian Philosophy* 4, nos. 1–2 (1976): 109–25.

48. Breau and Gillis-Smith, "Psychometric *Brahman*," 6–7. See Wilhelm Halbfass, *India and Europe*, 378–402.

49. Breau and Gillis-Smith, "Psychometric *Brahman*," 8. See also Partridge, *High Culture*, 201–24.

50. Breau and Gillis-Smith, "Psychometric *Brahman*," 8.

51. Pahnke and Richards, "Implications of LSD," 177.

52. Stace, *Mysticism and Philosophy*, 61–131.

53. Stace, *Mysticism and Philosophy*. 131–32. Elsewhere, Stace lists five characteristics of the mystical experience, which is defined largely in terms drawn from the Hindu *Upanishads*: 1) experience of undifferentiated unity; 2) dissolution of individuality; 3) feeling of peace, blessedness, joy; 4) revelation of some transcendent reality

(God, Nirvana, the Absolute); 5) transformative effects on one's life and character—transforms life (Stace, *Man Against Darkness*, 24–35).

54. Pahnke, "Drugs and Mysticism," xi.

55. Pahnke, "Drugs and Mysticism," 34; quoting from Kenneth Walker, *The Conscious Mind: A Commentary on the Mystics* (London: Rider, 1962). See Partridge, *High Culture*, 241.

56. Pahnke, "Drugs and Mysticism," 126ff. See also Baier, "High Mysticism," 385; Sabrina Eisenberg, "What Is the Mystical Experience Questionnaire?," *Psychedelic Review*, January 7, 2021, https://psychedelicreview.com/what-is-the-mystical-experience-questionnaire/.

57. Pahnke and Richards, "Implications of LSD," 192.

58. Pahnke, "Drugs and Mysticism," 130.

59. Breau and Gillis-Smith, "Psychometric *Brahman*," 2. See also Karl Baier, "High Mysticism—On the Interplay Between the Psychedelic Movement and Academic Study of Mysticism," in *Constructions of Mysticism as a Universal: Roots and Interactions Across Borders*, ed. by Annette Wilke, Robert Stephanus, and Robert Suckro (Wiesbaden: Harrassowitz Verlag, 2021), 363–96.

60. Porter, *Trust in Numbers: The Pursuit of Objectivity in Science and Scientific Life* (Princeton, NJ: Princeton University Press, 2020). See also Sally Engle Merry, *The Seductions of Quantification: Measuring Human Rights, Gender Violence and Sex Trafficking* (Chicago: University of Chicago Press, 2016).

61. Pahnke, "Drugs and Mysticism," 238.

62. See Pahnke and Richards, "Implications Of LSD and Experimental Mysticism"; William A. Richards, "Counseling, Peak Experiences and the Human Encounter with Death: An Empirical Study of the Efficacy of DPT-Assisted Counseling in Enhancing the Quality of Life of Persons with Terminal Cancer and Their Closest Family Members," PhD diss., Catholic University of America, 1975.

63. Katherine A. Maclean, Jeannie-Marie S. Leoutsakos, Matthew W. Johnson, and Roland R. Griffiths, "Factor Analysis of the Mystical Experience Questionnaire: A Study of Experiences Occasioned by the Hallucinogen Psilocybin," *Journal for the Scientific Study of Religion* 51, no. 4 (2012): 721–37; Frederick S. Barrett, Matthew W. Johnson, and Roland R. Griffiths, "Validation of the Revised Mystical Experience Questionnaire in Experimental Sessions with Psilocybin," *Journal of Psychopharmacology* 29, no. 11 (2015): 1182–90, DOI:10.1177/0269881115609019.

64. Breau and Gillis-Smith, "Psychometric *Brahman*," 3. See Taves, "Mystical and Other Alterations," 669–90.

65. Breau and Gillis-Smith, "Psychometric *Brahman*," 5. See Taves, "Mystical and Other Alterations," 673.

66. Taves, "Mystical and Other Alterations," 673. Taves further argues that "Stace's (1960) definition of mystical experience was driven by his quest to identify an unassailable 'common core' of the various religions: a pure experience that allegedly gives access to reality. Scales that operationalize this criteria have a number of limitations. They isolate features Stace viewed as authentic and overlook the potentially more widespread presence of others that he viewed as less authentic: for example, dissociative and sensorially rich experience" (685).

A similar point is made by Sharday Mosurinjohn, Leor Roseman, and Manesh Girn, "Psychedelic-Induced Mystical Experiences: An Interdisciplinary Discussion and Critique," *Frontiers in Psychiatry* 14 (2023), https://doi.org/10.3389/fpsyt.2023.1077311.

In their view, "existing operationalizations of mystical experiences in psychedelic science fail to historicize the concept and therefore fail to acknowledge its perennialist and specifically Christian bias."

67. Taves, "Mystical and Other Alterations," 671.

68. See Taves, "Mystical and Other Alterations," 669–90. For other criticisms of universalist and perennialist approaches to mysticism, see Steven T. Katz, "The 'Conservative' Character of Mysticism," in *Mysticism and Religious Traditions*, ed. Steven T. Katz (New York: Oxford University Press, 1983), 33; Robert M. Gimello, "Mysticism in Its Contexts," in *Mysticism and Religious Traditions*, ed. Steven T. Katz (New York: Oxford University Press, 1983), 63. As Gimello argues, "Buddhist mystical experiences . . . are precisely *experiences* of emptiness (*sunyata*), of dependent origination (*pratityasamutpada*), of the buddha-nature (*buddhata*) . . . of all sentient beings. . . . These are in no sense the same as the Christian mystic's experience of the Trinity, Christ or the Godhead; nor the same as the Jewish mystic's experience of Einsof; nor even the same as the Vedantist's experience of the identity of atman and brahman. . . . Mysticism is inextricably bound up with, dependent upon, and usually subservient to the deeper beliefs and values of the traditions, cultures, and historical milieux which harbour it" (63).

69. Breau and Gillis-Smith, "Psychometric *Brahman*," 14. See Taves, "Mystical and Other Alterations."

70. Barron, "The Problem with Pain Scores," *Scientific American*, July 15, 2021, https://www.scientificamerican.com/article/the-problem-with-pain-scores/.

71. Pahnke, "First Impressions of First LSD Experience, of March 30, 1964," March 31, 1964, William Richards Collection on Walter Pahnke, Purdue University Libraries and School of Information Studies, MSP 68.

72. Pahnke, "Psychedelic Mystical Experience in the Human Encounter with Death," *Harvard Theological Review* 62, no. 1 (1969): 1–21.

73. Leary, *Flashbacks*, 109. See Leary, *High Priest*, 317: "The miracle of Marsh Chapel was not just a scientific study; it was authentic spiritual ceremony. And like every valid Good Friday experiment our spring solstice death-rebirth-celebration (because it worked) invited excommunication and persecution. We were involved, not in a controversial research project, but in a classic religious struggle."

74. Leary, "In the Beginning, Leary Turned on Ginsberg and Saw That It Was Good," *Esquire*, July 1, 1968, 117.

75. Timothy Leary, Ralph Metzner, and Richard Alpert, *The Psychedelic Experience: A Manual Based on the Tibetan Book of the Dead* (New Hyde Park, NY: University Books, 1969), 11.

76. Leary et al., *The Psychedelic Experience*, 53. See David Jay Brown and Rebecca McClen Novick, *Mavericks of the Mind: Conversations for the New Millennium* (Freedom, CA: Crossing Press, 1993), 137.

77. Leary, *High Priest*, 318.

78. Leary, *Start Your Own Religion*, 5.

79. Leary, *Start Your Own Religion*, 6.

80. Leary, *Start Your Own Religion*, 11. See also "Playboy Interview: Timothy Leary," *Playboy*, September 1966, 12: "Each person will become his own Buddha, his own Einstein, his own Galileo. Instead of relying on canned, static, dead knowledge passed on from other symbol producers, he will be using his span of 80 or so years on

this planet to live out every possibility of the human, prehuman, and even subhuman adventurer."

81. Leary, quoted in Lee and Shlain, *Acid Dreams*, 77.

82. See "The IFIF Program," Tina and R. Gordon Wasson Ethnomycological Collection, Botany Libraries, Harvard University, Cambridge, MA: "IFIF. . . . seeks to return to the wisdom of the tribe, to the wisdom of the body, to the wisdom of the nervous system."

83. Leary, *High Priest*, note (np). See Leary, *Start Your Own Religion* (Millbrook, NY: Kriya Press, 1967), 13: The goals of this religion are "the discovery of the God within and worship through acts of glorification . . . The sacramental methods for contacting the inner divinity included psychedelic foods and drugs—marijuana, hashish, sacred mushrooms, peyote, LSD, etc."

84. Leary, *Start Your Own Religion*, 13.

85. Leary, *Start Your Own Religion*, 18.

86. See Kripal, *Esalen*; Hugh. B. Urban, *Zorba the Buddha: Sex, Spirituality, and Capitalism in the Global Osho Movement* (Berkeley: University of California Press, 2016).

87. See Nick Schou, *Orange Sunshine: The Brotherhood of Eternal Love and Its Quest to Spread Peace, Love, and Acid to the World* (New York: Thomas Dunne Books, 2010).

88. Quoted in Lee and Shlain, *Acid Dreams*, 237.

89. Lee and Shlain, *Acid Dreams*, 240.

90. Lee and Shlain, *Acid Dreams*, 236.

91. Leary, *Flashbacks*, 264–65. See Lee and Shlain, *Acid Dreams*, 238–40.

92. Leary, *Flashbacks*, 265.

93. Art Kleps, *The Boo Hoo Bible: The Neo-American Church Catechism* (San Cristobel, NM: Toad Books, 1971), 3.

94. Kleps, *Boo Hoo Bible*, 4.

95. See Omer C. Stewart, *Peyote Religion* (Norman: University of Oklahoma Press, 1993). The Supreme Court clearly acknowledges the peyote exemption for Native Americans in its ruling: United States v. Kuch, U.S. District Court for the District of Columbia. 288 F. Supp. 439 (D.D.C. 1968), July 1, 1968.

96. United States v. Kuch, U.S. District Court for the District of Columbia. 288 F. Supp. 439 (D.D.C. 1968), July 1, 1968.

97. Employment Division, Department of Human Resources of Oregon v. Smith, 494 US 872 (1990). See also Hugh B. Urban, *New Age*, chap. 1. In a 6–3 decision, the court concluded that religious freedom does not mean that groups can violate existing laws, such as the ban on substances such as peyote.

98. See Porter, *Trust in Numbers*.

99. See Matthew W. Johnson, "Consciousness, Religion, and Gurus: Pitfalls of Psychedelic Medicine," *ACS Pharmacology and Translational Science* 4, no. 2 (2021): 578–81.

100. Timothy Leary, "In the Beginning, Leary Turned on Ginsberg and Saw That It Was Good," *Esquire*, July 1, 1968, 117.

101. Wasson letter to Huston Smith, August 2, 1971, Tina and R. Gordon Wasson Ethnomycological Collection, Harvard University Botany Libraries, Cambridge, MA.

102. Bob Gaines, "Hollywood's Status-Symbol Drug," *Cosmopolitan*, November 1963, 78, 78–81.

103. Lee and Shlain, *Acid Dreams*, 224; Lattin, *Changing*, 49. As Lee and Shlain note, Nixon also "pushed through a series of no-knock laws allowing police to break into homes suspected of drug users, unannounced and armed to the hilt, to search for a tiny tab of LSD or a pipeful of pot . . . the targets of these antidrug campaign were often involved in radical politics" (*Acid Dreams*, 225).

104. Lincoln, *Authority*.

105. See Grace Jantzen, *Power, Gender and Christian Mysticism* (Cambridge: Cambridge University Press, 1996).

106. See Steven Ozment, *The Age of Reform, 1250–1550* (New Have, CT: Yale University Press, 2020).

107. Lattin, *Changing*, 10.

CHAPTER FOUR

1. McKenna, *True Hallucinations: Being an Account of the Author's Extraordinary Adventures in the Devil's Paradise* (San Francisco: HarperSanFrancisco, 1993), 41.

2. Pesce, quoted in Erik Davis, "Terence McKenna's Last Trip," *Wired*, 2000, https://www.wired.com/2000/05/mckenna/.

3. Hutton, *Shamans*, 159.

4. See Terence McKenna and Dennis McKenna, *The Invisible Landscape: Mind, Hallucinogens and the I Ching* (San Francisco: HarperSanFrancisco, 1993); Dennis McKenna, "The Experiment at la Chorrera: A 50-Year Retrospective," *McKenna Academy*, February 17, 2021, https://mckenna.academy/the-experiment-at-la-chorrera-a-50-year-retrospective/. For McKenna's full biography, see Graham St. John, *Strange Attractor: The Hallucinatory Life of Terence McKenna* (Cambridge, MA: MIT Press, 2025).

5. McKenna and McKenna, *Invisible Landscape*, 43.

6. See in particular Davis, *High Weirdness*.

7. Davis, *High Weirdness*, 45.

8. Stamets, *Psilocybe Mushrooms*, 3. See also Terence McKenna, Interview with Erik Davis, November 1999, *Library of Consciousness*, https://www.organism.earth/library/document/interview-with-erik-davis: "The mushroom is the most insidious and amusing, because it seems to associate itself with human beings. Like, for instance, one of the densest psilocybin ecologies in the world is Oregon and western Washington. Well, one of the main industries of those areas where these mushrooms are so dense is the production of sod to be shipped all over the country and world, to be pushed into malls and hotel lawns and golf courses. So it's essentially an enormous economic engine for spreading psilocybin spores throughout the planet."

9. Davis, *High Weirdness*, 401.

10. McKenna, *True Hallucinations*, 42. See also McKenna, *The Archaic Revival: Speculations on Psychedelic Mushrooms, the Amazon, Virtual Reality, UFO's, Evolution, Shamanism, the Rebirth of the Goddess, and the End of History* (San Francisco: HarperSanFrancisco 1991). As Wouter Hanegraaff notes, "contemporary neoshamanism as represented by a central author like McKenna is . . . a typical form of entheogenic esotericism in the narrow sense of the world. McKenna's 'archaic revival' means a revival of *cosmotheism* against the worldviews of classic monotheism and rational science; and he highlights entheogenic substances as providing a direct doorway to gnosis" ("Entheogenic Esotericism," 406–7).

11. As various authors have noted, the category of "shamanism" is notoriously problematic and has a complex history. As Hutton explains, the term "shaman" was first circulated in Russian literature on Siberian religions in the seventeenth century, and the general term "shamanism" was created much later to refer (even more problematically) to a wide range of phenomena found in many Indigenous cultures: "The word 'shaman' was apparently first printed in the memoirs of the existed Russian churchman Avvakum, in 1672, and seems to have reached Western and Central European scholarship twenty years later in the work of Nicholas Witsen. . . . 'Shamanism,' by contrast is recognized among experts to be a scholarly construct, used to group together beliefs and activities across the world which have some apparent relationship with those observed in Siberia. It is also generally admitted that no commonly agreed definition has ever been ascribed to the term, and that the recent boom in studies associated with it have only worsened the confusion and diversity in its use" (Hutton, *Shamans*, vii).

12. Torgovnick, *Gone Primitive: Savage Intellects, Modern Lives* (Chicago: University of Chicago Press, 1990), 246. See Torgnovnick, *Primitive Passions: Men, Women, and the Quest for Ecstasy* (Chicago: University of Chicago Press, 1996), 18–19.

13. On the New Age movement, see Hugh B. Urban, *New Age, Neopagan and New Religious Movements: Alternative Spirituality in Contemporary America* (Berkeley: University of California Press, 2015); Paul Heelas, *The New Age Movement: The Celebration of the Self and the Sacralization of Modernity* (Oxford: Blackwell, 1996); Kathryn Lofton, *Oprah: The Gospel of an Icon* (Berkeley: University of California Press, 2011).

14. Davis, *High Weirdness*, 91.

15. Mircea Eliade, *Shamanism: Archaic Techniques of Ecstasy* (Princeton, NJ: Princeton University Press, 1964). On the problematic history of the category of shamanism, see Hutton, *Shamans*.

16. Robert Marshall, "The Dark Legacy of Carlos Castaneda," *Salon*, April 12, 2007, https://www.salon.com/2007/04/12/castaneda/.

17. Fikes, *Carlos Castaneda*, 12. See Hutton, *Shamans*, 159.

18. Letter from Castaneda to Wasson, September 6, 1968, Castaneda, Carlos, 1962, Series I, 139, Tina and R. Gordon Wasson Ethnomycological Collection, Botany Libraries, Harvard University, Cambridge, MA.

19. See the correspondence between Wasson and Castaneda from April 8, 1962, to August 26, 1968, Castaneda, Carlos, 1962, Series I, 139, Tina and R. Gordon Wasson Ethnomycological Collection, Botany Libraries, Harvard University, Cambridge, MA.

20. Walter Goldschmidt, foreword to Carlos Castaneda, *The Teachings of Don Juan: A Yaqui Way of Knowledge* (New York: Washington Square Press, 1985), xxiii.

21. Castaneda, *The Teachings of Don Juan*, xxxiv.

22. Castaneda, *The Teachings of Don Juan*, 51.

23. Fikes, *Carlos Castenada*, 59.

24. Fikes, "Carlos Castaneda (1925–1998), Reading Between His Lines, a Summary Judgment," *The International Journal of Ethnopsychology* 2, no. 1 (2021): 1–8.

25. De Mille, letter to Wasson, November 21, 1975, Tina and R. Gordon Wasson Ethnomycological Collection, Botany Libraries, Harvard University, Cambridge, MA, Series I, 149. See also de Mille, *Castaneda's Journey: The Power and the Allegory* (Santa Barbara, CA: Ross-Erikson Publishers, 1980).

26. See Richard de Mille manuscript, Series I, 139, Tina and R. Gordon Wasson Ethnomycological Collection, Botany Libraries, Harvard University, Cambridge, MA:

"Carlos' friend Bill could introduce him to Don Juan in the Nogales bus station in the summer of 1960 because earlier that year in the special collections reading room at UCLA Gordon Wasson had introduced Castaneda to Don Aurelio, Maria Sabina and Aristeo, three curing shamans some of whose attributes found their way into the character of don Juan."

27. Fikes, "Carlos Castaneda."

28. James Kent, "Terence McKenna Interview, Part 1," *Tripzine*, 2003, https://www.tripzine.com/listing.php?id=terencel.

29. Dennis McKenna, "The Brotherhood of the Screaming Abyss," quoted in Tao Lin, "Psilocybin, the Mushroom, and Terence McKenna," *Vice*, August 12, 2014, https://www.vice.com/en/article/yvqqpj/psilocybin-the-mushroom-and-terence-mckenna-439.

30. McKenna, *Archaic Revival*, 7; Partridge, *High Culture*, 319.

31. Terence McKenna, Interview with Erik Davis, November 1999, *Library of Consciousness*, https://www.organism.earth/library/document/interview-with-erik-davis: "I discovered shamanism through an interest in Tibetan folk religion. Bon, the pre-Buddhist religion of Tibet, is a kind of shamanism. In going from the particular to the general with that concern, I studied shamanism as a general phenomenon."

32. See McKenna, *Archaic Revival*, 7.

33. Davis, *High Weirdness*, 91.

34. McKenna, *Archaic Revival*, 7. See also Davis, "Terrence McKenna's Last Trip."

35. Mark Jacobsen, "Is Terence McKenna the Brave Prophet of the Next Psychedelic Revolution or Is His Cosmic Egg Just a Little Big Cracked?," *Esquire*, June 1992, 107–38.

36. McKenna, *Archaic Revival*, 7.

37. McKenna, "Experiment at La Chorrera." See Partridge, *High Culture*, 321; Schultes, "Virola as an Orally Administered Hallucinogen," *Botanical Museum Leaflets* 22, no. 6 (1969): 239–40.

38. Davis, "Terence McKenna's Last Trip"; Davis, *High Weirdness*, 105; David Jay Brown and Rebecca McClen Novick, *Mavericks of the Mind: Conversations for the New Millennium* (Freedom CA: Crossing Press, 1993), 11.

39. Tao Lin, "Psilocybin, the Mushroom, and Terence McKenna," *Vice*, August 12, 2014, https://www.vice.com/en/article/yvqqpj/psilocybin-the-mushroom-and-terence-mckenna-439.

40. McKenna, *True Hallucinations*, 94.

41. Dennis McKenna, quoted in Alexander Price, "Immanentizing the Eschaton: An Interview with Dennis McKenna," *Reality Sandwich*, March 11, 2007, https://realitysandwich.com/interview_dennis_mckenna/.

42. Davis, *High Weirdness*, 129.

43. Partridge, *High Culture*, 328.

44. Davis, *High Weirdness*, 130.

45. Price, "Immanentizing the Eschaton."

46. Davis, *High Weirdness*, 131–32.

47. McKenna, *True Hallucinations*, 208.

48. McKenna, *True Hallucinations*, xi.

49. Davis, *High Weirdness*, 130. McKenna also believed that he discovered the secret key to understanding time itself. The *I Ching*, he determined, could be used to interpret the patterns of temporality and to work out time's basic structure and even to

calculate the year of the coming eschaton, which he eventually decided would be 2012 (Partridge, *High Culture*, 329).

50. Davis, "Terence McKenna's Last Trip."

51. Davis, *High Weirdness*, 159.

52. Davis, *High Weirdness*, 170.

53. McKenna, preface to *Psilocybin*, 7–8.

54. McKenna, preface to *Psilocybin*, 7–8.

55. Davis, "Terence McKenna's Last Trip."

56. Oss and Oeric, *Psilocybin*, 70.

57. McKenna, *Archaic Revival*, 13. See also McKenna, Interview with Erik Davis.

58. Dennis McKenna and Terence McKenna, "Shamanic Investigations Manuscript," 1972, Dennis and Terence McKenna Papers, Purdue University Libraries and School of Information Studies, MSP 213, 9.

59. McKenna and McKenna, "Shamanic Investigations Manuscript," 17.

60. McKenna, *Archaic Revival*, 2. See McKenna, *Food of the Gods*, 264: "Nature is ourselves, to be cherished and explored. Shamanism has always known this, and shamanism has always, in its most authentic expressions, taught that the path requires allies. These allies are the hallucinogenic plants and the mysterious teaching entities, luminous and transcendental, that reside in that nearby dimension of ecstatic beauty and understanding that have denied until it is now nearly too late."

61. McKenna, Interview with Erik Davis. See also McKenna, "Psilocybin and the Sands of Time," SEN Interview, 1982, ASKTMK.com, https://www.asktmk.com/talks/Psilocybin+and+the+Sands+of+Time.

62. McKenna, "Ethnobotany and Shamanism," 1988, ASKTKM.com, https://www.asktmk.com/talks/Ethnobotany+and+Shamanism+-+Psychedelics+Before+and+After+History. See also McKenna and McKenna, *Invisible Landscape*, 16.

63. McKenna, in Charles S. Grob, ed., *Hallucinations: A Reader* (New York: J. P. Tarcher, 2002), 46.

64. Davis, *High Weirdness*, 162. See Julian Silverman, "Shamans and Acute Schizophrenia," *American Anthropologist* 69, no. 1 (1967): 21–31.

65. McKenna, in David Jay Brown and Rebecca McClen Novick, *Mavericks of the Mind: Conversations for the New Millennium* (Freedom, CA: Crossing Press, 1993), 12. McKenna, "A Crisis in Consciousness, 1995," *Wisdom for Life*, https://www.youtube.com/watch?v=9E5eBqG0cds. See McKenna and McKenna, *The Invisible Landscape*, 3: "The search for liberation, a paradisiacal state of freedom that mythology insists is the ahistorical root of the historical process, has always been the *raison d'être* of the human species' conscious pilgrimage through time. . . . The entire human experience, individual and collective, can be described as the pursuit of that which frees."

66. Torgovnick, *Primitive Passions: Men, Women, and the Quest for Ecstasy* (Chicago: University of Chicago Press, 1996), 109; see Torgovnick, *Gone Primitive*, 246.

67. Partridge, *High Culture*, 324. See also Davis, *High Weirdness*, 160: "In more recent Western discourse, psychedelic and otherwise, the indigenous shaman transforms into an ecognostic healer, a spiritual leader, and a psychopomp of global transformation."

68. Hutton, *Shamans*, 159.

69. "High Times Greats: Interview with Terence McKenna," *High Times*, November 18, 2019, https://hightimes.com/culture/interview-with-terence-mckenna/. See McKenna, *Food of the Gods*, xviii: "The early hominids' adoption of an omnivorous

diet and their discovery of the power of certain plants were decisive factors in moving early humans out of the stream of animal evolution and into the fast-rising tide of language and culture. Our remote ancestors discovered that certain plants, when self-administered, suppress appetite, diminish pain, supply bursts of sudden energy, confer immunity against pathogens and synergize cognitive activities. These discoveries set us on the long journey to self-reflection."

70. McKenna, "Mushrooms, Evolution, and the Millennium," ASKTKM.com, 2020, https://www.asktmk.com/talks/Mushrooms%2C+Evolution+and+the+Millenium. As Dennis McKenna similarly argued, "Over the course of several million years, the human brain tripled in size from approximately 500 cubic centimeters in the earliest humans to 1500 cc today. . . . What triggered that? . . . I think psilocybin was a tool for learning cognition. It was essentially the software that programmed the neurological hardware to think, to have cognition, to have language, and language is essentially synesthesia, the association of an inherently meaningless uttered sound with a complex meaning" (McKenna, in Paul Stamets, ed., *Fantastic Fungi: How Mushrooms Can Heal, Shift Consciousness and Save the Planet* [San Rafael, CA: Earth Aware, 2019], 154).

71. McKenna, "What's So Great About Mushrooms?," ASKTMK.com, 1987, https://www.asktmk.com/talks/What%27s+so+Great+About+Mushrooms%3F.

72. McKenna, quoted in Pollan, *How to Change Your Mind*, 115. See McKenna, *Food of the Gods*.

73. See, for example, Church of Ambrosia, "Religious Evolution (the New Stoned Ape Theory)," Ambrosia Church, 2024, https://ambrosia.church/religious-evolution/.

74. Lin, "Psilocybin."

75. McKenna, *True Hallucinations*, 160.

76. See Francis Crick, *Life and Its Origins* (New York: Simon and Schuster, 1981).

77. Tao Lin, "Psilocybin, the Mushroom, and Terence McKenna," *Vice*, August 12, 2014, https://www.vice.com/en/article/yvqqpj/psilocybin-the-mushroom-and-terence-mckenna-439. See also David Jay Brown and Rebecca McClen Novick, *Mavericks of the Mind: Conversations for the New Millennium* (Freedom, CA: Crossing Press, 1993), 1.

78. McKenna, *True Hallucinations*, 210.

79. Oss and Oeric, *Psilocybin*, 14–15.

80. McKenna, *True Hallucinations*, xii.

81. Oss and Oeric, *Psilocybin*, 15.

82. McKenna, "Psilocybin and the Sands of Time," ASKTMK.com, 2020, https://www.asktmk.com/talks/Psilocybin+and+the+Sands+of+Time.

83. Oss and Oeric, *Psilocybin*, 18–19.

84. See John Markoff, *What the Dormouse Said: How the Sixties Counterculture Shaped the Personal Computer Industry* (New York: Penguin, 2006).

85. McKenna, Interview with Erik Davis, November 1999, *Library of Consciousness*, https://www.organism.earth/library/document/interview-with-erik-davis.

86. John Horgan, "Was Psychedelic Guru Terence McKenna Goofing About 2012 Prophecy," *Scientific American*, June 6, 2012, https://blogs.scientificamerican.com/cross-check/was-psychedelic-guru-terence-mckenna-goofing-about-2012-prophecy/.

87. Davis, "Terence McKenna's Last Trip."

88. Stamets, Interview on *The Joe Rogan Experience*, 2017, https://www.youtube.com/watch?v=mPqWstVnRjQ&t=7193s.

89. Partridge, *High Culture*, 334.

90. McKenna, "Psilocybin and the Sands of Time," ASKTMK.com, 2020, https://www.asktmk.com/talks/Psilocybin+and+the+Sands+of+Time.

91. Mckenna, *Food of the Gods*, xix.

92. Hutton, *Shamans*, 159.

93. McKenna, in Charles S. Grob, ed., *Hallucinations: A Reader* (New York: J. P. Tarcher, 2002), 46.

94. See Markoff, *What the Dormouse Said*; Grim, *This Is Your Country on Drugs*, 226: "Psychedelic drugs . . . pushed the computer and Internet revolutions forward by showing that reality can be profoundly altered through unconventional, highly intuitive thinking."

95. Davis, "Terence McKenna's Last Trip." "Psychedelics have certainly left their mark on computer graphics, virtual reality, and animation. . . . As VRML cocreator Mark Pesce notes, 'How often do you go to a Web site and say, "This is really trippy!"? Well, why? C'mon—it's because it was created by tripsters'" ("Terence McKenna's Last Trip").

CHAPTER FIVE

1. Stamets, "How Psilocybin Mushrooms Can Help Save the World," SXSW, 2023, https://www.youtube.com/watch?v=qry8K7KPHIQ.

2. Stamets, *Psilocybin Mushrooms of the World: An Identification Guide* (Berkeley, CA: Ten Speed Press, 1996), 19.

3. Sheldrake, *Entangled Life*, 183.

4. Stamets, *Psilocybin Mushrooms*, 4.

5. Stamets, "6 Ways Mushrooms Can Save the World."

6. Stamets, *Mycelium Running*, x.

7. Jules Peck, "Psychedelics for System Change: Could Drugs Helps Us Save the Planet?," *Open Democracy*, February 15, 2020, https://www.opendemocracy.net/en/oureconomy/psychedelics-systems-change-could-drugs-help-us-save-planet/.

8. See Stamets, "Mushrooms Are Spiritual Medicine for Everyone," *The New Health Club with Ann Phillipi*, https://www.youtube.com/watch?v=qj00RSTDnWQ; Stamets, "Paul Stamets on Mushrooms, Religion and Psychotherapy," *The Joe Rogan Experience*, https://ogjre.com/clip/paul-stamets-on-mushrooms-religion-and-psychotherapy; Stamets, "A Time for Deep Reflection," PaulStamets.com, July 18, 2002, https://paulstamets.com/news/a-time-in-life-for-deep-reflection; Tree Media, "Paul Stamets on How Mushrooms Can Save Us from Ourselves," YouTube.com, https://www.youtube.com/watch?v=T-9zzXuZ2h4.

9. Pew Research Center, "Religious Nones in America," *Pew Research*, 2024, https://www.pewresearch.org/religion/2024/01/24/religious-nones-in-america-who-they-are-and-what-they-believe/.

10. "Host Defense Products Currently Available," HostDefense.com, 2024. https://hostdefense.com/collections/in-stock?utm_source=google&utm_medium=cpc&utm_campaign=14043236575&utm_content=126022548435&utm_term=host%20defense&gad_source=1&gclid=Cj0KCQjw-r-vBhC-ARIsAGgUO2CfEuaa99tfFwFjXjupPTHZiO6hMPmRcr0j00IJl_9XnMhv5GAL-swaAmCtEALw_wcB.

11. Nat Segnit, "Hippie, Inc: How the Counterculture Went Corporate," *The Economist*, November 14, 2019, https://www.economist.com/1843/2019/11/14/hippie-inc-how-the-counterculture-went-corporate'; Joshua Clark Davis, *From Head

Shops to Whole Foods: Activist Businesses of the 1960s and '70s and the Roots of the New Economy (New York: Columbia University Press, 2017); Joshua Clark Davis, "The Business of Getting High: Head Shops, Countercultural Capitalism and the Marijuana Legalization Movement," *The Sixties* 8, no. 1 (2015): 27–49; David Farber, "Building the Counterculture, Creating Right Livelihoods: The Counterculture at Work," *The Sixties* 6, no. 1 (2013): 1–24.

12. Lau, *New Age Capitalism: Making Money East of Eden* (Philadelphia: University of Pennsylvania Press 2015). See also Jeremy Carrette and Richard King, *Selling Spirituality: The Silent Takeover of Religion* (New York: Routledge, 2005); Mara Einstein and Sarah Macfarland Taylor, *Selling the Sacred: Religion and Marketing from Crossfit to QAnon* (New York: Routledge, 2024).

13. On neoliberalism, see David Harvey, *A Brief History of Neoliberalism* (New York: Oxford University Press, 2007). On neoliberalism and religion, see Hugh B. Urban, *Zorba the Buddha: Sex, Spirituality and Capitalism in the Global Osho Movement* (Berkeley: University of California Press, 2016); Andrea R. Jain, *Peace, Love, and Yoga: The Politics of Global Spirituality* (New York: Oxford University Press, 2020).

14. I take this phrase from Daniel Bell's famous essay "The Cultural Contradictions of Capitalism," *The Journal of Aesthetic Education*, 6, nos. 1/2 (1972): 38.

15. "Fungi Perfecti Impact Report," FungiPerfecti.com, 2024, https://fungi.com/pages/impact-report.

16. Center for Geological Consciousness, "About Us," EcologicalConsciousnes.org, 2024. https://www.ecologicalconsciousness.org/.

17. Mary Carreon, "Paul Stamet's Employees Push to Unionize over Allegations of Low Pay and Insurance Disruptions," *Double Bind Magazine*, May 31, 2024, https://doubleblindmag.com/paul-stamets-fungi-perfecti/; "Psychedelic Union Busting," *The Stand*, June 4, 2024, https://www.thestand.org/2024/06/060424-news/.

18. Paul Stamets at TEDMED, 2011, https://www.youtube.com/watch?v=pXHDoROh2hA&t=4s.

19. "Paul Stamets—Mushrooms Are Spiritual Medicine for Everyone," *The New Health Club with Ann Phillipi*, https://www.youtube.com/watch?v=qj00RSTDnWQ.

20. Tim Ferris, "The Tim Ferris Show Transcripts: Paul Stamets," *Tim Ferris*, October 15, 2018, https://tim.blog/2018/10/15/the-tim-ferriss-show-transcripts-paul-stamets/.

21. Stamets, *Psilocybin Mushrooms*, 1.

22. Paul Stamets and Matthew Johnson, "Psilocybin on the Psyche," *Whalebone Magazine*, 2021, https://whalebonemag.com/psilocybin-on-the-psyche/.

23. Matt Powers, "Paul Stamets: The Origin Story of Fungi Perfecti," *Regenerative Soil and Permaculture*, 2021, https://www.youtube.com/watch?v=DnVtobZ13Fk.

24. Stamets, "Mushrooms Are Spiritual Medicine for Everyone," *The New Health Club with Ann Phillipi*, https://www.youtube.com/watch?v=qj00RSTDnWQ.

25. Paul Stamets, Interview on *The Joe Rogan Experience*, 2017, https://www.youtube.com/watch?v=mPqWstVnRjQ&t=7193s.

26. Stamets, Interview on *The Joe Rogan Experience*. See also Tree Media, "Paul Stamets on How Mushrooms Can Save Us."

27. Pollan, *How to Change*, 100.

28. Stamets, Interview on *The Joe Rogan Experience*, 2017.

29. Stamets, Interview on *The Joe Rogan Experience*, 2017.

30. Stamets, "Mushrooms Are Spiritual Medicine for Everyone," *The New Health Club with Ann Phillipi*, https://www.youtube.com/watch?v=qj00RSTDnWQ.

31. Stamets, *Psilocybin Mushrooms*, 5.

32. Stamets, *Psilocybin Mushrooms*, 6.

33. Stamets, *Psilocybin Mushrooms*, 7.

34. Tree Media, "Paul Stamets on How Mushrooms Can Save Us."

35. Joe Rogan Experience, "Paul Stamets on Mushrooms, Religion, and Psychotherapy," Ojre.com, 2020, https://ogjre.com/clip/paul-stamets-on-mushrooms-religion-and-psychotherapy.

36. Stamets, "Mushrooms Are Spiritual Medicine for Everyone," *The New Health Club with Ann Phillipi*, https://www.youtube.com/watch?v=qj00RSTDnWQ.

37. Stamets, "6 Ways Mushrooms Can Save the World," TED.com, 2009, https://www.youtube.com/watch?v=XI5frPV58tY.

38. Matt Powers, "Paul Stamets: The Origin Story of Fungi Perfecti," *Regenerative Soil and Permaculture*, 2021, https://www.youtube.com/watch?v=DnVtobZ13Fk.

39. Stamets, "Mushrooms Are Spiritual Medicine."

40. New Hope Network Staff, "The Natural List: Exclusive Interview with Paul Stamets," *New Hope Network*, October 12, 2023, https://www.newhope.com/vitamins-and-supplements/the-natural-list-exclusive-interview-paul-stamets: "The unanimity of being into a superconsciousness [is what] some people call God, and some religions try to navigate to this. There are some extant truths in life that are self-apparently obvious that you know in your core is true. I know in my core the most revolutionary understanding I have is that we're in this corporeal form, an assembly of molecules and atoms. We came from the soils that gave us birth, we came from stardust, we return. It's not a bad thing. It should give anyone solace that they are part of a much larger system and the dance of molecules, and the harmony and symphony of the universe is beautiful and fundamentally good."

41. Stamets, "Mushrooms Are Spiritual Medicine."

42. Joe Rogan Experience, "Paul Stamets on Mushrooms."

43. Tree Media, "Paul Stamets on How Mushrooms Can Save us from Ourselves."

44. Stamets, "A Time in Life for Deep Reflection," PaulStamets.com, July 18, 2020, https://paulstamets.com/news/a-time-in-life-for-deep-reflection. See also Stamets, Advertisement for TheraPsil: Therapeutic Psilocybin, Facebook.com, 2020. "There's two things certain in life: we are born, and we die. Where do come from, where are we going? With the psilocybin experience, you suddenly know that you are part of a giant oneness, and it gives you context and consolation about your own mortality. So I think it's critically important that at the end of your life, you have a right to these substances. . . . Everyone has a right for how they're going to leave this life."

45. Stamets, *Psilocybin Mushrooms*, 14–15.

46. Pollan, *How to Change*, 116. See Joe Rogan Experience, "Paul Stamets on Mushrooms."

47. Tree Media, "Paul Stamets on How Mushrooms Can Save Us."

48. Stamets, *Mycelium Running*, 2. "The mycelial archetype is seen throughout the universe: in the patterns of hurricanes, dark matter and the internet. The similarity in form to mycelium cannot be a coincidence. . . . The architecture of mycelium resembles patterns predicted in string theory, and astrophysicists theorize that the most energy-conserving forms in the universe will be organized as threads of matterenergy. The

arrangement of these strings resembles mycelium. When the internet was designed, a weblike structure maximized the pooling of data and computational power while minimizing critical points upon which the system is dependent. I believe the structure of the internet is simply an archetypal form . . . which is also seen in the human brain" (*Mycelium Running*, 6–7).

49. Stamets, *Mycelium Running*, 4.

50. "These are network-based organisms, they're externalized brains. . . . We are descendants of mycelium. . . . These are network-based organisms that have within them by their own design an innate ability to adapt and to store information and have a form of intelligence that gives us an opportunity to use them to have new discoveries" (Matt Powers, "Paul Stamets: The Origin Story of Fungi Perfecti," *Regenerative Soil and Permaculture*, 2021, https://www.youtube.com/watch?v=DnVtobZ13Fk).

51. Stamets, *Mycelium Running*, 4.

52. Stamets, *Mycelium Running*, 281.

53. Tree Media, "Paul Stamets on How Mushrooms Can Save Us." See also New Hope Network Staff, "The Natural List: Exclusive Interview with Paul Stamets," *New Hope Network*, October 12, 2023, https://www.newhope.com/vitamins-and-supplements/the-natural-list-exclusive-interview-paul-stamets: "This is a growing disease that's expanding over the surface mass of the planet. . . . Humans are literally becoming a disease blight on the ecosystem of the planet. Unless we rein in and start looking downstream, you have a responsibility for your grandchildren's grandchildren's grandchildren's future."

54. Stamets, *Psilocybin Mushrooms*, 19.

55. Stamets in Pollan, *How to Change*, 125.

56. Stamets, quoted in Pollan, "What It's Like to Trip on the World's Most Potent Mushroom," *The Atlantic*, June 4, 2018, https://www.theatlantic.com/science/archive/2018/06/what-its-like-to-trip-on-the-most-potent-magic-mushroom/561860/.

57. Paul Stamets and Matthew Johnson, "Psilocybin on the Psyche," *Whalebone Magazine*, 2021, https://whalebonemag.com/psilocybin-on-the-psyche/.

58. New Hope Network Staff, "The Natural List: Exclusive Interview with Paul Stamets," *New Hope Network*, October 12, 2023, https://www.newhope.com/vitamins-and-supplements/the-natural-list-exclusive-interview-paul-stamets.

59. Stamets "Mushrooms Are Spiritual Medicine for Everyone," *The New Health Club with Ann Phillipi*, https://www.youtube.com/watch?v=qj00RSTDnWQ. In another interview, Stamets explains, "It's truly a network that we need to reinforce and collaborate with. . . . Mushrooms give you the forethought into the ecosystem. You begin to understand that nature is alive all around you. We came from the fabric of nature, we are part of nature . . . it's so important we understand literally our roots and be good custodians of the ecosystem. You can't eat a microchip. You can't breath electricity . . . We have to protect the earth that gave us birth" (New Hope Network Staff, "The Natural List: Exclusive Interview with Paul Stamets," *New Hope Network*, October 12, 2023, https://www.newhope.com/vitamins-and-supplements/the-natural-list-exclusive-interview-paul-stamets).

60. Paul Stamets, ed., *Fantastic Fungi: How Mushrooms Can Heal, Shift Consciousness and Save the Planet* (San Rafael, CA: Earth Aware, 2019), 69.

61. See Ferguson, *The Aquarian Conspiracy: Personal and Social Transformation in the 1980s* (London: Routledge, 1981), 18.

62. New Hope Network Staff, "The Natural List: Exclusive Interview with Paul Stamets."

63. See Segnit, "Hippie Inc."; Farber, "Building the Counterculture"; Davis, "The Business of Getting High"; Wilson, "Commerce in Hippieland," *Los Angeles Times*, January 28, 1968, B16–B21.

64. Matt Powers, "Paul Stamets: The Origin Story of Fungi Perfecti," *Regenerative Soil and Permaculture*, 2021, https://www.youtube.com/watch?v=DnVtobZ13Fk.

65. Powers, "Paul Stamets."

66. Powers, "Paul Stamets."

67. Kenneth Miller, "How Mushrooms Can Save the World," *Discover*, May 31, 2013, https://web.archive.org/web/20191115020921/http://discovermagazine.com/2013/julyaug/13-mushrooms-clean-up-oil-spills-nuclear-meltdowns-and-human-health.

68. Host Defense, "Discover Wellness from Within," Hostdefense.com, 2024, https://hostdefense.com/.

69. Fungi Perfecti, "Gifts & Gear," 2024. https://fungi.com/collections/gifts-gear/.

70. Paul Stamets and Matthew Johnson, "Psilocybin on the Psyche," *Whalebone Magazine*, 2021, https://whalebonemag.com/psilocybin-on-the-psyche/.

71. Fungi Perfecti, "We're Climate Positive," FungiPerfect.com, March 10, 2020, https://fungi.com/blogs/articles/we-re-climate-positive; Fungi Perfecti, "The Materials Matter," FungiPerfecti.com, December 16, 2020, https://fungi.com/blogs/articles/packaging?_pos=5&_sid=beb2277a2&_ss=r.

72. Headcount, "Interview: Mushroom Master Paul Stamets Launches Life Box," Headcount.org, https://www.headcount.org/politics-and-elections/interview-mushroom-master-paul-stamets-launches-life-box/.

73. See Davis, "The Business of Getting High," 27–49; Davis, *From Head Shops to Whole Food.*

74. Davis, "The Business of Getting High," 27–49.

75. Mary Carreon, "Paul Stamets' Employees Push to Unionize over Allegations of Low Pay and Insurance Disruptions," May 31, 2024, *Double Blind Magazine*, https://doubleblindmag.com/paul-stamets-fungi-perfecti/. See also "Workers at Fungi Perfecti Are Pushing for a Union, but Facing Obstacles from a Consulting Firm Known for Its Union Avoidance Services," *Cannabis Law Report*, 2024, https://cannabislaw.report/double-blind-reprt-workers-at-fungi-perfecti-are-pushing-for-a-union-but-facing-obstacles-from-a-consulting-firm-known-for-its-union-avoidance-services/.

76. "Remove Paul Stamets as TESC Commencement Speaker," Actionnetwork.org, 2024, https://actionnetwork.org/petitions/remove-paul-stamets-as-tesc-commencement-speaker.

77. Carreon, "Paul Stamets' Employees Push to Unionize."

78. Carreon, "Paul Stamets' Employees Push to Unionize."

79. Carreon, "Paul Stamets' Employees Push to Unionize."

80. "Remove Paul Stamets as TESC Commencement Speaker," Actionnetwork.org, 2024, https://actionnetwork.org/petitions/remove-paul-stamets-as-tesc-commencement-speaker.

81. Bell, "The Cultural Contradictions of Capitalism," *The Journal of Aesthetic Education* 6, nos. 1/2 (1972): 38.

82. See Jane Wilson, "Commerce in Hippieland," *Los Angeles Times*, January 28, 1968, B16–B21; "The Age of Acquireous," *Good Times*, December 11, 1970, 10; Farber, "Building the Counterculture."

83. Pace and Devenot, "Right Wing Psychedelia."

84. Tsing, *Mushroom at the End of the World.*

85. Marilyn Ferguson, *The Aquarian Conspiracy: Personal and Social Transformation in the 1980s* (London: Routledge, 1981), 18.

86. See Hartmut Berghoff and Adam Rome, eds., *Green Capitalism? Business and Environment in the Twentieth Century* (Philadelphia: University of Pennsylvania Press, 2017); L. Hunter Lovins and Boyd Cohen, *Climate Capitalism: Capitalism in the Age of Climate Change* (New York: Hill and Wang, 2011).

87. A good example of a strong case against capitalism is Kohei Seito, *Slow Down: The Degrowth Manifesto* (New York: Astra House, 2024). See also Daniel Susskind, *Growth: A History and a Reckoning* (Cambridge, MA: Belknap Press, 2024); Daniel Tanuro, *Green Capitalism: Why It Can't Work* (Halifax: Fernwood Publishing, 2014).

88. Seito, *Slow Down*, xi, 34. See also Adrienne Butler, *The Value of a White Whale: On the Illusions of Green Capitalism* (Manchester: Manchester University Press, 2022); Richard Smith, *Green Capitalism: The God That Failed* (Rickmansworth: College Publications, 2016).

89. Berghoff and Rome, *Green Capitalism?*, 12.

CHAPTER SIX

1. Griffiths, "Psilocybin and Mystical Experience: Implications for Healthy Psychological Functioning, Spirituality, and Religion," *Harvard Divinity School*, September 20, 2020, https://cswr.hds.harvard.edu/news/2020/09/29/video-psilocybin-and-mystical-experience-implications-healthy-psychological.

2. McKenna, *Food of the Gods*, xiii.

3. Andrew Jacobs, "The Psychedelic Revolution Is Coming," *The New York Times*, May 9, 2021, https://www.nytimes.com/2021/05/09/health/psychedelics-mdma-psilocybin-molly-mental-health.html.

4. Roland R. Griffiths, "The Science of Psilocybin and Its Use to Relieve Suffering," TEDMED, 2016, https://www.youtube.com/watch?v=81-v8ePXPd4.

5. Griffiths, Richards, McCann, and Jesse, "Psilocybin Can Occasion Mystical Experiences."

6. Brendan Borrell, "The Psychedelic Evangelist," *The New York Times*, March 21, 2024, https://www.nytimes.com/2024/03/21/health/psychedelics-roland-griffiths-johns-hopkins.html. See also Travis Kitchens, "The Pseudo-Religion of Psychedelics," *Compact Magazine*, December 18, 2023, https://www.compactmag.com/article/the-pseudo-religion-of-psychedelics/.

7. Hood, "The Construction and Preliminary Validation of a Measure of Reported Mystical Experience," *Journal for the Scientific Study of Religion* 14 (1975): 29–41. See also Travis Kitchens, "A Channel for Magic: Ralph Hood's Mysticism Scale and the Occult Roots of the Johns Hopkins Psychedelic Research Program," *Psymposia*, September 9, 2022, https://www.psymposia.com/magazine/a-channel-for-magic-ralph-hoods-mysticism-scale-and-the-occult-roots-of-the-johns-hopkins-psychedelic-research-program/.

8. See Taves, "Mystical and Other Alterations"; Breau and Gilles-Smith, "Psychometric *brahman*"; Mosurinjohn, Roseman, and Girn, "Psychedelic-Induced Mystical Experiences"; Kitchens, "A Channel for Magic"; James W. Sanders and Josjan Zijlmans, "Moving Past Mysticism in Psychedelic Science," *ACS Pharmacology & Translational Science* 4 (2021): 1253–55.

9. Rick Strassman, quoted in Kitchens, "A Channel for Magic." See Borrell, "Psychedelic Evangelist."

10. Devenot, Conner, and Doyle, "Dark Side of the Shroom," 278.

11. See Martinez-Cruz, "María-Sabina"; Devenot, Conner, and Doyle, "Dark Side of the Shroom,"

12. Evans, "Immortality Key." See also Jonathan Smith, "UK Venture Round Shines Spotlight on Europe's Psychedelic Scene," *Labiotech*, August 24, 20921, https://www.labiotech.eu/trends-news/beckley-psytech-compass-psychedelics/; "Eleusis Is Joining Beckley Scitech," Eleusisltd.com, 2024, https://www.eleusisltd.com/. On the broader growth of the drug industry, see Dumit, *Drugs for Life*.

13. On this history, see Langlitz, *Neuropsychedelia*.

14. Strassman, "Human Hallucinogenic Drug Research in the United Staes: Present Day Case History and Review of the Process," *Psychoactive Drugs* 23, no. 1 (1991): 29–38. See Shaunacy Ferro, "Why Doctors Can't Give You LSD (but Maybe They Should)," *Popular Science*, April 17, 2013.

15. Langlitz, *Neuropsychedelia*, 43.

16. Marianne Williamson podcast, "Psychedelics and Spirituality with Rick Doblin, PhD," Maps.org, 2002, https://maps.org/2021/03/11/marianne-williamson-podcast-psychedelics-and-spirituality-with-rick-doblin-ph-d/.

17. Center for Psychedelic and Consciousness Research, "About," Hopkinspsychedelic.org, 2024, https://hopkinspsychedelic.org/.

18. On Siddha Yoga, see Douglas Renfrew Brooks, ed., *Meditation Revolution: A History and Theology of the Siddha Yoga Lineage* (New Delhi: Motilal Banarsidass, 2024). On the scandals surrounding the movement's leaders, see Jeffrey J. Kripal, "Inside-Out, Outside-In: Existential Place and Academic Practice in the Study of North American Guru-Traditions," *Religious Studies Review* 24, no. 3 (1999): 233–38; Sarah Caldwell, "The Heart of the Secret: A Personal and Scholarly Encounter with Shakta Tantrism in Siddha Yoga," *Nova Religio* 5, no. 1 (2001): 9–51.

19. Griffiths in Pollan, *How to Change*, 33.

20. Julie Scharper, "Crash Course in the Nature of the Mind," *Johns Hopkins Magazine*, Fall 2017, https://hub.jhu.edu/magazine/2017/fall/roland-griffiths-magic-mushrooms-experiment-psilocybin-depression/.

21. Scharper, "Crash Course."

22. Griffiths, "Science of Psilocybin."

23. Pollan, *How to Change*, 77.

24. Griffiths, "Science of Psilocybin." See also Griffiths, "Psilocybin and Mystical Experience."

25. Barrett and Griffiths, "Classic Hallucinogens and Mystical Experience." See also Matthew W. Johnson, Peter S. Hendricks, Frederick S. Barrett, and Roland R. Griffiths, "Classic Psychedelics: An Integrative Review of Epidemiology, Therapeutics, Mystical Experience, and Brain Network Function," *Pharmacology & Therapeutics* 197 (May 2019): 83–102. See also David Yaden, Khoa D. Le Nguyen, Margarat Kern, Alexander B. Belser, Johannes Eichstaedt, Jonathan Iwry, Mary E. Smith, Nancy A. Wintering, Ralph W. Hood Jr., and Andrew B. Newberg, "Of Roots and Fruits: A Comparison of Psychedelic and Nonpsychedelic Mystical Experiences," *Journal of Humanistic Psychology* 57, no. 4 (2016), https://doi.org/10.1177/0022167816674625.

26. Roland R. Griffiths, Ethan S. Hurwitz, Alan K. Davis, Matthew W. Johnson, and Robert Jesse, "Survey of Subjective 'God Encounter Experiences': Comparisons

Among Naturally Occurring Experiences and Those Occasioned by the Classic Psychedelics, Psilocybin, LSD, Ayahuasca, and DMT," *PLOS One* 14, no. 4 (2019), https://doi.org/10.1371/journal.pone.0214377. As the authors write, "Salient experiences interpreted as personal encounters with God, gods, or emissaries of God, have been documented for millennia. . . . God encounter and mystical experiences have also been described after ingestion of classic psychedelic drugs such as psilocybin, lysergic acid diethylamide (LSD), N,N-dimethyltryptamine (DMT), and mescaline, all of whose actions are mediated at the serotonin 2A receptor."

27. Smith quoted in Pollan, *How to Change*, 81.

28. See Stephen Ross, Anthony Bossis, Jeffrey Guss, Gabrielle Agin-Liebes, Tara Malone, Barry Cohen, Sarah E. Mennenga, Alexander Belser, Krystallia Kalliontzi, James Babb, Zhe Su, Patricia Corby, and Brian L. Schmidt, "Rapid and Sustained Symptom Reduction Following Psilocybin Treatment for Anxiety and Depression in Patients with Life-Threatening Cancer: A Randomized Controlled Trial," *Journal of Psychopharmacology* 30, no. 12 (2016): 1165–80.

29. McCullough et al., "Psilocybin-Induced Mystical Type Experiences." See also Frederick S. Barrett, Matthew W. Johnson, and Roland R. Griffiths, "Validation of the Revised Mystical Experience Questionnaire in Experimental Sessions with Psilocybin," *Journal of Psychopharmacology* 29, no. 11 (2015): 1182–90.

30. McCullough et al., "Psilocybin-Induced Mystical Type Experiences."

31. Breau and Gillis-Smith, "Psychometric *Brahman*," 3. See Griffiths, Richards, McCann, and Jesse, "Psilocybin Can Occasion Mystical-Type Experience," where they reiterate Stace's and Pahnke's domains of mystical experience: internal unity (pure awareness; a merging with ultimate reality); external unity (unity of all things; all things are alive; all is one); transcendence of time and space; ineffability and paradoxicality (claim of difficulty in describing the experience in words); sense of sacredness (awe); noetic quality (claim of intuitive knowledge of ultimate reality); and deeply felt positive mood (joy, peace, and love).

32. Frederick S. Barrett and Roland R. Griffiths, "Classic Hallucinogens and Mystical Experiences: Phenomenology and Neural Correlates," *Currents Topics in Behavioral Neuroscience* 36 (2018): 398–99.

33. Breau and Gillis-Smith, "Psychometric *Brahman*," 14.

34. Taves, "Mystical and Other Alterations," 677.

35. Hood, "The Construction and Preliminary Validation of a Measure of Reported Mystical Experience," *Journal for the Scientific Study of Religion* 14, no. 1 (1975): 29–41.

36. Hood quoted in Kitchens, "A Channel for Magic."

37. Hood quoted in Kitchens, "A Channel for Magic."

38. Kitchens, "A Channel for Magic."

39. Taves, "Mystical and Other Alterations," 670.

40. Latour and Woolgar, *Laboratory Life: The Construction of Scientific Facts* (Princeton, NJ: Princeton University Press, 1987), 17.

41. Geraci, "Laboratory Ritual: Experimentation the Advancement of Science," *Zygon* 37, no. 2 (2002): 891. See also Denis R. Alexander, "Scientists' Rituals Are Ripe for Investigation," *Nature* 494 (2013): 314: "many aspects of the ritual behaviour being investigated by anthropologist Harvey Whitehouse and his colleagues . . . could well apply to academia, and to the scientific community in particular."

42. Leary, "In the Beginning," 84.

43. Charles Grob, Anthony R. Bossis, and Roland R. Griffiths, "Use of the Classic Hallucinogen Psilocybin for Treatment of Existential Distress Associated with Cancer," in *Psychological Aspects of Cancer*, ed. B. I. Carr and J. Steel (New York: Springer, 2022), 300. Griffiths et al., "Psilocybin Can Occasion Mystical Experiences," 268–83.

44. Julie Scharper, "Crash Course in the Nature of the Mind," *Johns Hopkins Magazine*, 2017, https://hub.jhu.edu/magazine/2017/fall/roland-griffiths-magic-mushrooms-experiment-psilocybin-depression/#:~:text=Participants%20pluck%20a%20capsule%20of,more%20real%20than%20everyday%20life.

45. "Rooms," InnerGuidance.com, 2024, https://innerguidanceinc.com/services-copy/. See also Jacobs, "Psychedelic Revolution": "The future of psychedelic medicine can already be glimpsed at a suite of plush, soothingly decorated 'journey rooms' that occupy the top floor of an office building in Midtown Manhattan. The clinic, run by Field Trip Health, is a year-old venture where patients wear eyeshades and listen to electronic music and Tibetan chanting as they are administered drugs."

46. NYU Langone Health, "The Effects of Psilocybin-Facilitated Experience on the Psychology and Effectiveness of Religious Professionals," ClinicalTrials.gov, 2022, https://clinicaltrials.gov/study/NCT02421263.

47. Quoted in Lattin, *God on Psychedelics*, 2.

48. Lattin, *God on Psychedelics*, 5.

49. Lattin, *God on Psychedelics*, 5.

50. Lattin, *God on Psychedelics*, 3.

51. Quoted in Lattin, *God on Psychedelics*, 9.

52. Quoted in Lattin, *God on Psychedelics*, 2.

53. Ligare, "About," Ligare.org, 2024, https://www.ligare.org/about.

54. Strassman, "The Psychedelic Religion of Mystical Consciousness," *Journal of Psychedelic Studies* 2, no. 1 (2018): 4.

55. Strassman, in Kitchens, "A Channel for Magic."

56. Kitchens, "A Channel for Magic."

57. Alex Grey, Instagram.com, October 18, 2023, https://www.instagram.com/alexgreycosm/p/Cyi-b8YrK2Z/?img_index=1.

58. Borrell, "Psychedelic Evangelist."

59. Johnson, "Consciousness, Religion, and Gurus: Pitfalls of Psychedelic Medicine," *ACS Pharmacology and Translational Science* 4, no. 2 (2021): 580. See Borrell, "Psychedelic Evangelist": "Dr. Johnson wasn't the only researcher who was uncomfortable with the mystical atmosphere. 'I've seen people do some "namastes" in there,' said Manoj Doss, a former postdoctoral researcher at the center. Dr. Doss was also taken aback by the incense burner and the preparatory sessions done at Dr. Richards's home."

60. Johnson, "Consciousness, Religion and Gurus."

61. Borrell, "Psychedelic Evangelist."

62. Sanders and Zijlmans, "Moving Past Mysticism in Psychedelic Science," *ACS Pharmacology & Translational Science* 4 (2021): 1255. A similar point is made by Mosurinjohn, Roseman, and Girn, "Psychedelic-Induced Mystical Experiences": "the mysticism concept [is] fraught with metaphysical assumptions and cultural biases which have not been sufficiently recognized or reckoned with in the psychedelic science literature."

For a discussion of this debate, see Chris Letheby, Jaipreet Mattu, and Eric Hochstein, "How to End the Mysticism Wars in Psychedelic Science," in *The Palgrave*

Handbook of Philosophy and Psychoactive Drug Use, ed. Rob Lovering (London: Palgrave, 2024), 127–54.

63. Mosurinjohn, Roseman, and Girn, "Psychedelic-Induced Mystical Experiences." Strassman makes a similar point in "The Psychedelic Religion," 4: "There are clearly phenomenological similarities between certain religious experiences in long-time, dedicated practitioners of spiritual traditions and those brought on by psychedelics. But to equate the two is a categorical error." See also Sanders and Zijlmans, "Moving Past Mysticism in Psychedelic Science," 1255: "The current blend of mysticism and science in psychedelic research risks damaging the credibility and potential of psychedelic science. A theoretical shift is needed to clarify the division between psychedelic science and supernatural or nonempirical belief systems."

64. Pollan, *How to Change*, 80.

65. Griffiths, interviewed in Lattin, *God on Psychedelics*, 25. On the potentially harmful effects of *Psilocybe* mushrooms, see Jan van Amsterdam, Antoon Opperhuizen, and Wim van den Brink, "Harm Potential of Magic Mushroom Use: A Review," *Regulatory Toxicology and Pharmacology* 59 (2011): 423–29.

66. Kitchens, "Pseudo-Religion of Psychedelics." See Borrell, "Psychedelic Evangelist": "The drugs also come with unpredictable risks, such as psychotic episodes, increased suicidality or extended emotional difficulties, which are most likely underreported."

67. Petersen, "Taking Mushrooms." See also Kripal, *Superhumanities*, 210–11.

68. Petersen, "Taking Mushrooms."

69. Kripal, *Superhumanities*, 210–11.

70. Petersen, "Taking Mushrooms."

71. Gimello, "Mysticism in Its Contexts," 62.

72. Petersen, "Taking Mushrooms." See also Petersen, "A Theological Reckoning with Bad Trips," *Harvard Divinity Bulletin*, Autumn/Winter 2022, https://bulletin.hds.harvard.edu/a-theological-reckoning-with-bad-trips/: "Psychedelic science does an odd dance with the spiritual. On the one hand, studies . . . have popularized the notion that a mystical-type experience leads to better therapeutic outcomes. This frame reduces transcendence to its therapeutic potential—a breathtakingly transactional posture to the divine that creates a sort of tautology whereby the mystical is therapeutic because the therapeutic is mystical."

73. Kripal, *Superhumanities*, 210–11.

74. Petersen, "Theological Reckoning."

75. Petersen, "Theological Reckoning."

76. Petersen, "Theological Reckoning."

77. Daniele Fanelli, "Negative Results Are Disappearing from Most Disciplines and Countries," *Scientometrics* 90 (2012): 891–904, https://doi.org/10.1007/s11192-011-0494-7.

78. Devenot, Conner, and Doyle, "Dark Side of the Shroom," 478.

79. Petersen, quoted in Lattin, 29–30.

80. Bethany Halford, "Drug Companies Are Investing Big in Psychedelics," *Chemical & Engineering News*, March 6, 2022, https://cen.acs.org/pharmaceuticals/drug-development/Drug-companies-investing-big-psychedelics/100/i9.

81. Jacobs, "Psychedelic Revolution."

82. Zoe Cormier, "Psilocybin Is Headed for the Mainstream—It's Bringing the Problems of Big Pharma with It," *Elemental*, August 12, 2019, https://elemental

.medium.com/psilocybin-is-headed-for-the-mainstream-its-bringing-the-problems-of-big-pharma-with-it-45354b4836fc. See also W. F. Yacowicz, "The Future of Psychedelic Medicine Might Skip the Trip," *Forbes*, June 23, 2021, https://www.forbes.com/sites/willyakowicz/2021/06/23/the-future-of-psychedelic-medicine-might-skip-the-trip-rick-doblin-bryan-roth-mindmed-darpa-maps/?sh=6ade98f1244f; Cameron Coata and Sam Shead, "Peter Thiel–Backed Psychedelic Start-Up Shares Pop in Wall Street Debut," CNBC.com, June 18, 2021, https://www.cnbc.com/2021/06/18/peter-thiel-backed-psychedelic-start-ups-shares-pop-in-wall-street-debut.html; Olivia Goldhill, "A Millionaire Couple Is Threatening to Create a Magic Mushroom Monopoly," November 18, 2018, https://qz.com/1454785/a-millionaire-couple-is-threatening-to-create-a-magic-mushroom-monopoly.

83. Kitchens, "A Channel for Magic."

84. Devenot, Conner, and Doyle, "Dark Side of the Shroom," 477–78.

85. Ross Murdick, "Are Magic Mushrooms the Next Cannabis Industry? How Entrepreneurs Can Prepare," *Business News Daily*, April 28, 2023, https://www.businessnewsdaily.com/magic-mushrooms-business-opportunities.

86. Jacobs, "Psychedelic Revolution." In the words of Compass Pathways' CEO, Kabir Nath, "A lot of our time is spent thinking about: How will this commercialise? How will this scale? And that's the question we get a lot from investors. So what we've done is we've identified a number of potential different settings of care where psilocybin could be used" (Psychedelic Alpha, "Interview: Compass Pathways Kabir Nath Discusses Commercialisation, Psychological Support, and Competitive Landscape," *Psychedelic Alpha*, January 31, 2024, https://psychedelicalpha.com/news/interview-compass-pathways-ceo-kabir-nath-discusses-commercialisation-psychological-support-and-competitive-landscape).

87. James Hallifax, "Compass Pathways Psilocybin Patent Upheld," *Psychedelic Spotlight News*, June 24, 2022, https://psychedelicspotlight.com/compass-pathways-psilocybin-patent/. See also Martinez-Cruz, "María Sabina," 190.

88. Devenot, Conner, and Doyle, "Dark Side of the Shroom," 278.

89. Jonathan D. Grinstein, "Go Higher: Atai Life Sciences Is Moving the Dial on Psychedelic Medicine Clinical Trial Outcomes," *Genetic Engineering and Biotechnology News*, April 7, 2023, https://www.genengnews.com/gen-edge/go-higher-atai-life-sciences-is-moving-the-dial-on-psychedelic-medicine-clinical-trial-outcomes/.

90. Bethany Halford, "Drug Companies Are Investing Big in Psychedelics," *Chemical & Engineering News*, March 6 2022, https://cen.acs.org/pharmaceuticals/drug-development/Drug-companies-investing-big-psychedelics/100/i9.

91. Costa and Shead, "Peter Thiel–Backed Psychedelic Start-Up's Share Pop."

92. Kitchens, "A Channel for Magic." See Kitchens, "Pseudo-Religion of Psychedelics."

93. Thiel, "Competition Is for Losers," *The Wall Street Journal*, September 12, 2014, https://www.wsj.com/articles/peter-thiel-competition-is-for-losers-1410535536. See also Pace and Devenot, "Right Wing Psychedelia."

94. Julie Lythcott-Haims, "My Conversation with Peter Thiel About Apartheid . . . and Its Unfolding Aftermath," *Medium*, November 2, 2016, https://medium.com/indian-thoughts/my-conversation-with-peter-thiel-about-apartheid-and-its-aftermath-3fdf4249b08d.

95. Thiel, "The Education of a Libertarian," *Cato Unbound*, April 13, 2009, https://www.cato-unbound.org/2009/04/13/peter-thiel/education-libertarian. In this piece,

Thiel also suggest that the idea of a "capitalist democracy" is an oxymoron, since the two systems are inherently at odds.

96. See Love, "The Case Against Psychedelic Utopianism": "It's remarkably easy to find examples of psychedelic use associated with extreme right-wing or fascist beliefs instead. Or, just as common in today's booming for-profit psychedelic industry, examples of when psychedelics are associated with advocacy for capitalism, IP protection, and monopolies."

97. Pace and Devenot, "Right-Wing Psychedelia." See New York Times Audio, "The C.E.O.s Are Tripping. Can Psychedelics Help the C-Suite?," *The New York Times*, December 12, 2024, https://www.nytimes.com/audio/app/2024/12/12/business/psychedelic-retreats-ceos.html?referringSource=sharing: "A growing cottage industry is dedicated to the theory that mind-altering drugs can improve business leadership."

98. Devenot, Conner, and Doyle, "Dark Side of the Shroom," 478.

99. Benjamin Adams, "Is Mescaline a Key Component of the Future of Medicine?," *Forbes*, July 7, 2021, https://www.forbes.com/sites/benjaminadams/2021/07/07/is-mescaline-a-key-component-in-the-future-of-medicine-xphyto-aims-to-find-out/?sh=48f69ea61e90.

100. Annette McGivney, "Peyote Is the Darling of the Psychedelic Renaissance," *The Guardian*, December 19, 2023, https://www.theguardian.com/us-news/2023/dec/19/indigenous-communities-protecting-psychedelics-peyote-corporations?CMP=share_btn_link.

101. See Joseph Dumit, *Drugs for Life: How Pharmaceutical Companies Define Our Life* (Durham, NC: Duke University Press, 2012), back cover: "underlying the continual growth in medications, disease categories, costs, and insecurity is a relatively new perception of ourselves as inherently ill and in need of chronic treatment. This perception is based on clinical trials that we have largely outsourced to pharmaceutical companies. Those companies in turn see clinical trials as investments and measure the value of those investments by the size of the market and profits that they will create. They only ask questions for which the answer is more medicine."

102. Evans, "The Immortality Key." See also Jonathan Smith, "UK Venture Round Shines Spotlight on Europe's Psychedelic Scene," *Labiotech*, August 24, 20921, https://www.labiotech.eu/trends-news/beckley-psytech-compass-psychedelics/.

103. Evans, "The Immortality Key." See Dumit, *Drugs for Life*.

104. Hood, quoted in Kitchens, "A Channel for Magic."

105. Petrie-Flom Center for Health Law Policy, Biotechnology, and Bioethics at Harvard Law School, "Disclosed: Conflicts of Interest in the Psychedelics Ecosystem," *Petrie-Flom Center for Health Policy*, December 6, 2022, https://petrieflom.law.harvard.edu/events/details/conflicts-interest-psychedelics-ecosystem.

106. See Stephen Ross, Anthony Bossis, and Brian L. Schmidt, "Rapid and Sustained Symptom Reduction Following Psilocybin Treatment for Anxiety and Depression in Patients with Life-Threatening Cancer," *Journal of Psychopharmacology* 30, no. 12 (2016), https://doi.org/10.1177/0269881116675512; "Psilocybin Eases Depression in Patients with Life-Threatening Cancer, Study Says," *Dana-Farber Cancer Institute*, December 202, 2023, https://www.dana-farber.org/newsroom/news-releases/2023/psilocybin-eases-depression-in-patients-with-cancer-study-finds.

107. Kitchens, "Pseudo-Religion of Psychedelics."

CONCLUSION

1. Pollan, in Stamets, ed., *Fantastic Fungi*, 121.

2. Haraway, *Staying with the Trouble*, 98.

3. Scott F. Gilbert, Jan Sapp, and Alfred Tauber, "A Symbiotic View of Life: We Have Never Been Individuals," *Quarterly Review of Biology* 87, no. 4 (2012): 325–41.

4. Foucault, "Nietzsche, Genealogy, History," 146.

5. I take this metaphor from Arjun Appadurai, *Modernity at Large: Cultural Dimensions of Globalization* (Minneapolis: University of Minnesota Press, 1996). See also Urban, *Zorba the Buddha*.

6. "Odyssey: A Public Benefit Corporation," Odysseypbc.com, 2024. https://www.odysseypbc.com/.

7. On this point, see Tsing, *Mushroom*, 3: "Matsutake's willingness to emerge in blasted landscapes allows us to explore the ruin that has become our collective home."

8. See "America's Largest Mega-Church—Where Shrooms Are a Sacrament—Makes Millions," *Forbes Daily Briefing*, 2024, https://www.youtube.com/watch?v=NN5IGIxe94s; Natalia Gurevich, "Why Some San Franciscans Are Embracing Spirituality and Magic Mushrooms," *San Francisco Examiner*, April 19, 2024, https://www.sfexaminer.com/news/business/religion-and-psychedelics-collide-in-san-francisco-churches/article_19aa54ee-fcfc-11ee-b841-138d7e70a6bc.html; Lester Black, "Magic Mushroom Pastor Is Willing to Go to Jail for His New San Francisco Church," *San Francisco Gate*, April 12, 2023, https://www.sfgate.com/cannabis/article/oakland-magic-mushroom-church-sf-17885505.php.

9. See Jessica De La Torre, "Oakland's Psychedelic Mushroom Church Makes a Cautious Return," *The Oaklandside*, June 10, 2022, https://oaklandside.org/2022/06/10/zide-door-psycedelic-magic-mushroom-church-oakland/.

10. Gurevich, "Why Some San Franciscans Are Embracing Spirituality."

11. Hodges, "The Religious Use of High Dose Magic Mushrooms," *Zide Door: Church of Ambrosia*, February 27, 2022, https://www.youtube.com/watch?v=R_qu_obA4Jw.

12. "America's Largest Mega-Church."

13. Church of Ambrosia, "Religious Evolution Doctrine," Ambrosia.Church.com, 2024, https://ambrosia.church/religious-evolution/.

14. Zide Door, "Oakland's Church of Entheogenic Plants," Zidedoor.com, 2024, https://zidedoor.com/.

15. Church of Ambrosia, "High/Heroic," *Ambrosia Church*, 2024, https://ambrosia.church/safety-dose-guides/high-dose/.

16. Church of Ambrosia, "High/Heroic."

17. Gurevich, "Why Some San Franciscans Are Embracing Spirituality."

18. Miles Dilworth, "Pastor Behind Psychedelic San Francisco Church Raking in $5m a Year Supplying Mushrooms and Weed to Members," *The Daily Mail*, April 14, 2024, https://www.dailymail.co.uk/news/article-13292963/dave-hodges-shrooms-weed-supplier-san-francisco-church.html.

19. Gurevich, "Why Some San Franciscans Are Embracing Spirituality."

20. See Urban, *New Age*, chap. 1, and Urban, *Church of Scientology*, chap. 5.

21. See Urban, *Church of Scientology*, chap. 5 and conclusion.

22. Gurevich, "Why Some San Franciscans Are Embracing Spirituality."

23. Pace and Devenot, "Right-Wing Psychedelia." See Love, "The Case Against Psychedelic Utopianism."

24. Love, "The Case Against Psychedelic Utopianism"; Woolfe, *Altered States*. On Aum Shinrikyo and Manson, see Juergensmeyer, *Terror in the Mind of God*, chap. 6; Guinn, *Manson*.

25. Pace and Devenot, "Right-Wing Psychedelia."

26. Metzner, Pacific Radio Archives, 1988, quoted in Lattin, *Changing Our Minds*, 173.

27. Lattin, *Changing Our Minds*, 173.

28. As Sam Woolfe put it, "it is unrealistic and naïve to trust that widespread psychedelic use will transform the world into a utopia. Most of the people I see promoting the idea of a revolution in collective consciousness through psychedelics are the kind of people I would least trust to be in charge of social and political change" ("A Case for Psychedelic Scepticism," Samwoolfe.com, July 15, 2024, https://www.samwoolfe.com/2024/07/psychedelic-scepticism.html).

29. Here I follow David Harvey, who aptly defines neoliberalism as "the commodification of everything." See Harvey, *A Brief History of Neoliberalism* (New York: Oxford University Press, 2017).

30. Haraway, *Staying with the Trouble*, 98. I am also sympathetic to Eduardo Kohn's call for a posthuman politics that critiques the idea that humans are fundamentally separate from the rest of the world and instead explores human relations to nonhuman beings: "In the hopeful politics we seek to cultivate, we privilege heterarchy over hierarchy, the rhizomatic over the arborescent, and we celebrate the fact that horizontal processes—lateral gene transfer, symbiosis, commensalism, and the like—can be found in the non-human world" (*How Forests Think*, 19).

31. Haraway, *Staying with the Trouble*, 67.

32. Haraway, *Staying with the Trouble*, 67. See also Kohn, *How Forests Think*.

33. See Gilbert, Sapp, and Tauber, "A Symbiotic View of Life," 325–41.

34. Sheldrake, *Entangled Life*, 5.

35. Sheldrake, *Entangled Life*, 4.

36. Sheldrake, *Entangled Life*, 124.

37. Center for Biological Diversity, "Halting the Extinction Crisis," BiologicalDiversity.org, 2024, https://www.biologicaldiversity.org/programs/biodiversity/elements_of_biodiversity/extinction_crisis/.

38. Kolbert, *The Sixth Extinction: An Unnatural History* (New York: Henry Holt, 2014), 2–3. See Joshua Trey Barnett, *Mourning in the Anthropocene: Ecological Grief and Earthly Coexistence* (East Lansing: Michigan State University Press, 2022).

39. See Curtis W. Marean, "How Homo Sapiens Became the Ultimate Invasive Species," *Scientific American*, August 1, 2015, https://www.scientificamerican.com/article/how-homo-sapiens-became-the-ultimate-invasive-species/; Daniel Pauly, "Homo Sapiens: Cancer or Parasite?," *Ethics in Science and Environmental Politics* 14, no. 7 (2104): 7–10.

40. Sheldrake, *Entangled Life*, 176.

41. Haraway, *Staying with the Trouble*, 97.

42. Devenot, Conner, and Doyle, "Dark Side of the Shroom," 478.

43. Devenot, Conner, and Doyle, "Dark Side of the Shroom," 478. As Ralph Metzner similarly put it, "We need to look at the way these plants are used in traditional cultures—the whole framework and pattern. . . . The whole emphasis should be on looking at these earth-wisdom cultures and preserving native knowledge from being lost" (Pacific Radio Archives, 1988, quoted in Lattin, *Changing Our Minds*, 173).

44. On the "possibilities of coexistence within environmental disturbance" and different forms of "collaborative survival," see Tsing, *Mushroom*, 4.

45. On this point, see Katherine May, *Enchantment: Awakening Wonder in an Anxious Age* (New York: Riverhead Books, 2023), 8–9: "Enchantment is small wonder magnified through meaning, fascination caught in the web of fable and memory. It relies on small doses of awe. . . . It is a sense that we are all joined together in one continuous thread of existence with the elements constituting the earth, and that there is a potency trapped in this interconnection. . . . It is the forgotten seam in our geology . . . the ability to sense magic in the everyday, to channel in through our minds and bodies, to be sustained by it."

See also Patrick Curry, *Enchantment: Wonder in Modern Life* (Edinburgh: Floris Books, 2020); Rachel Carson, *The Sense of Wonder: A Celebration of Nature for Parents and Children* (New York: Harper Perennial, 2017).

Selected Bibliography

Archives and Special Collections

Albert Hofmann Correspondence and Other Materials. MSP 89. Purdue University Libraries and School of Information Studies, Purdue, IN.

Correspondence and Papers, General Mycological Research, 1925–87. Tina and R. Gordon Wasson Ethnomycological Collection. Harvard University Botany Libraries, Cambridge, MA.

Dennis and Terence McKenna Papers. MSP 213. Purdue University Libraries and School of Information Studies, Purdue, IN.

Field Notebooks, June 28–July 10, 1955. Tina and R. Gordon Wasson Ethnomycological Collection. Botany Libraries. Harvard University. Cambridge, MA.

Harvard Psilocybin Project Records, 1961–62. MSP 98. Purdue University Libraries and School of Information Studies, Purdue, IN.

LSD Professional Study Results, Maryland Psychiatric Research Center, 1970–74. MSP 170. University Libraries and School of Information Studies, Purdue, IN.

Photographic Material, 1950–80. Tina and R. Gordon Wasson Ethnomycological Collection. Harvard University Botany Libraries, Cambridge, MA.

Pocket Diaries and Field Notebooks, 1949–83. Tina and R. Gordon Wasson Ethnomycological Collection. Harvard University Botany Libraries, Cambridge, MA.

William Richards Collection on Walter Pahnke. MSP 68. Purdue University Libraries and School of Information Studies, Purdue, IN.

Books, Articles, and Other Materials

Adams, Benjamin. "Is Mescaline a Key Component in the Future of Medicine?" *Forbes*, July 7, 2021. https://www.forbes.com/sites/benjaminadams/2021/07/07/is-mescaline-a-key-component-in-the-future-of-medicine-xphyto-aims-to-find-out/?sh=48f69ea61e90.

Adelhofer, Otto, ed. *Codex Vindobonensis Mexicanus 1: Vollständige Faksimile-Ausgabe im Originalformat*. Graz: Akademische Druck- und Verlagsanstalt, 1974.

Akers, Brian. "A Cave in Spain Contains the Earliest Known Depictions of Mushrooms." *Mushroom: The Journal of Wild Mushrooming*, 2010. https://www.mushroomthejournal.com/a-cave-in-spain-contains-the-earliest-known-depictions-of-mushrooms/.

Akers, Brian, Juan Francisco Ruiz, Alan Piper, and Carl A. P. Ruck. "A Prehistoric Mural Depicting Neurotropic Mushrooms?" *Economic Botany* 65, no. 2 (2011): 121–28.

Allegro, John. *The Sacred Mushroom and the Cross: A Study of the Nature and Origins of Christianity Within the Fertility Cults of the Ancient Near East.* New York: Bantam, 1971.

Amsterdam, Jan van, Antoon Opperhuizen, and Wim van den Brink. "Harm Potential of Magic Mushroom Use: A Review." *Regulatory Toxicology and Pharmacology* 59 (2011): 423–29.

Andersson, Christer, Jakob Kristinsson, and Jorn Gry. *Occurrence and Use of Hallucinogenic Mushrooms Containing Psilocybin Alkaloids.* Copenhagen: Nordic Council of Ministers, 2009.

Appadurai, Arjun. *Modernity at Large: Cultural Dimensions of Globalization.* Minneapolis: University of Minnesota Press, 1996.

Baier, Karl. "High Mysticism—On the Interplay Between the Psychedelic Movement and Academic Study of Mysticism." In *Constructions of Mysticism as a Universal: Roots and Interactions Across Borders*, edited by Annette Wilke, Robert Stephanus, and Robert Suckro, 363–96. Wiesbaden: Harrassowitz Verlag, 2021.

Baker, Ian A. "Nectar of the Blue Goddess: A Living Tradition of Soma Consumption in West Bengal." In *Expanding Mindscapes: A Global History of Psychedelics*, edited by Erika Dyck and Chris Elcock, 23–50. Cambridge, MA: MIT Press, 2023.

Barnard, G. William. *Liquid Light: Ayahuasca Spirituality and the Santo Daime Tradition.* New York: Columbia University Press, 2022.

Barrett, Frederick S., and Roland R. Griffiths. "Classic Hallucinogens and Mystical Experiences: Phenomenology and Neural Correlates." *Currents Topics in Behavioral Neuroscience* 36 (2018): 393–430.

Barrett, Frederick S., Matthew W. Johnson, and Roland R. Griffiths. "Validation of the Revised Mystical Experience Questionnaire in Experimental Sessions with Psilocybin." *Journal of Psychopharmacology* 29, no. 11 (2015): 1182–90.

Bell, Daniel. "The Cultural Contradictions of Capitalism." *The Journal of Aesthetic Education* 6, nos. 1/2 (1972): 11–38.

Benjamin, Denis R. *Mushrooms: Poisons and Panaceas.* New York: W. H. Freeman and Company, 1995.

Bird, Paul. "There Is More to a Mushroom than Meets the Eye." *The New York Times*, July 14, 1957, 185.

Black, Lester. "Magic Mushroom Pastor Is Willing to Go to Jail for His New San Francisco Church." *San Francisco Gate*, April 12, 2023. https://www.sfgate.com/cannabis/article/oakland-magic-mushroom-church-sf-17885505.php.

Boone, Elizabeth Hill. *The Codex Magliabechiano and the Lost Prototype of the Magliabechiano Group.* Berkeley: University of California Press, 1983.

Borrell, Brendan. "The Psychedelic Evangelist." *The New York Times*, March 21, 2024. https://www.nytimes.com/2024/03/21/health/psychedelics-roland-griffiths-johns-hopkins.html.

Breau, Jeffrey, and Paul Gillis-Smith. "Psychometric *Brahman*, Psychedelic Science: Walter Stace, Transnational Vedanta and the Mystical Experience Questionnaire." *Interdisciplinary Science Reviews* (2023). https://doi.org/10.1080/03080188.2023.2266322.

Breen, Benjamin. *Tripping on Utopia: Margaret Mead, the Cold War, and the Birth of Psychedelics.* New York: Grand Central Publishing, 2024.

Brough, John. "Soma and *Amanita muscaria*." *Bulletin of the School of Oriental and African Studies* 34, no. 2 (1971): 331–62.

Carhart-Harris, Robin L. "How Do Psychedelics Work?" *Current Opinion in Psychiatry* 32, no. 1 (2019). https://doi.org/10.1097/YCO.0000000000000467.

Carhart-Harris, Robin L., David Erritzoe, Tim Williams, James M. Stone, Laurence J. Reed, Alessandro Colasanti, Robin J. Tyacke, Robert Leech, Andrea L. Malizia, Kevin Murphy, Peter Hobden, John Evans, Amanda Feilding, Richard G. Wise, and David J. Nutt. "Neural Correlates of the Psychedelic State as Determined by fMRI Studies with Psilocybin." *Proceedings of the National Academy of Science* 109, no. 6 (2012). https://doi.org/10.1073/pnas.1119598109.

Carhart-Harris, Robin L., Suresh Muthukumaraswamy, Leor Roseman, Mendel Kaelen, Wouter Droog, Kevin Murphy, Enzo Tagliazucchi, Eduardo E. Schenberg, Timothy Nest, Csaba Orban, Robert Leech, Luke T. Williams, Tim M. Williams, Mark Bolstridge, Ben Sessa, John McGonigle, Martin I. Sereno, David Nichols, Peter J. Hellyer, Peter Hobden, John Evans, Krish D. Singh, Richard G. Wise, H. Valerie Curran, Amanda Feilding, and David J. Nutt. "Neural Correlates of the LSD Experience Revealed by Multimodal Neuroimaging." *Proceedings of the National Academy of Science* 113, no. 17 (2016). https://doi.org/10.1073/pnas.1518377113.

Carod-Artal, F. J. "Hallucinogenic Drugs in Pre-Columbian Mesoamerican Cultures." *Neurología* 30, no. 1 (2015): 42–49.

Carrette, Jeremy, and Richard King. *Selling Spirituality: The Silent Takeover of Religion*. New York: Routledge, 2005.

Carson, Rachel. *The Sense of Wonder: A Celebration of Nature for Parents and Children*. New York: Harper Perennial, 2017.

Caso, Alfonso. "Representaciones de hongos en los codices." *Estudios de Cultura Náhuatl* 4 (1963): 27–36.

Castaneda, Carlos. Letter to R. Gordon Wasson, September 6, 1968. Series I, 140. Tina and R. Gordon Wasson Ethnomycological Collection. Harvard University Botany Libraries. Cambridge, MA.

Castaneda, Carlos. *The Teachings of Don Juan: A Yaqui Way of Knowledge*. New York: Washington Square Press, 1985.

Clark, Matthew. *The Tawny One: Soma, Haoma, and Ayahuasca*. London: Muswell Hill Press, 2017.

Clark, Walter Houston. "Walter Norman Pahnke, B.D., M.D., PH.D., 1931–1971." *Parapsychology Review* (November/December 1971): 27.

Cole, William D. "The Vegetable That Drives Men Mad." *True: The Men's Magazine*, December 1959, 54–56.

Cosmopoulos, Michael B. *Bronze Age Eleusis and the Origins of the Eleusinian Mysteries*. Cambridge: Cambridge University Press, 2015.

Curry, Patrick. *Enchantment: Wonder in Modern Life*. Edinburgh: Floris Books, 2020.

Davis, Erik. *High Weirdness: Drugs, Esoterica, and Visionary Experience in the Seventies*. Cambridge, MA: MIT Press, 2019.

Davis, Erik. "Terence McKenna's Last Trip." *Wired*, May 1, 2000. https://www.wired.com/2000/05/mckenna/.

De Mille, Richard. Letter to R. Gordon Wasson, November 21, 1975. Series I, 149. Tina and R. Gordon Wasson Ethnomycological Collection. Botany Libraries. Harvard University. Cambridge, MA.

De Mille, Richard. Untitled manuscript. Series I, 144. Tina and R. Gordon Wasson Ethnomycological Collection. Botany Libraries. Harvard University. Cambridge, MA.

Devenot, Neşe, Trey Conner, and Richard Doyle. "Dark Side of the Shroom: Erasing Indigenous and Counterculture Wisdoms with Psychedelic Capitalism, and Open Source Alternatives." *Anthropology of Consciousness*, August 22, 2022. https://anthrosource.onlinelibrary.wiley.com/doi/full/10.1111/anoc.12154.

Dirección de Turismo. "El Hongo: Sagrado de la Sierra Mazateca." Huautla de Jiménez, Oaxaca: Dirección de Turismo, n.d.

Doblin, Rick. "Pahnke's Good Friday Experiment: A Long-Term Follow-Up and Methodological Critique." *The Journal of Transpersonal Psychology* 23, no. 1 (1991): 1–28.

Doniger, Wendy. "'Somatic' Memories of R. Gordon Wasson." In *The Sacred Mushroom Seeker: Essays for R. Gordon Wasson*, edited by T. J. Riedlinger, 55–59. Portland: Dioscorides Press, 1990.

Dumit, Joseph. *Drugs for Life: How Pharmaceutical Companies Define Our Life*. Durham, NC: Duke University Press, 2012.

Dupuis, David, and Samuel Veissière. "Culture, Context and Ethics in the Therapeutic Use of Hallucinogens: Psychedelics as Active Super-Placebos?" *Transcultural Psychiatry* 59, no. 5 (2022). https://doi.org/10.1177/13634615221131465.

Durán, Fray Diego. *The History of the Indies of New Spain*. Translated by Ignacio Bernal. New York: Orion Press, 1964.

Dyck, Erika, and Chris Elcock, eds. *Expanding Mindscapes: A Global History of Psychedelics*. Cambridge, MA: MIT Press, 2023.

Eisenberg, Sabrina. "What Is the Mystical Experience Questionnaire?" *Psychedelic Science Review*, January 7, 2021. psychedelicreview.com/what-is-the-mystical-experience-questionnaire.

Eliade, Mircea. *Shamanism: Archaic Techniques of Ecstasy*. Princeton, NJ: Princeton University Press, 1964.

Estrada, Alvaro. *María Sabina: Her Life and Chants*. Santa Barbara, CA: Ross-Erikson, 1981.

Evans, Jules. "The Immortality Key." *Medium*, October 16, 2020. https://julesevans.medium.com/the-immortality-key-f66fef6e650f.

Falk, Harry. "Soma I and II." *Bulletin of the School of Oriental and African Studies* 52, no. 1 (1989): 77–90.

Faudree, Paja. *Singing for the Dead: The Politics of Indigenous Revival in Mexico*. Durham, NC: Duke University Press, 2013.

Feeney, Kevin M., ed. *Fly Agaric: A Compendium of History, Pharmacology, Mythology, and Exploration*. Ellensburg, WA: Fly Agaric Press, 2021.

Feinberg, Benjamin. *The Devil's Book of Culture: History, Mushrooms, and Caves in Southern Mexico*. Austin: University of Texas Press, 2010.

Feinberg, Benjamin. "Undiscovering the Pueblo Mágico: Lessons from Huautla for the Psychedelic Renaissance." In *Plant Medicine, Healing and Psychedelic Science*, edited by Beatriz Caiuby Labate and Clancy Clavnar, 37–54. Cham, Switzerland: Springer, 2018.

Fikes, Jay C. *Carlos Castaneda: Academic Opportunism and the Psychedelic Sixties*. Victoria, BC: Millennia Press, 1993.

Foscati, Alessandra, ed. *Saint Anthony's Fire from Antiquity to the Eighteenth Century*. Amsterdam: University of Amsterdam Press, 2019.

Foucault, Michel. "Nietzsche, Genealogy, History." In *Language, Counter-Memory, and Practice*, ed. D. F. Bouchard, 139–64. Ithaca, NY: Cornell University Press, 1977.

Fuller, Robert C. *Spiritual, but Not Religious: Understanding Unchurched America.* New York: Oxford University Press, 2001.

Fuller, Robert C. *Stairways to Heaven: Drugs in American Religious History.* New York: Basic Books, 2000.

Furst, Jill Leslie. *Codex Vindobonensis Mexicanus I: A Commentary.* Albany: State University of New York, 1978.

Gaines, Bob. "Hollywood's Status-Symbol Drug." *Cosmopolitan*, November 1963, 78–81.

Ginzburg, Carlo. *Ecstasies: Deciphering the Witches' Sabbath.* New York: Penguin, 1992.

Graves, Robert. "Food of the Gods." *The Atlantic*, August 1957, 73–77.

Griffiths, Roland R., Ethan S. Hurwitz, Alan K. Davis, Matthew W. Johnson, and Robert Jesse. "Survey of Subjective 'God Encounter Experiences': Comparisons Among Naturally Occurring Experiences and Those Occasioned by the Classic Psychedelics, Psilocybin, LSD, Ayahuasca, or DMT." *PLOS One* 14, no. 4 (2019). https://doi.org/10.1371/journal.pone.0214377.

Griffiths, Roland R., Matthew W. Johnson, William A. Richards, Brian D. Richards, Robert Jesse, Katherine A. MacLean, Frederick S. Barrett, Mary P. Cosimano, and Maggie A. Klinedinst. "Psilocybin-Occasioned Mystical-Type Experience in Combination with Meditation and Other Spiritual Practices Produces Enduring Positive Changes in Psychological Functioning and in Trait Measures of Prosocial Attitudes and Behaviors." *Journal of Psychopharmacology* 32, no. 1 (2018): 49–69.

Griffiths, Roland R., Matthew W. Johnson, William A. Richards, Brian D. Richards, Una McCann, and Robert Jesse. "Psilocybin Occasioned Mystical-Type Experiences: Immediate and Persisting Dose-Related Effects." *Psychopharmacology* 218, no. 4 (2011): 649–65.

Griffiths, Roland R., William A. Richards, Una McCann, and Robert Jesse. "Psilocybin Can Occasion Mystical Experiences Having Substantial and Sustained Personal Meaning and Spiritual Significance." *Psychopharmacology* 187 (2006): 268–83.

Grim, Ryan. *This Is Your Country on Drugs: The Secret History of Getting High in America.* Hoboken, NJ: John Wiley & Sons, 2009.

Guzmán, Gastón. *The Genus Psilocybe: A Systematic Revision of the Known Species Including the History, Distribution and Chemistry of the Hallucinogenic Species.* Vaduz: J. Cramer 1983.

Guzmán, Gastón. "Hallucinogenic Mushrooms in Mexico: An Overview." *Economic Botany* 62, no. 3 (2008): 404–12.

Halford, Bethany. "Drug Companies Are Investing Big in Psychedelics." *Chemical and Engineering News*, March 6, 2022. https://cen.acs.org/pharmaceuticals/drug-development/Drug-companies-investing-big-psychedelics/100/i9.

Halifax, Joan. *Shamanic Voices: A Survey of Visionary Narratives.* Harmondsworth: Arkana, 1979.

Hanegraaff, Wouter. "Entheogenic Esotericism." In *Contemporary Esotericism*, edited by Egil Asprem and Kennet Granholm, 392–409. Cambridge: Cambridge University Press, 2012.

Haraway, Donna. *Staying with the Trouble: Making Kin in the Chthulucene.* Durham, NC: Duke University Press, 2016.

Hartogsohn, Ido. "Constructing Drug Effects: A History of Set and Setting." *Drug Science, Policy, and Law*, January 1, 2017. https://doi.org/10.1177/2050324516683325.

Hartogsohn, Ido. "Set and Setting in Santo Daime." *Frontiers in Pharmacology* 12 (2021). https://doi.org/10.3389/fphar.2021.651037.

Harvey, Graham, and Robert J. Wallis, eds. *Historical Dictionary of Shamanism.* Lanham, MD: Rowman and Littlefield, 2007.

Heim, Roger, and R. Gordon Wasson. *Les Champignons hallucinogènes du Mexique: Études ethnologiques, taxonomiques, biologiques, physiologiques et chimiques.* Paris: Éditions due Muséum, 1958.

Heineman, Karin. "The Not-So-Trippy Reason Mushrooms Are Psychedelic." *Inside Science,* October 4, 2018. https://ww2.aip.org/inside-science/the-not-so-trippy-reason-mushrooms-are-psychedelic.

Herald, George W. "Curse or Cure? The Truth About the 'Devil's Drugs.'" *Real for Men,* February 1958.

Hofmann, Albert. *LSD: My Problem Child; Reflections on Sacred Drugs, Mysticism, and Science.* Los Angeles: J. P. Tarcher, 1983.

Hood, Ralph W. "The Construction and Preliminary Validation of a Measure of Reported Mystical Experience." *Journal for the Scientific Study of Religion* 14, no. 1 (1975): 29–41.

Hutton, Ronald. *Shamans: Siberian Spirituality and the Western Imagination.* New York: Humbledon and London, 2001.

Huxley, Aldous. *The Doors of Perception.* New York: Harper & Row, 1954.

Huxley, Aldous. "Drugs That Shape Men's Minds." *The Saturday Evening Post,* October 18, 1958.

Huxley, Aldous. *Island.* New York: Harper & Brothers, 1962.

Huxley, Aldous. *Moksha: Aldous Huxley's Classic Writings on Psychedelics and the Visionary Experience.* Rochester, VT: Park Street Press, 1999.

Irvin, Jan R. *God's Flesh: Teonanacátl: The True History of the Sacred Mushroom.* Crestline, CA: Logos Media, 2022.

Irvin, Jan R. "R. Gordon Wasson: The Man, the Legend, the Myth." In *Entheogens and the Development of Culture,* edited by John Rush, 565–619. Berkeley, CA: North Atlantic Books, 2013.

Jacobs, Andrew. "With Promise of Legalization, Psychedelic Companies Joust over Future Profits." *The New York Times,* October 25, 2022. https://www.nytimes.com/2022/10/25/health/psychedelic-drug-therapy-patents.html.

James, William. *The Varieties of Religious Experience: A Study in Human Nature.* New York: Modern Library 1902.

Jamison, Stephanie W., and Joel P. Brereton, trans. *The Rigveda: The Earliest Religious Poetry of India.* New York: Oxford University Press, 2014.

Jay, Mike. *Psychonauts: Drugs and the Making of the Modern Mind.* New Haven, CT: Yale University Press, 2023.

Johns Hopkins Center for Psychedelic and Consciousness Research. "About." 2023. https://hopkinspsychedelic.org/.

Johnson, Jean Bassett. "The Elements of Mazatec Witchcraft." *Ethnological Studies* 9 (1939): 128–50.

Johnson, Matthew W. "Consciousness, Religion, and Gurus: Pitfalls of Psychedelic Medicine." *ACS Pharmacology and Translational Science* 4, no. 2 (2021): 578–81.

Johnson, Matthew W. "How Psychedelics Work, Explained in Under 6 Minutes." *Big Think,* 2022. https://www.youtube.com/watch?v=yS9FBB19Ws0.

Johnson, Matthew W., Peter S. Hendricks, Frederick S. Barrett, and Roland R. Griffiths. "Classic Psychedelics: An Integrative Review of Epidemiology, Therapeutics, Mystical Experience, and Brain Network Function." *Pharmacology & Therapeutics* 197 (May 2019): 83–102.

Josephson-Storm, Jason. *The Myth of Disenchantment: Magic, Modernity and the Birth of the Human Sciences*. Chicago: University of Chicago Press, 2017.

Katz, Steven T. "The 'Conservative' Character of Mysticism." In *Mysticism and Religious Traditions*, edited by Steven T. Katz, 3–60. New York: Oxford University Press, 1983.

Katz, Steven T. "Language, Epistemology, and Mysticism." In *Mysticism and Philosophical Analysis*, edited by Steven T. Katz, 22–74. New York. Oxford University Press, 1978.

Kitchens, Travis. "A Channel for Magic: Ralph Hood's Mysticism Scale and the Occult Roots of the Johns Hopkins Psychedelic Research Program." *Psymposia*, September 9, 2022. https://www.psymposia.com/magazine/a-channel-for-magic-ralph-hoods-mysticism-scale-and-the-occult-roots-of-the-johns-hopkins-psychedelic-research-program/.

Kitchens, Travis. "The Pseudo-Religion of Psychedelics." *Compact Magazine*, December 18, 2023. https://www.compactmag.com/article/the-pseudo-religion-of-psychedelics/.

Kohn, Eduardo. *How Forests Think: Toward an Anthropology Beyond the Human*. Berkeley, CA: University of California Press, 2013.

Kripal, Jeffrey J. *Comparing Religions: Coming to Terms*. Malden and Oxford: John Wiley & Sons, 2014.

Kripal, Jeffrey J. *Esalen: America and the Religion of No Religion*. Chicago: University of Chicago Press, 2008.

Kripal, Jeffrey J. *The Superhumanities: Historical Precedents, Moral Objections, New Realities*. Chicago: University of Chicago Press, 2022.

Lajoux, Jean-Dominique. *The Rock Paintings of Tassili*. New York: World Publishing, 1963.

Langlitz, Nicolas. *Neuropsychedelia: The Revival of Hallucinogen Research Since the Decade of the Brain*. Berkeley: University of California Press, 2012.

Lara, Jaime. "A Meaty Incarnation: Making Sense of Divine Flesh." In *Image and Incarnation: The Early Modern Doctrine of the Pictorial Image*, edited by Walter Melion and Lee Palmer Wandel, 109–36. Leiden: Brill, 2013.

Latour, Bruno, and Steve Woolgar. *Laboratory Life: The Construction of Social Facts*. Princeton, NJ: Princeton University Press, 1986.

Lattin, Don. *Changing our Minds: Psychedelic Sacraments and the New Psychotherapy*. Santa Fe, NM: Synergetic Press, 2017.

Lattin, Don. *God on Psychedelics: Tripping Across the Rubble of Old-Time Religion*. Hannacroix, NY: Apocryphile Press, 2023.

Lattin, Don. *The Harvard Psychedelic Club: How Timothy Leary, Ram Dass, Huston Smith and Andrew Weil Killed the Fifties and Ushered in a New Age for America*. New York: HarperOne, 2010.

Lau, Kimberly. *New Age Capitalism: Making Money East of Eden*. Philadelphia: University of Pennsylvania Press, 2015.

Leary, Timothy. *Flashbacks: An Autobiography*. Los Angeles: J. P. Tarcher, 1983.

Leary, Timothy. *High Priest*. New York: World Publishing Group, 1968.

Leary, Timothy. "In the Beginning, Leary Turned on Ginsberg and Saw That It Was Good." *Esquire*, July 1, 1968, 83–116.

Leary, Timothy. *Start Your Own Religion*. Lexington, KY: Forgotten Books, 2012.

Letcher, Andy. *Shroom: The Cultural History of the Magic Mushroom*. New York: Harper Collins, 2007.

Lim, Michael, and Yun Shu. *The Future Is Fungi: How Fungi Feed Us, Heal Us, and Save the World*. London: Thames and Hudson, 2022.

Lincoln, Bruce. *Authority: Construction and Corrosion*. Chicago: University of Chicago Press, 1994.

Lincoln, Bruce. *Holy Terrors: Thinking About Religion After September 11*. Chicago: University of Chicago Press, 2003.

Love, Shayla. "The False Promise of Psychedelic Utopia." *Vice*, November 1, 2021. https://www.vice.com/en/article/the-false-promise-of-psychedelic-utopia/.

Lovering, Rob, ed. *The Palgrave Handbook of Philosophy and Psychoactive Drug Use*. London: Palgrave, 2024.

Lutkajtis, Anna. "Lost Saints: Descralization, Spiritual Abuse, and Magic Mushrooms." *Fieldwork in Religion* 14, no. 2 (2019): 118–39.

MacLean, Katherine A., Roland R. Griffiths, and Matthew M. Johnson. "Mystical Experiences Occasioned by the Hallucinogenic Psilocybin Lead to Increases in the Personality Domain of Openness." *Journal of Psychopharmacology* 29, no. 3 (2015): 1453–61.

MacLean, Katherine A., Jean-Marie S. Leoutsakos, Matthew W. Johnson, and Roland R. Griffiths. "Factor Analysis of the Mystical Experience Questionnaire: A Study of Experiences Occasioned by the Hallucinogen Psilocybin." *Journal of the Scientific Study of Religion* 51, no. 4 (2012): 721–37.

Magliocco, Sabina, and Sadie Rittman. "Faeries, Environmental Justice, and Re-Enchantment in Modern Pagan Narratives." *Journal for the Study of Religion, Nature, and Culture* 17, no. 3–4 (2023): 1–20.

Markoff, John. *What the Dormouse Said: How the Sixties Counterculture Shaped the Personal Computer Industry*. New York, Penguin, 2005.

Marley, Greg A. *Chanterelle Dreams, Amanita Nightmares: The Love, Lore, and Mystique of Mushrooms*. White River Junction, VT: Chelsea Green Publishing, 2010.

Marshall, Robert. "The Dark Legacy of Carlos Castaneda." *Salon*, April 12, 2007. https://www.salon.com/2007/04/12/castaneda/.

Martinez-Cruz, Paloma. "María Sabina as Vanishing Indian: Writing Mazatec Culture Out of Mushroom Medicine." In *Human Rights on the Move*, edited by Wendy S. Hesford, Momar K. Nduaye, and Amy Shuman, 177–93. Columbus: Ohio State University Press, 2024.

Martinez-Cruz, Paloma. *Women and Knowledge in Mesoamerica: From East L.A. to Anahuac*. Tucson: University of Arizona Press, 2011.

May, Katherine. *Enchantment: Awakening Wonder in an Anxious Age*. New York: Riverhead Books, 2023.

McCulloch, Drummond E-Wen, Maria Zofia Grzywacz, Martin Korsbak Madsen, Peter Steen Jensen, Brice Ozenne, Sophia Armand, Gitte Moos Knudsen, Patrick MacDonald Fisher, and Dea Siggaard Stenbaek. "Psilocybin-Induced Mystical-Type Experiences Are Related to Persisting Positive Effects: A Quantitative and Qualitative Report." *Frontiers in Pharmacology* 13 (2022). https://www.frontiersin.org/journals/pharmacology/articles/10.3389/fphar.2022.841648/full.

McGivney, Annette. "Peyote Is the Darling of the Psychedelic Renaissance." *The Guardian*, December 19, 2023. https://www.theguardian.com/us-news/2023/dec/19/indigenous-communities-protecting-psychedelics-peyote-corporations?CMP=share_btn_link.

McHugh, James. "Soma, Ancient Drugs and Modern Scholars." In *An Unholy Brew: Alcohol in Indian History and Religions*, edited by James McHugh, 289–97. New York: Oxford University Press, 2021.

McKenna, Dennis. "The Experiment at La Chorrera: A 50-Year Retrospective." *McKenna Academy*, February 17, 2021. https://mckenna.academy/the-experiment-at-la-chorrera-a-50-year-retrospective/.

McKenna, Terence. *The Archaic Revival: Speculations on Psychedelic Mushrooms, the Amazon, Virtual Reality, UFOs, Evolution, Shamanism, the Rebirth of the Goddess, and the End of History*. San Francisco: HarperSanFrancisco 1991.

McKenna, Terence. "A Crisis in Consciousness, 1995." *Wisdom for Life*. https://www.youtube.com/watch?v=9E5eBqG0cds.

McKenna, Terence. "Ethnobotany and Shamanism." ASKTKM.com, 2020. https://www.asktmk.com/talks/Ethnobotany+and+Shamanism+-+Psychedelics+Before+and+After+History.

McKenna, Terence. *Food of the Gods: The Search for the Original Tree of Knowledge*. New York: Bantam Books, 1992.

McKenna, Terence. Interview with Erik Davis, November 1999. *Library of Consciousness*. https://www.organism.earth/library/document/interview-with-erik-davis.

McKenna, Terence. "Mushrooms, Evolution, and the Millennium." ASKTKM.com, 2020. https://www.asktmk.com/talks/Mushrooms%2C+Evolution+and+the+Millenium.

McKenna, Terence. "Psilocybin and the Sands of Time." ASKTMK.com, 2020. https://www.asktmk.com/talks/Psilocybin+and+the+Sands+of+Time.

McKenna, Terence. *True Hallucinations: Being an Account of the Author's Extraordinary Adventures in the Devil's Paradise*. San Francisco: HarperSanFrancisco, 1993.

McKenna, Terence, and Dennis McKenna. *The Invisible Landscape: Mind, Hallucinogens and the I Ching*. San Francisco: HarperSanFrancisco, 1993.

Mercadante, Linda A. *Belief Without Borders: Inside the Minds of the Spiritual but Not Religious*. New York, NY: Oxford University Press, 2014.

Meyer, Matthew, and Jason Slot. "The Evolution and Ecology of Psilocybin in Nature." *Fungal Genetics and Biology* 167 (2023). https://doi.org/10.1016/j.fgb.2023.103812.

Miller, Kenneth. "How Mushrooms Can Save the World." *Discover*, May 31, 2013. https://web.archive.org/web/20191115020921/http://discovermagazine.com/2013/julyaug/13-mushrooms-clean-up-oil-spills-nuclear-meltdowns-and-human-health.

Mooney, James. "Eating the Mescal." *The Augusta Chronicle*, January 24, 1982, 11.

Mooney, James. "The Mescal Plant and Ceremony." *Therapeutic Gazette* 12 (1896): 7–11.

Moore, Peter. "Mysticism: Further Considerations." In Vol. 9, *The Encyclopedia of Religion*, edited by Lindsay Jones, 6355–59. New York: MacMillan, 2005.

"Morgan & Co. Announce Changes." *The New York Times*, July 17, 1941.

Mosurinjohn, Sharday, and Richard Ascough. "Psychedelics, Eleusis, and the Invention of Religious Experience." *Psychedelic Medicine* (2025). https://doi.org/10.1177/28314425251361835.

Mosurinjohn, Sharday, Leor Roseman, and Manesh Girn. "Psychedelic-Induced Mystical Experiences: An Interdisciplinary Discussion and Critique." *Frontiers in Psychiatry* 14 (2023). https://doi.org/10.3389/fpsyt.2023.1077311.

Motolinía, Fray Toribio de Benavente. *Memoriales o libro de las cosas de la Nueva España y de los naturales de ella*. Mexico: Universidad Nacional Autónoma de Mexico, 1971.

Müller-Ebeling, Claudia, Christian Rätsch, and Surendra Bahadur Shahi. *Shamanism and Tantra in the Himalayas*. Rochester, VT: Inner Traditions, 2002.

Munn, Henry. "The Mushrooms of Language." In *Hallucinogens and Shamanism*, edited by Michael J. Harner, 86–122. New York: Oxford University Press, 1973.

Muraresku, Brian C. *The Immortality Key: The Secret History of the Religion with No Name*. New York: St. Martin's Press, 2020.

New Hope Network Staff, "The Natural List: Exclusive Interview with Paul Stamets." *New Hope Network*, October 12, 2023. https://www.newhope.com/vitamins-and-supplements/the-natural-list-exclusive-interview-paul-stamets.

New York Times Audio. "The C.E.O.s Are Tripping. Can Psychedelics Help the C-Suite?" *The New York Times*, December 12, 2024. https://www.nytimes.com/audio/app/2024/12/12/business/psychedelic-retreats-ceos.html?referringSource=sharing.

Nuttall, Zelia. *The Book of the Life of the Ancient Mexicans, Containing an Account of Their Rites and Superstitions*. Berkeley: University of California Press, 1903.

Nyberg, Harri. "The Problem of the Aryans and the Soma: The Botanical Evidence." In *The Indo-Aryans of Ancient South Asia: Language, Material Culture, and Ethnicity*, edited by George Erdosy, 382–406. Berlin: Walter de Gruyter, 1995.

Nyberg, Harri. "Religious Use of Hallucinogenic Fungi: A Comparison Between Siberian and Mesoamerican Cultures." *Karstenia* 32 (1992): 71–80.

O'Connell, Brian. "Seven Best Psychedelic Stocks to Watch." *US News and World Report*, October 25, 2023. https://money.usnews.com/investing/articles/psychedelic-stocks-to-watch.

Ongaro, Alberto. Interview with María Sabina. *L'Europeo*, November 29, 1971.

Oss, O. T., and O. N. Oeric. *Psilocybin: Magic Mushroom Grower's Guide*. Berkeley, CA: Lux Natura, 1986.

Pace, Brian A. "Lucy in the Sky with Nazis: Psychedelics and the Right Wing." *Psymposia*, February 3, 2020. https://www.psymposia.com/magazine/lucy-in-the-sky-with-nazis-psychedelics-and-the-right-wing/.

Pace, Brian A., and Neşe Devenot. "Right-Wing Psychedelia: Case Studies in Cultural Plasticity and Political Pluripotency." *Frontiers in Psychology* 12 (2021). https://doi.org/10.3389/fpsyg.2021.733185.

Pahnke, Walter N. "Drugs and Mysticism: An Analysis of the Relationship Between Psychedelic Drugs and the Mystical Consciousness." PhD diss. Harvard University, 1963.

Pahnke, Walter N. "First Impressions of First LSD Experience, of March 30, 1964." March 31, 1964. William Richards Collection on Walter Pahnke, Purdue University Libraries and School of Information Studies. MSP 68.

Pahnke, Walter N. "Psychedelic Drugs and Mystical Experience." *International Journal of Psychiatry in Clinical Practice* 5, no. 4 (1969): 149–62.

Pahnke, Walter N. "Psychedelic Mystical Experience in the Human Encounter with Death." *Harvard Theological Review* 62, no. 1 (1969): 1–21.

Pahnke, Walter N., and William A. Richards. "Implications of LSD and Experimental Mysticism." *Journal of Religion and Health* 5, no. 3 (1966): 177–208.

Parsons, William, ed. *Being Spiritual but Not Religious: Past, Present, Future(s)*. New York: Routledge, 2020.

Partridge, Christopher. *High Culture: Drugs, Mysticism, and the Pursuit of Transcendence in the Modern World*. New York: Oxford University Press, 2018.

Partridge, Christopher. "Psychedelia Sub Rosa: The Eleusinian Mysteries and the Psychedelic Imagination." In *The Routledge Handbook of Religion and Secrecy*, edited by Hugh B. Urban and Paul Christopher Johnson, 57–70. New York: Routledge, 2022.

Partridge, Christopher. *The Re-Enchantment of the West*, vol. 1, *Alternative Spiritualities, Sacralization, Popular Culture, and Occulture*. London: T&T Clark, 2005.

Petersen, Rachael. "Taking Mushrooms for Depression Cured Me of My Atheism." *The Outline*, April 29, 2019. https://theoutline.com/post/7367/taking-mushrooms-for-depression-cured-me-of-my-atheism.

Petersen, Rachael. "A Theological Reckoning with 'Bad Trips.'" *Harvard Divinity Bulletin*, Autumn/Winter, 2022. https://bulletin.hds.harvard.edu/a-theological-reckoning-with-bad-trips/.

Pfister, Donald H. "R. Gordon Wasson: 1898–1986." *Mycologia* 80, no. 1 (1988): 11–13.

Piña Alcántara, Saraí. "Turismo y chamanismo, dos mundos imbricados: el caso de Huautla de Jiménez, Oaxaca." *Cuicuilco: Revista de ciencias antropológicas* 26, no. 75 (2019): 43–66.

Pollan, Michael. *How to Change Your Mind: What the New Science of Psychedelics Teaches Us About Consciousness, Dying, Addiction, Depression, and Transcendence*. New York: Penguin, 2018.

Pollan, Michael. "What It's Like to Trip on the World's Most Potent Mushroom." *The Atlantic*, June 4, 2018. https://www.theatlantic.com/science/archive/2018/06/what-its-like-to-trip-on-the-most-potent-magic-mushroom/561860/.

Regan, Holly. "Psyched Out." *Altered States*, January 27, 2023. https://www.goodbeerhunting.com/altered-states/2023/1/27/psyched-out.

Richards, William A. "Counseling, Peak Experiences and the Human Encounter with Death: An Empirical Study of the Efficacy of DPT-Assisted Counseling in Enhancing the Quality of Life of Persons with Terminal Cancer and Their Closest Family Members." PhD diss. Catholic University of America, 1975.

Richards, William A. *Sacred Knowledge: Psychedelics and Religious Experiences*. New York: Columbia University Press, 2016.

Riedlinger, Thomas J., ed. *The Sacred Mushroom Seeker: Essays for R. Gordon Wasson*. Portland: Dioscorides Press, 1990.

Rolfe, R. T., and F. W. Rolfe. *The Romance of the Fungus World: An Account of Fungus Life in Its Numerous Guises, Both Real and Legendary*. London: Chapman and Hall, 1925.

Romero, Osiris Gonzáles. "Ritual and Religious Uses of Psilocybe Mushrooms in Mesoamerica." *Center for the Study of World Religions*. October 9, 2024. https://cswr.hds.harvard.edu/news/2024/10/ritual-and-religious-uses-psilocybe-mushrooms-mesoamerica.

Sabina, María. *Selections*, edited by Jerome Rothenberg. Berkeley: University of California Press, 2003.

Sahagún, Fray Bernardino de. *The Florentine Codex: General History of the Things in New Spain*. Translated by A. J. O. Anderson and C. E. Dibble. Salt Lake City: University of Utah Press, 1950–1963.

Sanders, James W., and Josjan Zijlmans. "Moving Past Mysticism in Psychedelic Science." *ACS Pharmacology & Translational Science* 4 (2021): 1253–55.

Sarbacker, Stuart. *Tracing the Path of Yoga: The History and Philosophy of Indian Mind-Body Discipline*. Albany, NY: SUNY Press, 2021.

Schulberg, Budd. "The Night We Ate Magic Mushrooms." *Esquire*, December 1961, 129–30, 312–16.

Schultes, Richard E. "Plantae Mexicanae II: The Identification of Teonanácatl, a Narcotic Basidiomycete of the Aztecs." *Botanical Museum Leaflets, Harvard University* 7 (1939): 37–56.

Schultes, Richard E. "Teonanácatl: The Narcotic Mushroom of the Aztecs." *American Anthropologist* 42 (1940): 429–43.

Schultes, Richard Evans, and Albert Hofmann. *The Botany and Chemistry of Hallucinogens*. Springfield, IL: Charles C. Thomas, 1980.

Schwartzberg, Louie, dir. *Fantastic Fungi*. Moving Art, 2019.

Severus, Alex. "Drugs and the Mind's Hidden Powers." *Cosmopolitan*, January 1960, 43–45.

Sheldrake, Merlin. *Entangled Life: How Fungi Make Our Worlds, Change Our Minds and Shape Our Future*. New York: Random House, 2020.

Shipley, Morgan. *Psychedelic Mysticism: Transforming Consciousness, Religious Experiences, and Voluntary Peasants in Postwar America*. Lanham, MD: Lexington Books, 2015.

Siff, Stephen I. *Acid Hype: American Media and the Psychedelic Experience*. Champaign: Illinois University Press, 2015.

Siff, Stephen I. "R. Gordon Wasson and the Publicity Campaign to Introduce Magic Mushrooms to Mid-Century America." *Revue française d'études américaines* 156, no. 3 (2018): 91–104.

Smausz, Rebecca, Joanna Neill, and John Gigg, "Neural Mechanisms Underlying Psilocybin's Therapeutic Potential—The Need for Preclinical in vivo Electrophysiology." *Journal of Psychopharmacology* 36, no. 7 (2022): 781–93.

Smith, Huston. "The Good Friday Experiment." In *Hallucinations: A Reader*, edited by Charles S. Grob, 64–71. New York: J. P. Tarcher, 2002.

Spiers, Nicholas, Beatriz Caiuby Labate, Anna O. Ermakova, Patrick Farrell, Osiris Sinuhé Gonzáles Romero, Ibrahim Gabriell, and Nidia Olivera. "Indigenous Psilocybin Mushroom Practices: An Annotated Bibliography." *Journal of Psychedelic Studies* 8, no. 1 (2024): 3–25.

Spiteller, Peter. "Chemical Defense Strategies of Higher Fungi." *Chemistry: A European Journal* 14, no. 30 (2008). https://doi.org/10.1002/chem.200800292.

St. John, Graham. *Strange Attractor: The Hallucinatory Life of Terence McKenna*. Cambridge, MA: MIT Press, 2025.

Stace, W. T. *Man Against Darkness and Other Essays*. Pittsburgh: University of Pittsburgh Press, 1967.

Stace, W. T. *Mysticism and Philosophy*. London: MacMillan, 1960.

Stace, W. T. *The Teachings of the Mystics*. New York: New American Library, 1960.

Stamets, Paul, ed. *Fantastic Fungi: How Mushrooms Can Heal, Shift Consciousness and Save the Planet*. San Rafael, CA: Earth Aware, 2019.

Stamets, Paul. Interview on *The Joe Rogan Experience*, 2017. https://www.youtube.com/watch?v=mPqWstVnRjQ&t=7193s.

Stamets, Paul. "Mushrooms Are Spiritual Medicine for Everyone." *The New Health Club with Ann Phillipi*, 2021. https://www.youtube.com/watch?v=qj00RSTDnWQ.

Stamets, Paul. *Mycelium Running: How Mushrooms Can Help Save the World*. Berkeley, CA: Ten Speed Press, 2005.

Stamets, Paul. *Psilocybin Mushrooms of the World: An Identification Guide*. Berkeley, CA: Ten Speed Press, 1996.

Stamets, Paul. "Six Ways Mushrooms Can Save the World." TED.com, 2008. https://www.ted.com/talks/paul_stamets_6_ways_mushrooms_can_save_the_world.

Stamets, Paul, and Matthew Johnson. "Psilocybin on the Psyche." *Whalebone Magazine*, 2021. https://whalebonemag.com/psilocybin-on-the-psyche/.

Strassman, Rick. "Human Hallucinogenic Drug Research in the United Staes: Present Day Case History and Review of the Process." *Psychoactive Drugs* 23, no. 1 (1991): 29–38.

Strassman, Rick. "The Psychedelic Religion of Mystical Consciousness." *Journal of Psychedelic Studies* 2 (2018): 1–4.

Strauss, Dominique, Soumya Ghosh, Zurika Murray, and Marieka Gyrzenhout. "An Overview of the Taxonomy, Phylogenetics, and Ecology of the Psychedelic Genera of *Psilocybe, Panaeolus, Pluteus* and *Gymnopilus*." *Frontiers in Forests and Global Change* 5 (2022). https://www.frontiersin.org/articles/10.3389/ffgc.2022.813998/full.

Taves, Ann. "Mystical and Other Alterations in Sense of Self: An Expanded Framework for Studying Nonordinary Experiences." *Perspectives on Psychological Science* 15, no. 3 (2020): 669–90.

Tempone-Wiltshire, Julien, and Floren Matthews. "Evaluating the Role of Psychedelic Psychotherapy in Addressing Societal Alienation." *Journal of Psychedelic Studies* 7, no. 3 (2023). https://akjournals.com/view/journals/2054/7/3/article-p238.xml.

Torgovnick, Marianna. *Gone Primitive: Savage Intellects, Modern Lives*. Chicago: University of Chicago Press, 1990.

Torgovnick, Marianna. *Primitive Passions: Men, Women, and the Quest for Ecstasy*. Chicago: University of Chicago Press, 1996.

Tree Media. "Paul Stamets on How Mushrooms Can Save Us from Ourselves." YouTube.com, 2016. https://www.youtube.com/watch?v=T-9zzXuZ2h4.

Tsing, Anna Lowenhaupt. *The Mushroom at the End of the World: On the Possibility of Life in Capitalist Ruins*. Princeton, NJ: Princeton University Press, 2021.

Urban, Hugh B. *New Age, Neopagan and New Religious Movements: Alternative Spirituality in Contemporary America*. Berkeley: University of California Press, 2015.

Urban, Hugh B. *Tantra: Sex, Secrecy, Politics and Power in the Study of Religion*. Berkeley: University of California Press, 2003.

Urban, Hugh B. *Zorba the Buddha: Sex, Spirituality, Capitalism in the Global Osho Movement*. Berkeley: University of California Press, 2016.

Wagh, Manasee. "Magic Mushrooms May Have Shaped Our Consciousness." *Popular Mechanics*, July 23, 2024. https://www.popularmechanics.com/science/a61678397/magic-mushrooms-psilocybin-human-consciousness/.

Wall Street Journal. "Magic Mushrooms. LSD. Ketamine. The Drugs That Power Silicon Valley." *Wall Street Journal*, June 27, 2023. https://www.wsj.com/articles/silicon-valley-microdosing-ketamine-lsd-magic-mushrooms-d381e214?mod=hp_lead_pos7.

Wasson, R. Gordon. "Drugs: The Sacred Mushroom." *The New York Times*, September 26, 1970, 21.

Wasson, R. Gordon. *The Hall Carbine Affair: A Study in Contemporary Folklore*. New York: Pandick Press, 1941.

Wasson, R. Gordon. "The Hallucinogenic Fungi of Mexico." *Botanical Museum Leaflets* 19 (1961): 137–62.

Wasson, R. Gordon. Letter to Albert Hofmann, July 2, 1965. Series I, 360. Tina and R. Gordon Wasson Ethnomycological Collection. Harvard University Botany Libraries. Cambridge, MA.

Wasson, R. Gordon. Letter to Albert Hofmann, June 14, 1971. Series I, 361. Tina and R. Gordon Wasson Ethnomycological Collection. Harvard University Botany Libraries. Cambridge, MA.

Wasson, R. Gordon. Letter to Richard de Mille, January 10, 1976. Series I, 149. Tina and R. Gordon Wasson Ethnomycological Collection. Harvard University Botany Libraries. Cambridge, MA.

Wasson, R. Gordon. Letter to Robert Graves, August 8, 1955. Series I, 255. Tina and R. Gordon Wasson Ethnomycological Collection. Harvard University Botany Libraries. Cambridge, MA.

Wasson, R. Gordon. "The Role of Flowers in the Nahuatl Culture: A Suggested Interpretation." *Botanical Museum Leaflets* 25, no. 8 (1978): 305–24.

Wasson, R. Gordon. "Seeking the Magic Mushroom." *Life*, May 13, 1957, 100–102, 109–20.

Wasson, R. Gordon. *Soma: Divine Mushroom of Immortality*. New York: Harcourt Brace, 1968.

Wasson, R. Gordon. *The Wondrous Mushroom: Mycolatry in Mesoamerica*. New York: McGraw-Hill, 1980.

Wasson, R. Gordon, George Cowan, Florence Cowan, and Willard Rhodes. *María Sabina and Her Mazatec Mushroom Velada*. New York: Harcourt Brace Jovanovich, 1974.

Wasson, R. Gordon, Albert Hofmann, and Carl A. P. Ruck. *The Road to Eleusis: Unveiling the Secret of the Mysteries*. New York: Harcourt Brace Jovanovich, 1978.

Wasson, R. Gordon, Stella Kramrisch, Jonathan Ott, and Carl A. P. Ruck, *Persephone's Quest: Entheogens and the Origins of Religion*. New Haven, CT: Yale University Press, 1986.

Wasson, R. Gordon, and Valentina Pavlovna Wasson. *Mushrooms, Russia, and History*. New York: Pantheon, 1957.

Wasson, Valentina P. "I Ate the Sacred Mushrooms." *This Week*, May 19, 1957, 1, 18–10, 36.

Weil, Andrew T. "The Strange Case of the Harvard Drug Scandal." *Look Magazine*, November 8, 1963, 38, 43–44, 46, 48.

Whitaker, Jarrod. *Strong Arms and Drinking Strength: Masculinity, Violence, and the Body in Ancient India*. New York: Oxford University Press, 2011.

Woolfe, Sam. *Altered States: Critical Essays on Psychedelic Consciousness*. Iff Books, 2025.

Yaden, David B., and Andrew B. Newburg. *The Varieties of Spiritual Experience: Twenty-First Century Research and Perspectives*. New York: Oxford University Press, 2022.

Yaden, David, Khoa D. Le Nguyen, Margarat Kern, Alexander B. Belser, Johannes Eichstaedt, Jonathan Iwry, Mary E. Smith, Nancy A. Wintering, Ralph W. Hood Jr., and Andrew B. Newberg. "Of Roots and Fruits: A Comparison of Psychedelic and Nonpsychedelic Mystical Experiences." *Journal of Humanistic Psychology* 57, no. 4 (2016): https://doi.org/10.1177/0022167816674625.

Zaehner, R. C. *Mysticism Sacred and Profane: An Inquiry into Some Varieties of Praeter-Natural Experience*. Oxford: Clarendon, 1957.

Index